The 4th
North Carolina Cavalry
in the Civil War

The 4th
North Carolina Cavalry
in the Civil War

A History and Roster

by NEIL HUNTER RAIFORD

McFarland & Company, Inc., Publishers
Jefferson, North Carolina, and London

LIBRARY OF CONGRESS CATALOGUING-IN-PUBLICATION DATA

Raiford, Neil Hunter, 1969–
    The 4th North Carolina Cavalry in the Civil War : a history and roster
/ by Neil Hunter Raiford.
        p.   cm.
    Includes bibliographical references and index.

    ISBN 0-7864-1468-5 (illustrated case binding : 50# alkaline paper) ∞

    1. Confederate States of America. Army. North Carolina Cavalry
Regiment, 4th.   2. North Carolina—History—Civil War,
1861–1865—Regimental histories.   3. United States—History—Civil War,
1861–1865—Regimental histories.   4. Confederate States of America.
Army. North Carolina Cavalry Regiment, 4th—Registers.   5. North
Carolina—History—Civil War, 1861–1865—Registers.   6. United
States—History—Civil War, 1861–1865—Registers.   7. Soldiers—North
Carolina—Registers.   8. North Carolina—Genealogy.   I. Title: Fourth
North Carolina Cavalry in the Civil War.   II. Title.
E573.64th.R35   2003
973.7'456—dc21   2003002227

British Library cataloguing data are available

On the cover: Private William Samuel Pleasant, Company B, Caswell County
(Henry N. Pleasant); background image ©2003 PhotoSpin and Art Today

Manufactured in the United States of America

*McFarland & Company, Inc., Publishers
    Box 611, Jefferson, North Carolina 28640
        www.mcfarlandpub.com*

To the memory of Grandma Raiford
(Mary Norman Turner Raiford)

Table of Contents

Preface and Acknowledgments

THIS LABOR OF LOVE STARTED WHEN I began searching for my Civil War ancestors. I found three in the 4th North Carolina Cavalry: Private John Robert Early (my third great grandfather), Private Joseph Teaster (my third great granduncle), both of Company D, and 3rd Lieutenant Dallas Beale (my third great granduncle) of Company K. With their names discovered I set out to find a book to read more about their experience and to make a connection with my past.

I quickly discovered that no such volume existed. I then began the task of collecting primary and secondary source material on the regiment. The project continued to grow in scope and the only logical next step was to write the book I wanted to read. My effort is what follows. I hope that it is a fitting tribute and account to all of the men who served in the unit.

In any research project, the historian must stand upon the shoulders of others. The research for this book would not have been possible without the help of many individuals. Chris Calkins, at the Petersburg National Battlefield, read the chapters related to Petersburg and gave wonderful direction to me regarding the campaign. Kathryn L. Bridges, at the Local History Room, Charles A. Cannon Memorial Library in Concord, NC, made available to me their fine collection of local history and genealogical material that greatly added to the roster, especially regarding Cabarrus County. Kimberly A. Cumber and the staff at the NC Division of Archives and History helped me with a lot of the source material and photographs included in the book. Mary Boccaccio and Martha Elmore at the J. Y. Joyner Library, East Carolina University, provided a couple of key letter collections that helped me trace the 4th NC Cavalry through some hard-to-document periods.

Jeff H. Stepp, the project editor for the NC Confederate Burial Project, provided over a hundred burial locations of soldiers from the unit. (Anyone with NC Confederate burial information is encouraged to contribute to his important project. He can

1

be reached at 2139 Buffalo Shoals Road, Catawba, NC 28609 or via the links section at www.26nc.org.) Harriet Oliver Byrum, of the Ahoskie Public Library, helped make copies of some local research materials that were not readily available elsewhere. Patrick Bowmaster freely shared his thesis research on Brigadier General Beverly H. Robertson and other primary source material relating to the unit. Andrew Duppstadt, of the CSS Neuse Historic Site in Kinston, NC, provided key materials relating to the Battle of Whitehall.

I am also grateful to the staff members at the following institutions, who provided essential materials from their collections: the Library of Virginia, Richmond; the Southern Historical Collection, University of North Carolina at Chapel Hill; the Museum of the Confederacy, Richmond; the United States Military Academy, West Point, NY; the Perkins Library, Duke University, Durham, NC; the United States Military History Institute in Carlisle, PA, and the Naval Historical Center in Washington, DC.

No student ever develops the desire to learn without wonderful teachers. I was blessed with several exceptional ones, three in high school and two in college. Mrs. Betsy Overton, Mrs. Jenks Johnson and Mr. Ron Kelly of Ridgecroft School in Ahoskie fostered my interest in learning. Each of them challenged me and made me a better student. At Wake Forest University, I had a wonderful advisor in Richard L. Zuber. There I also had the great fortune to study under James P. Barefield—he is the reason that I became a history major in college. He taught me how to be a historical detective and that the most important part of a book is its bibliography. Unknowingly, each of them had a part in making this book a reality.

During the course of research I was fortunate to meet and correspond with other people who also had ancestors in the 4th North Carolina Cavalry. They freely provided family information and photos, and the book is more complete because of their contributions. They are (in alphabetical order): Doug Acree, Richard P. Aldridge, Carrie Baker, Pat Barr, Rufus Barringer, Robert Allen Beale, Holley Mack Bell, Clay Brenke, Bill Burkett, Ken Burton, Ben Callahan, Allen Churchill, Joy Skipper Cornwell, Chris Davis, Elwood E. Davis, Charles Dunn, Ernie Evans, G. Hunter Ferrell, Reese Ferrell, Neal F. Ganzert, Jr., John L. German, Norma Gordon, Jack Hagler, John Hagler, Clark Harrell, Becky Hollen, Mary Hope, Melba Bonham Jones, Jerry T. Kendall, Debbie Loefgren, Michael Manning, Mrs. R. C. Mason, Jr., David C. Michael, Carolyn Mitchell, Betty Pace, Henry N. Pleasant, Elizabeth Plumblee, Peter Rascoe, J. B. Rhyne, Cindy Rubio, Mike Rudd, Jean Schroeder, Essie Sciamanna, Bob Stokley, Doug Terrell, Sammy Vaughan, Ronald Weiss, H. Mark Whitley, John R. Woodard, Benjamin Wrenn, and Bettie Morris Young.

I would also like to acknowledge the staff at McFarland & Company, who were very patient and supportive throughout the entire project.

No undertaking of this kind is possible without the encouragement of friends and family. I could not have completed it without their love and support. My grandmother, the late Mrs. Norman Turner Raiford, instilled in me a sense of appreciation for my past and was the primary source for my love of history and genealogy. My parents, Hunter and Arlene Raiford, have always believed in me and given me the confidence that I could do anything I set my mind to do. My wife's parents, Larry and Katrina Gilliam, have also been very supportive throughout the project. Finally and most importantly, I must thank my wife Karen and son Benjamin. Their love and encouragement inspire me each day and I could not have written this book without them.

Neil Hunter Raiford
February 2003

CHAPTER 1

Independent Companies of Partisan Rangers

I N APRIL 1862 THE CIVIL WAR was entering its second year and North Carolina was rallying to supply more troops for the Confederacy. A stimulus for recruitment came on April 21, 1862 when the Confederate Congress passed the Partisan Ranger Act, which read as follows:

> Section 1. The Congress of the Confederate States of America do enact, That the President be, and he is hereby authorized to commission such officers as he may deem proper with authority to form bands of partisan rangers, in companies, battalions or regiments, to be composed of such members as the President may approve.
> Section 2. Be it further enacted, That such partisan rangers, after being regularly received in the service, shall be entitled to the same pay, rations, and quarters during their term of service, and be subject to the same regulations as other soldiers.
> Section 3. Be it further enacted, That for any arms and munitions of war captured from the enemy by any body of partisan rangers and delivered to any quartermaster at such place or places as may be designated by a commanding general, the rangers shall be paid their full value in such manner as the Secretary of War may prescribe.

The act prompted local leaders to recruit companies of irregular soldiers for service in the Confederate Army. Seven such companies were banded together into a regiment to form the 4th North Carolina Cavalry. The regiment was a true cross-section of North Carolina, having enlistment in the largest urban areas and smallest rural areas from over 15 counties across the state.

The regiment's colonel, Dennis Dozier Ferebee, was born November 9, 1815 in Currituck County, North Carolina. He was the son of Samuel Ferebee and Margatte "Peggy" Dauge. He attended the University of North Carolina at Chapel Hill, graduating in 1839. Ferebee married Sarah McPherson on February 3, 1842. He resided in Camden County, North Carolina as a lawyer and planter before the war. Ferebee was a member of the state legislature and was a delegate for Camden County in the

May 1861 North Carolina Secession Convention. Ferebee, a staunch Unionist, voted against secession. However, when the vote for secession passed, he did take up arms for the Confederacy. He was colonel of Camden County's local militia, the 2nd Regiment of the 1st Brigade. He saw action at the Battle of South Mills in Camden County on Saturday, April 19, 1862. On Sunday, August 10, 1862, at age 45, he was appointed colonel of the 4th North Carolina Cavalry.

The first company to begin organization and form what would become Company A of Ferebee's 4th North Carolina Cavalry (59th Regiment North Carolina State Troops) was Capt. Lewis A. Johnson's company from Anson County, North Carolina. As early as Thursday, December 12, 1861 Johnson placed an advertisement in Wadesboro's *North Carolina Argus*, in the hopes of forming a cavalry regiment from the western part of the state by the beginning of spring 1862. The ad informed the prospective cavalrymen that they would be "required by the Government to furnish their own horses, saddles and bridles, and side arms." However, once mustered into service, their mounts and weapons would be assessed and if the soldier made the company's roster, he would be paid for their value. Also, 40 cents per day would be paid for the use and risk of their horses.[1]

Johnson tried to instill the imminent need for such a regiment to be formed, claiming that the "war-cloud is darkening around us. Our enemies are putting forth all their strength, and unless we do the same, our fair land will be laid to ruins"[2] This need also echoed from Col. Zebulon Baird Vance of the 26th North Carolina Infantry, who writing on Tuesday, March 4, 1862 to Allen Turner Davidson, a member of the Confederate Congress, wanted permission to raise another regiment of infantry, two companies of cavalry, and one company of artillery. Vance stated that he already had the offer of some new companies from the mountains with which to begin his effort.[3] This group would form what Vance called his "Legion."[4]

Judging from the notice placed in the Thursday, May 1, 1862 *North Carolina Argus*, there is no doubt that Capt. Johnson offered his company to Vance's Legion. However, at the time, Johnson was a few cavalrymen short of the 80 needed to complete the company.[5] Vance never raised his Legion, which he hoped would make him a general. This was due mainly to the fact that he had difficulty getting leave to recruit for it. Vance contended that the "Confederate authorities in Raleigh and Richmond blocked his efforts because they did not desire a popular general whose politics differed from their own."[6] Despite Vance's eventual failure to raise his Legion, Johnson continued to complete his company of cavalry in hopes of joining it.

Capt. Johnson began official enlistment of his company of "Anson Troopers" on Saturday, May 10.[7] Some of those enlisting were local Anson County militia units, the 80th and 81st Regiments of the 20th Brigade.[8] His company was completed by Tuesday, May 20, when he ordered his "troopers" to report to Wadesboro on Wednesday, May 28 at 2:30 P.M., with five days' rations. From here they would head to Kittrell's Springs in Granville County (now in Vance County), near the Raleigh and Gaston Railroad.[9] It was here that the Legion was to be formed.

Many tears were shed as the company left their homes and loved ones in Wadesboro. A trooper writing to the *North Carolina Argus* reports the scene as follows: "we were given many beautiful nosegays from our fair lady friends, as emblems of memory to cheer us on in the road of duty assigned to us by the lamentable condition of our beloved country." After many heartfelt good-byes, the company rode out of town to the cheers of those remaining.[10]

Johnson planned to march the company first to Salisbury, in Rowan County. From there he planned to move the baggage by rail to Kittrell, with the troops moving across the countryside on their mounts. The Anson Troopers first passed through Cedar Hill, where they were cheered on by the young and old, and of course, the beautiful ladies. Here the boys once again received encouraging words and flowers from the grateful townspeople. However, this merriment could not last, and they once again had to take up the line of march for Salisbury.[11]

Along the way, they were hosted

Colonel Dennis Dozier Ferebee, Camden County (North Carolina Office of Archives and History, Raleigh, NC).

by many grateful and gracious people. The region allowed plenty of forage for their mounts as well as for themselves. Just north of Cedar Hill Johnson's company crossed the Pee Dee River into Stanly County. The troopers found the river so swollen from recent rains that it "rendered ferrying necessary." This proved to be a slow process, which forced some troopers to mount their horses and cross the angry stream, without the benefit of the ferry. After all of the men had crossed, some saturated from the trip, they headed for Norwoods, a small town in southeast Stanly County. Once the horses were fed, the troops' appetites were satisfied with a large meal at Norwoods's local hotel. "After resting a short time, at the sound of the bugle, we saddled, mounted and marched for Albemarle," reaching the town "just as the golden sun was passing behind the blue horizon in the west."[12]

Once in Albemarle, the company broke ranks to find forage for the horses and put up in one of the town's several hotels. After the horses were attended to, the signal sounded for dinner and the troops wasted no time in sitting down before another large meal. They rose early the next morning and reluctantly said good-bye to the gracious town. The quartermaster and several others headed for Salisbury with the baggage, while the rest of the Anson Troopers headed for Stoke's Ferry to cross the Yadkin River.[13]

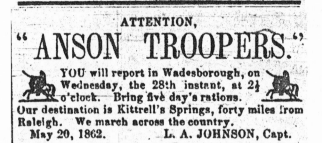

ATTENTION,

"ANSON TROOPERS."

YOU will report in Wadesborough, on Wednesday, the 28th instant, at 2½ o'clock. Bring five day's rations. Our destination is Kittrell's Springs, forty miles from Raleigh. We march across the country.
May 20, 1862.   L. A. JOHNSON, Capt.

Captain Lewis A. Johnson's Anson Trooper advertisement in the May 22, 1862, Wadesboro *North Carolina Argus* (Wadesboro, *North Carolina Argus*, May 22, 1862).

Johnson's boys continued their march through the beautiful countryside. They soon reached Trinity College (present day Trinity) in northwest Randolph County. From there they proceeded on to Jim Town (Jamestown). In Jim Town the company found a host in Dr. Coffin, who put them up for the night and fed the stock and the men. Most of the troops spent the night in the comfort of the hay in the doctor's barn. The dark and rainy night inspired a few of the boys to play a practical joke on their tired friends. The guilty parties caught a sheep and let it loose among the sleepers. After the excitement, the sheep was let out of the barn, with the culprits, and the rest of the boys finished their evening rest.[14]

After leaving Jim Town, the Anson Troopers headed for Greensboro, which they reached about 10 o'clock in the morning on Sunday, June 1, 1862. The local citizens were starting to church, which, as a letter from a member of the 4th NC to the *North Carolina Argus* reports: "made us feel like we were from home more than ever, hearing the church bell ringing, and we on march, and could not enjoy the pleasure of going as we did when we were home." Greensboro offered much the same hospitality that they had received from the other generous towns on their journey.[15]

The boys from Anson continued on their trip, crossing the Haw River near dusk on Sunday night. They did so in the midst of a violent summer thunderstorm. The country being sparsely settled forced the company to break up to find lodgings of their own. Some found comfort from local patriots, while others spent a tough night exposed in the drenching rain. The company reformed in the morning on June 2 and began riding toward Hillsboro and then to Oxford. From Oxford, the troops reached their destination at Kittrell's Springs. They went into camp there at Camp Vance by June 4, 1862, still with the belief that they would join Vance's Legion.[16]

Despite the fact that the Legion never materialized, Capt. L. A. Johnson's Anson Troopers were mustered into Confederate service on Wednesday, July 16, 1862.[17] By the first part of August, Johnson and his troops were in and around Petersburg, Virginia. D. D. McLaurin, a private in the company, writing home to his brother Hugh in Anson County on Saturday, August 23, 1862, gives their location as Prince George Court House. They arrived there on Thursday, August 21. The company received orders around midnight Monday, August 18 to march to Petersburg early on Tuesday morning. McLaurin describes traveling through "the thickest dust I ever saw." Johnson's men arrived in Petersburg late on August 19 and made camp there that evening. In Petersburg there was hardly any feed for their horses, only some clove hay. At seven o'clock Wednesday morning they took up a line of march for Richmond, but were ordered to turn back when they were within sight of the city, never even getting out of their saddles. They camped that night in Petersburg, moving the next day to Prince George Court House.[18]

The writer to the *North Carolina Argus* from the Anson Troopers described Prince George Court House as:

> not even a cross-road, no dwelling, no grog shop, nor Doctor shop to relieve the suffering humanity by giving them speedy transit to another world; no lawyer's office to gain suits for the guilty and blast the character of the innocent; but if my recollection serves me rightly, there was a little twenty foot square brick house standing out in the field, alone, with one window on the back side, a foot square, with quite ominous looking iron bars across it. There you have Prince George Court House.

From here Johnson's company went on picket duty to the James River. There pickets covered a space of 10 miles up and down the river, most of the time in full view of the Yankee gunboats. These boats occasionally shelled the countryside, but always missed the Anson pickets. On Thursday, August 28, after five days of picketing, they received orders from Maj. Gen. Daniel Harvey Hill to move to Garysburg, North Carolina and report to Col. Dennis D. Ferebee. The boys from Anson were designated as Company A of the 4th North Carolina Cavalry (59th Regiment North Carolina State Troops).[19]

Johnson's company was only one of seven companies that comprised the regiment's original enlistment. Capt. James "Jim" T. Mitchell's company of partisan rangers began enlisting at Yanceyville, in Caswell County, on Tuesday, July 8, 1862.[20] Mitchell was a 31-year-old resident of Caswell County when he was appointed captain in the summer of 1862. The group found enlistments throughout the county and surrounding area, as well as from their local militia, the 47th Regiment, 12th Brigade.[21] They were mustered into Confederate Service a month later on Tuesday, August 12 in Yanceyville. Mitchell's company became Company B in Ferebee's 4th NC Cavalry, when assigned to the unit on Wednesday, August 20.[22]

Capt. Andrew McIntire's company began enlisting at Wilmington in New Hanover County on Monday, May 5.[23] McIntire was born and raised in New Hanover County. He was a local physician, and upon enlisting at age 50 was appointed captain. Andrew's nephew, Robert Motier McIntire, a local merchant, actually raised the company, and "he furnished sabres, saddles, and twelve horses." He was elected 1st lieutenant and later captain of the company. The McIntires had some recruits come from New Hanover County's two militia units, the 22nd and 23rd Regiments, 6th Brigade. They also had recruits from the surrounding counties of Onslow, Brunswick and Duplin.[24] They were mustered into Confederate service on Wednesday, July 16, 1862, the same day as Johnson's company.[25] On Friday, August 29 the company was at Camp Herring in Academy Grove, one mile west of Kenansville.[26] From here McIntire's men headed for Garysburg to become Company C under Ferebee.

Capt. William Sharp's company began enlisting on Tuesday, July 8, 1862. Sharp was a native of Hertford County, where he practiced law. Enlistment took place primarily at Harrellsville in Hertford County, but recruits also signed up in St. Johns, Ahoskie, Murfreesboro, and Jackson (in Northampton County).[27] Sharp's company also had the advantage of local militia recruits coming form the 6th Regiment, 2nd Brigade.[28] Sharp's men formed what became Company D of the 4th NC Cavalry. The men reported to Murfreesboro on Sunday, July 12 and began to organize. From there the company moved to Ahoskie, where they assembled into barracks. By Thursday, July 24, they occupied the local church house, which provided shelter and a meeting place. Here they drilled to prepare for the impending events. They also learned to cook and raced their horses for fun. On Tuesday, August 5, they received marching orders for Rich Square, some 20 miles away. They remained in the small town until muster orders came on Wednesday, August 20 to join Ferebee in Garysburg. Once in Garysburg, they "occupied another church house, near the railroad, with a pleasant grove surrounding it."[29]

As early as Tuesday, February 4, 1862, 2d Lt. Robert Gadd placed an advertisement in Charlotte's *Daily Bulletin* in hopes of trying to raise a group of cavalry in and around the Charlotte area.[30] This was followed on Wednesday, February 19, 1862 with an ad from Capt. John Y. Bryce, who had the same intention.[31] Recruiting began in April and May, while official enlistment began on Monday, July 7, 1862 at Charlotte, in Mecklenburg County. The recruits came primarily from the counties of Mecklenburg, Cabarrus and Rowan.[32] Many of the new recruits dropped out of the local militia units to serve under Bryce.[33] They were mustered into Confederate Service a week later on July 14 and became Company E, when they were assigned to Ferebee's cavalry in August. Capt. Bryce placed an ad in the Friday, July 18, 1862 Charlotte *Daily Bulletin* ordering all of his "Partisan Rangers" to report to Charlotte on Monday, July 21. They were to bring blankets.[34]

Capt. Joseph B. Cherry's company of partisan rangers began enlisting at Windsor, in Bertie County, on Saturday, August 9, 1862.[35] Prior to being appointed captain, Cherry was a 1st lieutenant in the 8th Regiment North Carolina State Troops, serving as an adjutant on the field staff. The company's recruits came primarily from Bertie County, with some dropping out of the local militia, the 8th Regiment, 2nd Brigade, to sign up with the new company of cavalry.[36] Cherry's company was mustered into Confederate Service in Garysburg on September 1, and became Company F when assigned to Ferebee's regiment that same day.[37]

On Monday, March 31, 1862 the "Currituck Light Cavalry" began enlisting at Currituck Court House in Currituck County under Capt. Demosthenes Bell.[38] Bell had served in Company I of the 5th Virginia Cavalry before his appointment to captain March 18, 1862. Several men dropped out of the local militia, the 1st Regiment, 1st Brigade, to join the new local cavalry.[39] Bell's company was mustered into Confederate Service on Tuesday, April 8, 1862, and was reported in Petersburg, Virginia in June, 1862.[40] They were at Sycamore Church, Prince George Court House, by early September. There Bell's detached company was under the command of Brig. Gen. S. G. French, in the department south of the James River. The returns for the month show four officers and 66 men present for duty at the time.[41] The company was officially assigned to Ferebee's cavalry and designated Company G on Monday, September 22, 1862.[42]

These seven companies made up Ferebee's 4th North Carolina Cavalry (59th

59th Regiment Officers. 1: Jos. B. Cherry, Captain, Co. F; 2: Lewis B. Sutton, 2d Lieut., Co. F; 3: D. W. Lewis, 2d Lieut. Co. D; 4: J. M. Wright, 2d Lieut., Co. A (North Carolina Office of Archives and History, Raleigh, NC).

Regiment North Carolina State Troops). They would be joined by three others before the end of the war, Companies H, I, and K. Companies A through E comprised the original regiment assigned to Col. Ferebee on Wednesday, August 20, 1862. The regiment began formal training in Garysburg, where their days consisted of learning bugle calls and formations, constant drilling, and a general introduction to army life. It would only be three and a half weeks before the new recruits would leave their new training ground and move east to Hertford County, then north up the Chowan River to Franklin, Virginia. It was here on the banks of the Blackwater River that the 4th NC Cavalry received their first taste of battle.[43]

CHAPTER 2

First Taste of Fire:
Skirmishes Along
the Blackwater

ON FRIDAY, SEPTEMBER 12, the 4th North Carolina Cavalry received marching orders for Franklin, Virginia, a small town on the Blackwater River in Southampton County. They left Garysburg early that morning, arriving in Murfreesboro late in the afternoon, where they made camp for the night. Early Saturday morning Ferebee and his men began the march to Franklin, reaching the town late that evening. Here they "found no church house for shelter and no tents." The men were forced to spread their blankets on the cold, damp ground and sleep under the elements for the first time since enlistment.[1]

When the troops awoke on Sunday, September 14, they began to get acquainted with their new surroundings in Franklin. They began to set up camp and began reconnaissance up and down the Blackwater. From here the 4th North Carolina Cavalry sent out pickets and performed guard duty, closely monitoring the Federals in Suffolk, some 20 miles east of Franklin on the Nansemond River. The Confederate operations at Franklin were coordinated under Col. J. K. Marshall of the 52nd North Carolina Infantry. The 4th NC Cavalry and the 52nd NC received artillery support from Edward Graham's Petersburg Artillery. The 20 miles between the Blackwater and Nansemond Rivers was a no man's land that was constantly patrolled by both the Confederate and Union forces.[2]

The Blackwater is a narrow, winding river that begins near Petersburg and runs just south of the Virginia and North Carolina state line. It joins the Nottoway River to form the Chowan River in North Carolina. The Chowan, which runs into the Albemarle Sound, became a gateway into Virginia for the Union boats after the fall of Roanoke Island and the burning of Winton (Hertford County). An Anson Trooper described the Blackwater as "a dull, sluggish stream, suited only for Yankee gunboats, alligators, and cypress knees." Their dislike for this place grew in the coming weeks, as picket and guard duty, along with the occasional shelling by the enemy, made the green troops yearn for home.[3]

In addition to picket and guard duty, Ferebee's first major assignment was to construct a bridge across the Blackwater at Franklin, to transport artillery and men across the river. On Monday, September 14, just two days after reaching the small town, Union troops fired upon the newly arrived Confederates. The shelling did little or no damage and construction continued on the bridge. Ferebee's pickets reported the Union strength at Suffolk on Monday to be 1,900 cavalry, five regiments of infantry, and 18 pieces of artillery. By midday on September 17, Col. Ferebee reported that the bridge was almost complete, and expected it finished within five hours. By Friday, the Col. reported the bridge finished. He also had an update on the Union strength at Suffolk, reporting it to have two full and three skeleton regiments of infantry numbering 3,800, 1,900 cavalry, and six pieces of artillery. Ferebee also stated that 140 of the enemy's cavalry was encamped within five miles of their position, monitoring their movements.[4]

This small Union cavalry force, which was a portion of Col. Samuel P. Spear's 11th Pennsylvania Cavalry, was dispatched by Maj.-Gen. John J. Peck, commanding at Suffolk. The 11th PA Cavalry, along with parts of the 96th New York Volunteers, 103rd Pennsylvania Volunteers, 13th Indiana Volunteer Infantry, Col. Charles C. Dodge's Mounted Rifles (7th New York Cavalry), and a portion of Frederick M. Follet's Artillery (4th Union Regiment, Battery D) made up the Union force under Peck at Suffolk.[5] On September 23 Peck sent Col. Spear out on reconnaissance west toward Franklin. Spear met the Confederate pickets about three miles east of the Blackwater and promptly engaged them. He pushed a mile farther and found the Confederates in force at the junction of the South Quay and Franklin roads. After falling back, Spear reported to Peck that the enemy had constructed a sturdy bridge across the Blackwater, capable of supporting artillery, and was keeping a strict guard on it.[6]

The news of Confederate concentration and their bridge across the Blackwater forced Peck to ask his commanding officer, Maj.-Gen. John A. Dix, for assistance. He wanted two or three gunboats to be sent up the Blackwater from the Chowan River to disperse the enemy and destroy the bridge. The next day, September 24, Dix forwarded Peck's request to Acting Rear-Admiral S. P. Lee, who passed it on to Lt.-Col. C. W. Flusser, on the USS *Commodore Perry*. On September 26, Flusser dispatched Lee, stating that he would be at Franklin at 6:00 A.M. on October 3 to coordinate with the Union land forces. Two other Union boats were to join Flusser at Franklin, the USS *Hunchback* commanded by Acting Lt. E. R. Colhoun and the USS *Whitehead* commanded by Acting Master Charles A. French. The *Commodore Perry* was a sidewheel steamer ferry built in 1859 by Stack & Joyce of Williamsburg, NY. Acquired by the US Navy in October 1861 for $38,000, she was 143 feet long with a displacement of 512 tons. The *Hunchback* was a steam ferryboat built in 1852 in New York City, measuring 179 feet long with a displacement of 517 tons. The U.S. Navy purchased her in December 1861. (After the war the New York & Brooklyn Ferry Company bought both the *Commodore Perry* and the *Hunchback*. The *Hunchback* remained in active

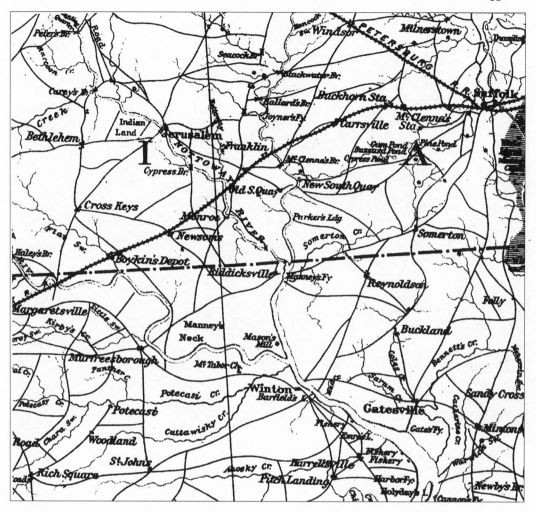

Northeastern North Carolina and Southeastern Virginia (Atlas to Accompany the Official Records, Plate CXXXVIII).

service until 1880). The *Whitehead* was a screw steamer built in 1861 at New Brunswick, NJ. She was acquired and commissioned by the US Navy later that same year. Much smaller than her two companions on the Blackwater River, she was 93 feet long with a displacement of 136 tons. (After the war the *Whitehead* was sold at public auction and redocumented as the *Nevada*, remaining in active mercantile service until 1872 when she was destroyed by fire).[7]

On Wednesday, October 1, the 4th NC Cavalry, 52nd NC, and Graham's Artillery were joined by Col. Collet Leventhorpe's 11th NC Infantry, which had been serving around Wilmington and other points along the North Carolina coast.[8] On Thursday, Confederate pickets were sent out to Carrsville, about six miles east of Franklin on the Seaboard and Roanoke Railroad. They were spotted by Union pickets who reported back to Maj.-Gen. Peck.[9] Peck was very concerned about the coordinated

USS Hunchback **(Department of the Navy—Naval Historical Center, Washington, DC).**

land and sea effort planned for Friday morning, feeling it better to wait until October 9.[10] However, reports of the Confederate pickets near Carrsville prompted Dix to order Peck to send a force of nearly 2,000 infantry, cavalry, and artillery from Suffolk to Franklin. They were to attack early Friday morning to disperse the Confederates and destroy the "floating bridge" in cooperation with the gunboats heading up the Blackwater.[11] Col. Spear commanded the Union force that left Suffolk at 9:00 P.M., arriving at Carrsville by morning.[12] Between 2:00 A.M. and 3:00 A.M. that night two deserters from Dodge's Mounted Rifles, one an orderly from Gen. Peck's headquarters, made their way to the Confederates.[13]

Late Thursday evening Confederate pickets, most likely from the Chesapeake Cavalry Company of the 14th Battalion Virginia Cavalry, which had headquarters in a schoolhouse half a mile from South Quay, spotted three Union gunboats passing South Quay a few miles below Franklin.[14] These were the *USS Commodore Perry*, the *USS Hunchback*, and the *USS Whitehead*, heading up the Blackwater for their rendezvous with Spear's force Friday morning. The three boats remained around South Quay that evening so that they could get an early start at Franklin the next morning. The Con-

USS *Commodore Perry* (Department of the Navy—Naval Historical Center, Washington, DC).

federates knew that they would meet their enemy the next day, but reported getting a good night's sleep nevertheless.[15]

At 5:45 A.M. Friday morning the Union boats began moving up the Blackwater toward Franklin, shelling the banks as they advanced.[16] These shells awoke the men of the 4th NC Cavalry on October 3, with one shell exploding just outside their camp. Their horses were soon removed and sent to the rear.[17] The regiment, now dismounted, armed with shotguns and carbines, received orders from commanding Col. J. K. Marshall. Marshall sent Lt. John M. Alexander, commanding Company A of the 52nd NC, to Crumpler's Bluff, with orders to commence firing upon the Union boats after the last ship passed that point. He sent Capt. John M. McCain, Capt. Eric Erson, and Lt. James M. Kincaid of the 52nd NC, along with Capt. James T. Mitchell (Company B) of the 4th NC Cavalry, with pickets in their respective commands to the neighboring bluffs, to fire upon the boats on their return down the river.[18]

Col. Ferebee, with a large portion of the 4th NC Cavalry, took a position along the road, where the old wharf once stood. From here, he sent Capt. William Sharp's Company D, under the command of Lt. Thomas Ruffin, with Company A, to the banks of the Blackwater. Ruffin formed the dismounted men into line and proceeded to the river. However, this was no easy task, as they had to cross an almost impenetrable swamp. After some trouble, they did make it to the river. Once there, Lt. Ruffin stationed his men behind trees and bushes to await the first boat.[19]

By 7:00 A.M. the USS Commodore Perry was within three-quarters of a mile Franklin. Flusser was having trouble turning his boat in a bend at that point of the narrow, crooked river. At this time, Lt. Ruffin's force, with the Confederate detachments on the bluffs overhead, began to open fire on the boat. They fired a sharp volley into the pilot house and all other exposed parts of the steamer. Flusser ordered his men to take cover on the boat and steam ahead of the fire. It was too close for Flusser to use his big guns. His only chance was to steam ahead out of the Confederate fire to a position where he could use his large guns, but the river was very narrow at this point and the boat ran into the bank. Ruffin and his men were so close to the boat they claimed to hear the Union officers cussing their crew. He thought they would surely capture the ship.[20]

However, after a few minutes the USS Commodore Perry got free and started up the river again. Now the Union steamer was in a position to use its guns again. Flusser started shelling Ruffin's men with 9-inch grape and shell, and with canister and shrapnel from their field piece. The canister rounds tore the trees covering the Confederates to shreds. This fire covered the USS Hunchback as it made its way through the tight bend. The Hunchback in turn covered the USS Whitehead as it turned in the bend. The fire from these boats forced Lt. Ruffin's force to retire.[21]

After turning the bend, the Union boats found the river barricaded in front of them. Flusser thought the barricade could be removed, but not under the sharp fire that the Confederates were showering on them. Therefore, the three boats were forced to hold their positions and wait for the Union land forces under Col. Spear to arrive. During this time a general fire commenced. The three boats began firing a number of shells at the Confederates. Flusser reported the following action on the Commodore Perry during this time:

> with the forward 9-inch gun I threw shells in the direction of Franklin; with the forward 32-pounder poured grape and canister into the woods on our left; with the after 32-pounder and field gun gave them the same on the right, and shelled the bluff ... with the after 9-inch gun.[22]

The Confederates kept up their firing on the boats from their various positions. By 10:15 A.M. the Union boats could no longer take the Confederate fire and started back down the river, without joining the Union land forces as planned.[23] Maj.-Gen. Dix sent a messenger to warn Flusser to wait a few days for the attack, feeling, like Peck, that it was too early to attack the Confederates. However, the messenger was delayed and did not make it to Flusser before he began the Friday morning assault.[24] As they made their way back down the Blackwater they were again showered with fire from the bluffs overhead. The Confederates had also cut down trees behind the boats, with hopes of stopping them on their return. This was not successful, because the Union boats were able to push through these obstacles with a full head of steam. Although the main engagement with the ships lasted nearly six hours, general fire continued for a few more hours until between 2:30 and 3:30 P.M., when the boats passed the last point of Confederate sharpshooters.[25]

During the fighting the *Commodore Perry* had two men killed and 10 wounded, the *Hunchback* had two killed and one wounded, while the *Whitehead* reported only four wounded. The *Commodore Perry* reported firing 319 shells, the *Hunchback* 132 shells, and the *Whitehead* 40 rounds. The Union boats headed back to the Albemarle Sound. They reported passing Winton, NC about 5:00 P.M. From there the *Hunchback* stopped at Plymouth, NC to bury the dead, while the *Commodore Perry* headed for Roanoke Island with the wounded. Six Federal seamen received the Medal of Honor for their part in this battle: Seaman Thomas Barton of the *Hunchback*, Boatswain's Mate John Breen, Seaman Daniel Lakin, Seaman Alfred Peterson, and Seaman John Williams of the *Commodore Perry*, and Ordinary Seaman Edwin Smith of the *Whitehead*. [26]

About 1:00 P.M., just as the skirmishing with the boats was coming to an end, the Union land force under Spear appeared across the Blackwater from the Confederates, missing their chance for a joint assault. Col. Marshall reported the force to consist of four regiments of infantry, one regiment of cavalry, and six pieces of artillery.[27] Spear was soon fired upon by a Confederate 32-pounder and other heavy guns in the Confederate battery. At this point, Spear placed Whitney's section of Follet's artillery and two small howitzers in a favorable position to fire upon the Confederates. He also put supports on this position and sent out parties to report on his flanks. A furious fire ensued for about an hour, at which time the Confederates fell back to await fresh troops.[28]

About this time, Edward Graham's Petersburg Artillery began the fight again for the Confederates. One of Graham's pieces was placed at the depot and another was carried to the bridge under Lt. Britton.[29] Spear then moved the 13th Indiana Regiment under Lt. Col. Dobbs down the right bank to open fire upon the Rebel position.[30] The fighting continued for another two hours, with the Union forces retiring between 3:30 and 4:00 P.M., leaving behind a brass field piece, a few overcoats and a horse.[31] Spear, who originally was supposed to leave with 2,000 men, left with what he believed to be 1,700 men. However, he discovered that he only had about 1,300 men. This and the fact that he was running out of ammunition forced the Federals to head back to Suffolk.[32] Dix also reported that he feared what the two deserters may have told the Confederates about their strength.[33]

Although the fight at Franklin on October 3 was only a minor skirmish, it served two important functions for the Confederates. It gave Ferebee's green regiment of cavalry its first taste of fire and a little confidence in its ability, and it also kept the Union gunboats from coming back up the Blackwater for a little while. The 4th NC Cavalry and the other Confederate forces at Franklin spent the rest of October watching their enemy across the Blackwater. Pickett duty continued and a few minor engagements ensued. On October 9 Edward Graham's artillery fired on a squadron of Union cavalry advancing near the railroad at Franklin forcing them to flee.[34] On October 15, there was a minor skirmish near Carrsville. It occurred when the regiment went on a scouting expedition across the Blackwater near Carrsville. The 4th NC Cavalry met a small force of Federal cavalry and succeeded in killing two horses and capturing two prisoners.[35]

In mid–October 1862, the 4th NC Cavalry was placed in the brigade of Brig. Gen. Beverly Holcombe Robertson, along with the 41st North Carolina (3rd North Carolina Cavalry), 63rd North Carolina (5th North Carolina Cavalry), 62nd Georgia Infantry (Mounted), and the 7th Confederate Cavalry. The rest of the brigade was at Garysburg, NC, in instructional camp under Robertson. It was another month before the 4th NC Cavalry met its new brigade in Garysburg.[36]

The new Brig. Gen., B. H. Robertson, was born at The Oaks in Amelia County, Virginia on June 5, 1827. He was the son of Dr. William H. Robertson. Robertson attended West Point from 1846 to 1849, graduating 25th in of a class of 43. He was commissioned 2nd lieutenant in the 2nd Dragoons on July 1, 1849, serving mainly on the western frontier. He was appointed first lieutenant on March 3, 1855 and captain on March 3, 1861. Shortly after this promotion he resigned from the US Army upon appointment as colonel of the 4th VA Cavalry. Robertson was promoted to Brig. Gen. on Monday, June 9, 1862. On Friday, September 5 he was assigned to the Department of North Carolina to take command of a cavalry brigade. During the fall of 1862 he organized and commanded the instruction camp in Garysburg, NC. Here he drilled his green troops daily in the fine art of cavalry.[37] One member of the brigade described him as "very strict, and sometimes irascible on military points."[38] Another member described this encounter with Robertson, who "came in the field where we were drilling yesterday evening and drilled our company a half hour or more. He is not the mildest man I ever saw by any means."[39] Despite whatever feelings the men had about his personality, they did respect his experience, knowledge and ability.

Picket and guard duty continued for the 4th North Carolina Cavalry and the other Confederates at Franklin through the end of October and into the first few weeks of November 1862. All remained quiet for the most part, notwithstanding an occasional encounter between picket forces. The weather was turning colder and the troops were still in their cotton tents. The wanted to begin making winter quarters soon. A soldier in Company A of the 4th NC Cavalry, writing to the Wadesboro *North Carolina Argus*, sarcastically described picket duty and camp life in Franklin as follows:

> There are many hardships in war that the uninitiated never dream of. It is excellent
> fun to be shot at in plain view of a man who takes sure aim, and will yell if he sees
> you fall. It is fine sport to stand picket near the enemy lines on a cold drizzly night
> with your toes aching, and your teeth chattering ... and, for fear a Yankee might pick
> you off, don't dare to kindle a blaze of fire. It is excellent to run your horse all day
> and to get to the dozen places you are ordered to at the same time, and then it is a
> great luxury, after fasting, to come in and find your mess with nothing cooked.[40]

The 4th NC Cavalry awoke on Wednesday, November 12 to find that it had snowed during the night. The cold, wet weather, especially in the cloth tents, made their camp life even more intolerable. Animal forage (hay or grass), "the Linchpin of mobility" in the 19th century, had become very scarce around Franklin and the surrounding countryside due to the constant skirmishing with their enemy on the Nansemond. What forage that "was not immediately eaten was soon ground into the dust or mud." The operations in the area prevented most of the locals from making their crops. Despite their complaining, the regiment was in good health and enjoying a few weeks of relatively light duty. On Thursday, November 13, the 4th NC Cavalry marched across the Blackwater on a foraging expedition. They found no sign of the enemy for miles, but did find a plantation from which forage could be obtained.[41]

On Sunday, November 16, the regiment received orders to prepare one day's rations and be ready to march at 4:00 A.M. on Monday. Ferebee's men, with the 11th NC and Graham's Artillery, were going to return to the plantation to obtain forage and other essentials for the Confederate forces at Franklin. The troops left at 4:00 A.M. and were accompanied by a long wagon train to be filled with the forage and other essentials. One squadron of the 4th NC Cavalry guarded the wagons

Brigadier General Beverly Holcombe Robertson (Massachusetts Commandery Military Order of the Loyal Legion and the US Army Military History Institute).

while another advanced beyond Carrsville to scout ahead for signs of any Union troops in the area. The wagon train reached the plantation and the wagons were filled with the much-needed forage. Sometime before lunch the troops headed back toward camp.[42]

On their return, one of the rear guards from the 4th NC returned to the main body and reported that a group of the enemy's cavalry was advancing in their direction.[43] This was a force of about 140 cavalry under Maj. Samuel Whitherill sent out from Suffolk by Col. Spear. They were halfway between Holland's Corners and Carrsville, about seven miles east of Franklin.[44] The 4th NC's rear guard quickly hid along both sides of the road to surprise the advancing enemy. However, Witherill was suspicious and sent two of his troopers to feel the way. They surrendered upon seeing the Confederates. When his two front men did not return, Witherill halted his force to survey the situation. About this time Edward Graham's artillery advanced up the road with the remainder of the 4th NC Cavalry and the 11th NC Infantry. Graham's guns opened on the Union troops and "they put their spurs in active service

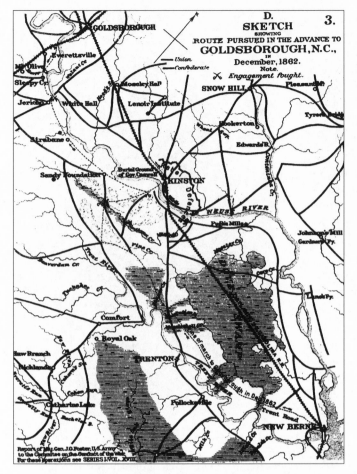

Movements in Eastern North Carolina (Atlas to Accompany the Official Records, Plate XCI).

towards Suffolk." They skirmished in the surrounding woods for a short time, but soon they could find nothing of the enemy. That evening they returned to camp in Franklin.[45]

The Confederates awoke the next morning, Tuesday, November 18, to the booming of Yankee cannon fire. There was a mad scramble in camp to prepare to meet the Union force. By 11:00 A.M. the Federal forces were within a mile and a half of Franklin. For three hours Graham's Artillery kept up a continual fire with the enemy across the Blackwater. By 2:00 P.M. the Union forces retired from the fight. The 4th NC Cavalry was dispatched to follow them. Local citizens reported the Yankees coming by, claiming that they found no Confederate force at Franklin. The local citizens also told members of the 4th NC that the Union forces had ready-built (pontoon) bridges with which to cross the Blackwater. It is clear that the Federals intended to take Franklin on November 18, but they did not expect the reception they got from the Confederates guarding the town. The Union forces made a similar advance on Col. Marshall, some seven miles up the river, but were met with the same reception.[46] On Friday, November, 21, the 4th NC Cavalry received orders to return to Garysburg to commence building its winter quarters.[47]

CHAPTER 3

The Battle of Whitehall

B Y MONDAY, NOVEMBER 24, Ferebee and his cavalrymen returned to Garysburg and joined the rest of Robertson's Brigade. They camped about a mile outside of Garysburg and began to build winter quarters. Since they thought they would remain in Northampton County for the entire winter, Robertson's men built very comfortable quarters. The troops split logs and notched them, creating small log cabin structures about three feet high with a chimney at one end. Barrels were placed atop some of the chimneys to help increase the draft. Over this frame they placed their tents. Inside these huts they made their beds on a layer of pine straw and blankets. At night they sat inside by the fire and told stories of their homes and loved ones. Daily drilling and routine camp life filled their days and nights for the next three weeks. This routine ended when the Union force in New Bern started on an expedition for Goldsboro.[1]

About 8 o'clock Thursday morning, December 11, Union Maj. Gen. John G. Foster, commanding the Department of North Carolina, left New Bern with a force of 10,000 infantry, 40 artillery guns, and 640 cavalrymen.[2] The Union's objective was to capture Kinston and Goldsboro, "therefore cutting the Wilmington and Weldon Railroad, which would isolate Wilmington and effectually cut off its supplies and reinforcements."[3] This mission was to coincide with Gen. Ambrose E. Burnside's movement on Fredericksburg, Virginia. Foster and his troops traveled only about 14 miles up the Trent Road before meeting a Confederate picket force about 3:00 P.M. After the advance guard of the 3rd New York Cavalry drove away the small force, the Union troops found the road blocked by felled trees. The dense blockade, which extended for several hundred yards, and the surrounding swamp, forced the Federals to stop for the evening. Foster ordered the obstructions cleared and the Union troops went into camp for the night.[4]

Foster and his men broke camp at sunrise on Friday morning and pushed on toward Kinston. About 9:30 A.M. Capt. Marshall, commanding Company B, 3rd New York Cavalry, skirmished with a Confederate picket force, taking a few prisoners. After minor encounters with the Confederate cavalry throughout the day, Foster's column halted for the evening about 11 miles from Kinston. On Saturday, December 13, the Union troops continued their advance at daybreak, reaching Southwest Creek, about five miles from Kinston, by 9:00 A.M. Here Foster found the bridge partially destroyed by a Confederate force on the opposite bank.[5] The Confederate force consisted of Col. James D. Radcliffe's 61st North Carolina, which was entrenched behind an earthwork.

About 10:00 A.M. Brig. Gen. N. G. Evans arrived on the field and assumed command of the Confederate force, which consisted of the 17th South Carolina, 22nd South Carolina, 23rd South Carolina, Holcombe Legion South Carolina Volunteers, 61st North Carolina, Maj. Mallett's North Carolina Infantry Battalion, Capt. Boyce's Light Battery South Carolina Volunteers, and Capt. Bunting's and Starr's Batteries North Carolina Light Artillery. The forces fought until sunset, when Evans decided to withdraw his troops due to the Union's superior numbers.[6] After repairing the bridge, Foster advanced a little farther, camping that evening about four miles from Kinston.[7]

On Sunday morning, December 14, Ferebee and his men received orders in Garysburg to march to the railroad and take the train to Goldsboro. Their horses were sent through the country to meet them there. The 4th NC Cavalry was sent in hopes of countering the Union forces heading to Goldsboro under Foster. They arrived at Mosely Hall (present day La Grange) later in the day.[8] At daybreak the Union column continued its advance toward Kinston, with the 3rd NY Cavalry and Henry W. Wessell's Brigade in the lead. Sometime between 9:00 and 10:00 A.M. the Confederates under Brig. Gen. Evans once again met Foster's troops, this time about a mile outside Kinston. Evans was posted in a strong position in the woods, his right being secured by a deep swamp. Realizing the strong position Evans held, Foster deployed his troops in waves.[9]

Foster first sent in Col. Heckman's 9th New Jersey, along with Wessell's Brigade and Morrison's 3rd New York Artillery. Col. Armory's 17th Massachusetts Volunteers were sent ahead next to support the 9th New Jersey on the Union right. The 23rd and 45th Massachusetts were then moved forward, along with Belger's 1st Rhode Island Artillery, Battery F. To support the Union left, Foster moved up the 24th Massachusetts and the 5th Rhode Island. To support his right, he employed the 10th Connecticut and 44th Massachusetts. After three hours, the Union's superior numbers and a gallant charge by the 10th Connecticut and 96th New York forced Evans to retreat across the Neuse back to Kinston, burning the bridge behind him. During the afternoon, Evans continued pulling back, reaching Falling Creek by evening. Due to the hour and feeling his immediate mission accomplished, Foster did not pursue Evans. Instead, the Union troops bivouacked in a field beyond Kinston for the night.[10]

Monday morning Foster recrossed the Neuse and started for Goldsboro. He left Maj. Charles Fitz Simmons of the 3rd NY Cavalry to guard Kinston and Col. Ledlie of the 3rd NY Artillery to repair the bridge. During the day, the Union column moved about 17 miles to within four miles of Whitehall.[11] After learning that Foster was heading to Whitehall, Gen. Evans sent a dispatch to Robertson at Mosely Hall. Evans

Bridge over the Neuse River at Whitehall; photograph taken in 1884 from the position of Company A, 44th Massachusetts Volunteer Militia (North Carolina Collection, University of North Carolina Library at Chapel Hill).

wanted him to hasten to that point to prevent the Union crossing the Neuse River, while he planned to attack Foster's rear from the south. At 11:30 A.M. the Confederates under Brig. Gen. B. H. Robertson left Mosely Hall, taking the Atlantic Road for Whitehall. Robertson's force consisted of Leventhorpe's 11th North Carolina, portions of Ferebee's 4th North Carolina Cavalry and Evans's 5th North Carolina Cavalry, and Lt. McCleese's Company B, 3rd Battalion North Carolina Light Artillery. His object was to burn the bridge at Whitehall to prevent the Union crossing and flanking Evans's right.[12]

Due to the lack of horses, which were on the way from Garysburg, Robertson drafted a citizen guide to reconnoiter with him in advance of his command. After arriving in Whitehall, he discovered that the Union forces had not yet arrived. Robertson then sent his citizen guide toward Kinston to scout for the enemy to prevent a surprise attack. Robertson's forces continued to Whitehall on foot and arrived about an hour after him, just before sunset. At this time he posted McCleese's battery on the north bank of the Neuse and made preparations to burn the bridge.[13]

Whitehall, North Carolina was a small town on the southern bank of the Neuse River between Kinston and Goldsboro. It was named for the plantation of William

View of Confederate riverbank at Whitehall. This 1884 photograph is the view directly opposite the position of the 44th Massachusetts Volunteer Militia (North Carolina Collection, University of North Carolina Library at Chapel Hill).

Whitefield built around 1741. The town became Seven Springs in 1881. In 1862, the small hamlet consisted of "two or three stores and warehouses, and a straggling street with some neat dwellings and enclosures." The town was situated on a high bluff on the southern bank, which overlooked a gentle rolling slope on the northern bank. The northern bank was bordered by a swamp, which contained a dense growth of tall timber. Although the Neuse was narrow at Whitehall, it was deep and navigable. In fact, the river was not fordable at Whitehall, making the bridge there all the more important for military purposes.[14]

On the northern bank, not far from the bridge, a gunboat, the *CSS Neuse*, was in the course of construction in December 1862. Local carpenters were hired to construct the ship's hull. The local stand of dense pines furnished timber for the boat's construction. Many felled pines were scattered on the river's bank when Robertson's troops arrived, and they served as much-needed cover for his men during the fighting.[15]

As mentioned earlier, Foster's column camped within four miles of Whitehall on the evening of Monday, December 15. From there Foster sent Maj. Garrard, with three companies of the 3rd New York Cavalry and Capt. Jenny's Battery F, 3rd New York Artillery, to reconnoiter in the direction of Whitehall.[16] It was this Union force that Robertson's advance guard discovered outside of Whitehall. The Confederates

View from the bridge at Whitehall showing the riverbank where the CSS *Neuse* was under construction during the battle (North Carolina Collection, University of North Carolina Library at Chapel Hill).

retreated, bringing down piles of crude rosin and barrels of turpentine from the high bluffs on the southern bank and placing the combustibles on the bridge on their return. They recrossed the bridge and set fire to the structure just as Foster's men arrived there.[17]

Upon arriving at the burning structure, the Union forces discovered the Confederate ship under construction on the opposite bank. Its destruction became a third priority for the Union, along with flanking Evans's right and taking Goldsboro. Maj. Garrard wanted a volunteer to swim the river and set fire to the Confederate ship. Pvt. Henry Butler of Company C, 3rd NY Cavalry, volunteered, but was quickly forced back to the southern bank by a sharp volley from Robertson's men before completing his task. These shots came from Capt. Francis Bird's Company C and Capt. Edward Small's Company F, both from the 11th North Carolina. A general fire soon commenced between these two companies and the Union troops.[18]

The other troops under Robertson were ordered into the surrounding woods to camp for the night. Most of Robertson's men were exhausted from the day's march, since they were not accustomed to traveling on foot. The Confederates had nothing to eat during the day on their way to Whitehall, so some of Ferebee's men were sent out to gather food for the regiment. The detail returned with a hog, which they made quick preparations to begin boiling. However, the Union troops soon discovered the

Construction of CSS *Neuse*, Whitehall, North Carolina (Modern-day Seven Springs, NC) (watercolor by Steven McCall. Courtesy of the CSS *Neuse* Gunboat Association, Inc.).

fire and began to shell the camp. This fire was immediately put out and Robertson ordered his men out of the range of the enemy's artillery. Ferebee's men were forced to spend the rest of the night in darkness without anything to eat.[19] Not all of the Confederates went hungry; some of the 11th NC were able to roast potatoes for supper.[20] The Union forces continued to shell the Confederates off and on throughout the night. Around midnight Foster's men set fire to Whitehall.[21]

About 9:00 A.M. on Tuesday, December 16, a picket skirmish commenced between a detachment of the 3rd NY Cavalry and Capt. Ransom's 23rd NY Artillery and two companies of the 11th North Carolina, led by Capt. M. D. Armfield. The Union troops returned fire until their main column arrived a short time later. After the skirmish began, Robertson went down to the bridge to survey the situation. He then placed Col. John V. Jordan's 31st North Carolina, which had arrived late Monday night from Wilmington, in a sheltered position near the bridge. He also posted Lt. Nelson McCleese's Company B, 3rd NC Light Artillery, adjacent to Jordan, to shell the Union troops. Robertson held the 4th and 5th NC Cavalries and Leventhorpe's 11th NC in reserve. The Confederates' fire was not as effective as it could have been due to Foster's advantage of the high ground on the southern bank.[22]

When Foster's main column arrived, Col. Charles A. Heckman and his 9th New Jersey Infantry were in the lead. They were followed by Col. Thomas J. C. Armory's 17th Massachusetts Volunteers. Armory commanded the 1st Brigade of the 2nd Divi-

Battle of Whitehall, December 16, 1862 (watercolor by Steven McCall. Courtesy of the CSS *Neuse* Gunboat Association, Inc.).

sion, which consisted of the 17th, 23rd, and 45th Massachusetts. Upon their arrival, Foster sent Garrard and the initial Union picket force on to Mt. Olive, a station on the Wilmington and Weldon Railroad, 14 miles below Goldsboro. Heckman's and Armory's men drew the fire of the Confederates and were immediately sent forward to the banks of the river to engage their enemy. Heckman ordered the fences on each side of the road torn down so that the artillery could take their position.[23]

Heckman's 9th New Jersey was deployed first, as a skirmish force. After firing sixty rounds, it was replaced by the 17th Massachusetts on the left and the 23rd Massachusetts on the right. The 17th led the way, followed by the 23rd. The 23rd Massachusetts marched through a small swamp under heavy fire from the Confederates. When it reached the edge of the Neuse River, the extreme left was resting where the bridge had been destroyed. Armory ordered Charles R. Codman's 45th Massachusetts to take a position along the Whitehall Road. The men were told to lie down to take cover and never actually engaged their enemy. Across the river, the Confederates were positioned behind trees and stumps. Some Confederates made a makeshift log fort out of the felled trees being used to construct the CSS *Neuse's* hull. A brisk fire immediately ensued and after firing 40 rounds the Union troops gave way to the 3rd NY Artillery, which had been placed behind them.[24]

Capt. Jenny's Battery F, 3rd NY Artillery, which was placed on a hill directly across from the Confederates, was the first Union artillery to engage. After firing about 20 rounds, one of Battery F's guns burst. About 10:30 A.M. Capt. Angel's Battery K, 3rd

The Battle of Whitehall, December 16, 1862, taken from *Harper's Weekly*, January 10, 1863 (North Carolina Collection, University of North Carolina Library at Chapel Hill).

NY Artillery, was moved forward to support Jenny's right. The right section of Jenny's battery under J. F. Dennis was then sent forward and posted on the left side of the bridge. Lt. George E. Ashby's Battery E, 3rd NY Artillery, and Capt. James Belger's Battery F, 1st Rhode Island Artillery, were then put in position on a hill behind Angel and Jenny to fire down on the Confederates.[25]

The Union firepower proved too heavy for Jordan's 31st NC and it withdrew without instructions. Brig. Gen. Robertson then ordered Leventhorpe's 11th NC forward into the swamp to replace Jordan's troops and engage the enemy. Col. Dennis D. Ferebee of the 4th NC Cavalry commanded a small skirmish force consisting of 18 men from the 11th NC. The small force fought the Union troops at close quarters for several hours and was praised by Robertson for its bravery after the battle. The fighting lingered on for several hours as the small Confederate force tried to hold its position.[26]

Meanwhile, Foster posted Capt. Jay E. Lee's 24th New York Battalion in the swamp to the right of the 3rd NY Artillery. Lt. George W. Thomas' Battery I, 3rd NY Artillery, and a section of Lt. Thomas J. Mersereau's Battery K, 3rd NY Artillery, were sent forward to the left of the bridge. Capt. William J. Riggs's Battery H, 3rd NY Artillery, and Capt. James Belger's Battery F, 1st Rhode Island Artillery, were then placed in the center of the Union line. They opened fire upon the Confederates at point-blank range. They were joined by Col. Francis L. Lee's 44th Massachusetts Volunteer Militia on the left of the road leading to the bridge. However, the Union fire had little effect on the concealed Confederate sharpshooters. Between noon and 1:00 P.M., almost five hours after the battle started, Foster deemed his mission at Whitehall accomplished, and decided to withdraw his force and continue on toward Goldsboro.[27]

At the time Foster withdrew his force, the 11th NC ran out of ammunition and was relieved by the 31st NC.[28] Foster left behind Capt. Job Arnold's 5th Rhode Island and a few sharpshooters from the 24th Massachusetts to engage the rebels until the rear of the Union column passed. They were also joined by small detachments from the 25th and 46th Massachusetts. Jordan's 31st NC returned fire with the Union sharpshooters. Foster's column arrived in Mt. Olive around 3:00 P.M. on Tuesday.[29]

At 4:30 P.M. Brig. Gen. Robertson sent a dispatch to Maj. Gen. S. G. French requesting ammunition for Leventhorpe's 11th NC Infantry. He also reported that the firing had nearly ceased. That afternoon the Confederates collected about 70 Union guns and a quantity of clothing from the battlefield. The 4th and 5th NC Cavalries were not actively engaged during the battle at Whitehall. However, they were constantly exposed to Union fire throughout the ordeal and two soldiers, Pvt. Benjamin F. Smith and Pvt. Elias Dulin, from Company E, 4th NC Cavalry, were killed in the battle. By sundown, Robertson and his troops were at Spring Bank Bridge, located in central Wayne County on the Neuse River. From here he requested rations for his tired and hungry troops. Robertson left behind four companies from the 31st NC, under the command of Capt. Edward R. Liles, to guard Whitehall. On December 19, a detachment from this group was sent across the river to bury the Union dead. Wednesday morning, December 17, Robertson reported holding the ferry at Spring Bank.[30] Later that same day in Goldsboro, Foster completed his mission by burning the railroad bridge and the depot, and destroying a train of four railroad cars and the water tower. Afterwards, Foster and his troops returned to New Bern.[31] The next day, December 18, Robertson and his Confederates reached Goldsboro, where they remained until January 12, 1863.[32]

CHAPTER 4

Movements in
Eastern North Carolina

FEREBEE AND HIS MEN SPENT the Christmas of 1862 in Goldsboro with the rest of Brig. Gen. B. H. Robertson's command. There they recovered from the action at Whitehall and received their horses, which finally arrived from Garysburg. Abe Jones, a member of the 5th NC Cavalry, wrote his brother Ellick from near Kinston on Christmas Eve, lamenting:

> Christmas is close at hand & I suppose you will have a nice time hunting rabbits, squirrels [sic] & I should like to be with you a day or two to take a hunt & see all. [B]ut it is useless to think about home in the army & especially when there are so many Yankees in our state. There is no Christmas in the army & Sunday is generally the day for long marches and fighting.

Although the battle at Whitehall could not compare to the larger battles elsewhere, it was quite enough fight for those involved and the quiet time in Goldsboro afterwards was much needed. The soldiers' daily life here consisted mainly of picket duty, drilling, and gathering forage for their horses.[1] Their spare time consisted of writing letters home to loved ones and other various activities, including dice and card games. Other entertainment was provided by the 4th NC Cavalry's brass band, which lifted the men's spirits each night. Potatoes, which grew in abundance in the area, served as the main staple for lunch and supper.[2] Despite the relatively quiet time in Goldsboro, Robertson did have to deal with the problem of deserters. The 4th NC Cavalry had no less than 39 deserters after the battle at Whitehall, while the 5th NC Cavalry had at least 13. Finding and retrieving these men became a top priority for Robertson and his staff.[3]

Although the majority of his command was at Goldsboro, Robertson did have a picket force along the Chowan River to keep an eye on the Union's activity there. Lt. Daniel W. Lewis, of Company D, 4th NC Cavalry, commanded these detached soldiers near Winton. On Monday, January 5, 1863, Lewis reported to Ferebee from Barefield (now Tuscarora Beach) that the Union troops in Gates and Chowan counties, numbering perhaps 12,000, were on the move toward New Bern to reinforce Foster. Although some doubted the accuracy of Lewis's report, there was no doubt that the Union's activity in and around New Bern needed to be investigated.[4]

Robertson, realizing the importance of finding out the Union's plans and movements around New Bern and eastern North Carolina, went on a scouting expedition to determine the enemy's intentions. Ferebee and his men began their reconnaissance on the morning of Wednesday, January 14, 1863, when they left Goldsboro for Kinston. That afternoon they passed through Kinston and camped on the south side of the Neuse. Ferebee and his cavalrymen, along with the other Confederates at Kinston, began building entrenchments around the town. On Sunday, January 18, Ferebee's men started south on an expedition to Jones and Onslow Counties. During this assignment the men slept on the ground, with single blankets as their only cover. That evening they reached Richlands, named for the fertile soil of the region, about 10 miles north of Jacksonville. In Richlands, they heard the Union's cannons in the distance.[5] Tuesday evening Robertson was informed by Maj. Gen. G. W. Smith, commanding at Goldsboro, that the Union force that was in Trenton on January 17 was within three miles of Jacksonville.[6] Upon learning of the Union position, Robertson and Ferebee proceeded immediately south to Jacksonville Wednesday morning. However, when they arrived the Union force was already gone. Although they did not engage the enemy, they did find a disabled Union wagon full of blankets, axes, and other much-needed supplies.[7] They pursued the Union force to within 10 miles of New Bern, but returned to Kinston by January 25.[8] By that time the entrenchments around Kinston were formidable.

On Wednesday, January 28, the 1st lieutenant of every company in the 4th NC Cavalry was sent home for 30 days to recruit new men and gather deserters. The rest of Ferebee's men remained in camp at Kinston, performing picket duty along the Neuse River. Events remained relatively quiet for the 4th NC Cavalry until Wednesday, February 11, when they marched to Snow Hill in Greene County. The unit set up camp about four miles from Snow Hill, where the main priorities were drilling and attending to the horses.[9]

Meanwhile in Virginia, Lt. Gen. James Longstreet was assigned by Gen. Lee to the south side of the James River to guard Richmond from any possible attack from that direction.[10] On Wednesday, February 25, Maj. Gen. D. H. Hill assumed command of the Department of North Carolina.[11] One of Longstreet's major concerns was to protect the supply lines in eastern North Carolina and gather as many provisions from the fertile region as possible. He felt that the only way to accomplish this was to contain the Union at its bases in Tidewater Virginia and eastern North Carolina. To contain the Union, Longstreet decided to move on Suffolk, while his subordinate was to attack the enemy at New Bern and Washington.[12]

Neither Longstreet nor Hill had any confidence in Brig. Gen. B. H. Robertson as a leader. Hill, in a February 23 dispatch, described Robertson's Brigade as "wonderfully inefficient."[13] He wanted Wade Hampton to command North Carolina's cavalry, while Longstreet preferred Robert Ransom for the job. Despite their misgivings about Robertson's ability to lead, Longstreet and Hill needed his cavalry troops in their upcoming plans. To keep the Federals at their bases and protect the crucial supply lines in eastern North Carolina, Longstreet wanted Hill to "make a diversion upon New Bern and surprise the garrison at Washington."[14] Heavy rains forced Hill to move on New Bern instead. Hill's strategy called for a three-pronged attack on the city originating in Kinston, 30 miles west. First, Brig. Gen. Junius Daniel was to move on New Bern along the Lower Trent Road. Second, Brig. Gen. Robertson's cavalry was to proceed along the south side of the Trent River, on the Upper Trent Road, with orders to tear up the Atlantic and North Carolina Railroad. Finally, Brig. Gen. James Johnston Pettigrew's troops, with Maj. John C. Haskell's artillery, were to move on the city around Barrington's Ferry, with orders to shell Fort Anderson and the Union gunboats in the Neuse River.[15]

On Monday, March 9, under orders from Hill, Robertson left Snow Hill for Kinston to begin his part in the expedition. Tuesday he left Kinston, proceeding along the south side of the Trent River with six squadrons, three each from the 4th and 5th North Carolina Cavalries. Robertson and his men had instructions to tear up the Atlantic and North Carolina Railroad south of New Bern. Robertson had information from Capt. Thomas Harris, Company E, 5th NC Cavalry (on picket duty between the White Oak River and Jacksonville), that the Union cavalry was in the vicinity of Deep Gully, on the Trent River. Harris had also discovered that the Union troops were building a bridge across the White Oak River. On Wednesday, March 11, Robertson met his picket commander, Capt. Harris, at the Huggins farm, only to learn that the Federals had recrossed the White Oak and headed back to New Bern. Thursday, Robertson learned that there was a Union force in Trenton. He headed there immediately, camping that evening in Comfort, located in southern Jones County.[16]

On Friday morning, March 13, Robertson and his troops headed for Pollocksville, to protect Daniel's right and reconnoiter the country. They believed that the enemy pickets were stationed there and strongly fortified. After arriving, Robertson discovered that the Union troops had crossed Mill Creek, burning the bridge behind them. Finding the stream impassable at that point due to recent rains, Robertson returned to McDaniel's Mill. He left Capt. Andrew McIntire's Company C on picket at Pollocksville and Mill Creek, "with orders to hold those places at all hazards." He then sent a detachment under Lt. William J. Wiley, Company F, 5th NC Cavalry, to cut the Atlantic and North Carolina Railroad between Sheppardsville (near present-day Newport) and New Bern, as Hill had ordered. He gave the detail a few axes and his only reliable guide, Pvt. Dennis of the 3rd NC Cavalry.[17]

Robertson then took the bulk of his command to make a move on the enemy either at Mill Creek or at Sheppardsville. After talking with a local citizen, Richard Oldfield, Robertson decided to try at both points. First he chose to attack at or near the Evans's farm on Mill Creek, about seven miles from New Bern. Col. Peter G. Evans, commanding the 5th NC Cavalry, volunteered for this mission, taking Capt. E. F. Shaw's Company C from his regiment. The rest of Robertson's men, including two of Ferebee's companies, headed south for Sheppardsville. By sunset Saturday evening they reached Peletier's Mill, 20 miles south of Pollocksville on the White Oak River. Robertson planned to attack Sheppardsville early Sunday morning, while a detachment under Ferebee would destroy the railroad above Newport Creek. However, Saturday night the brigadier general received dispatches from Maj. Gen. Hill and Col. Evans, which persuaded him to abandon his plans. Evans was forced back across Mill Creek, leaving Robertson's only route of return in jeopardy. Wiley reported that he had torn up the railroad track three miles above Sheppardsville, but was forced to do so at night due to their proximity to Union troops. Unfortunately, Wiley and his detail only partially cut the railroad, which was easily repaired by the enemy.[18]

Brig. Gen. Daniel's troops successfully forced the Federals out of their entrenchments at Deep Gully. However, Robertson's part in the expedition was a failure and Maj. Gen. D. H. Hill was very disappointed. Wiley only partially cut the railroad and Col. Evans was turned back at Mill Creek. Pettigrew also failed to complete his mission by not taking Fort Anderson. Their failures forced Hill to abandon his attack on New Bern.[19] The Confederates had done little more than harass the Union for a few days. Robertson returned to Snow Hill with his troops. He tried to justify his failure due to the weather, lack of forage in the area, and the absence of a good battery of artillery.[20]

After failing with his attempt on New Bern, Maj. Gen. Hill focused his attention on Washington, on the Tar-Pamlico River. By the end of March, Hill was ready to take the town. On Friday, March 27, Ferebee and his 4th NC Cavalry left Snow Hill for Greenville. His men and horses were rested from the failed expedition against New Bern. Some of Ferebee's men did not participate in the expedition and were very well rested. Once in Greenville, they reported to D. H. Hill, who placed them temporarily under the command of Brig. Gen. Richard Brooke Garnett. B. H. Robertson, with portions of the 5th NC Cavalry, was sent to guard the road between Williamston and Jamesville. Garnett ordered Ferebee to proceed toward Washington, which they reached by late evening on March 28.[21] Later that night a detail from Company D was sent to reconnoiter the town. Media Evans, a private in the detail, described the excursion as follows:

> It was dark and drisly [sic]. We went through apiece of woods that the enemy had cut down to obstruck [sic] and attack. Sometimes we were climbing up trees, falling out of the top over logs and that so dark we could hardly see the man before or next to us. That was a dreary night that I shall never forget. We went near enough to hear walking and talking in the enemys [sic] lines. They had extinguished all their lights. It was so dark it was impossible to get much information. After lying around on the suburbs of the town for some time we made our way back hungry and tired.[22]

The next morning, Sunday, March 29, a number of the men from the 4th NC Cavalry, including Pvt. Media Evans, left camp looking for food. Not far from camp they came upon a house where two women were cooking herrings. They immediately asked the women for breakfast and they kindly obliged, serving the troops fried fish, corn bread, and coffee. They each paid the women 25 cents for the meal.[23] Monday morning the 4th NC Cavalry dashed up to within gunshot of the Union batteries and drove the enemy pickets back inside their breastworks.[24]

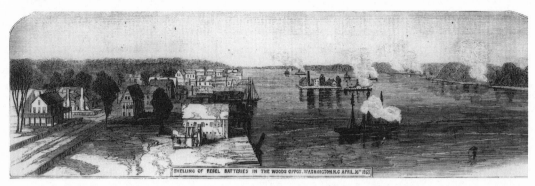

SHELLING OF REBEL BATTERIES IN THE WOODS OPPOS. WASHINGTON.N.C APRIL.16ᵗʰ 1863

Shelling of the Confederate batteries in the woods opposite Washington, NC on April 16, 1863, from *Frank Leslie's Illustrated Newspaper,* May 16, 1863 (North Carolina Collection, University of North Carolina Library at Chapel Hill).

Ferebee's men remained on picket duty around Washington for a couple of weeks, while Hill continued his direct assault on the town. The 4th NC Cavalry kept a close eye on the Union troops and often went on reconnaissance throughout the area to towns such as Bath, where Media Evans reported buying a ham. Keeping in mind Longstreet and Hill's original purpose of the mission, Ferebee's men gathered as many supplies and stores as possible from the region. They were able to secure great quantities of corn, bacon, and potatoes, as well as other much-needed items. However, like his attempt on New Bern, Hill's push on Washington also ended in failure and the 4th NC Cavalry left the town on Thursday, April 16, 1863. Company H was assigned to the 4th NC Cavalry in March—April 1863. The company began enlistment Wednesday, December 17, 1862 in Wilson County under Capt. Arthur Barnes. The company was originally mustered into Confederate service as Company C, 66th Regiment NC State Troops, but the regiment never completed its organization and the companies were incorporated into existing regiments.[25]

On April 16, Ferebee's 4th NC Cavalry moved about 10 miles northwest of Washington, stopping at Tranter's Creek Bridge to camp. They were followed for some distance by a force of Union cavalry and infantry. They remained under the temporary command of Brig. Gen. Garnett, who instructed Ferebee to guard the bridge and keep the enemy in check while he moved a great quantity of corn and other stores to Greenville. Recent rains made most roads impassable to wagons, so it was imperative that Ferebee hold off the Union long enough to get the much needed stores to Greenville.[26] To hinder any Union movement, Ferebee, under orders from Garnett, destroyed the bridge over Tranter's Creek. However, the Union made no attempt to attack Ferebee and he was able to conduct reconnaissance of the surrounding area. One such detail, under Capt. Joseph Cherry, Company F, and Capt. William Sharp, Company D, was sent to Plymouth where they learned that the Union force there expected to be attacked by Ferebee's men. In addition to the picket and reconnaissance duties, Ferebee's troops also helped ferry local citizens across the creek.[27]

On Sunday, April 26, the 4th NC Cavalry left Tranter's Creek and headed north to Woodville, North Carolina (adjacent to present day Lewiston in Bertie County), which they reached on April 27. On Saturday, May 2, after camping in Woodville for a few days, they proceeded toward Franklin, Virginia, stopping in Murfreesboro, North Carolina that evening. The next morning they left Murfreesboro for Franklin, arriving there that afternoon.[28] Upon arriving in Virginia, Ferebee and his men were temporarily placed in Maj. Gen. Samuel G. French's division under the command of Col. John A. Baker, 2nd NC Cavalry. They arrived in Franklin just as Longstreet's siege of Suffolk was coming to a close.[29] On Monday, May 4, Ferebee's troopers were ordered to Ivor to look for the enemy and wait for further instructions from French.[30]

CHAPTER 5

J.E.B. Stuart's Cavalry: Brandy Station

FEREBEE AND THE 4TH North Carolina Cavalry remained in the area around Ivor for a few days performing reconnaissance and picket duty. During this time they scouted east from Ivor to Isle of Wight Court House, south to Chuckatuck, north to Smithfield and the James River and back southwest to Ivor, finding no sign of Union troops. The men ate well during this time, roasting oysters from the local waters. However, forage for their horses was scare and their mounts were suffering. Capt. W. A. Graham's squadron, which consisted of Companies C and K, 2nd NC Cavalry, was also present at Ivor to help with picket duty. On Friday, May 8, by Special Order Number 21, Ferebee's regiment of cavalry was ordered to report to Gen. Robert E. Lee in Richmond for duty. All scattered companies were ordered to join there. Their Brig. Gen., B. H. Robertson, was still in eastern North Carolina with the 5th NC Cavalry. They would join the 4th NC Cavalry in Virginia by the end of May. However, Company E, 5th NC Cavalry, remained at Huggins Farm in Onslow County, NC, and would not rejoin the regiment until April 1864.[1]

On Saturday, May 9, the 4th NC Cavalry began its ride to Richmond, camping at Cypress Church that evening. The regiment soon learned of the death of Thomas Jonathan "Stonewall" Jackson. His death seemed to bring a cold dose of reality to the horrors of war, which for the most part the regiment had been spared, up to this point in the conflict. If the legendary Jackson could be killed, then certainly they could easily meet the same fate on the battlefield. One of Ferebee's men wrote: "We have no other Jackson—there can be but one such in any generation." The 4th NC Cavalry continued toward Richmond, reaching Petersburg on May 13. That day they saw about three thousand Yankee prisoners pass their camp on the way to City Point to be exchanged. Also on May 13, the regiment was placed in Maj. Gen. Arnold Elzay's Department of Richmond.[2]

Ferebee's cavalry reached Richmond on Thursday, May 14. Once there the men were equipped with new, much-needed supplies. They received Enfield rifles and sabers, as well as "brass spurs, flowing sword knots, pine saddle trees, heavy dragoon bridles and halters, haversacks and canteens, and saddlebags." They also received new uniforms, and their horses were shod for their upcoming journey north. Forage was just as scarce in Richmond as it had been in Ivor, but the men were issued a small amount of wheat-straw each day for their horses. The 4th NC Cavalry left Richmond on May 16, well supplied and rested. They were to head northwest to Orange Court House and report to James Ewell Brown Stuart at the cavalry headquarters there.[3]

As mentioned above, Ferebee's men were issued Enfield rifles while in Richmond. It is important to note that up until this point his regiment had been armed with their own weapons, which consisted mainly of shotguns. Before the war, they used these guns primarily for hunting. Some men were armed with pistols, which they either brought from home or captured from Union soldiers. The 4th NC Cavalry had also captured or procured Union rifles from various battlefields, but lack of ammunition for these weapons rendered them essentially useless. Neither the Enfield rifles nor pistols could compare to the carbines used by the Federals.[4]

By Monday, May 18, the 4th NC Cavalry was at Guinea Station, just south of Fredericksburg. On Tuesday, the soldiers camped near Orange Court House. The next day, May 20, J. E. B. Stuart moved the cavalry headquarters from Orange north to Culpeper Court House.[5] George M. Neese, a gunner in Chew's Battery of Stuart's horse artillery, described the town in his diary:

> Culpeper Court House is a pretty town pleasantly situated on the gently rising slope of a hill in a rather rolling and diversified section of the country. West of town toward the Blue Ridge [Mountains] the country is broken by wooded ridges, but looking east and south toward the lower Rapidan the country is beautiful and open, the land being nearly level and of good quality. The town is situated on the Orange and Alexandria Railroad about nine miles from the Rappahannock River.[6]

By Friday, May 22, Stuart was joined in Culpeper by the brigades of Wade Hampton, Fitzhugh "Fitz" Lee (Gen. Robert E. Lee's nephew), and William Henry Fitzhugh "Rooney" Lee (Gen. Robert E. Lee's second son). That same day he reviewed the three brigades (approximately 4,000 cavalrymen) on the broad open fields between Brandy Station and Culpeper. Shortly thereafter Brig. Gen. William E. "Grumble" Jones arrived from the Shenandoah Valley with his brigade. Ferebee and the 4th NC Cavalry camped at Orange Court House until Sunday, May 24. On May 25 they met Robertson and the rest of the brigade and joined Stuart at his headquarters in Culpeper. Here the Confederate cavalry constantly drilled and prepared for the review scheduled for Friday, June 5, with the hopes that Gen. Robert E. Lee would be in attendance.[7]

While Stuart was preparing his cavalry for the upcoming review, Lee was moving his army west from Fredericksburg to Culpeper. From Culpeper, Lee planned to move even farther west before turning north down the Shenandoah Valley. He then planned to cross the Potomac once again and launch another attack on Union soil. By doing this, Lee hoped to draw the Federals out of his beloved Virginia. Lee wanted

Stuart's massed cavalry to screen his crossing of the Rappahannock on June 9, so that he could begin his move north undetected.[8]

J. E. B. Stuart wanted the June 5 review to be a magnificent showcasing of his cavalry. Invitations were sent near and far for the occasion. The nearby hotels and private homes were made ready to accommodate the many guests expected to attend. In fact, so many attended that some guests had to stay in the soldier's tents.[9] The review was held on a "level plain about four miles northeast of Culpeper Court House about a mile southwest of Brandy Station on the west side of the Orange and Alexandria Railroad."[10] The broad pasture was on the Unionist John Minor Botts's plantation, Auburn.[11] Lt. Col. W. W. Blackford, a member of Stuart's staff, described the place as follows: "the ground was admirably adapted to the purpose, a hill in the centre affording a reviewing stand from which ... men present could be seen to great advantage."[12]

About 8:00 A.M. June 5, a bright and beautiful morning, Stuart and his staff, dressed in pristine new uniforms, mounted their horses and started for the plains near Brandy Station. By 10:00 A.M. the column, which extended about two miles, was ready to begin its processional.[13] The column was quite a sight to behold as Blackford describes: "cavalry show much larger than infantry, the mounted men produce the effect of at least three times their number of infantry." Once the column was formed, Stuart and his staff rode in front of the mass from one end to the other, taking position on a knoll by the railroad overlooking the plain. From there the "gallant knight" viewed the magnificent spectacle.[14] George M. Neese described Stuart as he dashed onto the plain:

> He was superbly mounted. The trappings on his proud, prancing horse all looked bright and new, and his side-arms gleamed in the sun like burnished silver. A long black ostrich feather plume waved gracefully from a black slouch hat cocked up on one side, and was held with a golden clasp which also stayed the plume. He is the prettiest and most graceful rider I ever saw. When he dashed past us I could not help but notice with what natural ease and comely elegance he sat on his steed as it bounded over the field, and his every motion in the saddle was in such strict accord with the movements of his horse that he and his horse appeared to be but one and the same machine.[15]

The column passed the review station first at a quick walk, then came by at a trot, taking the gallop a hundred yards before reaching the reviewing stand. The final and most memorable act of the day was a sham battle, with the cavalrymen charging at each other at full speed with sabers drawn. During these passes, Beckman's horse artillery fired blank rounds to heighten the effect of the scene. Several hundred spectators gathered to view the grand military display. They consisted mostly of women from Culpeper Court House and the surrounding area. However, many came by rail from all over the state. Many prominent men also came, including former Secretary of War George Wythe Randolph. Unfortunately, Robert E. Lee did not arrive for the review—Stuart's only disappointment of the day.[16]

The event was over by about four o'clock that afternoon, at which time the troops retired to their respective camps. B. H. Robertson's 4th and 5th NC Cavalries camped near John Minor Botts's plantation. That evening Stuart's staff hosted a dance for all the guests that came for the review. As Blackford described, "we gave a ball at head-quarters on the turf by moonlight, assisted by huge wood fires, firelight to dance by and moonlight for the strolls." Maj. Heros Von Borcke commented that the firelight produced a "wild and romantic effect." Lee arrived in Culpeper on Sunday, June 7, and Stuart hastily made preparations for yet another review. This news was met with mixed feelings among the cavalry, who had to once again polish and clean their equipment. That same day, Stuart moved his headquarters to Fleetwood, an old plantation residence on a hill by the same name, about a half mile east of Brandy Station.[17]

Stuart's review on Monday, June 8 for Lee took place on the same field. This time, however, the event was more of a "business affair, the spectators being all soldiers." Much less of a display was attempted this time, because Lee did not want to tax his cavalry unnecessarily. Rather, he wanted them to conserve their energy for the serious work which would soon begin. For this reason, there was no mock battle, nor did the artillery fire throughout the review as on the 5th. After the review the men again returned to their respective camps.[18]

Stuart, expecting no immediate fighting, positioned his troops alongside good roads on the evening of June 8 for a quick move in the morning. The next morning his cavalry was to move toward Gaines Crossroads and ford the Rappahannock, screening Longstreet's and R. S. Ewell's infantry as they moved north. Stuart placed his five brigades as follows on the evening of June 8: Fitz Lee's brigade was seven miles northwest of Fleetwood at Oak Shade Church; Rooney Lee was two miles west of the Rappahannock, along the Hazel River, near the Welford House; Grumble Jones's men were near St. James Church, two miles south of the Rappahannock on the road that led from Beverly's Ford to Brandy Station; Jones had Company A, 6th VA Cavalry, picketing at Beverly's Ford; Wade Hampton's brigade was near Stevensburg. B. H. Robertson's 4th and 5th NC Cavalries were southwest of Brandy Station between the Botts and Barbour farms. Robertson had a picket force near Kelly's Ford, with vedettes (solitary scouts out four to five hundred yards from the pickets) covering Kelly's, Wheatley's and Norman's Fords. Four of Beckman's five artillery batteries were also at St. James Church, between the camp of Jones's Brigade and Beverly's Ford.[19]

While the Confederates were planning their move north, the Federal troops had plans of their own. After their disappointing failure in the Chancellorsville Campaign in early May 1863, the Union's Army of the Potomac, commanded by Maj. Gen. Joseph Hooker, was put in a defensive stance. Hooker decided that he needed to be "watchful" of Lee. On Friday, May 22, Hooker replaced George Stoneman with Alfred Pleasonton. Two days earlier Stoneman had been granted a leave of absence due to a health problem—hemorrhoids. By late May, Pleasonton knew that Stuart had massed the Confederate cavalry in and around Culpeper Court House. He felt that this force was placed either for a raid or to conceal the movement of other troops. In either case, he knew that he must strike this force if he was to get to Lee. On June 6, in preparation for a move on Stuart, Pleasonton split his force into two wings.

The right wing, commanded by Brig. Gen. John Buford, consisted of Buford's own First Cavalry Division, Maj. Charles J. Whiting's Reserve Cavalry Brigade, Brig. Gen. Adelbert Ames's infantry command, and two batteries of horse artillery. The left wing, commanded by Brig. Gen. David McMurtrie Gregg, consisted of Col. Alfred N. Duffie's Second Cavalry Division and Gregg's Third Cavalry Division, along with Brig. Gen. Russell's infantry command and three batteries of horse artillery.[20]

Due to a lack of Confederate pickets north of the Rappahannock, Pleasonton's force was able to move undetected to within a half mile of the river by the evening of June 8. Believing that Stuart's force was still at Culpeper, some seven miles from Brandy Station, Pleasonton decided that he would simultaneously send the right wing of his force across the Rappahannock at Beverly's Ford, with his left wing crossing at Kelly's Ford early on the morning of June 9. His force would then reunite at Brandy Station and proceed toward Stuart at Culpeper.[21]

At about 5:00 A.M. on Tuesday, June 9, the first Union troops crossed the Rappahannock at Beverly's Ford. They were Grimes Davis's 8th New York, which was at the head of Buford's column. They were met by Jones's pickets from Company A, 6th VA Cavalry. The Union force soon overwhelmed the small Confederate picket and began moving southwest toward Brandy Station. However, the narrow roads and ditches on both sides of the road slowed the Union advance. This enabled Grumble Jones's brigade and Beckham's artillery to get in position to meet the enemy near St. James Church. Wade Hampton's men came up from Stevensburg about 6:00 A.M. and took position on Jones's and Beckham's right. Stuart soon ordered Robertson's 4th NC and 5th NC towards Beverly's Ford to assist in the action there.[22]

Events six miles downstream changed these orders for Robertson and his Tarheels. Pleasonton's left wing, commanded by Gen. Gregg, crossed the Rappahannock at Kelly's Ford at about 6:00 A.M.—an hour later than originally planned. They crossed an hour late because Col. Duffie was misled by a guide. Robertson's vedettes were the first to meet Gregg's force at Kelly's Ford. These North Carolinians were soon captured by the Union's advance guard, a squadron of the 1st New Jersey Cavalry. Their capture prevented any warning of the Federal advance. The 1st New Jersey met their first resistance at the position held by B. H. Robertson's out-posts (picket). However, they were only able to offer minimum resistance to the Union advance.[23]

Capt. William White, commanding Robertson's pickets, reported to his commander that the Union troops had crossed Kelly's Ford in force with infantry and cavalry. Robertson immediately relayed this intelligence to Stuart, who ordered the Brig. Gen. to take his two regiments to Kelly's Ford, instead of Beverly's Ford as previously directed. Robertson's men were to hold the Federals in check and protect the right flank of the Confederates engaged between the Rappahannock and Beverly's Ford. Before leaving camp, Robertson received another more detailed dispatch from his picket commander Capt. White, informing him that five regiments of infantry and several regiments of cavalry with artillery had crossed and were slowly advancing up the river.[24]

Robertson and his Carolinians proceeded toward their pickets at Kelly's Ford, along the Kelly's Mill Road. About a half mile from Kelly's Ford, at the Brown House, they met White and his picket falling back from the Union advance. White informed his brigadier general that the Union occupied the line of woods directly in front of them. Almost immediately after gaining this intelligence, the Union infantry appeared from behind the trees. Robertson dismounted some of his two regiments, using them as skirmishers.[25]

To ascertain the Union's strength, Robertson sent out scouts to his right, making a personal reconnaissance of the enemy in his front. From his reconnaissance, Robertson learned that a force had passed around their right flank and was heading toward Brandy Station, along the Brandy Station Road. This was Gregg's Third Division, and they were heading directly for the Confederate rear. Robertson immediately sent Capt. W. N. Worthington, of his staff, to inform Stuart of the enemy's movement. His scouts soon reported that another Union force had also passed their right flank. This was Col. Duffie's Second Division and they were heading toward Stevensburg, along the Willis Maddens Road. Robertson reported this to Stuart through Lt. W. P. Holcombe.[26]

Robertson then ordered his command to fall back a short distance down the Kelly's Mill Road, where they took up a new position. He considered attacking the rear of Gregg's column, but he was soon ordered by Stuart to hold his ground. Robertson is criticized for not attacking at this point or at least fighting some delaying effort. Nonetheless, Robertson, as Stuart admitted, "intended to do what was right."[27]

While Gregg was taking a southerly, indirect route to Brandy Station, Brig. Gen. Russell was to lead his Union infantry there by the most direct route. This route forced Russell's men to meet Robertson's Tarheels on the Kelly's Mill Road, bringing the Federal column to a halt. Their confrontation, which consisted mainly of a series of shot trading between Robertson's and Russell's forward skirmishers, was a stalemate from the beginning. Russell believed that he should remain close to Kelly's Ford to help guard a possible line of retreat for Gregg's and Duffie's columns. On the Confederate side, Robertson believed it to be of the utmost importance to prevent Russell's force from marching to help Pleasonton, who was engaged with the Confederates about six miles northwest of their position.[28]

The stalemate continued until later in the day when Russell employed a battery of artillery, which had been left behind to defend Kelly's Ford. When the Union guns opened on Robertson's cavalry, he placed his skirmishers behind an embankment to protect them from the artillery. Soon after this firing commenced, Robertson received a dispatch from Brig. Gen. Wade Hampton, informing Robertson of his movement from St. James Church to Fleetwood. Hampton's movement would leave Robertson's rear open to attack. Accordingly, Robertson withdrew with his men toward Brandy Station, abandoning his fight with Russell.[29]

Upon reaching the railroad at Brandy Station, Robertson discovered a considerable Union infantry force to his right. These Federals were the extreme left flank of Pleasonton's right wing, which had advanced from Beverly's Ford. Almost immediately after arriving at this point, Robertson received orders from Stuart directing him to advance rapidly toward his headquarters at Fleetwood to help support the Confederates fighting there. He selected the 5th NC Cavalry, which was in front, to move forward toward Stuart, while he sent Ferebee's 4th NC Cavalry to cover their right and rear and to support Gen. Hampton.[30]

By the time Robertson and the 5th NC Cavalry reported to Stuart, the Federals were withdrawing. The major general then ordered Robertson and the 5th NC Cavalry to rejoin the 4th NC Cavalry, to assist Hampton and a battery of artillery, who were preparing to pursue the retreating enemy force. Shortly after reporting to Hampton, a large Union force appeared directly in front of Robertson's Brigade, with the apparent intention of attacking. Reacting to this threat, Robertson formed the 4th and 5th NC Cavalries in a line of battle. The Union column advanced toward the Tarheels' left wing. Robertson was then ordered to advance with the 5th NC Cavalry to meet this force, leaving Ferebee's men under Hampton's command. Upon reaching the far left of the Confederate line, Robertson dismounted the 5th NC Cavalry and used the men as skirmishers to hold that end of the line.[31]

Although deployed, the dismounted troopers of the 5th NC Cavalry did not engage the Union force at this point. However, farther down the line to Robertson's right, Gen. W. H. F. "Rooney" Lee received a severe thigh wound while leading a charge against Buford's men on Pleasonton's right wing. Although Lee was successful in stopping the Federal advance, the wound forced him out of action. Robertson was then ordered to leave his command and replace Lee in command of the Confederate left wing. By that time, though, the battle was over and the Union forces were beginning to withdraw back across the Rappahannock.[32]

The Battle of Brandy Station took both sides by surprise. Though technically a draw, the battle did delay the Confederate plans to move northward. It also served to show that the Union cavalry had come of age and was now a force to be taken seriously. Despite the fact that Robertson's men encountered Union troops during the entire battle, they were not actually engaged. His command suffered no human casualties, losing only four horses in the action. Notwithstanding their inactivity, they did manage to capture two Sharps carbines and seven horses from the Federals. Robertson's ineffectiveness as a leader is highlighted in the battle. This performance would serve as a grim foreshadowing of the upcoming campaign.[33]

CHAPTER 6

Fights in
the Loudoun Valley

AFTER THE BATTLE OF BRANDY STATION, Stuart and the Confederate cavalry returned to their camps along the Rappahannock and Hazel Rivers, while Pleasonton's Federal cavalry withdrew to Warrenton Junction. It is important to note that during this time the area was experiencing a severe drought. The dust produced from this extended period without rain made camp life all the more miserable for soldiers on both sides. The 4th and 5th NC Cavalries remained in and around Culpeper Court House until June 15. During this time Lee's infantry was preparing for its delayed march north, while Stuart's cavalry went back to the tedium of picket duty.[1]

This period was also an active one for Hooker and the Army of the Potomac. On Thursday, June 11, Pleasonton reorganized his cavalry, reducing it from three divisions to two. The 1st Division was now commanded by Brig. Gen. John Buford, while Brig. Gen. David McMurtrie Gregg commanded the 2nd Division. Among those displaced in the consolidation was the Frenchman, Col. Alfred Duffie, who was demoted back to regimental command. Hooker was being pressed by Halleck's War Department for information on the Confederates. He wanted desperately to locate Lee's army and prevent its rumored move north. Hooker employed Pleasonton to gather this critical intelligence. The effort to find Lee led to several encounters between Stuart's cavalry and Pleasonton's mounted troopers in the Loudoun Valley.[2]

The Loudoun Valley of Virginia, spanning 18 miles, consists of the land between the Blue Ridge Mountains to the west and the Bull Run Mountains to the east. Lee's army was moving up the Blue Ridge, while Hooker was following the Bull Run chain. On Tuesday, June 16, Stuart's cavalry began to move north by crossing the upper tributaries of the Rappahannock River. This move was to serve as a screen for Longstreet's infantry as it moved north along the Blue Ridge. Fitz Lee's brigade, commanded by Col. Thomas T. Munford, crossed the Hedgeman River at Rock Ford. B. H. Robertson's brigade and Rooney Lee's brigade, commanded by Col. John R. Chambliss, crossed the Aesthem (Hazel) River at Hinson's Mill. Wade Hampton's and Grumble Jones's brigades were left behind to cover Longstreet's rear and screen A. P. Hill's advance. That evening Stuart camped with the 4th and 5th NC Cavalries and Chambliss's men at Salem, while Munford's men camped at Piedmont and Upperville.[3]

On Wednesday, June 17, Stuart ordered Munford to move his men toward Aldie via Middleburg, to hold the Aldie Gap, while Col. Chambliss was ordered to move Rooney Lee's brigade to Thoroughfare Gap. By holding these two gaps in the Bull Run Mountains, Stuart hoped to screen Longstreet's movements. Robertson's Tarheels were ordered to Rector's Crossroads (Rectortown), where they could support either Munford or Chambliss. Stuart and his staff made their headquarters in Middleburg, where they could remain in close communication with all three brigades.[4]

About 3:00 A.M. on June 17, Pleasonton ordered Col. Duffie to move his 1st Rhode Island Cavalry from Manassas Junction via the Thoroughfare Gap to Middleburg. Once there he was to camp for the night and relay any intelligence to Pleasonton. Their march from Manassas was fairly uneventful until they reached Hopewell. Just north of the town, Duffie's men captured a Confederate scout and learned that Stuart and a portion of his cavalry were in Middleburg. About 4:00 P.M. the 1st Rhode Island met Stuart's picket force about two miles outside of Middleburg. The picket consisted of troopers from the 4th VA Cavalry. Duffie's men galloped forward at a charge driving the pickets back into Middleburg, where they informed Stuart of the impending crisis. Stuart and his staff, who had been "taking their leisure" in Middleburg, immediately moved west toward Rector's Crossroads. Once in Middleburg, Duffie learned that Munford's troops had passed through just hours before and were now a threat from the south. Duffie decided to secure the town, barricading all entrances to prevent any access. Each of these barricades was manned by a strong picket force.[5]

After being driven out of Middleburg, Stuart rode eight miles west to Rector's Crossroads, where he met B. H. Robertson and his brigade. The major general made immediate plans to return to recapture the town. About 7:00 P.M., just about dark, Stuart and Von Borcke returned to Middleburg with Robertson's Carolinians. About a half mile west of town, Stuart and his force met the 4th VA Cavalry pickets, who had been skirmishing with sharpshooters from the 1st Rhode Island since 4:00 P.M. After a few moments the Confederates began their charge.[6]

Maj. Heros Von Borcke and Robertson led the 4th and 5th NC Cavalries, with the picket force from the 4th VA Cavalry, into Duffie's western barricade. Within seconds the Tarheels jumped the barricades and drove the Union pickets away from their stronghold, forcing them to retreat to Duffie's main defense south of Middleburg. Their main defense, located in a patch of woods south of town, consisted of a farmyard enclosed by stone walls. Here Duffie dismounted his men and dug in to prepare for the worst. Meanwhile, Robertson sent two squadrons to circle the outskirts of town to prevent a counterattack. After the charge, with Middleburg back in Confederate hands, Robertson and Von Borcke reformed their men near Mansion House. Robertson then divided his command to search for the Federals. He led one detachment of his Tarheels east, along the road to Aldie, while others searched north of town toward Union.[7]

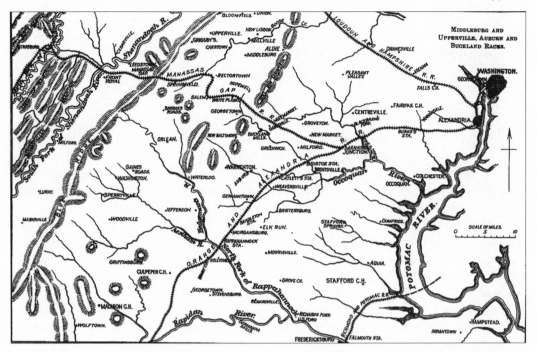

Fights in the Loudoun Valley (Clark's *Regiments,* Volume III, page 582).

Von Borcke led the remainder of Robertson's command south of Middleburg on the Hopewell Road. The Confederate advance guard located Duffie's main body in their stronghold, behind the stone wall in the farmyard. The Prussian led the eager Carolinians toward the Federals at a gallop, yelling the Rebel Yell. As one of the 1st Rhode Island Cavalry described: "down the road dashed the rebel column—men riding four abreast—yelling and firing like demons." Upon reaching the Federal line, the Tarheels received an abrading fire in their right flank from a range of six feet. This brought the head of the Confederate column to a halt about 250 yards south of Middleburg. From here Robertson's men made three mounted charges at the stone wall. Each time they were met with an intense volley of carbine and pistol fire, as one trooper described: "there was blaze after blaze of fire, out of the darkness into the charging Carolinians." After the third repulse, Stuart, who had arrived on the scene, dismounted the Tarheels and sent them in to flank and surround the Federals. The Federals were soon under fire from their flank and rear. Duffie realized the dire circumstances and decided to make a run for it. Many Federals were captured during this move, while many others hid in the woods under cover of darkness and returned to the safety of the Union lines on the morning of the 18th. Among the Confederate casualties was James H. McNeill of the 5th NC Cavalry, who was wounded in the hip and disabled for months.[8]

Thursday, June 18 was another day of constant skirmishing for Ferebee's men. The Carolinians encountered Col. J. Irvin Gregg's Brigade, which advanced from Aldie on reconnaissance. The Union force consisted of the 4th PA, 16th PA, and the 10th

NY Cavalries. This Union force met the Confederate picket (outpost) just east of Middleburg. After several hours of skirmishing the Federals drove the Confederates back through Middleburg and occupied the town by 3:00 P.M. About 6:00 P.M. Pleasonton ordered Gregg to a position halfway between Aldie and Middleburg, where he bivouacked for the night. Immediately after Gregg's withdrawal the Confederates reoccupied the village.[9]

Stuart did not want Middleburg shelled by the Union artillery, so that evening he placed his main body of troops on the wooded heights, known as Mount Defiance, about a mile west of town. This was a good defensive position divided by the Ashby's Gap Turnpike. Robertson placed his Tarheels south of the road on the ridge's highest peak, while one regiment of Chambliss's command was put just north of the road. Chambliss's other three regiments were mounted and placed further back of the Confederate center, to be used if needed in a counterattack. Maj. James F. Hart's battery was placed near an old blacksmith shop at the highest point in the ridge, to provide artillery support.[10]

Ferebee's men awoke on Friday, June 19 before dawn to a drenching thunderstorm. About 6:00 A.M. the 4th PA, 16th PA, and the 10th NY Cavalries, with a section of Battery C, 3rd U. S. Artillery, under the command of Col. J. Irvin Gregg, advanced toward Middleburg from their bivouac. By 7:00 A.M. Gregg's advance guard had driven the Confederate pickets out of Middleburg, to their main body, on the crest a mile west of town. About 8:00 A.M. the Confederate artillery opened fire on Col. Gregg's force as it approached Mount Defiance. For about and hour and a half Gregg made no attempt to attack. However, about 9:30 A.M. Gregg's cousin, Gen. David M. Gregg, arrived on the field and ordered J. Irvin Gregg to attack the Confederates.[11]

By 10:00 A.M. Col. Gregg had moved his brigade into action, across the open wheat field south of the turnpike toward the woods which concealed B. H. Robertson's cavalry. Gregg was joined by Kilpatrick's Brigade, which consisted of the 6th Ohio and 2nd New York, but they saw little action. The 4th PA were the first to meet Robertson's skirmishers, who were positioned in the old stone-walled cemetery of the Cocke family. Robertson's men held their ground for a while, but were forced from their stronghold by a dismounted charge of the 4th PA led by Maj. Biddle. This charge forced the Carolinians from the cemetery back into the woods. Biddle's advance was soon followed by a mounted charge from the 1st Maine. Companies E and M of the 1st Maine stormed into the woods under heavy fire from the dismounted Tarheels. One Federal claimed that the Rebels fought from tree to tree like a "swarm of bees." Eventually this second charge forced Robertson out of the woods. The Carolinians next took cover behind a stone wall in their rear. A third Union charge was made as the 4th and 5th NC Cavalries were mounting their horses, which forced many to surrender—37 from the 4th NC Cavalry, including Lt. Col. Edward Cantwell. Three members of the 4th NC Cavalry were wounded in the day's fight and one, Pvt. Peter Etheridge of Co. G, was killed.[12]

B. H. Robertson, once again, performed poorly under fire, which reflected badly on his leadership ability as well as on his men. Sensing the dire consequences of

Robertson's failure to hold his position, Stuart had to alter his plans. He was forced to fall back about a half mile west, where he formed a line on the next ridge. During this withdrawal Maj. Von Borcke was wounded in the neck.[13]

Pleasonton was satisfied with forcing Stuart from Mount Defiance and did not pursue the Confederates. Instead, both sides held their respective lines with pickets. About dark, Stuart's troopers withdrew a little farther, out of Union artillery range, while their counterparts bivouacked on the battlefield for the night. That evening Brig. Gen. Jones's brigade joined Stuart. A heavy rain began that evening and continued throughout Saturday, June 20. The rains slowed the action, with only an occasional shot being fired.[14]

By Saturday, June 20, Stuart had all five of his cavalry brigades in the Loudoun Valley. His objective still remained to screen Lee's movements from the Federals. With the Federals concentrated at Aldie, Stuart was concerned with the threat they posed to Upperville and Ashby's Gap. To protect these positions he strategically placed his brigades. He put Munford's brigade near Snickersville, Chambliss's and Jones's near Union, while Robertson's and Hampton's covered Middleburg. Meanwhile, the Federals had plans of their own. Pleasonton, frustrated by lack of success, now wanted to attack Stuart's entire force.[15]

Stuart did not want to fight on the Sabbath, but about 8:00 A.M. Sunday, June 21, Union artillery, under Capt. William Fuller, opened on the Confederates west of Middleburg. This fire was answered by Capt. James F. Hart's battery. Stuart sent Hampton's and Robertson's men to the front, where they took a position along a ridge overlooking a small stream, known as Kirk's Branch. The advancing Union troops included Col. Strong Vincent's infantry, which consisted of the 20th Maine, 16th Michigan, 44th New York, and the 83rd Pennsylvania. They were joined by Kilpatrick's cavalry from David M. Gregg's Brigade, which consisted of the 6th Ohio, 2nd New York, and the 4th New York.[16]

Due to the large Federal infantry force approaching, Stuart decided that he could do little more than fight a series of delaying actions to slow the Union advance. In accordance with this plan of action, Stuart directed Hampton and Robertson to withdraw when necessary. Hampton's men engaged the Federals for about an hour, while Robertson's Carolinians were held in reserve. Unable to hold their position any longer, the Confederates began to withdraw slowly. Hampton and Robertson reformed farther west of Middleburg on the high ground west of Crummey's (Crowell's) Run. When the action became too heated there, the Confederates once again withdrew. From Crummey's Run, the Confederates passed through Rector's Crossroads (present day Atoka) to Goose Creek, where they took up a defensive position near the bridge there. At Goose Creek Bridge, Robertson and Hampton received artillery support from Hart's and Moorman's batteries. As the Union force, consisting of the 2nd NY and 4th NY Cavalries and the 16th Michigan Infantry, approached the valley overlooking Goose Creek, Hart's battery opened on them from a range of 1,500 yards. Unfortunately for the Confederates, they did very little damage. The Union force was too much for Robertson and Hampton and they were forced to withdraw again.[17]

From Goose Creek, Hampton and Robertson hastily retreated toward Upperville, three miles to the west. During this withdrawal, the 4th and 5th NC Cavalries covered Hampton's rear, occasionally skirmishing with the Union troops in pursuit. They next took a position just east of Upperville on a low rise known as Vineyard Hill. Hampton's men were placed south of the Ashby's Gap Turnpike, while Robertson's men held the ground north of the road, near Panther Skin Creek. Stuart wanted to hold this ground to avoid any conflict in Upperville, due to the number of women and children still in the town.[18]

About 4:00 P.M., Kilpatrick, leading Gregg's advance, attacked the Confederates. He sent the 2nd NY and 4th NY south of the turnpike against Hampton, while the 6th Ohio attacked Robertson's men to the north. At about the same time that Kilpatrick ordered his attack, Brig. Gen. John Buford arrived with his command. Buford ordered Col. William Gamble's brigade to attack Robertson's left flank. Thus Robertson's Tarheels were being attacked by the 6th Ohio from the right and from Gamble's men on their left. The impending attack from two sides broke Robertson's men and they retreated into Upperville, pursued by about 30 men from the 6th Ohio. The Tarheels and 6th Ohio fought in the streets and back alleys of the town, often hand to hand. Eventually Robertson was able to rally a portion of the 4th NC Cavalry and in a countercharge they drove the Federals from Upperville.[19]

Robertson soon regrouped his entire brigade west of town on a knoll, west of Trappe Road. Stuart then directed Hampton, presently engaged with the Federals east of Upperville, to withdraw through the town. Stuart ordered Robertson's men to cover this retreat. Seeing the Confederate withdrawal, Pleasonton ordered the 1st Maine to charge the town and pursue the enemy. After passing untouched through Upperville, the 1st Maine encountered Robertson's Carolinians, who were posted behind stone walls on the knoll just north of Ashby's Gap Turnpike. The Tarheels fired a sharp volley into the blue column, slowing their advance and forcing them from the pike. However, after gathering themselves, the 1st Maine once again charged the Tarheels, forcing them from their strong position.[20]

As the Maine troopers began their pursuit, Robertson rallied his men for another counterattack. Their efforts were successful, and they drove the Federals back toward Upperville. Just outside of Upperville, the Tarheels came upon the 4th PA and 16th PA, as well as part of the 2nd NY. This Federal force put down Robertson's counterattack and the Confederates were once again on the run, but this time the Union troops did not pursue. Just as the 4th PA and 16th PA were attempting to gather themselves and reform around Upperville, the Carolinians came back for yet another charge. This charge was led by Col. Peter G. Evans of the 5th NC Cavalry, who took a detachment of the brigade with him. Due to mixed orders, only a portion of the 5th NC Cavalry followed Evans. After an initial surge into the Union ranks, the Tarheels were swarmed upon by the Yankees. The fight on June 21 proved costly for Robertson's men: Evans of the 5th NC Cavalry was mortally wounded; the 4th NC Cavalry had 26 captured, including Maj. J. M. Mayo, 10 wounded and three killed (Pvt. William Jasper Askew of Co. D, Pvt. Simon Peter Finks of Co. E, and Pvt. Eli Harmon of Co. F).[21]

That evening Stuart retreated to Ashby's Gap. Gregg's troops bivouacked just east of Upperville, while Vincent's infantry returned to Aldie. Pleasonton was content with the Union's effort during the five days of fighting in the Loudoun Valley. He felt that his men fought well and his mission of harassing Stuart was successful. Nevertheless, his paramount task of finding Lee was not completed. Although Robertson and his men performed poorly throughout most of the fighting, Stuart's ultimate goal was accomplished, and Lee's movement went undetected.[22]

CHAPTER 7

Gettysburg

O N MONDAY, JUNE 22, Stuart reestablished his headquarters at Rector's Cross-roads. That morning the Union cavalry was continuing its withdrawal from the area, leaving a group of pickets at Aldie to cover this movement. Media Evans and his fellow Carolinians from the 4th NC Cavalry were "ordered in the saddles" to track this Union movement. In their pursuit they found many of the dead and wounded left by the Union troops from the previous days of fighting. They cared for those they could, but pressed on with the task of locating the enemy. When it became apparent that the Union troops were in fact withdrawing, the Confederates ceased the pursuit upon reaching Middleburg.[1]

Lee had new orders for Stuart's cavalry on Tuesday, June 23. He left Stuart with the dual task of holding the Blue Ridge Gaps, the mountain passes at Ashby's and Snicker's Gaps and of crossing into Maryland to gain a position on Gen. Ewell's right. This left Stuart with a major command decision: What part of his command would he take into Maryland and whom would he leave to guard the passes? Stuart decided to leave W. E. "Grumble" Jones's and B. H. Robertson's brigades behind to guard the passes, while he took Hampton's, Fitz Lee's, and W. H. F. Lee's brigades north into Maryland. Stuart's decision may have been based on many factors. Jones had the largest brigade, while Robertson had the smallest. Robertson's effective strength was down because he had lost over 90 men (killed, wounded or captured) from the 4th NC Cavalry alone, during the fights in the Loudoun Valley. Jones had proven himself as an outpost leader. Robertson was also in disfavor at Confederate headquarters due to his recent performance. (A more personal reason on Stuart's part may have been the fact that Robertson had once courted his wife Flora). The combined factors seemed to make Jones's and Robertson's men the right choice to leave behind.[2]

On Wednesday, June 24, Stuart moved his headquarters to Salem. From there he issued the following orders to Robertson:

> GEN.: Your own and Gen. Jones' brigades will cover the front of Ashby's and
> Snicker's Gaps, yourself as senior officer, being in command. Your object will be to

watch the enemy; deceive him as to our designs, and harass his rear if you find he is retiring. Be always alert; let nothing escape your observation, and miss no opportunity which offers damage to the enemy. After the enemy has moved beyond your reach, leave sufficient pickets in the mountains, withdraw to the west side of Shenandoah, place a strong and reliable picket to watch the enemy at Harper's Ferry, cross the Potomac, and follow the army, keeping on its right and rear. As long as the enemy remains in your front on force, unless otherwise ordered by Gen. R. E. Lee. Lt.-Gen. Longstreet, or myself, hold the gaps with a line of pickets reaching across the Shenandoah, by Charlestown to the Potomac. If, in the contingency mentioned, you withdraw, sweep the Valley clear of what pertains to the army and cross the Potomac at different points crossed by it. You will instruct Gen. Jones from time to time as the movements progress, or events may require, and report anything of importance to Lt.-Gen. Longstreet, with whose position you will communicate by relays through Charlestown. I send instructions from Gen. Jones, which please read. Avail yourself of every means in your power to increase the efficiency of your command, and keep it to the highest number possible. Particular attention will be paid to shoeing horses, and to marching of the turnpike. In case of an advance of the enemy, you will offer such resistance as will be justifiable to check him and discover his intentions and, if possible, you will prevent him from gaining possession of the Gaps. In case of a move by the enemy upon Warrenton, you will counteract it as much as you can, compatible with previous instructions. You will have the two brigades [and] two batteries of horse artillery.[3]

Robertson was to march on Lee's *right* to keep between the Confederate and Union troops and act as a screen. On the evening of June 24, Hampton's, Fitz Lee's and W. H. F. Lee's brigades met Stuart near Salem Depot. At about 1:00 A.M. Thursday, June 25, the three brigades moved out on a "noiseless march" with Stuart, beginning their ride around the Union Army. Stuart would not be in communication with Lee during this ride around the Union rear. Therefore, B. H. Robertson and Grumble Jones would be the "eyes and ears" for Lee during this time.[4]

Robertson, with the 4th NC Cavalry and the 5th NC Cavalry, guarded Ashby's Gap. Jones, with the 6th VA Cavalry, 7th VA Cavalry, 11th VA Cavalry, 12th VA Cavalry, 35th VA Battalion, 1st Maryland Battalion and Brig. Albert Jenkins's brigade, guarded Snicker's Gap. As directed by Stuart, Robertson, as senior officer, was in command of the division.[5]

On June 25, Union Gen. Hooker's troops left Leesburg, crossing the Potomac near Edward's Ferry, on two pontoon bridges. This crucial movement went undetected by Robertson and Jones. That same day, Jones ordered the 12th VA Cavalry to form a picket line near Harpers Ferry, as directed in Stuart's orders. They remained at Harpers Ferry throughout the Gettysburg Campaign, thus reducing Robertson's effectives by one regiment. The next day, Friday, June 26, the Union's rear guard, consisting of John Buford's and David M. Gregg's brigades of cavalry, began their withdrawal toward Leesburg. This movement also went undetected by Robertson and Jones. On June 27 and 28, Robertson was at Oakley, the manor house owned by the Dulaney family located a mile east of Upperville.[6]

Important events in the campaign occurred on Saturday, June 28. That day Hooker was replaced by Gen. George Gordon Meade, as commander of the Army of the Potomac. Also that evening Gen. Robert E. Lee *first* learned of Hooker's movement and approach into Maryland, from one of James Longstreet's spies at Chambersburg, PA. Lee immediately sent orders for Jones and Robertson to "rejoin the army without delay." Unfortunately for the Confederates, these orders were not received by the cavalry until July 1 on its movement through Martinsburg, Maryland.[7]

On Monday, June 29, Robertson was confident that the enemy had left his immediate front and he decided to make his move north to join Lee's army. He instructed the division to meet at Berryville. Jones, who had been in Snickersville, immediately brought his brigade to Berryville to meet Robertson. The division camped four miles south of the town that evening. A detail from the 4th NC Cavalry, commanded by Capt. Lewis A. Johnson of Company A, was left behind at Ashby's Gap to guard the pass. On June 30 their march north began in a steady rain. As one of Robertson's men reported, their "old cloth capes" provided little protection from the drenching rains. They marched on the Charlestown Road to Millwood, leaving the road at Rippon, then passing through Summit Point and Smithfield. They camped that evening two miles north of Martinsburg on the Winchester Pike.[8]

On Wednesday, July 1, Robertson's division forded the Potomac at Williamsport, Maryland, and passed through Greencastle, Pennsylvania, before finally reaching Chambersburg, Pennsylvania. They remain camped in and around Chambersburg on the Baltimore Pike through July 2. While in Chambersburg, the 4th NC Cavalry grazed its horses. Robertson's division camped near the mill just outside of the town. The men enjoyed local hospitality as Robertson reported, "here, at a citizen's home, a German, we enjoyed the apple-butter and cold-loaf bread characteristic of the people."[9]

About 1:00 A.M. on Friday, July 3, Robertson received a report that Brig. Gen. John D. Imboden's brigade, which was in camp ten miles to the east, at the foot of South Mountain, was in danger of being attacked. Robertson's command immediately headed east down the Baltimore Pike toward Imboden. Upon reaching South Mountain, they learned their comrades were not in danger. They then headed toward Cashtown where they arrived "tired and hungry" around 10:00 A.M. Once there, breakfast was prepared. About 1:00 P.M. a courier arrived and reported that the Federal cavalry was heading toward Lee's right and rear. Lee, engaged at Gettysburg, ordered Robertson's command to Fairfield, seven miles south, to counter this threat. Robertson was absent when the orders arrived, so Jones immediately ordered the command into position. Robertson arrived before Jones left, but he let Jones take the lead.[10]

About two miles outside Fairfield, Jones's Brigade encountered Maj. Samuel H. "Paddy" Starr's 6th U.S. Cavalry. A fierce fight ensued, in which Jones's men routed the Federals. The division remained relatively inactive for the remainder of the day, as it guarded the Confederate Army's right as it withdrew from its three-day engagement at Gettysburg. That evening the men camped near the battle site at Fairfield. Robertson's Carolinians were very concerned with what was to happen next. One of Ferebee's officers reported that evening that "our men, careworn, tired and hungry, drenched by the rain, [were] anxiously awaiting orders."[11]

Their orders were to hold their position and the mountain pass. It was very important for Robertson's men to hold their position at Fairfield, because of the crucial pass through Jack Mountain at that point. The Jack Mountain Pass at Fairfield was the shortest possible route to Hagerstown, Maryland and the Potomac River ford at Williamsport. It was this route that the majority of the Confederates would take south on the retreat.[12]

On the retreat south, which commenced on Saturday, July 4, Lee divided his supplies and ambulances into two wagon trains. The largest train was assigned to Gen. Imboden to guard. It was to cross South Mountain at Cashtown Gap and march to the Williamsport Ford to cross the Potomac. The other, smaller train was to travel with the main army crossing west of South and Jack Mountains, moving through Hagerstown and on to Williamsport. B. H. Robertson's division was assigned to guard this train. Ferebee's 4th NC Cavalry and the rest of Robertson's men spent most of July 4 in drenching thunderstorms waiting to join in Lee's retreat.[13]

About 10:00 P.M. on the evening of July 4, Robertson learned that Brig. Gen. Judson Kilpatrick's cavalry, consisting of six regiments, was advancing along the unguarded Emmitsburg and Waynesboro Road. Kilpatrick's troops easily pushed aside Robertson's picket force, stationed at the road junction just southwest of Fairfield. The Union Gen. wanted to gain the Monterey Pass and cut off the wagon train.[14]

Realizing that Gen. Ewell's train of supply wagons and ambulances was in imminent danger, Grumble Jones immediately deployed the 6th VA Cavalry, 7th VA Cavalry, and Chew's Artillery to counter this threat. However, the 7th VA Cavalry was called back and replaced by the 4th NC Cavalry. As Jones later reported about the Emmettsburg and Waynesboro Road, it was a "narrow and difficult way rendered so by heavy rains." These conditions would prove fatal for many of Jones's and Robertson's men.[15]

After reaching Monterey, Kilpatrick was stopped by a small force, a company of the 1st Maryland Cavalry, led by Capt. G. M. Emack. The weather and road conditions prevented the remainder of Jones's men from reaching the pass, but Jones was finally able to get through to them with a portion of the 4th NC Cavalry. This force was able to hold off Kilpatrick's six regiments for nearly five hours. About 3:00 A.M. Kilpatrick's men finally broke the Confederate line, but the Rebels had held on long enough for the trains to pass southward safely. This engagement became known as Jack's (or South) Mountain. This would be the costliest engagement of the war for the 4th NC Cavalry. The regiment lost 72 captured, three wounded and two killed (Corp. W. H. Flowers of Co. C and Pvt. John Dempster of Co. E).[16]

The retreat south continued on Sunday, July 5. That day as Robertson's division was approaching Hagerstown, Maryland, they were confronted by Kilpatrick's brigade. A skirmish ensued, in which Kilpatrick's men drove the 4th NC Cavalry, 5th NC Cavalry, and Chambliss's brigade from the town. Late that afternoon, Alfred Iverson's infantry arrived, forcing the Federals to withdraw. The Confederates pursued the fleeing Kilpatrick, who counterattacked to buy time for his retreat. This was repulsed by a detachment of the 5th NC Cavalry. A later charge by the 11th VA Cavalry broke the Union lines. A detachment of the 4th NC Cavalry was then sent to pursue the fleeing Federals. Ferebee's men engaged the Union troops until nightfall, suffering 71 casualties. The Carolinians' pursuit ended in Williamsport, where they established pickets. Robertson's men continued picketing July 6, on Lee's extreme left, on the Cavetown Road.[17]

The days after Gettysburg during the retreat proved very stressful on all the men. As 2nd Lt. William Shaw, 4th NC Cavalry, recollected after the war, these were "days which will ever be remembered by those present as days of unprecedented hardships and anxiety, as with scant ration, amid country swept bare of provisions, with the enemy hanging 'round in every direction and the swollen waters of the Potomac at our backs." On Tuesday, July 7, the 4th NC Cavalry was still on picket duty around Williamsport. That night the "rain fell in torrents" adding further to the misery of the troops. The next day Ferebee's men were in Funkstown, Maryland, where they remained until about 5:00 P.M. on July 9, when they were driven back by a force of Federal cavalry.[18]

On Friday, July 10, Stuart's scouts reported Federals in the area. Lee advised Stuart to order Robertson to be on the lookout for them and to offer stiff resistance. That morning the Federal cavalry advanced once again on Robertson's men, about two miles below Funkstown. The force was too great, so the Carolinians retired, falling back about a mile.[19]

On the evening of Monday, July 13, the Confederate Army began recrossing the Potomac at Williamsport. Some of Lee's army crossed the river on pontoon bridges at Falling Waters, four miles below Williamsport. As one of Robertson's men recorded, the "crossing was a narrow, winding ledge of rock." His Tarheels were the last to cross back onto Confederate soil on the morning of July 14.[20]

Once back in Virginia, the Confederates moved to Leetown, while Robertson's brigade was sent to the fords of the Shenandoah River. The infantry was then withdrawn to the south side of the Rapidan, while the cavalry was withdrawn to the Rappahannock and "for some weeks the army enjoyed comparative rest." On Friday, July 17, the 4th NC Cavalry arrived at Millwood, near Ashby's Gap, where it remained at least through July 20. On Friday, July 24, Robertson's men were at the rear of Longstreet's train and had established pickets at Kelly's Ford. It was there on July 25 that the picket force left at Ashby's Gap during the Gettysburg Campaign under Capt. Johnson rejoined the brigade. From Kelly's Ford the brigade headed for Culpeper Court House. About this time, Robertson, who had requested on July 15 to leave the brigade, fell ill with bilious diarrhea. With Robertson ill, Ferebee became acting commander of the brigade, while Capt. Jim Mitchell of Company B assumed temporary command of the regiment.[21]

Picket duty along the Rappahannock River continued for the next month for Ferebee's men. There were a number of minor skirmishes during this time. On Friday, July 31, the 4th NC Cavalry encountered the 66th Ohio Volunteers at Kelly's Ford. The Carolinians reestablished their pickets after the Federals retired. By Wednesday, August 5, the 4th NC Cavalry was still on picket duty, camped near Cedar Run. That same day Lee officially relieved Robertson of command of the 4th and 5th NC Cavalries, due to his health and his July 15 request. By August 16, the 4th NC Cavalry had moved to Stevensburg. The months of movement and fighting had proven costly to the Tarheels morale and supplies. One of Ferebee's men wrote home from camp in Stevensburg, complaining that the men were "nearly barefoot, with no change of clothing." These factors and others, such as the desire of his men to protect their own homes and state, consumed Ferebee. He diligently campaigned to get his command back to North Carolina. However, picket duty along the Rappahannock from Ellis Ford to the junction of the two rivers continued for Ferebee's men into September.[22]

CHAPTER 8

The North Carolina Cavalry Brigade

O N WEDNESDAY, SEPTEMBER 9, 1863, the Army of Northern Virginia's cavalry was reorganized. In this reorganization the North Carolina regiments of cavalry were brigaded together under recently promoted Brig. Gen. Laurence S. Baker. The brigade consisted of the 1st NC Cavalry (9th Regiment N.C.S.T.), 2nd NC Cavalry (19th Regiment N.C.S.T), 4th NC Cavalry (59th Regiment N.C.S.T.), and the 5th NC Cavalry (N.C.S.T.).[1]

Brig. Gen. Laurence Simmons Baker of Gates County, North Carolina was born on May 15, 1830 at Coles Hill. He was the son of Dr. John Burgess Baker and Mary Wynn. He attended Norfolk Academy. In June 1847 Baker was appointed to West Point from North Carolina, graduating in the Class of 1851. (While he attended West Point, a clerk mistakenly spelled his name "Lawrence," and this error has caused many subsequent sources to erroneously record his name.) Upon graduation he was promoted to 2nd lieutenant of the Third Cavalry. He married Elizabeth Earl Henderson on March 15, 1855. He made 1st lieutenant and then captain, before resigning his commission on May 10, 1861 to serve in the Confederate Army. On May 8, 1861, Baker was appointed Lt. Col. of the 1st NC Cavalry. He was promoted to colonel of the regiment on March 1, 1862. He lost an arm at Brandy Station. Baker was promoted to Brig. Gen. in this reorganization. Due to Baker's injury, Ferebee temporarily assumed actual field command of the brigade.[2]

Picket duty continued along the Rappahannock for Ferebee's men. The 4th NC Cavalry was in camp near Raccoon Ford through about Sunday, September 20, when they were reported at Rapidan Station, about five miles from Orange Court House. That evening Meade decided to send Buford's and Kilpatrick's cavalry on reconnaissance across the Robertson River, through Madison County, to gather information and possibly flank Lee's left. The Federal reconnaissance began on Monday, September 21, when Kilpatrick left Stevensburg to meet Buford's men. That afternoon they crossed the Robertson River at Russell's Ford, near James City, nine miles southwest of Culpeper, reaching Madison Court House about sundown.[3]

On Tuesday, September 22 Buford split his command. Kilpatrick moved southwest, crossing the Rapidan at Burtonsville, while Buford, with Chapman's brigade, advanced south along the Madison and Gordonsville Turnpike. After learning that the Union cavalry was advancing on the turnpike, Ferebee's men were ordered into the saddles. They rode up the turnpike to within a few miles of Madison Court House, where they met Grumble Jones's brigade. Jones advised that the Union troops were in strength at Madison Court House. They continued onward, discovering no Union troops there. After proceeding just a little farther, the Confederate advance guard (a company of the 1st NC Cavalry) encountered the Federal pickets, about six miles south of Madison. The main Union force was just north of Jack's Shop (present day Roncelle).[4]

The Confederate force on the turn-

Brigadier General Laurence Simmons Baker, Gates County (North Carolina Office of Archives and History, Raleigh, NC).

pike consisted of J. E. B. Stuart, with Lt. Col. Oliver R. Funsten's brigade, Baker's NC Cavalry brigade (led by Ferebee), and a portion of P. M. B. Young's brigade. Stuart ordered part of Young's men to dismount and engage the Federals, who were in the surrounding woods. Ferebee and the Carolinians, and Young's mounted troopers, were ordered to wait in reserve behind their dismounted comrades. Soon Stuart ordered Ferebee's mounted troopers to charge the Federal line. They were met with a galling fire from the Union troops, who were hidden in the woods extending from each side of the road. They drove the Federals back and for some time held their position in the pines, but the conditions were impractical for mounted troopers. Therefore, Stuart ordered the men to dismount. Soon afterwards, Union artillery opened on the Confederate cavalry. Ferebee ordered sharpshooters from every company to pick off the Federal artillerists. The Carolinians put up a stubborn resistance, but were eventually overpowered, falling back 200 yards. They held this position for several hours.

Buford, sensing an opportunity to trap the Confederates, sent a courier to Kilpatrick in an attempt to have him attack Stuart's rear. Kilpatrick received the dispatch and was able to move up behind the Confederates undetected from the south. Surprisingly, Stuart now found himself fighting on two fronts. Desperate fighting ensued on both fronts as Stuart withdrew south toward Liberty Mills to cross the Rapidan. Kilpatrick's arrival forced Ferebee's men to fall back another mile. Buford slowly pursued Stuart, but met the Confederate reinforcements after crossing the Rapidan. This forced Buford and the Federals to withdraw back across the Rapidan, thus ending the day's fighting, which became known as Jack's Shop.[5]

The Confederates awoke on Wednesday, September 23 to find that the Federals had left their front. Buford's mission to gather intelligence of the area's roads, bridges, fords, etc., as well as information on Confederate troop strength, had been accomplished. Due to the Confederate victory at Chickamauga, in northern Georgia, the Federal move on Lee's left was postponed. On September 24, Maj. Gen. Oliver Otis Howard's XI Corps and Maj. Gen. Henry W. Slocum's XII Corps boarded trains and left the area to reinforce the Union troops in eastern Tennessee. Despite the loss of these troops, Meade still held a decisive troop advantage over Lee: 76,000 to 45,000. Meade took a defensive stand on the north side of the Rapidan. To take advantage of Meade's move, Lee decided to cut around Meade's right flank and rear. Lee hoped this movement would force the Federals to withdraw and allow him to provision his army in northern Virginia for the winter.[6]

Ferebee's men remained camped at Rapidan Station for a couple of weeks. They spent this relatively quiet time on picket duty and in writing letters home. Ferebee was still anxious about getting his men home to North Carolina. His men wrote to loved ones about the weather turning colder. The first hard frost of the season occurred on Sunday, September 27. Some men requested blankets, socks, shoes, coats, and other items needed for the upcoming winter in their letters home.[7]

On Monday, September 28, James B. Gordon was promoted to brigadier general of the North Carolina Cavalry Brigade, replacing the disabled Baker. James Byron Gordon was born on November 2, 1822, in Wilkesboro, North Carolina. He attended Emory and Henry College in Virginia, the same school J. E. B. Stuart attended. After school he operated a mercantile business and farmed. In 1850 he served as a member of the North Carolina legislature. In 1861 he enlisted as a private in the Wilkes Valley Guards. He was elected 1st lieutenant and later captain. He was then appointed major of the 1st NC Cavalry, being promoted to colonel of that regiment in the spring of 1863. Gordon brought a good deal of combat experience to the brigade. One member recalled, "Gordon was a genius of war, a veritable god of battle ... he did more than any other one man to make the brigade what it was."[8]

On Tuesday, October 6, Lee began making preparations for his movement around Meade. The series of actions became known as the Bristoe Campaign. On the evening of Friday, October 9, Gordon and his Carolinians bivouacked near Madison Court House. Here they received their orders from Stuart to begin their movement. Gordon's troops began moving toward the Robertson River at about 3:00 A.M. on October 10. Stuart wanted them to cross at Russell's Ford by about 6:30 A.M. The 4th NC Cavalry, under Lt. William A. Benton of Company A, led the Confederate advance, driving back the Federal vedettes of the 5th New York. The 4th NC Cavalry then charged the reserve Union pickets, capturing a few prisoners. They pursued the Federals until they reached their support, the 120th NY Infantry, at Bethsaida Church, three miles northeast on the road to James City.

Kilpatrick was in force at James City. Realizing this fact, Gordon halted his Carolinians and dismounted men for skirmishing. Shortly afterwards Stuart arrived with Gen. P. M. B. Young's brigade. Gordon then sent his dismounted troopers forward to attack the Union front, while Stuart with Young's troops made an advance on the Union flank. Stuart's and Gordon's simultaneous attack broke the Federal lines and they fled from the field in confusion. The Carolinians then moved toward James City, where Kilpatrick was making defensive preparations.[9]

The Confederates reached James City about 9:00 A.M. Here Gordon's troops squared off against Henry Davies's First Brigade, which consisted of the 2nd NY, 5th NY, 18th PA, and 1st WV Cavalries. Gordon's Carolinians, strategically

Brigadier General James Byron Gordon (North Carolina Office of Archives and History, Raleigh, NC).

placed by Stuart on a hill just south of James City, attacked the Union front, while Young tried to attack Davies's right flank. Both sides dismounted men in a skirmish that lasted several hours, with no decisive decision. That evening Gordon's men camped near James City.[10]

On Sunday, October 11, the Federals fell back toward Culpeper Court House. Stuart and Gordon's Tarheels moved toward Griffinsburg, intersecting the Sperryville-Culpeper Turnpike at Stone House Mountain. Stuart ordered Gordon to proceed down the pike and push the Union back to Culpeper. Finding Kilpatrick's cavalry in force near Culpeper, Gordon selected the 4th NC Cavalry to lead the charge. Ferebee's men charged the blue column, dispersing them. In this charge, Ferebee was wounded in the right foot and Lt. Benton of Company A was killed. (On Friday, October 23, Ferebee was admitted to Gen. Hospital No. 4 in Richmond. He was furloughed on Friday, November 27 and did not return to active command of the 4th NC Cavalry until early May 1864.)[11]

To take advantage of the Union retreat, Stuart directed a move toward Brandy Station, to hit the Union rear, which was guarded by their cavalry. Gordon's North Carolina Cavalry Brigade, the 7th VA Cavalry, and the 12th VA Cavalry were selected by Stuart for the task. One of Gordon's men recollected, "as we approached John Minor Botts' house there could be seen from the front of our column the dense columns of Federal cavalry moving along the railway towards Brandy. They had perceived our purpose to get in their rear and were in full retreat, across the plain to our right, towards Stevensburg." Col. Massie's 12th VA led the charge against Gen. Davies's Federals. The 4th NC and 5th NC Cavalries watched Massie's charge and awaited further orders from Stuart and Gordon. They held a position in a partly sunken road that obstructed the view of their right flank, which at the time was carelessly unprotected.[12]

In a sudden burst, the 2nd NY Cavalry came "over the open elevation which had concealed them" and fell on the Carolinians "like a tornado." The 4th and 5th NC Cavalries broke and fled in confusion. Stuart then sent in the 7th VA to stop the Union charge, but they were stopped by the 1st West Virginia Cavalry. The Federals now held Fleetwood Hill. Stuart, who had occupied the same hill at Brandy Station, realized its importance and decided to outflank the Federals to regain the position. Pleasonton detected Stuart's movement and ordered his troops to fall back slowly. About 8:00 P.M. the Federals crossed the Rappahannock River, where they camped for the night. That evening, the 4th NC Cavalry, fatigued and exhausted, camped with the rest of Gordon's brigade in and around Brandy Station.[13]

On Monday, October 12, the 4th NC Cavalry was in camp near Culpeper Court House. Later that day, they and the rest of Gordon's brigade were ordered toward Warrenton. They crossed the Hedgeman River about sunset and moved into Warrenton, where they camped for the night. On the morning of the 13th, Stuart ordered Gordon's brigade to follow Funsten's Brigade toward Catlett's Station on reconnaissance. Brig. Gen. Lunsford L. Lomax's brigade of Fitz Lee's division had advance scouts which reported the Federals in force at Warrenton Junction, approximately seven miles southeast of Warrenton. Gordon left Warrenton before noon, crossed Cedar Run, and arrived at Auburn about 1:00 P.M. From Auburn, Stuart, with Gordon's and Funsten's brigades, headed toward Catlett's Station along St. Stephens Road. Lomax remained at Auburn to guard the road there. Familiar with the region from previous battles, Stuart left Gordon and Funsten in a wooded area north of St. Stephens Episcopal Church, while he and a small party scouted toward Warrenton Junction. Near the junction, Stuart discovered the immense Federal wagon train, which extended nearly two miles.[14]

Meanwhile at Auburn, a Federal force under Col. Charles H. Collins, consisting of the 57th PA, 63rd PA, 68th PA, 105th PA, 114th PA, and the 141st PA Infantries, forced Lomax from his position. After Stuart learned of the Federal presence at Auburn, he rejoined Gordon and Funsten at St. Stephen's Church. After rejoining with them, Stuart's cavalry headed toward Auburn. About 6:00 P.M. Stuart approached Auburn only to discover that he was surrounded by a large Federal force. Stuart could do nothing but wait until morning, when he planned to make a break for Warrenton. He hoped a diversionary attack by Gen. Lee would help him and his men escape. Because his cavalry was trapped and forced to wait until dawn, Stuart's men went into a "silent, sleepless, cheerless bivouac." The desperate situation was described by one of Gordon's troopers: "all night long we could hear the tramp and the talk and the rumble of the wagons and artillery of the enemy along the road in our front ... not a word was allowed except in whispers, not a spark of fire could be struck, while through the long night we stood there listening to the sounds of the mighty column of armed foes passing near us." A scout got word of Stuart's desperate situation to Lee about 1:00 A.M. on October 14.[15]

On the morning of Wednesday, October 14, Gen. Lee sent A. P. Hill's and Ewell's Infantry toward Auburn to help Stuart. After helping Stuart they were to try to reach Meade's rear. About 6:30 A.M. Confederate and Union artillery began exchanging fire. Shortly thereafter, Union troopers from the 125th NY, under the command of Lt. Col. Levin Crandell, began advancing up the St. Stephen's Road. Stuart saw their approach through the morning mist. He dismounted Funsten's men as skirmishers and ordered Gordon's men to charge the New Yorkers. The Tarheels pushed them back, but the Federals regrouped with support from the 8th NY and 126th NY.

Gordon then reorganized his troops, selecting the 1st NC Cavalry, led by Col. Thomas Ruffin, to lead the second charge against the Federals. During this charge, Gordon was wounded and Col. Ruffin was shot and captured. Ruffin died four days later (October 18) in a Union Army hospital. This charge covered Stuart's withdrawal. The Confederate cavalry moved toward Bristoe Station, where it bivouacked for the night in a pouring rain.

On Thursday, October 15, Stuart's cavalry was ordered to Manassas Junction, where it encountered Federal pickets guarding the retreat of a large wagon train across the Bull Run River. Gordon's men dismounted and fiercely skirmished with the Federals for several hours, eventually driving them across the Bull Run. The Carolinians bivouacked for the night near Manassas. On Friday, during a torrential rain, Gordon moved his men, with Young's and Rosser's brigades, toward Frying Pan Church. Near Frying Pan Church, they made a demonstration upon the Union flank and rear, which lasted for several hours. On Saturday, October 17, the Confederate cavalry destroyed portions of the Orange & Alexandria Railroad to hinder Meade. That night the 4th NC Cavalry bivouacked near the Little River Turnpike.[16]

On Sunday, October 18, Gordon's Tarheels, with Rosser's and Young's brigades, met Kilpatrick's Federals near Groveton. They were pushed back to Gainsville, where they camped for the night. Kilpatrick's men camped near Groveton. Sunday evening, Stuart received intelligence that the Federals were intending to advance on Monday.[17]

At dawn on Monday, October 19, the last day of the Bristoe Campaign, Kilpatrick received orders from Pleasonton to move as soon as possible to Warrenton. Stuart coordinated his movement with Maj. Gen. Fitz Lee, setting up a line of defense on the west bank of the rain-swollen Broad Run. Stuart then began to slowly pull back, allowing Kilpatrick to remain just long enough for Fitz Lee to arrive at Buckland via Auburn to attack the Federal left flank. Once Lee arrived, making his charge on Kilpatrick's left, Stuart ended his fake retreat and turned on the Federals. Gordon's Brigade was in the center of Stuart's force, flanked by Young's and Rosser's brigades. Near Chestnut Hill, the 1st NC Cavalry led the charge. The Union lines broke and the "rout was soon complete." Stuart's men pursued Kilpatrick five and a half miles back to Buckland, "the horses at full speed the whole distance." The battle became known as the "Buckland Races." That evening Stuart's cavalry camped neared Warrenton.[18]

Stuart left his position at Warrenton on Tuesday morning, October 20, leisurely withdrawing across the Rappahannock at Faquier White Sulphur Springs to join the Confederate infantry, which had already crossed. With the Bristoe Campaign, Gen. Lee had wanted to engage the Federals camped around Culpeper Court House and drive them from the area. In this respect he succeeded, but the gains were only short term. The land gained could not be held, because the Confederates were too far from their supply base and the land could not support them. Forage had become very scarce with the constant battling in the area.

With the exception of some minor skirmishing along the picket lines, the 4th NC Cavalry was spared from any major fighting for the next month. Letters home from the men place the regiment in camp on the Rappahannock about four to five miles from Culpeper Court House through November 12, when they are reported near Orange Court House. (On November 5, the 4th NC Cavalry returned to Auburn, the farm of John Minor Botts, to participate in another cavalry review for Stuart. Six months earlier many of these same men paraded on the same pastures for Stuart before Brandy Station.) The 4th NC Cavalry was picketing the fords of the Rappahannock with little contact with the Federals. This quiet time was much needed for the Carolinians, many of whom were sick from the Bristoe Campaign. The weather was turning colder and snow was reported on November 9. On November 20, their period of rest came to an end when Gordon's men were put on stand-by for battle. They made preparations to move from camp, taking seven days' rations and ammunition for battle. They left at 10:00 P.M. and marched six miles toward the Rapidan, where they again set up camp.

By Thursday, November 26, Gordon's Carolinians were with Young's brigade near Twyman's Store. That day Meade was spotted moving in force south of the Rapidan near Germanna. Stuart put his cavalry on alert. At about 9:00 A.M. on November 27, Stuart and Gordon's brigade met the Union advance near New Hope Church, east of Verdiersville. The 4th NC Cavalry was mounted and in advance, while the 5th NC Cavalry and 2nd NC Cavalry were dismounted in the rear. The Tarheels were able to hold the Federals in check, keeping them some distance beyond Mine Run, until Heth arrived with his division. During this action, Capt. Bryce was severely wounded in the foot. The 4th NC Cavalry only had sporadic skirmishing on November 28. That evening Stuart received orders from Lee to advance on the enemy's left and rear.[19]

The engagement on Sunday, November 29, became known as "Parker's Store." It began that morning as Confederate Gen. Rosser, in the advance, surprised a camp of Union cavalry at Parker's Store. Brig. Gen. Gordon was about a mile away on Rosser's right, when the fierce skirmish began. Stuart ordered Gordon to support Rosser, who was being driven back. Gordon dismounted his brigade and attacked the Federals on the Confederate right. At about this same time, Lt. Bamberg, of Hart's Battery, opened within short range of the Union cavalry with artillery fire. The Federal troopers scattered in great confusion. Gordon's Tarheels, who were now mounted, then attacked Union skirmishers. During this charge, Gordon's horse was shot from under him. When Gordon took the pressure off Rosser's right, Gen. Young advanced on Rosser's left, making a joint attack with Rosser on the remaining Federals. Young and Rosser forced the Federals from the field, pursuing them for a while. Gordon's brigade remained at Parker's Store to hold the position during Young's and Rosser's pursuit. The Confederates were successful in capturing prisoners, horses, wagons, overcoats, blankets, guns and camp equipment.[20]

Meade then retired back across the Rapidan. From November 30 through December 2, Gordon's Brigade was held in readiness near Antioch Church, where it performed picket duty. Shortly afterwards Gordon's Tarheels went into winter quarters near Milford Station, picketing the Rapidan at Jacob's and other nearby fords. The 4th NC Cavalry established winter quarters at Guinea Station, east of Milford, and remained there through December 1863.[21]

CHAPTER 9

Defending Petersburg

GORDON'S TARHEELS WERE STILL PICKETING the fords of the Rapidan in January 1864, traveling up to 40 miles from their base camp. Forage was very scarce and Gordon was asking that his command be relieved of duty in Virginia, so that his men could return home to North Carolina. Ferebee was still absent on furlough due to the wound he received on October 11, 1863 during the Bristoe Campaign. A letter home from a member of Company A places the 4th NC Cavalry in camp in Caroline County, VA on January 24. The next day, Monday, January 25, the regiment was ordered home to recruit for the winter. They were to make their winter quarters in Woodville, NC. Sometime shortly after February 3, the 5th NC Cavalry was ordered home to North Carolina to recruit.[1]

On their way to Woodville, the 4th NC Cavalry stopped in nearby Rich Square, NC, where they were met with a warm reception and greatly entertained. One of the 4th NC Cavalry described the hospitality: "large presents were made to the whole regiment of bacon, beef, cabbages, lard, pepper, etc. ... the ladies—the beings we fight for—visited our camp, dined with us in our tents, and danced with us at their homes." They received a much colder welcome upon reaching their destination in Woodville. Letters from the regiment place the group in camp at Woodville through March into April. By April 13, the regiment was reported in camp near Oxford, NC. On Wednesday, April 20, the 4th NC Cavalry was ordered back to Virginia. On Friday, April 22, by Special Order 94, the 4th NC Cavalry was detached from Gordon's Brigade and ordered to report to Gen. P. G. T. Beauregard, commanding the Department of Southeastern Virginia and North Carolina. The 3rd NC Cavalry replaced the 4th NC Cavalry in Gordon's Brigade.[2]

The 4th NC Cavalry did not immediately go north to Virginia. On Saturday, April 23 the regiment was in Weldon, NC, near the border of North Carolina and Virginia. Here Capt. Cherry's Company F was detached to guard the Weldon Bridge. In early May the regiment was in Kinston, NC. Their time in North Carolina was limited; Special Order 105 put the 4th NC Cavalry in Brig. Gen. James Dearing's

Brigade, with Col. V. H. Taliaferro's 7th Confederate Cavalry, Col. Joel R. Griffin's 62nd GA Cavalry, and Col. George N. Folk's 65th NC Cavalry. Ferebee rejoined the regiment in early May, after recovering from his wounded foot.[3]

James Dearing, the 4th NC Cavalry's fourth brigadier general, was born April 25, 1840 at Otterburne, a 920-acre tobacco plantation in Campbell County, Virginia. He attended Hanover Academy and was appointed to West Point in July 1858. He resigned from West Point on April 22, 1861 to accept a lieutenant's commission in the Washington Artillery (New Orleans). He served with the group for about seven months, before being selected by the 38th Battalion VA Artillery (a.k.a. Latham's Battery and Lynchburg Artillery), becoming 2nd captain in Company D. He was promoted to major in January of 1863 and assigned to Pickett's division. In early 1864, he was promoted to colonel to lead a detached group of cavalry under Pickett. On Friday, April 29, 1864, just

Brigadier General James Dearing (Massachusetts Commandery Military Order of the Loyal Legion and the US Army Military History Institute).

four days after his 24th birthday, Dearing was promoted to the rank of brigadier general. He was mortally wounded during the retreat to Appomattox at High Bridge on April 6, 1865, in a pistol dual with Union Gen. Theodore Read. He died 17 days later, the last Confederate general officer to die from wounds received in action. He is buried in Lynchburg's Spring Hill Cemetery.[4]

In the spring of 1864, action in and around Richmond, VA was becoming heated. Events there would draw the 4th NC Cavalry back to extensive duty in Virginia. On Saturday, March 12, 1864, Lt. Gen. Ulysses S. Grant was named commander-in-chief of all the armies of the United States, replacing Maj. Gen. Henry W. Halleck. Grant was headquartered with the Army of the Potomac, 60 miles north of Richmond, just beyond the Rapidan. The new Union commander's chief objective was to capture the Confederate capitol of Richmond. To accomplish his objective, Grant decided a two-front attack would be best. He would lead the Army of the Potomac overland from the north directly toward Richmond, while Benjamin Butler would move his Army of the James up the James River from Fort Monroe and attack the city from the south. Butler was to secure a point at the junction of the Appomattox and James Rivers, known as Bermuda Hundred, and use it as his base of operations.[5]

Butler landed at Bermuda Hundred unhindered on Thursday, May 5. The next day Butler's men advanced a short distance in an effort to destroy the Richmond and Petersburg Railroad. They traveled only a short distance before they met Confederate resistance at Port Wathall Junction. This setback forced Butler to begin building defense works to guard the lines at Bermuda Hundred. On Saturday, May 7 Butler's men were once again driven back at Port Wathall Junction. The Federals advanced on May 9 as far as Swift Creek, a tributary of the Appomattox, before stopping. A Wednesday, May 11 dispatch from Gen. Beauregard states that Dearing's Brigade was "en route" to Petersburg.[6]

On Thursday, May 12, Dearing's Brigade, including Ferebee's 4th NC Cavalry, was ordered temporarily to Brig. Gen. Henry A. Wise to guard the lines between Swift Creek and Drewry's Bluff. The 4th NC Cavalry arrived in Petersburg on May 13 and reported to W. H. C. Whiting. The next day Whiting ordered Dearing's cavalry back to Petersburg, where on Sunday, May 15 they were ordered to guard all approaches to the city. There the Confederate command learned that the Union troops may have been moving toward Drewry's Bluff.[7]

On May 14 and May 15, Beauregard made plans for a Confederate offensive movement at Drewry's Bluff. Beauregard would advance south from the town toward the Federal front, while Whiting would move north from Petersburg around the Federal flank and rear. On May 15, Beauregard decided to attack the Federals at daybreak on May 16. That evening he ordered Whiting to move to Swift Creek, with Wise's and James G. Martin's brigades, part of Alfred H. Colquitt's brigade, Dearing's cavalry, and 20 artillery guns with the following instructions: "At daybreak you will march to Port Wathall Junction, and when you hear an engagement in your front you will advance boldly and rapidly by the shortest road in the direction of the heaviest firing, to attack the enemy in rear or flank."[8]

Whiting was very anxious about the entire situation, because he believed that Petersburg, not Drewry's Bluff, was the focus of the Federal movement. Therefore, he did not want to leave Petersburg undefended. Despite his misgivings, Whiting complied with Beauregard's orders and cautiously moved his column north toward Port Wathall Junction. Whiting had the 7th Confederate Cavalry on his left, Martin's and Ferebee's men in the center, and the 62nd GA on his right.[9]

The Federal force led by Brig. Gen. Adelbert Ames consisted of the 13th IN Infantry, the 169th NY Infantry, Battery E of the 3rd US Artillery, and a detachment of the 1st US Colored Cavalry. Beauregard was able to defeat the Army of the James on his front, but Whiting did not advance into the rear of the retreating Federals. Instead, he decided to fall back south toward Swift Creek, because there was no enemy in his front and he did not want to leave Petersburg undefended. Whiting did halt his withdrawal for a while, but his hesitation to pursue the fleeing Federals caused the Confederates to miss a great opportunity.[10]

The evening of Friday, May 20, Dearing's cavalry was on reconnaissance near Fort Powhatan. The next day, by Special Order #10, Ferebee and the 4th NC Cavalry were ordered to Finley's House to relieve the 3rd NC Cavalry to guard and protect the Confederate left flank. On May 25, Special Order #12 commanded Ferebee to divide his force. He was to leave two companies, or about 100 men, with Brig. Gen. Bushrod Johnson, commanding the Confederate left wing. These Tarheels would guard Johnson's left to Drewry's Bluff. Ferebee was to take the rest of his command and report to Maj. Gen. Robert F. Hoke commanding the right flank. They were to guard Hoke's right flank between Bake-House and Swift Creek. They were to relieve Col. Griffin's 62nd GA Cavalry, who were to report back to Dearing at or near Petersburg. Ferebee's divided force served mainly as a picket force for the next week in and around Petersburg. It drove in the Union picket at Gatlin's on Tuesday, May 31. Two days later Ferebee's Carolinians were ordered to protect the Confederate front and flank, "guarding with special care the approach from Bermuda Hundred."[11]

By late May Grant's strategy was beginning to change, due mainly to Butler's defeat at Drewry's Bluff. Afterwards Grant ordered Smith's XVIII Corps to join him at Cold Harbor, which greatly reduced Butler's strength. This also apparently reduced Butler's role at Bermuda Hundred to a defensive one, yet Butler was convinced, even with his reduced force, that he could still mount a successful offensive campaign against the Cockade City, Petersburg. (Petersburg was nicknamed the Cockade City by President James Madison to venerate the city's sacrifice and contribution in the War of 1812. The name came from the Cockade Monument in Blandford Cemetery, honoring the men of Petersburg who died in the War of 1812. The monument was named for the rosette insignia on the volunteer's hats.) By June 1, Butler had devised a plan whereby his force would attack Petersburg from the south, and destroy the city's public buildings and the railroad bridge over the Appomattox. By destroying this bridge, Butler would cut off Lee's direct supply line to Wilmington, NC.

Butler scheduled his offensive for Thursday, June 2. Unbeknownst to Butler, Beauregard had ordered a thorough reconnaissance of the area that same day. This Confederate reconnaissance inadvertently captured part of the Union advance picket, thus postponing Butler's advance. Even with this setback, Butler was still convinced that an attack on Petersburg was necessary and practical. However, he did not think his force could hold the city; rather they would quickly raid the city and destroy the railroad bridge, then retire to their defenses at Bermuda Hundred. Butler envisioned a three-pronged attack consisting of two columns of infantry and one of cavalry. Maj. Gen. Quincy Gillmore asked to lead the attack and Butler reluctantly agreed. The Union infantry was led by Brig. Gen. Edward Hincks, with Col. Joseph R. Hawley's four-brigade regiment, which was detached from Brig. Gen. Alfred Terry's division. Brig. Gen. August Kautz led the Federal cavalry.[12]

Meanwhile, Ferebee's men were building up the defenses around Petersburg, helping in the construction of defensive breastworks around the city. The Carolinians sensed something was about to happen due to the increased activity in the area. On Wednesday, June 8, the 4th NC Cavalry was on picket and guard duty near Dunn's Farm, about seven miles from Petersburg. That evening Butler put his offensive plan in motion, but his men were delayed by the nighttime travel through the swamps.[13]

At about 7 A.M. on Thursday, June 9, Hawley's brigade encountered Col. V. K. Taliaferro's 7th Confederate Cavalry near the City Point Railroad, about two miles northeast of Petersburg. They skirmished for over an hour. Taliaferro's men held the

Union advance until about 8:30 A.M., when they were forced to fall back toward the Cockade City. Meanwhile, things were "business as usual" in Petersburg on that bright, beautiful June day. As Taliaferro's men were retreating, the bustle of everyday life was beginning, the local stores were opening, local children were heading to school, women were doing their shopping, and the local militia was beginning to drill.[14]

Maj. Fletcher Archer commanded Petersburg's local militia, camped at the Rive's Farm just south of town, near the Dimmock Line. The Dimmock Line was a series of defenses around Petersburg, begun in 1862 by slaves under the guidance of Capt. Charles Dimmock, a Confederate engineer. The line, completed in 1863, was in the shape of a flattened horseshoe, with its points resting firmly against the Appomattox River to the east and west of Petersburg. It consisted of 55 batteries, connected by a series of rifle pits and long trenches. At one time the line's defenses were formidable, but by June 1864 weather had eroded the line somewhat, decreasing its effectiveness.[15]

Archer's group at the Dimmock Line consisted of men too young and too old for regular military service. By 9:00 A.M. on June 9, they had consumed their breakfast and were waiting for their morning drill to begin. At about that time, a courier from Col. Randolph Harrison's 46th VA reported that the Confederate forces east of the city were under attack, and that the Federals were heading for the Jerusalem Plank Road. Archer reacted quickly, calling his men to arms. Soon bells began to ring throughout the city, signaling the impending danger. By 10:00 A.M. all able-bodied men had joined Archer at the Dimmock Line, the bells had stopped and there was an unusual calm in the city.[16]

Upon learning of the Union advance on the outer defenses of Petersburg, Beauregard, headquartered at Dunlop's (about two miles north of Petersburg on the Richmond and Petersburg Railroad) ordered Dearing and Ferebee's 4th NC Cavalry to report to Brig. Gen. Henry Wise and offer any help it could. Wise, who reported directly to Beauregard, was in command of the forces in and around Petersburg. Beauregard also ordered Brig. Gen. Bushrod Johnson to open artillery fire on Butler at Bermuda Hundred, in case the move on Petersburg was a diversion.[17]

Fortunately for the Confederates, the defenses on the Dimmock Line were holding the Union advance in check. Hincks and Gillmore became discouraged with their lack of success. Kautz, commanding the cavalry, left Hincks's infantry force at Jordan Point Road and continued south on the Confederate flank. Shortly after Kautz left the infantry, Hincks learned that Gillmore was withdrawing his force back to the Union defenses at Bermuda Hundred. Hincks soon did the same, leaving Kautz alone to raid the Cockade City.[18]

Meanwhile, south of town, in the Confederate militia camp at Rives's Farm, Fletcher Archer was preparing his men for the impending Federal advance. His troops had outdated weapons and no uniforms, but they were fighting to defend their homes and families. Archer had his men deployed behind the fortifications between Batteries 27 and 25 of the Dimmock Line. About 11:30 A.M. two pickets from the 7th Confederate Cavalry came dashing up the Jerusalem Plank Road past Archer's positions and informed the militia leader that the Federals were on their heels.[19]

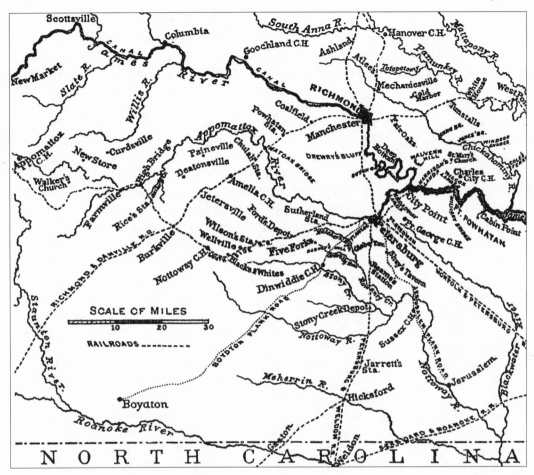

Petersburg and Appomattox Campaigns 1864–1865 (*Battles and Leaders*, Volume IV, page 569).

Seconds later Col. Spear's 2nd Brigade, led by Col. Stetzel's 11th PA, charged Archer's men at Battery 27 with their sabers drawn. Archer made his men hold their fire until the last possible second. The Confederates patiently did so and when they opened fire they were able to repulse the first wave of the Federal attack. Kautz soon arrived on the scene and postponed Spear's second charge, until they were able to reconnoiter the Confederate position. However, the Federals proved too much for Archer's small force, which consisted of only about 125 men on June 9, 1864. The 5th PA, 11th PA, and the 1st DC cavalries were flanking his left. It was only a matter of time before they broke through the Confederate line. Archer had to decide whether to retreat immediately or wait a while to buy his town more time. The Confederates decided to try to hold their line, but the were soon overrun and in full retreat back to Petersburg. Kautz's cavalry then destroyed the camp at Rives's Farm. Kautz, remembering his original mission to destroy the railroad bridges, began organizing Lt. Moton's artillery.[20]

Seven miles northeast of town between Dunn's Farm and Bermuda Hundred, Dearing and Ferebee, with Edward Graham's battery, obeying Beauregard's mid-morning order, broke camp and headed for Petersburg to offer assistance. They crossed the Appomattox at the Pocahontas Bridge and proceeded up Second Street. Dearing then sent Capt. William E. Hinton, Jr. to Wise for further instructions. Wise advised Hinton that he needed Dearing and his men at the Wilcox Farm, west of Battery 27. In town, Dearing was joined by Col. Taliaferro's 7th Confederate Cavalry.[21]

Realizing the importance of getting his men into position at the Wilcox Farm, Dearing ordered his men down Sycamore Street at a gallop, with Edward Graham's artillery in the lead. About halfway down Sycamore Street, Dearing was informed by a local militiaman, E. H. Osborne, that the Federals were approaching Petersburg on the Jerusalem Plank Road. This changed Dearing's plans; he stopped and divided his force. He sent the 7th Confederate Cavalry toward Blandford Church, while the 4th NC Cavalry and Graham's battery continued down Sycamore Street. Anticipating the Federal movement, Graham sent two guns to the crest of Reservoir Hill, which was located south of the water works. He and the other two guns continued down Sycamore Street with Ferebee's men. Graham eventually placed these guns on either side of William Cameron's house.[22]

With the artillery in place, Dearing ordered Lt. Col. Cantwell, with a portion of the 4th NC Cavalry, to charge the advancing Union column. The remaining troops of the 4th NC Cavalry were deployed as skirmishers between the reservoir (on their left) and the Cameron house (on their right). As the Federals approached, Graham's guns opened fire on them. Although the shells missed the advance guard of the 11th PA, they did greatly confuse the charging enemy. Combined with Cantwell's charge, the shells were enough to stop the Federal charge. Under cover from Graham's guns, the 4th NC Cavalry slowly moved forward, breaking the Federal lines and forcing them to retire hastily back to their defenses at Bermuda Hundred.[23]

After helping successfully defend Petersburg on June 9, Ferebee's men were placed on the Broadway and City Point Road to watch and guard against any Federal advance. One of Ferebee's troopers wrote from camp near Petersburg on June 10 about his blistered feet, and the fact that he was now wearing a pair of Union pants. By Sunday, June 12, Ferebee had reestablished his picket line within two and a half miles of City Point. The next day Dearing was reported at Swift Creek.[24]

On June 5, before Butler's attempted raid on Petersburg, Grant decided to move his army to the south side of the James River. He wanted to coordinate with Butler at Bermuda Hundred, attack Petersburg, then head on to Richmond and capture the Confederate capitol. He put his plan into motion on June 12. Some of his Army of the Potomac marched overland, while others boarded transports at White House Landing (Smith's 18th Corps, Army of the James), taking a journey down the Pamunkey River and back up the James to Bermuda Hundred. Amazingly, Grant's army slipped away from Lee's front at Cold Harbor. Grant met with Butler on Tuesday, June 14 at Bermuda Hundred and informed Butler of his plan to take Petersburg the next morning.[25]

Unfortunately for the Federals, unforeseen setbacks delayed Grant's plans for an early morning attack on Wednesday, June 15. At about 5:00 A.M. on the 15th the 3rd NY Mounted Rifles attacked Ferebee's "advanced pickets and drove them to the reserve post" at Baylor Farm. Capt. James T. Mitchell led the picket in the slow, orderly retreat. Mitchell's picket was able to offer some resistance, which helped to slow the Union advance. Mitchell's men were joined by more of the 4th NC Cavalry and Graham's artillery and were able to repulse the Federal charge.[26]

However, the 3rd NY was soon joined by Baldy Smith's XVIII Corps of infantry. The 4th NC Cavalry and Graham's battery held for about four hours, repulsing several more charges, but when their ammunition was exhausted they gave way to the Federals' superior numbers. During this time, Capt. Bell of Company G was sent out to Broadway Road on Ferebee's left to prevent a flanking movement, which he was able to do for a few hours. The 4th NC Cavalry's firm stand helped buy enough time for Petersburg to be secured on June 15. William Henry Edwards of Company H was killed during this battle. Fighting continued for the next three days, and despite being outnumbered the Confederates held their lines. On June 1, Ferebee's Tarheels were guarding the Appomattox River to prevent a Federal crossing and subsequent flanking movement. By June 18, the bulk of Lee's Army of Northern Virginia arrived at Petersburg, thwarting Grant's plans. The Union's failure to take the Cockade City resulted in a trench-warfare standoff between Lee and Grant around Petersburg.[27]

On Sunday, June 19, under Special Order No. 26, Dearing's Brigade, now consisting of the 4th NC Cavalry, 7th Confederate Cavalry, and 62nd GA Cavalry, was ordered to report to Gen. W. H. F. Lee on the Jerusalem Plank Road to guard and protect the Petersburg & Weldon Railroad. The next day Ferebee's men skirmished with Union pickets on the Jerusalem Plank Road. On Tuesday, June 21, Dearing and the 4th NC Cavalry moved to Reams' Station, 10 miles south of Petersburg on the Weldon Railroad.[28]

That same night the Federals were putting another raid into motion, with the purpose of destroying the South Side Railroad and the Richmond & Danville Railroad, as far south as the Staunton River Bridge. Grant chose James Harrison Wilson's Third Division and Kautz's cavalry for the task. Brig. Gen. Rufus Barringer described the Federal movement and subsequent destruction of June 21 and June 22 as follows:

> We first struck them at Reams' Station ... where they had destroyed the depot, and then made straight across the country by Dinwiddie Court House for the South Side road, on towards Burkeville. That night the work of destruction went ceaselessly forward; for twenty miles the entire track was taken up, the cross-ties made up into great piles and the iron laid across them so as to insure [sic] complete destruction by fire. In the same way the work was started the next day on the Richmond & Danville lines.

The entire area was overrun by the invading foe. The Confederates offered some resistance in small skirmishes, but none with any decisive results.[29]

The Federals' destruction continued on Thursday, June 23, when they were met by a Confederate force consisting of Dearing's (4th NC, 7th Confederate, and 62nd GA Cavalries) and Barringer's (1st NC, 2nd NC, and 5th NC Cavalries) brigades between Black and White's and Nottoway Court House. The action there started after noon and "for several hours the battle raged ... whole trees and saplings were cut down with shells and minie-balls, until night ended the conflict." That night the Federals retired from the field and headed for the Staunton River Bridge on the Richmond and Danville Railroad. The next morning, Friday, June 24, Barringer and Dearing separated their forces to pursue the Federals. Barringer's brigade followed the enemy's line of march, while Dearing's column moved on the Federal left flank. However, the Federal raid was a success, as it left the area completely overrun, with much destruction. Dearing's men spent the next week in camp recovering from the heavy action.[30]

CHAPTER 10

Reams' Station,
the Cattle Raid,
and Hatcher's Run

THE 4TH NC CAVALRY and the remainder of Dearing's Brigade remained in camp around Petersburg for most of July 1864. Their only action was picket duty and occasional contact with the Federals. On Monday, July 11, 1864, Dearing's cavalry was reorganized by Special Order 161. Dearing's mounted unit now consisted of the 8th GA Cavalry (created from 62nd GA), commanded by Col. Joel Griffin, the 4th NC Cavalry, under Col. Dennis D. Ferebee, the 65th NCST (6th NC Cavalry), led by Col. George Folk, and the newly formed 16th Battalion of NC Cavalry, commanded by Lt. Col. John Kennedy. Kennedy's force was formed from parts of the 7th CS Cavalry, the 62nd GA and the 12th Battalion NC Cavalry. In this same consolidation, Companies A and B of the 12th Battalion became Companies K and I, respectively, of the 4th NC Cavalry. The 12th Battalion was organized May 3, 1863 and consisted of three companies. Companies A and C enlisted in Northampton County, while Bertie and Hertford counties supplied the men for Company B. In the reorganization under Special Order 161, Company C was assigned to the 16th Battalion NC Cavalry (75th NCST).[1]

The war was beginning to wear on the soldiers of the 4th NC Cavalry by the summer of 1864. The stalemate around Petersburg was allowing the Carolinians to see the wholesale carnage of war for the first extended period. One of Ferebee's men described the scene in the following passage written to his hometown newspaper:

> Human life is nothing. Some thirty negroes are busily employed digging narrow trenches, perhaps fifty yards long and three or four feet deep. Ambulances are arriving from all quarters at full speed, wheeled into position and two stalwart hands seize the dead soldier and throw him, without regard to position, in the trench. They are thus thrown two deep along the whole trench without boxes even, and the dirt from the next row serves as a covering. Sometimes, but rarely, a headboard tells the name of him beneath the sod.[2]

Brigadier General Rufus Barringer (top right), Cabarrus County (North Carolina Office of Archives and History, Raleigh, NC).

On Thursday, July 28, the 4th NC Cavalry was still in the same camp it had occupied since July 3. A letter from Richard P. Allen (Company A) to a friend notes that forage for the horses was getting scarce around Petersburg. Each man was only issued two small bundles of oats a day, with no corn to be distributed. Allen also states that Rufus Barringer's men left that morning, heading toward Petersburg. Another Allen letter on Monday, August 1 describes the very hot weather and the tremendous amount of dust that the soldiers endured each day while on picket duty. He also mentions hearing an explosion the day before, which was no doubt, the Battle of the Crater.[3]

Picket duty around Reams' Station continued for the 4th NC Cavalry until Thursday, August 4, when the men were relieved by the 2nd NC Cavalry and returned to their previous position just south of Petersburg. The main Federal objective south of Petersburg during the summer of 1864 was the destruction of the Petersburg & Weldon Railroad, Lee's vital supply line to and from North Carolina. By mid–August, Dearing's Brigade consisted of the 4th NC Cavalry, the 7th Confederate Cavalry, and the 8th GA Cavalry. Company H of the 8th GA served as artillery. Dearing's command was brigaded with Rufus Barringer's Brigade, which at the time consisted of the 1st, 2nd, 3rd, and 5th NC Cavalries. Barringer was in command of the division, since W. H. F. Lee was ill and absent. On the morning of August 14 Ferebee's Tarheels and Dearing met Barringer's Brigade at Reams' Station. The Confederates, anticipating a Federal move to destroy the railroad, left Reams' Station about 11:00 A.M. heading toward Globe Tavern, with Barringer in advance.[4]

On Wednesday, August 17, the Federal Fifth Corps, commanded by Gouverneur Warren, was ordered to move its entire four-division corps, with Brig. Gen. August Kautz's two-brigade cavalry division, to raid the Weldon Railroad in the vicinity of Gurley House. They were to destroy the tracks as far south as possible. Kautz's cavalry was to protect Warren's southern flank. This mission would have been a chance for Warren to redeem himself for his poor performance in June and at the Battle of the Crater, but he was held in reserve and did not participate. The Union movement began August 18 at 5:00 A.M., an hour later than planned, as Brig. Gen. Charles Griffin's infantry division began marching south along the Jerusalem Plank Road, with Kautz's cavalry under Samuel Spear in the lead.[5]

According to the *War of the Rebellion* records, "The Halifax Road ran alongside the Weldon tracks, a little over a mile north of Globe Tavern, it threw off a branch, the Vaughan Road, which diverged to the southwest. Near this intersection was the Davis House and farm." It was here that Dearing's men and a two-gun Confederate artillery met the initial Union advance. Dearing's pickets were driven back and he reported to Beauregard that the Federals were moving in force upon both the railroad and the Vaughan Road. Dearing's men were able to check the Union advance at the Davis House, but they formed a "strong line of battle at his front." On August 19 rain poured in torrents all day and into the night. That day Confederate forces under Maj. Gen. William Mahone and Maj. Gen. Henry Heth halted the Union advance north of Globe Tavern. The struggle for the railroad continued through August 21, when the Confederates stopped their efforts. As a result of the battle, the Union lines extended across the tracks north of Globe Tavern and along the Weldon Railroad. Although the Confederates still controlled the railroad as far north as Reams' Station, the Federals had accomplished their goal of cutting the line into Petersburg.[6]

On Sunday, August 21, Union Gen. Winfield S. Hancock was ordered from Deep Bottom to Reams' Station. Hancock was to follow up on the Federal success of the last few days by planning a move on Reams' Station to destroy the tracks there. He arrived there on Tuesday, August 22 and commenced his task. Dearing's Brigade was on the Confederate right flank. On Wednesday, August 23, Maj. Gen. Wade Hampton made a personal reconnaissance of the Federal activity around Reams' Station. He felt that the Union lines could be broken with the help of the Confederate infantry. On August 24, Union destruction of the line continued. The Federals (Barlow's Division) established a skirmish line in front of Malone's Crossing. That same day Barringer's cavalry scouts at Stony Creek were searching for the Union cavalry. On August 25, under Hampton's recommendation, a combined Confederate force of cavalry, infantry, and artillery attacked the Federals around Reams' Station. Cavalry under the overall command of Wade Hampton attacked the Union right flank, while A. P. Hill's infantry attacked the entrenched Union front along the railroad. The Battle of Reams' Station was a complete Confederate success.[7]

In a Friday, August 26, 1864, letter to Maj. Gen. Wade Hampton, Gen. Robert E. Lee requested that Dearing's Brigade "do all the picketing if practical, so as to give the rest of the cavalry a good period of repose for refreshing their horses." A member of the 4th NC Cavalry wrote home to the Wadesboro *North Carolina Argus* on Wednesday, August 31, stating that "since the fights last week ... the lines around Petersburg have been remarkably quiet." The regiment remained in camp around Petersburg for the next few weeks, performing picket duty and recuperating from the recent fighting. The Thursday, September 1, 1864 Organization of Troops, Department of North Carolina and Southern Virginia, commanded by Gen. P. G. T. Beauregard, listed the following regiments in Dearing's cavalry: the 7th Confederate Cavalry, commanded by Col. V. H. Taliaferro, the 8th GA Cavalry, commanded by Col. Joel R. Griffin, the 4th NC Cavalry, under Col. Ferebee, and the 6th NC Cavalry, under Col. George N. Folk. They were joined by Capt. Edward Graham's battery of horse artillery. (The 6th NC Cavalry never joined Dearing's brigade, having been detained by events in North Carolina. Companies D and E of the 7th Confederate Cavalry were on duty at Masonborough Sound under Col. George Jackson and also did not join Dearing's brigade).[8]

The 4th NC Cavalry was still in camp around Petersburg in early September. A letter from Brantley H. Saunders (Company E) says that the regiment was without a chaplain, but that the men of the regiment were holding prayer meetings every night on their own. In September 1864 the Federals controlled the James River, with a small fleet of converted ferryboats, tugboats, and schooners. This fleet also helped to supply the Union troops. The Federal lines around Petersburg were stretched thin. The Union cavalry under Brig. Gen. August Kautz was responsible for protecting Grant's Army of the Potomac's rear supply lines, which at this time included a cattle herd of 3,000 head. The cattle were penned near Cocke's Mill at Coggin's Point.[9]

Lack of refrigeration was a problem for both the North and South in providing fresh meat to the troops. The Union had developed a solution in which they shipped cattle to the lines between Richmond and Petersburg, where they could graze along the fertile pastures along the James River. Once a Union request for beef was made to the Quartermaster Department, the appropriate number were slaughtered and sent fresh to the troops. In early September 1864, Capt. George D. Shadburne, the chief Confederate scout, reported to Wade Hampton that he had discovered the 3,000-head herd near Cocke's Mill. Hampton advised Gen. Robert E. Lee of Shadburne's suggestion for a raid on the Union rear to capture the herd.

Lee welcomed Shadburne's suggestion and on the chilly morning of Wednesday, September 14, Wade Hampton, with Tom Rosser's brigade, Dearing's brigade (including the 4th NC Cavalry), Rooney Lee's division, and a detachment of 100 men from Young's and Dunovant's brigades began the raid to capture the cattle. To prevent detection from the Union pickets, Hampton made a wide circle around Grant's left flank. The raiders moved south from Petersburg along the Boydton Plank Road for about 13 miles. They then turned southeast on Flat Foot Road for about seven miles, until they reached Wilkinson's Bridge on Rowanty Creek, where they bivouacked for the night.

On Thursday, September 15, the Confederates were silently awoken by word of mouth two hours before dawn. From their bivouac, they headed northeast toward Ebenezer Church, crossing the Norfolk and Petersburg Railroad by noon. The line had been dismantled by Federal troops. Upon reaching the Blackwater River they found the Cook's Bridge out. Supposedly, Hampton "took this route because ... the absence of a bridge averted suspicion of any approach that way." The cavalry rested and the horses were fed as the engineers made repairs to the 100-foot long bridge. Once the repairs were complete, Hampton's column crossed the Blackwater. That evening, once all had crossed the river, Hampton split his command for a three-pronged attack. Rooney Lee, Hampton's largest unit, was sent northwest toward Prince George Court House. Lee was to attack to the Federals camped there. Tom Rosser's Brigade was sent north toward Coggin's Point. Rosser was the key to Hampton's plan, because it would be his men who would capture the herd. Dearing's troopers, Hampton's smallest unit, were positioned on Hines Road to Rosser's right. They were to move toward Cocke's Mill, via Stage Road. From there they could block any Federal interference from the east.

The next day, Friday, September 16, about 5:00 A.M., the Confederates put their battle plan into action. Rosser made a charge on the Federal line near Sycamore Church. He first met the vedettes of the 1st DC Cavalry, which were armed with 16-shot Henry rifles. They slowed the Confederate advance, but Rosser's men eventually broke through the initial Union resistance, making their way to the cattle pen guarded by the 13th PA Cavalry. Dearing and Lee moved into position as planned. By 8:00 A.M. the Confederates had captured the herd and were leading it south toward Cook's Bridge. By 10:00 A.M. the four-mile long Confederate column was at the bridge. The herd was counted as it crossed the bridge, with the final tally being 2,486 head. Once all of Hampton's men and the captured herd had crossed, the bridge was destroyed to slow the Union pursuit.

Union Brig. Gen. Henry Davies, Jr. pursued Hampton's column, engaging it near Ebenezer Church. He held the Confederates in position until about 8:00 P.M. He hoped that Kautz would arrive and attack the Confederate rear, but Kautz was slowed by Hampton's rear guard. By dawn on September 17 Hampton's column near Ebenezer Church was in motion. They were safely behind Confederate lines by 9:00 A.M., reestablishing the same camp southwest of Petersburg.[10]

After the raid Dearing became ill with chills, fever, and severe headaches. Later in the month, Tom Rosser's Brigade was transferred to the Shenandoah Valley to reinforce Jubal Early, who was engaged with the Union forces led by Maj. Gen. Phil Sheridan. This greatly diminished the Confederate cavalry force around Petersburg. On Thursday, September 29 the Federals took advantage of this by making an advance on the Confederate lines on the Vaughan and Squirrel Level roads. Rooney Lee's and Matthew Butler's brigades held off the initial Union advance. However, early on the morning of Friday, September 30, a strengthened Union column attacked the breastworks held by Dearing's Brigade. The defenders were led by senior Col. Joel R. Griffin of the 8th GA Cavalry in Dearing's absence. The Federals broke the Confederate line and captured the breastworks at the Squirrel Level Road line (Fort Archer). All was not lost though, because Hampton was able to stop Grant's general advance. Hampton blamed Griffin's men for the loss of the breastworks, which ultimately reflected poorly on Dearing. The Confederates held their positions that night and waited for another attack, which seemed imminent but never came.[11]

The next month the 4th NC Cavalry and the rest of Dearing's Brigade were dismounted and placed in the trenches near Hatcher's Run, guarding the Boydton Plank Road. A Saturday, October 1, 1864 supply request by Lt. Dallas M. Beale places the 4th NC Cavalry's camp at Burgess Mill. It was still in the same camp at Burgess Mill in Hampton's October 11 letter to Robert E. Lee. During this time Ferebee was vying for a promotion. He was angered that Joel R. Griffin led the brigade in Dearing's absence. He had been wanting a brigadiership since the initial dissatisfaction with B. H. Robertson.[12]

Grant's main objective was still to cut Lee's supply lines around Petersburg, but politics were also playing a role in the Union operations. The 1864 presidential election was just weeks away and Lincoln was in a battle against the former commander of the Army of the Potomac, George B. McClellan, who was running on the peace-oriented Democratic platform. McClellan's election might hamper Grant's job against Lee. With this in mind, George Meade, the Union leader at Gettysburg, who had lost political favor due to recent inefficiencies, suggested that Grant go on the offensive again before the election. This time they could silence the critics and "finally close the ring around Petersburg."[13]

On Monday, October 24 Grant ordered Meade to march out early on Thursday, October 27, gain possession of the South Side Railroad and Boydton Plank Road, cut both and destroy the railroad. Grant was planning a simultaneous attack north of the James River, to prevent the Confederates from being reinforced. Grant chose Benjamin Butler to face James Longstreet, commanding the Confederates north of the James. On October 27, the Union troops south of the James were in columns by

3:00 A.M. and were marching by 3:30 A.M. However, they did not travel quickly. As Horace Porter describes, the "morning was dark and gloomy, a heavy rain was falling, the roads were muddy and obstructed, and tangled thickets, dense woods, and swampy streams confronted the troops at all points."[14]

The attack began 12 miles southwest of Petersburg as Hampton's pickets were quickly driven in from their position along Hatcher's Run. Hampton's counterattack plan was to attempt an envelopment of David Gregg's cavalry. To accomplish this he moved Rooney Lee's men up from the south, while Matthew Butler's division was to screen his movement north and west. Dearing's brigade was to guard his rear along the Boydton Plank Road. A. P. Hill arrived on the scene and advised Dearing's men to hold their position in the trenches near Burgess Mill. This left Hampton's rear flank unguarded. Hampton was unaware of this because the courier relaying this information, Maj. Venable, was captured. Hampton continued with his attack along the Quaker Road in ignorance, discovering that his rear flank was unprotected only after Union infantry appeared behind him.[15]

Hampton described the action following the Federal approach in his Monday, November 21, 1864 report:

> This made it necessary for me to change my front so as to meet the enemy on the [Boydton] plank road and the White Oak road, both of which were by this time in his possession ... I ordered Butler to withdraw his command promptly from the Quaker Meeting House and to take position near Wilson's house on the plank road ... I passed rapidly over to the White Oak road. The skirmish line of the enemy was advancing up this road when we reached it, but it was quickly driven back. I then formed line of battle across this road, my left resting on Burgess mill pond, and repulsed an attack.

Skirmishing continued throughout the afternoon, but darkness and heavy rains brought an end to the day's fighting. Hampton ordered that his line of battle be held through the night. That evening the Confederate gathered reinforcements and made preparations for a morning attack on the Federals, who wisely retreated during the night.[16]

On the morning of Friday, October 28, the Confederates discovered that the Union troops had retreated. Hampton immediately ordered a search for the enemy. He reports: "Dearing's brigade being in advance ... [I] struck his rear guard between Dabney's and Armstrong's Mills. Dearing charged and drove him across the creek. He formed near Armstrong's house and was again charged and driven, when he fell back behind his infantry lines." Hampton then withdrew his command and returned to camp. Instead of celebrating a victory, the Federals were forced to downplay a tactical loss. They referred to the effort as a reconnaissance, rather than a battle. Nonetheless, Lincoln was reelected in November. After the battle at Hatcher's Run, the Union operations around Petersburg and Richmond were mainly defensive.[17]

The Monday, October 31, 1864, Army of Northern Virginia returns showed that Dearing's Brigade was at the time unassigned. It consisted of Col. V. H. Taliaferro's 7th Confederate Cavalry, Col. Joel R. Griffin's 8th GA, Col. Dennis D. Ferebee's 4th

NC Cavalry, and Capt. Edward Graham's artillery battery. A Tuesday, November 1, 1864 request for forage by Dallas M. Beale places the 4th NC Cavalry again at Burgess Mill. A November 11 return listed Dearing's strength at 442 dismounted men. On Wednesday, November 16, the regiment was reported three miles south of Burgess Mill, encamped along the new military road. By month's end Dearing's Brigade was assigned to W. H. F. Lee's division. It consisted of Griffin's 8th GA, Ferebee's 4th NC Cavalry, and Capt. William K. Lane's 16th NC Battalion. Only 127 dismounted troopers were listed as present for duty.[18]

Preparations were underway for the 4th NC Cavalry to go into winter quarters. Dallas M. Beale's December 1 request for forage places the regiment at Belfield, VA (now north Emporia). Spending another winter in Virginia did not sit well with many of Ferebee's Tarheels, who wanted to return home. On Thursday, December 8, a pleasant but cold day, Company C of the 2nd NC Cavalry was relieved on picket by part of Dearing's Brigade, so that they could move to Stony Creek Station. Ferebee's men spent the remainder of December 1864 building winter quarters around Belfield and picketing for the infantry near Burgess Mill.[19]

CHAPTER 11

To Appomattox:
The Final Months
of the War

FEREBEE'S TARHEELS SPENT THE LAST winter of the war in southeastern Virginia, either in Belfield or Hicksford (now Emporia). The 4th NC was not happy about spending the winter away from North Carolina. Maj. John M. Galloway of the 5th NC Cavalry described the hardships of the Tarheels: "we suffered unspeakably, the ration was not enough to keep a man in vigor, even if regularly issued. It frequently was not so issued, and we of the cavalry would parch corn and eat it." Several of Ferebee's men mentioned the freezing weather that they endured during this time, often without ample supplies or shelter. A January 10, 1865 return listed W. H. F. Lee's division strength at 762 dismounted men, of which the 4th NC was a part. A January 23 letter from Neill McLaurin, of Company A, 4th NC, to his sister listed the Tarheel's position as Hicksford, VA. In the letter he asked her to send gloves, sewing thread, and soap. He also mentions a rumor that the regiment will move back to Stony Creek in a few weeks.[1]

The Tuesday, January 31, 1865, returns for the Army of Northern Virginia reported Ferebee's 4th NC, with Lt. Col. John T. Kennedy's 16th Battalion of NC Cavalry, and Col. Joel R. Griffin's 8th GA in Brig. Gen. James Dearing's Brigade, in W. H. F. Lee's division, in Lt. Gen. Wade Hampton's corps. (Company G of the 8th GA, under Capt. Patrick Gray, was on detached service in Kinston.) Several dispatches in early February 1865 place W. H. F. Lee's division and the 4th NC around Hicksford. Here the 4th NC was once again performing picket duty and making preparations for the coming spring campaign. During this time the Tarheels were "not entirely restrained from excitement and pleasure." On February 4 members of the 4th NC Cavalry were entertained by members of Barringer's Brigade with a mock jousting tournament.[2]

Also in early February, Brig. Gen. Dearing was ordered to the command of Rosser's

Brigadier General William Paul Roberts, Gates County (North Carolina Office of Archives and History, Raleigh, NC).

brigade. His vacancy was filled on Tuesday, February 21, when William Paul Roberts was promoted to brigadier general. Roberts's new brigade consisted of the 4th NC and the 7th Confederate Cavalry (75th Regiment NCST). William P. Roberts, the youngest general officer in Confederate service, was born on July 11, 1841 in Gates County, NC. Before the war he had received no former military training; instead, he was a schoolteacher in his native Gates County. He enlisted as a sergeant at the age of 19 in the 19th Regiment of North Carolina State Troops, which became known as the 2nd NC Cavalry. He quickly moved through the ranks. He made 3rd lieutenant on August 31, 1861, 1st lieutenant on September 13, 1862, captain on November 19, 1863, major on May 7, 1864, and colonel in June of 1864. He served with notable achievement in many battles with the 2nd NC Cavalry and upon promotion to brigadier general was presented with Gen. Robert E. Lee's gauntlets "as a mark of personal recognition of the young hero's distinguished gallantry."[3]

Roberts's promotion was a bittersweet one for Ferebee's Tarheels. They were certainly glad to once again be commanded by a North Carolinian. There had been great dissatisfaction among the Carolinians with a Virginian as their brigadier general. Nevertheless, they felt that Ferebee should have been the recipient of the promotion. The 4th NC's colonel had been vying for the brigade command since the regiment's inception under Robertson. Lee recommended Roberts for the promotion, but left the final choice up to Rufus Barringer, a brigadier general and North Carolinian in Hampton's Cavalry Corps. Barringer selected Roberts "because he had many times proven himself a tenacious and effective fighter [and] was more regular in the enforcement of camp discipline." Ferebee could not accept the fact that he was overlooked once again for promotion. On Friday, March 3, 1865, writing to Col. G. W. Little, Ferebee reluctantly resigned his commission "in protection of his honor." On March 7 the resignation was officially submitted and on Friday, March 24 it was officially accepted. The reason Ferebee was never promoted to brigadier general may have been a political one. Ferebee had been campaigning throughout the war to get his regiment back to North Carolina, and this may have been viewed as insubordinate. Ferebee had also not voted for secession, which may have left some officials questioning his loyalty or judgment. After leaving the cavalry, Ferebee served on Governor Vance's staff for a brief time until the war ended.[4]

On Wednesday, February 22, the day after receiving his commission, Roberts moved his brigade from Belfield to Stony Creek, as intimated in the January 23 McLaurin letter. To say that Roberts had inherited a brigade in less than full complement would be a gross understatement. His men were in need of clothing, horses, and countless other supplies. They were also "suffering for want of field officers." This made Ferebee's resignation on March 3 all the more difficult. Capt. Demosthenes Bell of Company G took command of the 4th NC after Ferebee's departure. On Monday, March 13, a pleasant spring-like day, W. H. F. Lee's division, including Roberts's Brigade, was ordered to move from Stony Creek toward Dinwiddie Court House. Second Lt. William Shaw of Company D, 4th NC, states that on March 14 they were "encamped on the White Oak Road about six miles from Dinwiddie Court House."[5]

On Thursday, March 16, a Union dispatch from Maj. Gen. G. K. Warren reported that the Confederate cavalry was stationed at Stony Creek, but was camped between Rooney's Mill and Dinwiddie Court House. That evening there was a hard rain and windstorm in the area. On the morning of March 17, Robert E. Lee ordered them back to Stony Creek, due to a lack of forage around Dinwiddie Court House. The next day Union Bvt. Brig. Gen. George H. Sharpe wrote Maj. Gen. George Meade that W. H. F. Lee was at Dinwiddie Court House. He also reported that Lee's cavalry "pickets the whole line from Stony Creek to Boydton Plank Road." Sharpe thought the Confederate line to be very thin, but that their position along the White Oak Road was very strong.[6]

On Monday, March 20, W. H. F. Lee's Division was assigned William M. McGregor's Battalion and McClanahan's battery. That same day two deserters from the 16th NC Battalion reported to Union Maj. Gen. G. K. Warren that the Confederates were very tired. Two days later on March 22, three deserters from the 4th NC reported that their regiment was at Hatcher's Run on picket duty and that Roberts's brigade consisted of about 650 men. Barringer's Brigade, near Stony Creek, was reported to be about 1,000 strong. A March 22 Confederate return shows that Roberts's Brigade consisted of the 4th NC, the 16th Battalion NC Cavalry, the 8th GA, four pieces of Graham's battery and Lyon's battery.[7]

In the spring of 1865 the Federals' main objective was to cut Lee's two main supply lines into Petersburg, the Boydton Plank Road and the South Side Railroad. Grant's plan was to draw Lee out of the trenches in Petersburg and to engage him, before Lee could retreat from Petersburg and possibly join forces with Joseph E. Johnston's troops in North Carolina. Heavy rains in the last week of March 1865 complicated both Union and Confederate movements, swelling creeks and muddying roads. Sensing Grant's objective, the South Side Railroad, Lee deduced that the Federals would attempt to flank his right near Hatcher's Run, via Dinwiddie Court House and Five Forks. Lee chose Pickett to move southwest from Petersburg to protect his right flank, which was on the Claiborne and White Oak roads near Hatcher's Run.[8]

During the last two weeks of March 1865, the 4th NC Cavalry, which was encamped about six miles from Dinwiddie Court House on the White Oak Road, enjoyed "some weeks of comparative rest and quiet recuperation." Their rest ended on Wednesday, March 29 when the Union began to move on the Confederate right flank. That morning Roberts's Brigade, with the 4th NC picketing in front, met a superior force of Federals and was forced to fall back to the White Oak Road. Shaw describes what happened next in his narrative:

> Soon after meeting the enemy the greater part of the regiment had been dismounted and formed in line on either side of the road, while the writer [Shaw], in charge of a squadron of mounted men, was directed by General Roberts, to remain in the road and watch closely any movement of the Federal cavalry in front and in case of a charge, to meet the charge, but with orders to retire before the fire of the advancing infantry as we came in range of their guns.[9]

On March 30 and March 31, the 4th NC was "continually in the immediate front of Sheridan's cavalry and had a number of sharp encounters with the enemy at Dr. Boisseau's and other points along the line of White Oak road." On Thursday, March 30, a windy day, Pickett arrived at Five Forks via White Oak Road. The next day he moved toward the Federal position at Dinwiddie Court House in a heavy rain. The Confederates had to cross the swampy creek bottom, Chamberlain's Bed, at two fords, Danse's and Fitzgerald's. They made several assaults on Sheridan's position, but were unable to move the entrenched Federals from their position. Pickett was able to move to within a mile of the town before nightfall, but darkness brought an end to his movement and the fighting. Pickett decided that he needed to protect his position at Five Forks. Later that night he retired back to Five Forks, meeting heavy resistance again. The action of March 31, which became known as the Battle of Dinwiddie Court House (Chamberlain's Bed), was tactically a draw.[10]

Once back at Five Forks, the Confederates began strengthening their breastworks along White Oak Road. On Saturday, April 1 Pickett had the following cavalry support: Rooney Lee and Barringer's men were guarding the Confederate right flank; William P. Roberts "covered the four mile gap between Pickett and Anderson, on the Claiborne Road"; Munford's cavalry guarded the Confederate left flank; and Capt. William M. McGregor's battery provided artillery support. This morning marked the beginning of the Battle of Five Forks. East of the main battle, where Warren's Federals were engaging Pickett's infantry, Roberts's Carolinians were attacked at the intersection of Crump and White Oak roads by some of Gen. Mackenzie's cavalry, with Col. Samuel P. Spear's 11th PA Cavalry in the lead. The Federals broke Roberts's line with little resistance, but Spear was wounded in the charge. The Union rout cleared White Oak road of Confederates from Claiborne Road to Gravelly Run Church Road, and allowed Mackenzie to return to the main battle with Warren.[11]

The Confederate main force under Pickett did not fare much better than Roberts's Tarheels. The Union forces under Maj. Gen. Philip H. Sheridan completely routed the beleaguered Confederates. The Battle of Five Forks settled the fate of Confederate resistance in Virginia. Following on Sheridan's success, Grant ordered a general assault along all lines. The 4th NC learned early on the morning of April 2 that Lee was evacuating Petersburg. Robert E. Lee and his staff evacuated about 8:00 P.M. Lee's objective was to join Joseph E. Johnston and the Army of Tennessee along the Richmond & Danville Railroad.[12]

Roberts's brigade was ordered to take up the line of retreat along the South Side Railroad. By nightfall the 4th NC reached a point near Namozine Church. On the morning of Monday, April 3 the Confederate forces crossed the Namozine Creek. Roberts's brigade and a Virginia regiment were to erect a defensive position on the west bank of Namozine Creek, guard the ford and bring up the rear. Early on the 3rd, Union Maj. Gen. George A. Custer appeared on the creek's opposite bank. A diversionary artillery assault of canister on Roberts's Tarheels by Company A of the 2nd US Artillery allowed the 1st Vermont Cavalry to cross farther downstream unnoticed. The Vermont troopers attacked Roberts's flank, forcing them to retreat. The remaining Federals crossed the creek unmolested. Later in the day Brig. Gen. Barringer relieved Roberts in command of the rearguard action. At Namozine Church and the intersection of Green's, Cousin's and Namozine roads, Barringer placed his troops (1st NC Cavalry, 2nd NC Cavalry, and 5th NC Cavalry) to meet the advancing Union cavalry.[13]

The Federal force proved too much for the Confederates, who were forced to retreat west down Green's Road, following Johnson's division and Rooney Lee's Brigade. Munford's and Rosser's Divisions retreated west along Cousin's Road. During the withdrawal Brig. Gen. Barringer and a few members of his staff became separated from the other Tarheels after turning onto Cousin's Road. Barringer and his men came upon what they thought to be a Confederate cavalry picket. Upon stopping, they discovered the picket to be some of Sheridan's scouts in disguise. Gen. Barringer and his men were taken prisoner and taken to Sheridan's headquarters at Mrs. Cousin's house. Brig. Gen. Roberts assumed command of Barringer's brigade after his capture. The Confederates crossed Deep Creek at Brown's Bridge, bivouacking near the Bevil's Bridge Road intersection.[14]

The 4th NC continued the retreat west, crossing through High Bridge, Farmville, and other points. Second Lt. William P. Shaw (4th NC, Co. D) described the journey as "marked by skirmish battles, frequently under artillery fire, and enduring the most severe fatigue and hardship.... On Saturday, 8 April, our march was almost unmolested and it was the most quiet day of this memorable retreat." That clear, warm evening the 4th NC Cavalry and 7th CS Cavalry went into camp "in a piece of woodland" just east of Appomattox Court House on the Richmond and Lynchburg Road.[15]

> From here the writer [Shaw] with a detachment of his regiment, was sent to the home [Wildway] of the Hon. Thos. S. Bocock, who was then Speaker of the Confederate House of Representatives, to obtain corn for the regiment. Here we were most generously entertained. The barns were opened to us, and a supper prepared for the tired and hungry men, and in his parlor Mr. Bocock stated to the writer that the great struggle was fast nearing the end, and that with our departure he would leave his home to escape capture.[16]

"About 4 A.M. the morning of the 9th [Palm Sunday] we mounted and were marched through the village to about one-third of a mile west of the Court House and formed in line facing the southwest on the right of Grimes' Division next to Cox's Division." Roberts's horsemen, consisting of the 4th NC Cavalry and the 75th NC (7th CS Cavalry), took a position on the Confederate right. W. H. F. Lee's Division was ordered to advance after the Federal artillery opened on their position. 1st Lt. E. J. Holt (75th NC) recounted that the Federal artillery "was a little to the left of our front and about 700 or 800 yards distant. The battery was in an open field and near to woodland on its left and rear, and was very much lower than the position held by us." Roberts ordered "sabers drawn" and "charge." Holt continues, "when we got within 200 yards of them they began to run. Some went into the woods, some took shelter under the gun carriage and all quit firing." Roberts's men captured about 50 prisoners and the Union ordnance, which consisted of four Napoleons. This is reported to be the last capture of arms at Appomattox. After the capture the Tarheels returned to the point of their original line to reform their command. Shortly before 9:00 A.M. they skirmished with a small force of Bvt. Brig. Gen. Charles H. Smith's men, but fell back due to the terrain and the superior Spencer rifles wielded by the Federals.[17]

As the Tarheels fell back, Holt noticed that there was no firing taking place on the field. Despite Roberts's limited success on the morning of April 9, Lee's ANV was in trouble around Appomattox Court House. He found his army trapped on three fronts. His only possible route for escape was northwest. However, lack of sufficient roads and the fact that it was in the opposite direction of reinforcements from North Carolina prevented this option. With no other alternative, Lee decided to meet Grant to discuss terms of surrender. Between 10:00 A.M. and 11:00 A.M. truce flags were sent out along the Confederate lines. Early on the afternoon of April 9, 1865 Gen. Robert E. Lee surrendered his Army of Northern Virginia to Gen. Ulysses S. Grant.[18]

The 4th NC Cavalry's 2nd Lt. William P. Shaw eloquently summarized the end in his 1904 recollection. "The advance is stopped. The physical valor and human endurance can go no further. The last act in the tragic drama is closed. The rattle of musketry and the roar of artillery cease. The curtain drops. The Army of Northern Virginia has surrendered."[19]

The Roster of Troops

Brigade Command

Baker, Laurence Simmons: Brigadier General

Appointed brigadier general on 9/9/1863; his first name also appears with the spelling "Lawrence" due to a clerk's error at West Point; born May 15, 1830 at Coles Hill in Gates Co., NC; son of Dr. John Burgess Baker and Mary Wynn; attended Norfolk Academy; admitted to West Point on July 1, 1847, graduating last in a class of 42 members on July 1, 1851; commissioned brevet 2nd lieutenant of 2nd Cavalry (Mounted Rifles) upon graduation; assigned to western frontier, spending most of the time in New Mexico and Texas; married Elizabeth Earl Henderson (of Salisbury, NC) on March 15, 1855; promoted to 1st lieutenant and captain; resigned commission on 5/10/1861; 5/8/1861 appointed lieutenant colonel of 1st NC Cavalry; promoted colonel of 1st NC Cavalry 3/1/1862; lost arm 6/89/1863 at Brandy Station; due to injury never assumed field command as Brig. Gen.; forced to give up command due to health 9/28/1863; later given district command in Dept. of NC and SE VA; led a brigade of reserves in March 1865 in Bentonville, NC; after the war he farmed from 1866 to 1878; during this time he also sold life insurance in New Bern; from 1878 until his death he worked as a station agent for Seaboard & Roanoke RR and the Southern Express Company; he also served as a manager for Western Union Telegraph Company in Suffolk, VA and was in the trucking business in Norfolk; active in the Tom Smith Camp, United Confederate Veterans in Suffolk; died on April 10, 1907 in Suffolk, VA (funeral service held at St. Paul's Parish).

Dearing, James: Brigadier General

Appointed brigadier general on 4/29/1864; born April 25, 1840 at Otterburne (a few miles north of Altavista) in Campbell Co., VA; son of James Griffin Dearing and Mary Anna Lynch; he attended Hanover Academy; admitted to West Point on July 1, 1858; resigned on 4/22/1861 to accept commission as lieutenant in Washington Artillery (New Orleans); transferred to Company D, 38th Battalion VA Artillery;

promoted Jan. 1863 to major and assigned to Pickett's division; promoted to Brig. Gen. 4/29/1864; February 1865 assigned command of Rosser's Brigade; wounded in action on 4/6/1865 at High Bridge, VA in a pistol dual with Fed. Gen. Theodore Read (who was killed); died 4/23/1865 in Ladies' Aid Hospital, Lynchburg, VA, the last Confederate general officer to die of wounds received in battle; buried Spring Hill Cemetery, Lynchburg, VA.

Gordon, James Byron: Brigadier General

Appointed brigadier general on 9/28/1863; born November 2, 1822 in Wilkesboro, NC (Wilkes Co.); son of Nathaniel Gordon and Sarah Gwyn; as a child he attended Peter S. Ney's school in Iredell Co.; he later attended Emory and Henry College (VA); merchant and farmer; in 1850, he served in the NC legislature; 1861 enlisted in Wilkes Valley Guards (later Company B, 1st NCST), elected 1st lieutenant then captain; later joined 1st NC Cavalry as major, promoted to colonel on 6/18/1863; promoted to brigadier general on 9/28/1864 (commanded NC Cavalry Brigade); wounded near Meadow Bridge on 5/12/1864; died 5/18/1864 in Richmond hospital; buried St. Paul's Episcopal Cemetery, Wilkesboro, NC.

Roberts, William Paul: Brigadier General

Appointed brigadier general on 2/21/1865; born on 7/11/1841 in Gates Co., NC; prewar schoolteacher; enlisted as sergeant in 2nd NC Cavalry (19th NCST) at age 19; promoted to 3rd lieutenant 8/31/1861, 1st lieutenant on 9/13/1862, captain 11/19/1863, major 5/7/1864, colonel June 1864; 2/21/1865 appointed Brig. Gen.; youngest general officer in Confederate service; wife, Eliza Ann Roberts (1847–1924); postwar served in state legislature 1876–1877; elected state auditor in 1880 and 1884; appointed consul general to Victoria, British Columbia by Pres. Grover Cleveland; died on March 28, 1910 in a Norfolk hospital after falling in his home; buried in Gatesville, NC.

Robertson, Beverly Holcombe: Brigadier General

Appointed brigadier general on 9/5/1862; born on June 5, 1827 at The Oaks, Amelia Co., VA; son of Dr. William H. Robertson; admitted to West Point on July 1, 1845 at age 18, graduating in 1849 (25th in class of 43); upon graduation on July 1, 1849 he was commissioned a brevet 2nd lieutenant in Col. Chas. A. May's 2nd Dragoons (Co. E), stationed in Socorro, New Mexico; he was appointed 2nd lieutenant on July 25, 1850; fought in the Indian wars on the western frontier, actively engaging the Sioux, Apache, Navajo and Comanche tribes; appointed first lieutenant on March 3, 1855 and captain on March 3, 1861; resigned from US Army upon appointment as colonel of 4th VA Cavalry; promoted to Brig. Gen. on 6/9/1862, and assigned to Dept. of NC on 9/5/1862; 7/15/1863 resigned post; 10/15/1863 given command of 2nd Militia District of SC, GA and FL; after the war he lived in Chicago, Memphis, and Washington, DC; sold insurance and real estate; died on November 12, 1910 in Washington, DC, buried at The Oaks in Amelia Co., VA.

Field and Staff

Barnes, Edwin: Asst. Surgeon

Member of regiment's Field & Staff, assigned to 4th NC Cavalry on 9/19/1862; born 1/27/1839; resident of Wilson Co.; appointed Asst. Surgeon 6/5/1862; detached from Dec. 1862–January 1863 to serve with detached companies of 3rd NC Cavalry (41st NCST) in Jacksonville, NC and Richland, NC; admitted 7/3/1863 to Richmond hospital with "febris typhoides"; returned to duty 7/14/1863; postwar physician; died 6/15/1882, buried Maplewood Cemetery, Wilson, NC.

Barringer, Rufus: Lieutenant Colonel

Member of regiment's Field & Staff, temporarily assigned from Jan. 1864–June 1864; took temporary command of 4th NC Cavalry regiment while serving as lieutenant colonel on Field and Staff of 1st NC Cavalry (9th NCST); left upon appointment to brigadier general 6/1/1864; born on December 2, 1821 in Cabarrus Co.; son of Paul Barringer and Elizabeth Brandon; prior to college he attended Sugar Hill Academy in Concord; in 1842 he graduated from the University of North Carolina; studied law with his brother, Daniel Moreau Barringer and Chief Justice R. M. Pearson; he settled in Concord, living there until 1866; represented Cabarrus Co. in the House of Commons from 1848–1850; married three times, first to Eugenia Morrison in 1854; after Eugenia's death in 1858 he married Rosalie Chunn in 1861; he later married Margaret Long; promoted to major on August 26, 1863; captured on April 3, 1865 at Namozine Church and confined at City Point prison, where he met Abraham Lincoln; after the war he moved to Charlotte, where he practiced law until retiring from the bar in 1884 (he maintained offices in Charlotte and Concord); after the war he remained active in politics (Republican), serving at the NC Constitutional Convention in 1875; made an unsuccessful bid for lieutenant governor in 1880; died February 3, 1895 in Charlotte.

Cantwell, Edward Payne: Lieutenant Colonel

Member of regiment's Field & Staff, appointed lieutenant colonel on 9/28/1862; born 12/22/1825 in Charleston, SC; served as a lieutenant in Mexican war; editor in Wilmington, NC; moved to Raleigh serving as city commissioner and attorney; previously served as lieutenant colonel on Field and Staff of 12th NC Infantry (2nd NC Vol.) and as an aide-de-camp to Gen. Clingman; captured 6/19/1863 in Middleburg, VA, held at Old Capitol Prison; transferred 8/8/1863 to Johnson's Island, 2/9/1864 to Baltimore then to Pt. Lookout; paroled and exchanged 3/10/1864 at Aiken's Landing, VA; promoted 10/15/1864 to colonel of cavalry, Prov. Army of CSA; transferred as Judge on Mil. Court, 3rd Corps, ANV; married Ellen Denning; died 4/11/1891.

Eves, Abram E.: Asst. Surgeon

Member of regiment's Field & Staff, assigned to regiment in or after June 1863; resident of VA; appointed Asst. Surgeon 4/17/1863; present or accounted for on muster rolls through February 1864.

Ferebee, Dennis Dozier: Colonel

Member of regiment's Field & Staff, appointed colonel on 8/10/1862; born on November 9, 1815 in Currituck Co., NC; son of Samuel Ferebee and Peggy Dauge (later the family changed the last name from Dauge to Dozier); graduated from UNC-Chapel Hill in 1839 (in a class of 13); while a student there he was described as being "more regular than the college bell"; after college he studied law with Judge William Gaston of New Bern; he married Sarah R. McPherson on February 3, 1842 and they resided in Camden Co.; he was a lawyer, planter and politician; after marriage he devoted more time to farming; member of state legislature, elected to the House of Commons in 1846, 1848, 1856, 1858, and 1860; delegate for Camden Co. in November 1861 to the NC Secession Convention; served as colonel of 2nd Regiment (Camden Co.), 1st Brigade NC Conf. Militia; fought at Battle of South Mill 4/19/1862; appointed colonel 4th NC Cavalry 8/10/1862; wounded in action (right foot) 10/13/1863 in Bristoe, VA; absent wounded through April 1864; resigned 3/7/1865, officially accepted 3/24/1865; served on Gov. Vance's staff until end of war; served as a prominent member in the State Convention of 1865; worked on a report for Governor Worth regarding the state university; he then backed out of public life, except for serving one term as sheriff; married a second time on October 28, 1878 to Mary E. Davenport; described as having "distinguished appearance and elegant manners" exemplifying "what a gentleman should be"; died 4/26/1884 Camden Co.; buried on Hodges Farm, McPherson Rd., Camden Co., NC.

Harris, W. H.: Asst. Surgeon

Member of regiment's Field & Staff, appointed on Oct. 10, 1862; no service records found.

Hutchings, John W.: Surgeon

Member of regiment's Field & Staff, appointed on 9/16/1862; previously served as surgeon on Field and Staff of 14th NC Infantry (4th NC Vol.); present or accounted for until he resigned 4/28/1863; later reappointed surgeon serving on Field and Staff of 68th NC Infantry.

Luck, William Jordan: Surgeon

Member of regiment's Field & Staff, appointment date unknown; resident of VA; appointed Asst. Surgeon 5/2/1862; served in Lynchburg, VA hospital; 9/22/1863 ordered to report to medical director, Wilmington, NC; later assigned to Dearing's brigade, serving as asst. surgeon there through October 1864; paroled 4/9/1865 at Appomattox Court House, listing rank as surgeon and 4th NC Cavalry as unit.

Mayo, James Micajah: Major

Member of regiment's Field & Staff, appointed on 9/11/1862; born 1841; attended Univ. of VA; resident of Tarboro, NC; previously served as captain in Company F (Pamlico Artillery), 2nd NC Artillery (36th NCST); captured 6/21/1863 in Upperville, VA, held at Old Capitol Prison; transferred 8/8/1863 to Johnson's Island; transferred 2/24/1865 to City Point, VA for exchange; admitted 3/3/1865 to Richmond hospital; lived in Whitaker, NC after war as a planter.

Michie, Junius: Surgeon

Member of regiment's Field & Staff, appointed surgeon on 5/22/1863; resident of VA; appointed asst. surgeon 10/16/1861, serving in Medical Dept.; assigned 2/3/1862 to Field and Staff of 15th GA Infantry as Asst. Surgeon; transferred 5/22/1863 to 4th NC Cavalry upon appointment to Surgeon; captured 7/12/1863 in Hagerstown, MD, held at Ft. McHenry; transferred 7/20/1863 to Ft. Delaware; date of parole and exchange not known; Fall 1864 transferred to Field and Staff of 4th VA Cavalry; first name appears as "James" on Moore's roster.

Moore, Thomas J.: 1st Lieutenant (Adj.)

Member of regiment's Field & Staff, transferred on 1/14/1863 as 1st lieutenant; previously served in Company B, 1st NC Infantry (6 months, 1861); served as an aide-de-camp, 1st lieutenant and ordnance officer on staff of Gen. D. H. Hill; also served as adjutant with rank of 1st lieutenant on Field and Staff of 33rd NC Infantry; present or accounted for until he was paroled 5/13/1865 in Charlotte, NC.

Sessoms, Joseph W.: Asst. Surgeon

Member of regiment's Field & Staff, assigned on 10/2/1862 to 4th NC Cavalry; appointed Asst. Surgeon 9/28/1862; submitted resignation 6/1/1863, officially accepted 6/19/1863.

Thompson, Thomas: Captain

Member of regiment's Field & Staff, transferred to 4th NC Cavalry on 8/16/1862; previously served as quartermaster sergeant in Quartermaster Dept.; appointed captain and asst. commissary of subsistence 8/16/1862 for 4th NC Cavalry; dropped from rolls by General Order 70, Adj. and Inspector Gen. Office, 5/29/1863 which stated that regimental commissary was to be abolished and all such officers relieved of duty no later than 7/31/1863.

Company A

Adam, William M.: Private

Enlisted in Co. A; "issued clothing at General Hospital No. 24, Richmond, VA, January 6, 1864."

Allen, A. W.: 3rd Corporal

Enlisted in Co. A in Anson Co.; listed on June 12, 1862 Wadesboro *North Carolina Argus* muster roll. This may be William Alexander Allen.

Allen, James F.: Private

Enlisted in Co. A on 5/10/1862 in Anson Co. at age 21; born November 11, 1839; served as regimental mail carrier and regimental musician; present or accounted for on muster rolls through September 1864; died February 4, 1914 and buried in the Leggett Cemetery on Whites Store Road in Anson Co.

Allen, James T.: Private

Enlisted in Co. A on 5/10/1862 in Anson Co.; born January 20, 1833; resident of Anson Co. at the time of enlistment; present or accounted for on muster rolls through September 1864; captured 4/5/1865 near Amelia Court House, confined to Pt. Lookout until taking Oath of Allegiance 6/22/1865; died 5/23/1911, buried Philadelphia Church Cemetery, Pageland Rd., Union Co., NC.

Allen, Richard Paul: Corporal

Enlisted in Co. A on 3/1/1863 in Anson Co. at age 37; born 12/17/1826; resident of Anson Co. at the time of enlistment; mustered in as a private; appointed corporal May/June 1864; listed as a 2nd corporal in Moore's roster; died 12/17/1901, buried Allen Family Cemetery, Allen Rd., Anson Co., NC.

Allen, William Alexander: Corporal

Enlisted in Co. A on 5/10/1862 in Anson Co. at age 25; mustered in as a corporal; listed as a 1st corporal on Moore's roster; present or accounted for on muster rolls through September 1864.

Allen, Y. C.: Private

Enlisted in Co. A on 8/22/1864 (conscripted); assigned clothing on 8/22/1864; this may be W. C. Allen of Anson Co., son of William Allen.

Alsobrooks, William M.: Bugler

Enlisted in Co. A on 5/10/1862 in Anson Co. at age 25; born in Union Co., where he resided at the time of enlistment; mustered in as bugler; transferred to Field and Staff 12/25/1862 to join regimental band; present or accounted for on muster rolls until he returned to Co. A (November/December 1864); received gunshot wound 3/29/1865, admitted to Petersburg hospital; transferred to Richmond hospital 3/31/1865, captured there on 4/3/1865, confined to Pt. Lookout until taking Oath of Allegiance 6/28/1865.

Atkins, John S.: Private

Enlisted in Co. A on 3/1/1863 in Anson Co.; captured 7/12/1863 at Ashby's Gap, VA, held at Old Capitol Prison until transferred to Pt. Lookout 8/8/1863; paroled and exchanged 2/18/1865 at Aiken's Landing, VA.

Atkinson, Robert: Private

Enlisted in Co. A in 1864 (conscripted).

Austin, Calvin S.: Private

Enlisted in Co. A on 3/1/1863 in Anson Co.; present or accounted for on muster rolls through September 1864.

Austin, James H.: Private

Enlisted in Co. A on 5/10/1862 in Anson Co. at age 23; born March 27, 1844; never mustered into service; died on May 10, 1923, buried in the Pleasant Grove Baptist Church Cemetery in Richmond Co.

Avitt, James A.: Private

Enlisted in Co. A on 8/9/1862 in Anson Co.; present or accounted for on muster rolls through September 1864.

Baldwin, Frank T.: Private

Enlisted in Co. A on 10/1/1864 "for the war"; born April 4, 1832; died March 8, 1910 and buried in the Jim Ingram Cemetery in Richmond Co.

Bennett, John G.: Private

Enlisted in Co. A on 3/1/1863 in Anson Co.; born circa 1839 in Anson Co. (Burnsville District); son of Neville Bennett and Catherine Harris; previously served as a private in Company B, 31st NC Infantry; present or accounted for on muster rolls through September 1864; after the war he moved to Mississippi.

Bennett, John Washington: Private

Enlisted in Co. A on 8/21/1862 in Anson Co.; born 11/30/1829 Anson Co., where he resided as a farmer at the time of enlistment; attended Univ. of VA and Jefferson Medical College (Philadelphia); married Rosa Elizabeth Boggan on 11/12/1854; served as hospital steward through 2/6/1863; appointed captain and assistant surgeon by governor; transferred to Medical Dept. (Chimborazo Hospital, Richmond, VA), later promoted to major and appointed chief surgeon at the Soldier's Home hospital in Richmond; died 5/6/1899, buried Eastview Cemetery Wadesboro, Anson Co., NC.

Bennett, William H.: Private

Enlisted in Co. A on 5/10/1862 in Anson Co. at age 35; died in Raleigh, NC hospital 1/31/1863 of "pneumonia."

Benton, Archibald Caraway: Private

Enlisted in Co. A on 5/10/1862 in Anson Co. at age 32; born in Anson Co.; son of William Henry Benton and Elizabeth Caraway; he married Nannie W. Ingram, 5/31/1859 near Ansonville, NC; wounded in action on 10/11/1863 at Culpeper Court House; present or accounted for on muster rolls through September 1864; paroled 5/20/1865 in Salisbury, NC.

Benton, William A.: 2nd Lieutenant

Enlisted in Co. A on 5/10/1862 in Anson Co. at age 37; killed in action at Culpeper Court House 10/11/1863.

Beverly, Henry L.: Private

Enlisted in Co. A on 8/9/1862 in Anson Co.; present or accounted for on muster rolls through September 1864; buried Mt. Vernon Church, Anson Co., NC.

Beverly, William C.: Private

Enlisted in Co. A; admitted to Petersburg hospital 3/24/1865 with "rubeola"; returned to active duty 4/2/1865.

Biles, John W.: Private
Enlisted in Co. A on 5/10/1862 in Anson Co. at age 32; born 1830; captured 7/12/1863 at Ashby's Gap, VA, held at Old Capitol Prison, until transferred to Pt. Lookout 8/8/1863; transferred to Elmira, NY 8/16/1864; transferred for exchange 10/11/1864, exchanged 10/29/1864; died 1909, buried Rehobeth Methodist Church, Plank Rd., Stanly Co., NC.

Billingsley, William M.: Private
Enlisted in Co. A on 12/27/1864.

Boggan, William H.: Private
Enlisted in Co. A on 9/25/1862 in Southampton Co., VA; born circa 1842 in Anson Co.; married Sally Dumas (daughter of James Dumas) on 10/12/1859 at Edmund Lilly's house (bride's grandfather); present or accounted for on muster rolls through September 1864.

Braswell, William A.: Private
Enlisted in Co. A on 8/8/1864 in Petersburg, VA born 1842; present or accounted for on muster rolls through September 1864; buried Red Hill Baptist Church, Anson Co., NC.

Bright, D. H.: Private
Enlisted in Co. A; resident of Montgomery Co., NC at the time of enlistment; paroled 5/5/1865 in Greensboro, NC; took Oath of Allegiance 6/7/1865 in Salisbury, NC.

Buchanan, Henry W.: Private
Enlisted in Co. A on 5/10/1862 in Anson Co. at age 18; present or accounted for on muster rolls through September 1864.

Burns Josiah C.: Private
Enlisted in Co. A on 5/10/1862 in Anson Co. at age 28; mustered in as a farrier; reported as musician March/April 1863; reduced to ranks May/June 1863; present or accounted for on muster rolls through September 1864.

Carelock, William A.: Private
Enlisted in Co. A on 4/1/1864 in Granville Co., NC; born 12/22/1844 in Union Co.; present or accounted for on muster rolls until his death; died on 8/24/1864, buried Carelock Family Cemetery, Union Co., NC.

Carter, Jack R.: Private
Enlisted in Co. A on 5/10/1862 in Anson Co. at age 25; captured 7/12/1863 at Hagerstown, MD, held at Pt. Lookout; paroled and exchanged 11/15/1864 at Venus Point, Savannah River, GA; paroled 5/3/1865 in Charlotte.

Carter, James: Private
Enlisted in Co. A on 5/10/1862 in Anson Co. at age 30; present or accounted for on muster rolls through September 1864.

Carter, William Henry: Private

Enlisted in Co. A on 5/10/1862 in Anson Co. at age 34; present or accounted for on muster rolls through September 1864.

Clark, E. J. S.: Private

Enlisted in Co. A; captured 8/3/1863 in Landmark, VA, held at Pt. Lookout; exchanged 12/23/1864.

Collins, William H.: Bugler

Enlisted in Co. A on 5/10/1862 in Anson Co. at age 34; mustered in as a private; transferred to Field and Staff of regiment 1/25/1862 and assigned to band as chief bugler; present or accounted for on muster rolls through September 1864.

Cottingham, James Bridges: Private

Enlisted in Co. A on 5/10/1862 in Anson Co. at age 23; born 1838; married Judah L. Gatewood 1/27/1859 in Anson Co.; present or accounted for on muster rolls through September 1864; died 1918, buried Morven Town Cemetery, Morven, NC.

Covington, James M.: Private

Enlisted in Co. A on 3/1/1864 in Granville Co., NC; born circa 1841 in Richmond Co., NC; son of Calvin C. Covington and Rachel Crawford; he married Ella McRae in Richmond Co. circa 1861; present or accounted for on muster rolls through September 1864.

Covington, Lemuel M.: Private

Enlisted in Co. A on 12/1862 in Anson Co.; present or accounted for on muster rolls through September 1864.

Covington, S. H.: Private

Enlisted in Co. A on 3/1/1864 in Granville Co., NC; listed in Moore's roster.

Crowder, James A.: Sergeant Major

Enlisted in Co. A on 10/6/1862 in Southampton Co., VA; mustered in as a private; transferred to Field and Staff of regiment 8/10/1863 when appointed sergeant major; present or accounted for on muster rolls through October 1864.

Crump, James F.: Corporal

Enlisted in Co. A on 5/10/1862 in Anson Co. at age 18; mustered in as a corporal, reduced to ranks March/April 1864 for "neglect of duty"; present or accounted for on muster rolls through August 1864.

Crump, William F.: Sergeant

Enlisted in Co. A on 5/10/1862 in Anson Co. at age 23; mustered in as a sergeant; present or accounted for on muster rolls through September 1864; wounded in action (right knee) on 3/30/1865 and admitted to Petersburg hospital, captured there 4/3/1865; transferred to Ft. Monroe hospital 3/30/1865; took Oath of Allegiance 7/13/1865 and released; listed as a 4th sergeant in Moore's roster.

Curlee, J. F.: Private
    Enlisted in Co. A.

Currin, Joseph Fleming: Private
    Enlisted in Co. A on 3/1/1863 in Anson Co.; born 12/30/1847; present or accounted for on muster rolls through September 1864; furloughed from Petersburg hospital 9/23/1864 due to wounds; died 6/10/1898, buried Elmwood Cemetery, Oxford, NC.

Davis, Benjamin Franklin: Private
    Enlisted in Co. A on 9/25/1862 in Southampton Co., VA; wounded in action on 8/18/1864 and admitted to Petersburg hospital; furloughed for 40 days 8/25/1864; buried Davis Family Cemetery on property of Mrs. Jesse Caudle, Stanly Co., NC.

Davis, H. H.: Private
    Transferred to Co. A on 12/4/1864; previously served in Company G, 1st Reg. NC Junior Reserves.

Davis, John E.: Sergeant
    Enlisted in Co. A on 5/10/1862 in Anson Co. at age 32; mustered in as a 2nd sergeant ; present or accounted for on muster rolls through September 1864.

Davis, William E.: Private
    Enlisted in Co. A on 5/10/1862 in Anson Co. at age 23; present or accounted for on muster rolls through September 1864; paroled at Appomattox Court House 4/9/1865.

Doster, E. C.: Private
    Enlisted in Co. A on 5/10/1862 in Anson Co. at age 33; born circa 1828 in Anson Co.; killed in action on 9/16/1864.

Dunn, C. F.: Private
    Enlisted in Co. A on 3/1/1863 in Anson Co.; present or accounted for on muster rolls through September 1864.

Eason, John B.: Private
    Enlisted in Co. A on 5/10/1862 in Anson Co. at age 26; served as commissary sergeant 10/31/1862–2/28/1863; transferred to CS Navy 9/3/1863; transferred back to regiment 1/7/1865.

Eason, William: 4th Corporal
    Transferred to Co. A on 1/7/1864; previously served in Company I, 43rd NC Infantry; reported as a "deserter from the enemy" by the provost marshal general, Army of the Potomac 3/12/1865; sent to City Point, VA 3/13/1865; took Oath of Allegiance in Washington, DC 3/18/1865, furnished transportation to New York City.

Edwards, John W.: Private
    Enlisted in Co. A on 5/10/1862 in Anson Co. at age 17; born 4/6/1846; resident of Anson Co. at the time of enlistment; present or accounted for on muster rolls

through August 1864; captured in Petersburg 4/3/1865, held at Hart's Island, NY Harbor; released after taking Oath of Allegiance 6/19/1865; died 9/19/1865, buried Eastview Cemetery, Wadesboro, NC.

Flake, James M.: Private

Enlisted in Co. A on 5/10/1862 in Anson Co. at age 25; present or accounted for on muster rolls through September 1864.

Flake, S. Thomas: Private

Enlisted in Co. A on 5/10/1862 in Anson Co. at age 21; listed as "S. F. Flake" on June 12, 1862 *North Carolina Argus* muster roll; wounded in action (leg) on 6/21/1863 in Upperville, VA.

Gaddy, E. T.: Private

Enlisted in Co. A on 3/1/1863 in Anson Co.; present or accounted for on muster rolls through September 1864.

Gaddy, J. N.: Private

Enlisted in Co. A on 5/10/1862 in Anson Co. at age 27; never mustered into service.

Gaddy, Risden B.: Captain

Enlisted in Co. A on 5/10/1862 in Anson Co. at age 23; born circa 1838 in Anson Co., where he resided at the time of enlistment; mustered in as a private; transferred to Field and Staff of regiment 10/1/1862 upon appointment as sergeant major; promoted to captain 2/19/1863 serving as assistant commissary of subsistence; served in that position through February 1864.

Gatewood, Samuel: Private

Enlisted in Co. A on 5/10/1862 in Anson Co. at age 26; married Nancy Covington (daughter of Elijah Covington) on December 9, 1858 in Anson Co.; present or accounted for on muster rolls through August 1864.

Gatewood, William T.: Private

Enlisted in Co. A on 5/10/1862 in Anson Co. at age 26; died in Petersburg hospital 11/22/1862 of "typhoid fever."

George, Ely: Private

Enlisted in Co. A; listed on June 12, 1862 *North Carolina Argus* muster roll.

George, Fleming M.: Musician

Enlisted in Co. A on 9/25/1862 in Anson Co. at age 22; residing in Anson Co. as a farmer at the time of enlistment; previously served as a private in Company K, 26th NC Infantry; mustered in as a private; transferred to Field and Staff of regiment 12/25/1862, assigned to band as a musician; discharged 12/23/1863 in Lynchburg, VA due to "valvular disease of the heart."

Gillis, James B.: Private

Enlisted in Co. A on 5/10/1862 in Anson Co. at age 23; present or accounted for on muster rolls through September 1864.

Gillis, William H.: Private

Enlisted in Co. A on 5/10/1862 in Anson Co. at age 21; wounded in action (wrist) near Upperville, VA on 6/21/1863; present or accounted for on muster rolls through September 1864.

Grandy, E. T.: Private

Enlisted in Co. A on 5/10/1862 in Anson Co.

Gray, James Madison: Private

Enlisted in Co. A on 8/9/1862 in Anson Co.; married Laura A. Lee 8/1/1860 in Anson Co.; present or accounted for on muster rolls through August 1864; wounded in action on 9/16/1864, admitted to Petersburg hospital; furloughed for injuries 9/23/1864; never returned to regiment.

Gray, William B.: Private

Enlisted in Co. A on 8/9/1862 in Anson Co.; born 1/20/1827; son of Jerimiah and Miriah Gray; present or accounted for on muster rolls through September 1864; died 5/29/1907, buried in Gray Family Cemetery, three miles north of Wadesboro, NC off of NC Highway 515.

Griffin, A. T.: Private

Enlisted in Co. A on 5/10/1862 in Anson Co. at age 22; never mustered into service.

Griffin, E. A.: Private

Enlisted in Co. A on 5/10/1862 in Anson Co. at age 23; never mustered into service.

Griffin, J. W.: Private

Enlisted in Co. A on 5/10/1862 in Anson Co. at age 22; never mustered into service.

Harris, Jonathan T.: Private

Enlisted in Co. A on 5/10/1862 in Anson Co. at age 34; served as wagoner from 10/31/1862–June 1864; present or accounted for on muster rolls through September 1864.

Harris, Thomas J.: Private

Enlisted in Co. A on 3/1/1863 in Pitt Co., NC; enlisted "under the pretense of having received a discharge from the 48th Regiment NC Troops"; however, he was actually absent on furlough from Co. H of the 48th NC. He was "seized and taken back to said regiment by his officers of the 48th on the 15 October 1863."

Hathcock, J. A.: Private

Transferred to Co. A on 6/2/1864; previously served in McRae's Battalion NC Cavalry, which was organized in 9/1863 for arresting conscripts and deserters in NC, disbanded 6/1/1864; present or accounted for on muster rolls through September 1864; paroled in Albemarle, NC 5/19/1865.

Hayes, H. S.: Private
Enlisted in Co. A on 5/10/1862 in Anson Co. at age 31; furnished a substitute
(C.A. Hoyt) 6/15/1862 and discharged.

Hill, H. N.: Private
Enlisted in Co. A; listed on June 12, 1862 *North Carolina Argus* muster roll.

Hill, Henry W.: Private
Enlisted in Co. A on 5/10/1862 in Anson Co. at age 24; present or accounted
for on muster rolls through August 1864.

Hill, James P.: Private
Enlisted in Co. A on 5/10/1862 in Anson Co. at age 20; present or accounted
for on muster rolls through September 1864.

Hill, John E.: Chief Bugler
Enlisted in Co. A on 5/10/1862 in Anson Co. at age 25; mustered in as a trum-
peter; transferred to Field and Staff of regiment 12/25/1862 and assigned to band as
chief bugler; captured 9/22/1863 at Jack's Shop, VA, held at Pt. Lookout; paroled
and exchanged February 14–15, 1865 at Coxes Landing, James River, VA; present on
2/17/1865 roll of paroled and exchanged prisoners at Camp Lee, Richmond, VA.

Horne, James: Private
Enlisted in Co. A on 5/10/1862 in Anson Co. at age 32; admitted to Petersburg
hospital 3/28/1865, captured at same 4/3/1865; 4/9/1865 transferred to Point of
Rocks, VA 4/9/1865, no record of release.

Horne, Thomas J.: Private
Enlisted in Co. A on 3/1/1863 in Anson Co.; captured 10/11/1863 at Brandy
Station, VA; held at Old Capitol Prison, until transferred to Pt. Lookout 10/27/1863;
paroled and exchanged at Coxes Landing, James River, VA 2/14/1865; admitted to
Richmond hospital 2/15/1865 with "diarrhea chronic," furloughed for 60 days
3/6/1865.

Hoyt, C. A.: Private
Enlisted in Co. A on 7/15/1862 in Anson Co. at age 17; substitute for H.S. Hayes;
deserted from Camp Ferebee, Garysburg, NC 12/6/1862.

Ingraham, Eban Nelms: Private
Enlisted in Co. A on 5/10/1862 in Anson Co. at age 22; born 2/23/1841; mustered in as a private; transferred to Field and Staff of this regiment 12/25/1862 and
assigned to band and appointed musician; present or accounted for on muster rolls
until he transferred back to company July/August 1863 serving in the Ambulance
Corps; died 4/14/1926, buried Bethel Baptist Church, Montgomery Co., NC.

Ingram, E. D., Jr.: Private
Enlisted in Co. A; listed on June 12, 1862 *North Carolina Argus* muster roll.

Ingram, William A.: Private

Enlisted in Co. A on 5/10/1862 in Anson Co. at age 25; born 4/6/1836; present or accounted for on muster rolls through September 1864; died 4/29/1909, buried Eastview Cemetery, Wadesboro, NC (grave marker states that he was a surgeon for the regiment, no data to support claim).

Jarman, John J.: Private

Enlisted in Co. A on 5/10/1862 in Anson Co. at age 41; married Julia A. Ricketts and was the father of six children; son of William Jarman (War of 1812 veteran) and Polly Currin (1st wife); brother of Joseph Jarman, also in Co. A; a 4/24/1863 letter by Corp. Richard Paul Allen (Co. A, 4th NC Cavalry) to his wife states that Jarman had been "shocked by a shell until he was very deaf" and that he had suffered an attack of rheumatism; the letter states he was sent to hospital and not heard from again; on 8/15/1864 rolls reported as "absent sick" since 10/31/1862; moved with Joseph and family to Carrol Co. Mississippi after war.

Jarman, Joseph Pinkney: Private

Enlisted in Co. A on 5/10/1862 in Anson Co. at age 27; resident of Anson Co. at the time of enlistment; son of William Jarman (War of 1812 veteran) and Polly Currin (1st wife); brother of John Jarman, also of Co. A; captured 7/4/1863 or 7/5/1863 during retreat from Gettysburg; held at Ft. McHenry until transferred to Ft. Delaware 7/9/1863; released 6/16/1865, took Oath of Allegiance 6/19/1865; moved with John and family to Carroll Co. Mississippi after war.

Henry Douglas Kendall, Company A, Anson County (Jerry T. Kendall).

Johnson, A. H.: Private

Enlisted in Co. A on 5/10/1862 in Anson Co. at age 34; admitted to Petersburg hospital 7/13/1864 with "hepatitis acute"; died in hospital either 8/12/1864 or 9/1/1864.

Johnson, Lewis A.: Captain

Enlisted in Co. A on 5/10/1862 in Anson Co. at age 40; wounded in action (thumb) on 6/21/1863 near Upperville, VA; present or accounted for on muster rolls through January 1865.

Kendall, Henry Douglas: Private

Enlisted in Co. A on 5/10/1862 in Anson Co. at age 42; born on February 29, 1820 in Anson Co.; son of Dr. John Spilman Douglas (also a Methodist minister) and Winifred "Wincy" Harrison Turner; his brother John Patrick Kendall also served in Co. A; before the war Henry was a physician in Stanly Co., NC; also served as a magistrate in the county; married Caroline E. Locke on November 19, 1846 in Stanly Co.; sometime in the 1850s he got into financial trouble and moved back to Anson Co., living beside his father's farm; served as hospital steward in Wilson, NC; reported as "absent sick" several times in various hospitals; in 1870 he moved to Washington Co., GA, where he practiced as a physician until his death on January 12, 1894; buried in Harrison, GA (Washington Co.) in the City Cemetery.

Kendall, John Patrick: 3rd Lieutenant

Enlisted in Co. A on 5/20/1862 in Anson Co. at age 24; born on February 27, 1837 in Anson Co.; son of Dr. John Spilman Douglas (also a Methodist minister) and Winifred "Wincy" Harrison Turner; his brother Henry Douglas Kendall also served in Co. A; he was appointed postmaster in Cedar Hill (Anson Co.) on December 5, 1859; he married Frances "Fannie" Josaphene Palmer on February 8, 1860 in Stanly Co.; mustered in as sergeant; appointed 3rd lieutenant in May/June 1864; killed in action on 9/16/1864—buried, unknown; listed as a 2nd corporal on Moore's roster; on August 16, 1997 a tombstone (located beside his mother's) was placed in his memory in the Concord United Methodist Church Cemetery in Anson Co. by his descendant Jerry T. Kendall.

Kilgore, John W.: Private

Enlisted in Co. A on 5/10/1862 in Anson Co. at age 28; listed as "J. N. Kilgore" on June 12, 1862 *North Carolina Argus* muster roll; married Miss C. A. Pratt 3/7/1861 in Anson Co.; previously served in the 80th Regiment (Anson Co.), 20th Brig. NC Confederate Militia, commissioned captain 9/18/1861; present or accounted for on muster rolls through August 1864.

Kirk, Adam: Private

Transferred to Co. A on 6/2/1864; previously served in McRae's Battalion NC Cavalry, which was organized in 9/1863 for arresting conscripts and deserters in NC, disbanded 6/1/1864; present or accounted for on muster rolls through September 1864.

Knotts, Harvey T.: Private

Enlisted in Co. A on 5/10/1862 in Anson Co. at age 32; present or accounted for on muster rolls through September 1864.

Leak, R. S.: Private

Enlisted in Co. A on 3/1/1864 in Anson Co.; present or accounted for on muster rolls through September 1864.

Ledwell, Luke: Blacksmith

Enlisted in Co. A on 5/10/1862 in Anson Co. at age 41; mustered in as a blacksmith; died in Raleigh hospital 1/10/1863 of "variola."

Lee, George T.: Private

Enlisted in Co. A on in 1864; born on October 27, 1847; died on April 5, 1924, buried in the Wightman Methodist Church Cemetery in Anson Co.

Lee, James A.: Private
Enlisted in Co. A on 5/10/1862 in Anson Co.; present or accounted for on muster rolls through September 1864.

Lee, S.: Private
Enlisted in Co. A on 5/25/1864 in Petersburg, VA; present or accounted for on muster rolls through September 1864.

Lockhart, R. A.: Private
Enlisted in Co. A on 6/18/1863 in Anson Co.; present or accounted for on muster rolls through September 1864.

Lockhart, William: Private
Enlisted in Co. A on 5/10/1862 in Anson Co. at age 19; discharged 8/15/1862.

Louder, L.: Private
Enlisted in Co. A on 6/1/1864 in Petersburg, VA; last name appears as "Lander" in Moore's roster; present or accounted for on muster rolls through August 1864.

Lowder, Benjamin F.: Private
Enlisted in Co. A on 2/23/1864 in Perquimans Co., NC; born 1846; died 5/1/1864 in Raleigh hospital of "pneumonia"; buried Oakwood Cemetery, Raleigh, NC.

Ludwell, L.: Private
Enlisted in Co. A; listed on June 12, 1862 *North Carolina Argus* muster roll.

Mainer, William M.: Private
Enlisted in Co. A on 3/1/1863 in Anson Co.; resident of Stanly Co., NC at the time of enlistment; present or accounted for on muster rolls through September 1864; captured 3/30/1865 at Dinwiddie Court House; held at Pt. Lookout, released 6/29/1865 after taking Oath of Allegiance.

McLaurin, D. T.: Private
Enlisted in Co. A on 5/10/1862 in Anson Co. at age 32; mustered in as a wagoner, served in that function through 10/1863; listed as "prisoner of war" on company rolls March–June 1864, no record of date/place of capture; admitted 10/28/1864 to Richmond hospital, furloughed for 60 days 11/27/1864.

McLaurin, Daniel D.: Private
Enlisted in Co. A on 5/10/1862 in Anson Co.; born May 8, 1830; son of Scottish immigrant parents, Daniel McLaurin and Nancy Ann Stewart; brother of Neill McLaurin, also in Co. A; captured 7/4/1863 at South Mountain; held at Ft. McHenry until transferred 7/9/1863 to Ft. Delaware, died there 12/18/1863 of "apoplexy"; buried National Cemetery Finn's Pt. (Salem), NJ.

McLaurin, Neill: Private
Enlisted in Co. A on 8/9/1862 in Anson Co.; born September 15, 1831; son of Scottish immigrant parents, Daniel McLaurin and Nancy Ann Stewart; brother of Daniel

D. McLaurin, also of Co. A.; wounded in action on 9/22/1863 at Jack's Shop, VA; present or accounted for on muster rolls through September 1864; married Eliza Jane Meachum on May 30, 1872 in Anson Co. (she was 17 and he was 41 years old)—family history claims that Eliza called him "Mr. Mac"; died on October 6, 1895.

McLester, W. P.: Private
Enlisted in Co. A on 3/1/1863 in Anson Co.; last name spelled "McLister" on Moore's roster; present or accounted for on muster rolls through September 1864.

Mendenhall, W. A.: Private
Enlisted in Co. A on 3/1/1863 in Anson Co.; died 6/1/1863 in Danville, VA hospital of "febris conntinua."

Mills, John Q.: Private
Enlisted in Co. A on 5/10/1862 in Anson Co. at age 35; discharged 8/28/1862.

Mitchum, Jesse C.: Private
Enlisted in Co. A on 5/10/1862 in Anson Co. at age 23; present or accounted for on muster rolls through September 1864.

Moore, R. A.: Private
Enlisted in Co. A on 8/9/1862 in Anson Co.; present or accounted for on muster rolls through August 1864.

Myers, Hampton: Private
Enlisted in Co. A on 8/9/1862 in Anson Co.; present or accounted for on muster rolls through September 1864.

Myers, James W.: Private
Enlisted in Co. A on 5/10/1862 in Anson Co. at age 25; married Rebecca Rivers 2/28/1861 in Chesterfield, SC; previously served in the 80th Reg. (Anson Co.) 20th Brig. NC Conf. Militia, commissioned 2nd lieutenant on 9/18/1861; also served as 2nd lieutenant in 81st Reg.; captured 7/4/1863 at South Mountain; held at Ft. McHenry until transferred to Ft. Delaware 7/9/1863; died there 9/5/1863 of "acute dysentery"; buried National Cemetery Finn's Pt. (Salem), NJ.

Myers, Stephen H.: Private
Enlisted in Co. A on 3/1/1863 in Anson Co.; present or accounted for on muster rolls through September 1864.

Myers, William Alex: Private
Transferred to Co. A on 9/10/1864; previously served in Company K, 26th NCST; present or accounted for on muster rolls through September 1864.

Odom, William H.: Private
Enlisted in Co. A on 5/10/1862 in Anson Co. at age 31; present or accounted for on muster rolls through August 1864; in August 1864 reported as "absent home on horse detail"; captured 3/4/1865 in Anson Co.; held at Pt. Lookout, died there 5/12/1865 of "pneumonia"; buried in the Confederate Cemetery, Pt. Lookout, MD.

Palmer, Hezekiah W.: Sergeant

Enlisted in Co. A on 5/10/1862 in Anson Co.; previously served in Co. H, 14th NC Infantry; mustered in as a corporal, appointed sergeant May/June 1864; listed as 5th sergeant on Moore's roster; present or accounted for on muster rolls through September 1864; paroled 5/12/1865 in Salisbury, NC.

Palmer, John L.: Private

Enlisted in Co. A on 5/10/1862 in Anson Co. at age 18; present or accounted for on muster rolls through September 1864.

Palmer, T. A.: Private

Enlisted in Co. A on 5/10/1862 in Anson Co. at age 23; listed as "F. A. Palmer" on June 12, 1862 *North Carolina Argus* muster roll; present or accounted for on muster rolls through September 1864; from March/April 1863–June 1864 served as a hospital attendant and ambulance driver.

Porter, J. J.: Private

Enlisted in Co. A on 2/1/1864 in Perquimans Co., NC; present or accounted for on muster rolls through September 1864.

Porter, John D.: Private

Enlisted in Co. A on 5/10/1862 in Anson Co.; born 7/12/1840; married Elizabeth Threadgill 3/11/1861 in Anson Co.; present or accounted for on muster rolls through September 1864; died 10/5/1904, buried Eastside Cemetery, Rockingham, NC.

Porter, W. M.: Private

Enlisted in Co. A on 2/1/1864 in Perquimans Co., NC; present or accounted for on muster rolls through September 1864.

Redfearn, A. T.: Private

Enlisted in Co. A on 5/10/1862 in Anson Co. at age 23; captured 7/12/1863 at Hagerstown, MD; held at Pt. Lookout until 3/20/1864 when paroled and exchanged at City Point, VA.

Redfearn, Alfred: Private

Enlisted in Co. A on 3/1/1863 in Anson Co.; previously served as a private in Company A, 23rd NC Infantry (13th NC Vol.); captured 7/4/1863 or 7/5/1863 on retreat from Gettysburg (near South Mt.); held at Ft. McHenry until transferred to Ft. Delaware 7/9/1863; remained there until 2/14/1865 or 2/15/1865 when exchanged at Coxes Landing, James River, VA; 2/15/1865 admitted to Richmond hospital with "debilitas"; furloughed for 60 days 3/2/1865.

Redfearn, David A.: Private

Transferred to Co. A in August 1864; previously served in Capt. James I. Kelly's Co., SC Light Artillery; present or accounted for on muster rolls through September 1864.

Redfearn, George W.: Private

Enlisted in Co. A on 5/10/1862 in Anson Co. at age 26; wounded in action (neck) on 6/21/1863 at Upperville, VA; present or accounted for on muster rolls through September 1864.

Redfearn, William D.: Private

Enlisted in Co. A on 9/8/1862 in Northampton Co.; previously served in Co. A, 23rd NC Infantry; captured 7/4/1863 or 7/5/1863 on retreat from Gettysburg (near South Mt.); held at Ft. McHenry until transferred to Ft. Delaware 7/9/1863; transferred to Pt. Lookout 10/22/1863; 4/30/1864 paroled and exchanged at City Point, VA; admitted 5/1/1864 to Richmond hospital with "rheumatism chronic", furloughed 5/6/1864 for 60 days.

Richardson, Amos: Private

Enlisted in Co. A on 5/25/1864 in Anson Co.; present or accounted for on muster rolls through August 1864.

Richardson, Clement L.: 1st Sergeant

Enlisted in Co. A on 5/10/1862 in Anson Co. at age 20; son of Purdie Richardson; brother of James P. Richardson, also of Co. A; previously served as a sergeant in Co. A, 23rd NC Infantry (13th NC Vol.); mustered in as a 1st sergeant; captured 7/4/1863 on retreat from Gettysburg (near South Mt.); held at Ft. McHenry until transferred to Ft. Delaware 7/9/1863; transferred to Pt. Lookout 10/22/1863; paroled and exchanged 3/15/1864 at City Point, VA; 5/10/1865 admitted to Danville, VA hospital; according to Purdie Richardson's Anson Co. will (probated Jan. 1872), Clement L. Richardson was living in a "distant state."

Richardson, James P.: Private

Enlisted in Co. A on 5/10/1862 in Anson Co. at age 27; son of Purdie Richardson; brother of Clement L. Richardson, also of Co. A; married Annie E. Simons 4/30/1861 in Anson Co.; captured 8/19/1864 on "Weldon Railroad," held at Pt. Lookout until paroled and exchanged 3/19/1865 at Aiken's Landing, VA.

Robards, James: Private

Enlisted in Co. A; paroled 4/9/1865 at Appomattox Court House, VA.

Sibley, George D.: 1st Lieutenant

Enlisted in Co. A on 5/10/1862 in Anson Co. at age 24; mustered in as a 3rd lieutenant ; appointed 1st lieutenant 9/1/1863; present or accounted for on muster rolls through January 1865.

Sibley, H. C.: Private

Enlisted in Co. A on 2/1/1864 in Halifax Co., NC; present or accounted for on muster rolls through September 1864; paroled 5/15/1865 in Charlotte, NC.

Sibley, James A.: Private

Enlisted in Co. A on 5/10/1862 in Anson Co. at age 32; present or accounted for on muster rolls through August 1864.

Sides, George M.: Private

Transferred to Co. A on 6/2/1864; previously served in McRae's Battalion NC Cavalry, which was organized in 9/1863 to arrest conscripts and deserters in NC, disbanded 6/1/1864; present or accounted for on muster rolls through September 1864; paroled in Albemarle, NC 5/19/1865.

Simons, Eugene Robertson: Private

Enlisted in Co. A on 5/10/1862 in Anson Co. at age 18; resident of Anson Co. at the time of enlistment; present or accounted for on muster rolls through September 1864; admitted to Petersburg hospital 3/22/1865 with "rubiola"; returned to duty 4/2/1865.

Sinclair, Gideon D.: Private

Enlisted in Co. A on 5/10/1862 in Anson Co. at age 31; mustered in as a corporal; listed as 4th corporal on June 12, 1862 *North Carolina Argus* muster roll; March–April 1864 "reduced to ranks for disobedience of orders"; present or accounted for on muster rolls through September 1864.

Sinclair, Lot: Private

Enlisted in Co. A on 3/1/1863 in Anson Co.; wounded in action on 8/6/1863 at Madison's Cross Roads, VA and sent to hospital in Charlottesville, VA; furloughed 10/20/1863 for 60 days; reported absent home on furlough through 8/1864.

Smith, David A.: Private

Enlisted in Co. A on 5/10/1862 in Anson Co. at age 27; listed as "Davis Smith" on June 12, 1862 *North Carolina Argus* muster roll; present or accounted for on muster rolls through September 1864.

Smith, John A.: Private

Enlisted in Co. A on 5/10/1862 in Anson Co. at age 22; present or accounted for on muster rolls through September 1864.

Smith, W. T.: Private

Enlisted in Co. A on 3/1/1864 in Anson Co.; present or accounted for on muster rolls through September 1864.

Stubbs, James R.: Private

Enlisted in Co. A on 5/10/1862 in Anson Co. at age 29; born 9/22/1835; wounded in action on 9/22/1863 at Jack's Shop, VA; admitted to Richmond hospital; there until 11/7/1863 when furloughed for 60 days; admitted to Raleigh hospital 6/6/1864, absent from regiment through August 1864 rolls; admitted to Raleigh hospital 4/10/1865, captured there 4/13/1865; released 4/22/1865 after taking Oath of Allegiance; paroled 4/23/1865; died 10/20/1905, Pleasant Hill Cemetery, US Highway 52, Anson Co., NC.

Sturdivant, Edmund A.: 1st Lieutenant

Enlisted in Co. A on 5/10/1862 in Anson Co. at age 24; mustered in as a 1st lieutenant ; wounded in action at Charlottesville, VA on 7/12/1863 and admitted to hospital there same day; transferred to Richmond hospital 7/13/1863; submitted resignation due to health 9/1/1863, officially accepted 9/22/1863.

Swaine, J. R.: Private
Enlisted in Co. A; wounded in action on 7/1863 at Gettysburg.

Talton, Davis L.: Private
Enlisted in Co. A on 8/9/1862 in Anson Co.; last name also appears as "Tarlton"; present or accounted for on muster rolls through September 1864.

Teal, William R.: Corporal
Enlisted in Co. A on 5/10/1862 in Anson Co. at age 28; mustered in as a private; appointed corporal in May/June 1864; listed as 3rd corporal on Moore's roster; present or accounted for on muster rolls through September 1864; admitted 4/7/1865 to Farmville, VA hospital with gunshot wound in left hip; captured in hospital, died there 5/24/1865.

Thomas, R.: Private
Enlisted in Co. A; listed on June 12, 1862 *North Carolina Argus* muster roll.

Threadgill, William B.: Private
Enlisted in Co. A on 5/10/1862 in Anson Co.; born 8/22/1839; present or accounted for on muster rolls through September 1864; died 6/21/1916, buried Threadgill Family Cemetery, Anson Co., NC.

Townsend, W.: Private
Enlisted in Co. A; first appears on May/June 1864 muster roll; present or accounted for on muster rolls through September 1864; admitted 12/23/1864 to Petersburg hospital; returned to duty 1/8/1865.

Treadway, E. W.: Private
Enlisted in Co. A on 8/9/1864; "issued clothing on September 18, 1864."

Troutman, M.: Private
Enlisted in Co. A on 5/10/1862 in Anson Co. at age 37; never mustered into service.

Turner, George W.: Private
Enlisted in Co. A on 5/10/1862 in Anson Co. at age 27; wounded in action (neck) on 10/11/1863 at Brandy Station, VA; present or accounted for on muster rolls through September 1864.

Turner, W. P.: Private
Transferred to Co. A on 6/2/1864; previously served in McRae's Battalion NC Cavalry, which was organized in 9/1863 to arrest conscripts and deserters in NC, disbanded 6/1/1864; present or accounted for on muster rolls through September 1864.

Tyson, William Franklin: Private
Enlisted in Co. A on 2/1/1864 in Anson Co.; born in Anson Co.; wounded in

action near Petersburg, admitted to hospital there 8/18/1864; furloughed for 60 days 9/9/1864.

Wall, Henry Clay: Private
Enlisted in Co. A on 3/1/1864 in Richmond Co., NC; previously served as sergeant in Company D, 23rd NC Infantry (13th NC Vol.); wrote a postwar memoir in 1876 *Historical Sketch of the Pee Dee Guards (Co. D, 23rd N. C. Regiment) From 1861 to 1865*; present or accounted for on muster rolls through September 1864.

Wall, James Marshall: 2nd Lieutenant
Enlisted in Co. A on 5/10/1862 in Anson Co.; previously served in Co. A, 23rd NC Infantry; mustered in 9/8/1862 in Northampton Co. as a private; captured 7/5/1863 sent to Ft. McHenry, transferred to Ft. Delaware 7/9/1863, paroled and exchanged at City Point, VA 8/1/1863; elected 2nd lieutenant 12/12/1863; present or accounted for on muster rolls through February 1865.

Watson, Calvin: Private
Enlisted in Co. A on 8/19/1862 in Anson Co.; present or accounted for on muster rolls through September 1864; deserted on 3/12/1865; received as a "deserter from the enemy" by Federal Provost Marshall 3/18/1865.

Watson, H. C.: Private
Enlisted in Co. A on 3/1/1864 in Granville Co., NC; present or accounted for on muster rolls through September 1864.

Watson, Stephen: Private
Enlisted in Co. A on 9/9/1862 in Anson Co.; present and accounted for on muster rolls until he transferred to James I. Kelly's Co. SC Light Artillery as stated on the July/August 1864 roll.

Webb, J. T.: Private
Enlisted in Co. A; "reported on an undated receipt roll as a member of this Company."

Webb, John W.: Private
Enlisted in Co. A on 5/10/1862 in Anson Co. at age 20; present or accounted for on muster rolls through September 1864.

Whitley, T.: Private
Transferred to Co. A on 6/2/1864; previously served in McRae's Battalion NC Cavalry, which was organized in 9/1863 to arrest conscripts and deserters in NC, disbanded 6/1/1864; present or accounted for on muster rolls through September 1864.

Wright, James M.: 2nd Lieutenant
Enlisted in Co. A on 5/10/1862 in Anson Co. at age 23; previously served in 81st Reg. (Anson Co.), 20th Brig. NC Confederate Militia; commissioned 2nd lieutenant on 9/11/1861, promoted to captain on 12/21/1861; mustered into 4th NC Cavalry as a sergeant; served as acting regimental commissary sergeant from May–Aug.

1864; promoted to 2nd lieutenant on 9/20/1864; present or accounted for on muster rolls through September 1864.

Company B

Aldridge, Rufus Graves: Private

Enlisted in Co. B on 7/8/1862 in Caswell Co. at age 21; born July 31, 1836 in Caswell Co.; son of Joseph Aldridge and Martha "Pattie" Graves; present or accounted for on muster rolls through October 1864; married Annie Elizabeth Wyatt on July 31, 1870.

Austin, Joseph B.: Private

Enlisted in Co. B on 7/8/1862 in Caswell Co. at age 27; captured 7/19/1863 at Ashby's Gap, VA; held at Pt. Lookout where died 12/1863.

Barker, Eaton A.: Private

Enlisted in Co. B on 7/8/1862 in Caswell Co. at age 27; present or accounted for on muster rolls through October 1864; married Mary C. Farley on October 12, 1865 in Caswell Co.

Barnwell, W. S.: Private

Enlisted in Co. B in 1864.

Beavers, James: Private

Enlisted in Co. B on 7/8/1862 in Caswell Co. at age 24; born in Caswell Co.; died 12/30/1862 in Petersburg hospital of "pneumonia."

Beavers, William T.: Private

Enlisted in Co. B on 7/8/1862 in Caswell Co. at age 27; married Sarah Jane Smithy on November 6, 1854 in Caswell Co.; on 11/2/1864 admitted to a Richmond hospital with "rheumatism"; furloughed 3/12/1865 for 60 days.

Bennett, C. G.: Private

Enlisted in Co. B; paroled 4/9/1865 at Appomattox Court House, VA.

Bennett, Edward W.: Private

Enlisted in Co. B on 7/8/1862 in Caswell Co. at age 31; present or accounted for on all muster rolls through October 1864.

William Samuel Barnwell, Company B, Caswell County (Tom Barnwell).

Bennett, John N.: Private

Enlisted in Co. B on 7/8/1862 in Caswell Co. at age 28; married Julia Bennett on November 11, 1857 in Caswell Co.; present or accounted for on all muster rolls through October 1864.

Bennett, Thomas G.: Private

Enlisted in Co. B on 7/8/1862 in Caswell Co. at age 18; present or accounted for on all muster rolls through October 1864.

Bennett, William T.: Private

Enlisted in Co. B on 7/8/1862 in Caswell Co. at age 33; mustered in 8/12/1862; "no further records."

Bishop, Amos: Private

Enlisted in Co. B on 2/13/1863 in Lenoir Co., NC; 4/15/1864 transferred to Co. G, 2nd NC Infantry.

Boney, Thomas E.: Private

Enlisted in Co. B on 2/13/1863 in Lenoir Co., NC; captured 7/4/1863 during retreat from Gettysburg, held at Ft. McHenry; transferred 7/9/1863 to Ft. Delaware, DE; transferred 10/18/1863 to Pt. Lookout, died there 10/28/1863 of "dropsy of lungs"; buried in Confederate Cemetery, Pt. Lookout.

Boswell, Thomas E.: Private

Enlisted in Co. B on 7/8/1862 in Caswell Co. at age 33; married Eliza Ann Bird on September 28, 1861 in Caswell Co.; on 7/4/1863 captured on retreat from Gettysburg (South Mountain), held at Ft. McHenry; transferred 7/9/1863 to Ft. Delaware where he died 8/24/1863 of "typhoid pneumonia"; buried in National Cemetery, Finn's Point (Salem), NJ.

Botton , W. H.: Private

Enlisted in Co. B; paroled 5/18/1865 in Raleigh.

Bradsher, David Y.: Private

Enlisted in Co. B on 7/8/1862 in Caswell Co. at age 33; last name also appears as "Bradshear"; on 7/4/1863 captured on retreat from Gettysburg (South Mountain), held at Ft. McHenry; transferred 7/9/1863 to Ft. Delaware; 10/31/1864 paroled and exchanged; 5/16/1865 took Oath of Allegiance.

Bradsher, William G.: Private

Enlisted in Co. B on 7/8/1862 in Caswell Co. at age 29; last name also appears as "Bradshear"; mustered in as a private; 2/1/1863 transferred to Field and Staff of regiment and assigned to band serving as a musician; present or accounted for on muster rolls until he returned to Co. B on 7/31/1863; married Mattie E. Bradshear on July 8, 1865 in Caswell Co.

Bradsher, Wilson: Private

Enlisted in Co. B on 7/8/1862 in Caswell Co. at age 33; last name also appears as "Bradshear"; married Martha Martin on February 11, 1858 in Caswell Co.; on

7/4/1863 captured on retreat from Gettysburg (South Mountain), held at Ft. McHenry; transferred 7/9/1863 to Ft. Delaware; died there 12/6/1863 of "inflammation of the lungs."

Brandon, James C.: Private
Enlisted in Co. B on 7/8/1862 in Caswell Co. at age 18; captured 7/4/1863 on retreat from Gettysburg (South Mountain), held at Ft. McHenry; transferred 7/9/1863 to Ft. Delaware, died there 10/3/1863; buried in National Cemetery, Finn's Point (Salem), NJ.

Brannock, William H.: Private
Enlisted in Co. B on 7/8/1862 in Caswell Co. at age 21; present or accounted for on all muster rolls through October 1864.

Bray, Lewis R.: Private
Enlisted in Co. B on 7/8/1862 in Caswell Co. at age 30; muster roll of 7/31/1863 reports him as "acting courier for Brigadier General Robertson"; September/October 1863 reported "absent at home on detail"; AWOL November/December 1863–August 1864.

Brincefield, Thompson A.: Private
Enlisted in Co. B on 7/8/1862 in Caswell Co. at age 25; captured 7/4/1863 on retreat from Gettysburg (South Mountain), held at Ft. McHenry; transferred 7/9/1863 to Ft. Delaware; remained there until released 6/8/1865 after taking Oath of Allegiance.

Brintle, James H.: Private
Enlisted in Co. B on 7/8/1862 in Caswell Co. at age 28; present or accounted for on all muster rolls through October 1864.

Brintle, Zachariah: Private
Enlisted in Co. B in Jan/Feb 1864 in Caswell Co.; "deserted at Taylor's Ferry, Mecklenburg County, VA, April 25, 1864"; he married Eliza A. Smith on January 1, 1866 in Caswell Co.

Brooks, H. M.: Private
Enlisted in Co. B; paroled 5/13/1865 in Salisbury, NC.

Brown, Thomas: Private
Enlisted in Co. B on 5/16/1863 in Caswell Co.; substitute for George W. Pinnix; AWOL 7/1863 through 8/1864.

Bryant, William W. R.: Corporal
Enlisted in Co. B on 7/8/1862 in Caswell Co. at age 19; born 11/17/1843; mustered in as a private; appointed corporal Nov/Dec 1863; married V. E. Poteat on February 12, 1867; died 12/5/1919, buried Bryant Family Cemetery, NC Highway 62 N., Caswell Co., NC.

Burke, William T.: Private

Enlisted in Co. B on 7/8/1862 in Caswell Co. at age 28; married Nancy Boswell on May 4, 1858 in Caswell Co.; captured 7/4/1863 on retreat from Gettysburg (South Mountain), held at Ft. McHenry; transferred to Ft. Delaware 7/9/1863, died there 9/6/1863 of "typhoid fever"; buried in the National Cemetery, Finn's Point (Salem), NJ.

Burns, Lawrence: Private

Enlisted in Co. B on 7/8/1862 in Caswell Co. at age 47; farmer; born in Polk Co., TX.

Burton, George Moses: Private

Enlisted in Co. B in April 1864 in Caswell Co.; son of Drury Burton, Jr. and Catherine McMullen; previously served as a private in Company D, 13th NC Infantry (3rd NC Vol.); captured 3/30/1865 at Dinwiddie Court House, VA; released 6/23/1865 after taking Oath of Allegiance; married F. E. Smith on September 29, 1866 in Caswell Co.

Burton, John Richard: Private

Enlisted in Co. B on 4/1/1864 in Caswell Co.; born 4/27/1845; paroled 4/9/1865 at Appomattox Court House, VA; died 6/23/1921, buried Bethesda Presbyterian Church, Aberdeen, NC (remains moved here in 1993).

Butler, Moses M.: Private

Enlisted in Co. B on 7/8/1862 in Caswell Co. at age 34; married Elizabeth Summers on February 18, 1855 in Caswell Co.; resident of Caswell Co. at the time of enlistment; transferred to Co. G, 45th NC Infantry.

Chance, Yancey: Private

Enlisted in Co. B on 5/1/1863 in Caswell Co.; wounded in action in September 1864 at Brandy Station, VA; reported AWOL after January 1864; married Martha Horton on January 8, 1864 in Caswell Co.; on 11/5/1864 admitted to a Danville, VA hospital with "erysipelas"; 11/5/1864 returned to duty; may have previously served as a private in Company C, 13th NC Infantry (3rd NC Vol.).

Chandler, George W.: Private

Enlisted in Co. B on 7/8/1862 in Caswell Co. at age 28; born Jan. 4, 1832 in Caswell Co.; son of Pleasant Chandler and Martha Jeffreys; married Elizabeth Boswell on November 5, 1857 in Caswell Co.; hospitalized for several weeks in mid–1864 for "chronic hepatitis"; paroled 4/9/1865 at Appomattox Court House, VA; after the war he returned to Caswell Co. where

George W. Chandler, Company B, Caswell County (Elizabeth Chandler Plumblee).

became a Justice of the Peace in 1872; died "suddenly " at home on 3/30/1883, buried with his father "on a periwinkle covered knoll" in the Chandler Family Cemetery, Caswell Co., NC; obituary in Milton *Chronicle* states, "He was a middle-aged man, a most excellent citizen and neighbor and was a faithful member of the Presbyterian Church."

Chandler, James M.: Private
Enlisted in Co. B on 1/1/1863 in Caswell Co.; captured either 7/4/1863 or 7/5/1863 on retreat from Gettysburg; held at Ft. McHenry; transferred 7/9/1863 to Ft. Delaware; paroled and exchanged 9/22/1864 at Aiken's Landing, VA.

Chandler, Joseph W.: Private
Enlisted in Co. B on 7/8/1862 in Caswell Co.; present or accounted for on all muster rolls through October 1864.

Chapman, C. S.: Private
Enlisted in Co. B on 3/6/1863 in Caswell Co.; present or accounted for on all muster rolls through October 1864.

Cheek, Alexander C.: Private
Enlisted in Co. B on 7/8/1862 in Caswell Co. at age 26; paroled 4/9/1865 at Appomattox Court House, VA.

Cooper, Warren: Private
Enlisted in Co. B on 9/1/1863 in Caswell Co.; son of Allen Cooper and Fannie Warren; brother of Will Cooper, also of Co. B; married Elizabeth A. Corbitt on July 17, 1851 in Caswell Co.; 11/29/1864 admitted to Danville, VA hospital with "diarrhea chronic"; 12/23/1864 furloughed for 60 days.

Cooper, William: Private
Enlisted in Co. B on 3/1/1864 in Caswell Co.; son of Allen Cooper and Fannie Warren; brother of Warren Cooper, also of Co. B; called "Will"; married Mary A. Warren on February 6, 1847 in Caswell Co.; present or accounted for on all muster rolls through October 1864.

Couch, G. W.: Private
Enlisted in Co. B; paroled 5/16/1865 in Salisbury, NC.

Covington, Nathaniel R.: Private
Enlisted in Co. B on 3/1/1864 in Caswell Co.; son of Thomas Covington (ruling elder at Grier's Presbyterian Church and Justice of the Caswell Co. Court in 1854) and Elizabeth Willis Stanfield; brother-in-law to Iverson Oliver, also of Co. B; paroled 4/9/1865 at Appomattox Court House, VA.

Craft, Andrew J.: Private
Enlisted in Co. B on 3/6/1863 in Caswell Co.; married Mary J. Lockard on May 8, 1861 in Caswell Co.

Davis, George W.: Private

Enlisted in Co. B on 7/8/1862 in Caswell Co. at age 30; son of Enoch Davis and Dicie Johnson; paroled 4/9/1865 at Appomattox Court House; died Jan. 14, 1893.

Davis, Henry W.: Private

Enlisted in Co. B on 3/6/1863 in Caswell Co.; wounded in action on 10/14/1863 at Brandy Station, VA and admitted to Richmond hospital; furloughed 10/17/1863 for 60 days; absent wounded through August 1864.

Dickie, James B.: Sergeant

Enlisted in Co. B on 7/8/1862 in Caswell Co. at age 26; mustered in as a corporal; captured 7/4/1863 on retreat from Gettysburg; held at Ft. McHenry; transferred 7/9/1863 to Ft. Delaware; promoted to sergeant in Sept/Oct 1863 while a POW; died 1/26/1864 at Ft. Delaware of "dysentery chronic."

Dillard, Joseph F.: Private

Enlisted in Co. B on 7/8/1862 in Caswell Co. at age 24; wounded in action 6/15/1864 near Petersburg.

Donoho, Charles D.: Private

Enlisted in Co. B on 7/8/1862 in Caswell Co. at age 18; married Caroline Boswell on May 8, 1861 in Caswell Co.; mustered into service on 8/12/1862.

Duffy, Philip W.: Private

Enlisted in Co. B on 5/16/1863; born in Ireland; substitute for Cicero Love; "deserted at Brandy Station, VA, June 17, 1863"; held at Old Capitol Prison until 7/16/1863 when he took Oath of Allegiance and was sent to Philadelphia, PA.

Dunnevant, Thomas: Private

Enlisted in Co. B on 7/8/1862 in Caswell Co. at age 27; August 1864 reported as "absent wounded at hospital"; 10/2/1864 admitted to Danville, VA hospital with a gunshot wound to left leg; 10/8/1864 furloughed for 60 days; married Elizabeth Fuqua on April 7, 1866 in Caswell Co.

Dupont, George: Private

Enlisted in Co. B on 7/8/1862 in Caswell Co.; present or accounted for on muster rolls through February 1863.

Elliott, William M.: Corporal

Enlisted in Co. B on 7/8/1862 in Caswell Co. at age 32; mustered in as a private; appointed corporal Nov/Dec 1863.

Evans, Bazley H.: Private

Enlisted in Co. B on 4/1/1864 in Caswell Co.; present or accounted for on muster rolls through August 1864.

Evans, Thomas L.: Private

Enlisted in Co. B on 7/8/1862 in Caswell Co. at age 33; paroled 4/9/1865 at Appomattox Court House.

Foard, Wyatt: Private
Enlisted in Co. B; paroled 4/9/1865 at Appomattox Court House.

Ford, James T.: Sergeant
Enlisted in Co. B on 7/8/1862 in Caswell Co. at age 38; mustered in as a private; appointed corporal Sept/Oct 1863; promoted to sergeant in Jan/Feb 1864; July/August 1864 reported as "absent wounded prisoner of war."

Foster, John: Private
Enlisted in Co. B on 7/8/1862 in Caswell Co.; "deserted at Williamsport, MD, July 14, 1863."

Foster, William A.: Private
Enlisted in Co. B on 7/8/1862 in Caswell Co. at age 27; born in Caswell Co.; farmer; married Ann P. Jones on December 20, 1860 in Caswell Co.; discharged 11/12/1862 because of "tuberculosis."

Fowler, Charles J.: Private
Enlisted in Co. B on 7/8/1862 in Caswell Co. at age 21; wounded in action on 6/21/1863 in Upperville, VA; muster rolls indicate that on 11/11/1863 he was in a Danville, VA hospital.

Fullington, Lorenzo L.: Private
Enlisted in Co. B on 7/8/1862 in Caswell Co. at age 31; captured 7/4/1863 in retreat from Gettysburg, held at Ft. McHenry; transferred 7/9/1863 to Ft. Delaware; released 6/19/1865 after taking Oath of Allegiance.

Fuquay, Augustus W.: Private
Enlisted in Co. B on 7/8/1862 in Caswell Co. at age 18.

Glidewell, Lewis F.: Private
Enlisted in Co. B on 7/8/1862 in Caswell Co. at age 23; captured 7/4/1863 on retreat from Gettysburg, held at Ft. McHenry; transferred 7/9/1863 to Ft. Delaware; died there 9/1/1863 of "typhoid fever"; buried in National Cemetery, Finn's Point (Salem), NJ.

Graham, Alexander R.: Private
Enlisted in Co. B on 7/8/1862 in Caswell Co. at age 22; present or accounted for on muster rolls through October 1864.

Grant, Joseph: Private
Enlisted in Co. B on 7/8/1862 in Caswell Co. at age 26; 12/3/1864 admitted to Danville, VA hospital with "rheumatismos"; 3/24/1865 furloughed for 60 days.

Groom, Calvin: Private
Enlisted in Co. B on 7/8/1862 in Caswell Co. at age 27; married Elizabeth Martin on November 8, 1859 in Caswell Co.; present or accounted for on muster rolls through October 1864.

Gwynn, Iverson R.: Private
Enlisted in Co. B on 7/8/1862 in Caswell Co. at age 31; present or accounted for on muster rolls through October 1864.

Hall, Caleb F.: Private
Enlisted in Co. B on 2/1/1863 in Lenoir Co., NC; resident of Jones County at the time of enlistment; transferred on enlistment date to Field and Staff of regiment to serve in band as musician; present or accounted for on muster rolls until 7/31/1863 when he returned to Co. B as a private; absent on furlough Jan/Feb 1864; AWOL after May 1864.

Harrelson, John L.: Private
Enlisted in Co. B on 7/8/1862 in Caswell Co. at age 32; captured 7/4/1863 on retreat from Gettysburg, held at Ft. McHenry; transferred 7/9/1863 to Ft. Delaware; transferred 10/22/1863 to Pt. Lookout; paroled and exchanged Feb. 20–21, 1865 at Boulware's Wharf, James River, VA; present on 2/23/1865 roll of exchanged prisoners at Camp Lee, Richmond.

Haymes, John B.: Sergeant
Enlisted in Co. B on 7/8/1862 in Caswell Co. at age 26; mustered in as a private; appointed corporal July/August 1863; promoted to sergeant in Nov/Dec 1863; 8/20/1864 admitted to Petersburg hospital (gunshot wound right jaw); 8/24/1864 furloughed for 30 days; married Martha E. Rice on July 12, 1865 in Caswell Co.

Hendricks, Thomas W.: Private
Enlisted in Co. B on 7/8/1862 in Caswell Co. at age 28; married Aderlaid V. Burton on December 13, 1859 in Caswell Co., where he was residing as a farmer at the time of enlistment; detailed as a courier for Brig. Gen. B. H. Robertson from November 1862 to August 1863.

Henry, John: Private
Enlisted in Co. B; paroled 4/9/1865 at Appomattox Court House.

Henry, Robert L. D.: Private
Enlisted in Co. B; born 7/8/1827; paroled 5/16/1865 at Greensboro, NC; died 5/25/1896, buried Maplewood Cemetery, Durham, NC.

Hensley, William J.: Private
Enlisted in Co. B on 3/6/1863 in Caswell Co.; captured 7/4/1863 on retreat from Gettysburg (South Mountain), held at Ft. McHenry; transferred 7/9/1863 to Ft. Delaware; died there 10/6/1863; buried in the National Cemetery, Finn's Point (Salem), NJ.

Hensly, Buford Brown: Private
Enlisted in Co. B on 7/8/1862 in Caswell Co. at age 32; last name also appears in records as "Henslee"; married Annis Underwood on November 10, 1853; died 11/17/1862 in Franklin, VA.

Hester, Louis C.: Private

Enlisted in Co. B on 4/1/1864 in Caswell Co.; born on October 29, 1844 in Person Co.; paroled 5/16/1865 in Greensboro, NC; married Margaret Burton in 1869; member of Clement Church, where he was a faithful member until his death; died on December 11, 1909; a brief obituary appears in the April 1910 *Confederate Veteran* (Vol. XVIII, No. 4), p. 183.

Hightower, William Daniel: Private

Enlisted in Co. B on 1/1/1863 in Caswell Co.; born 1844 in Caswell Co.; son of John A. and Mary Jackson Hightower; the Hightowers were staunch Methodists and leading members of the Bethel M. E. Church, South; captured near Petersburg during Appomattox campaign and soon paroled; after the war he returned to Caswell Co. to farm; later moved to Rockingham Co., NC where he became a prominent farmer and merchant; also held several public offices including deputy register of deeds; died 1925.

Holden, Emory Brock: 1st Lieutenant

Enlisted in Co. B on 7/8/1862 in Caswell Co. at age 32; married Bettie R. Currie on October 4, 1855 in Caswell Co.; previously served as 1st lieutenant of Company D, 13th NC Infantry (3rd NC Vol.); present or accounted for on muster rolls through August 1864.

Hooper, Henry: Private

Enlisted in Co. B on 3/6/1863 in Caswell Co.; married Elizabeth Bennett on September 23, 1854.

Hooper, James: Private

Enlisted in Co. B on 9/1/1863 in Caswell Co.; paroled 4/9/1865 at Appomattox Court House.

Hooper, Woodlieff: Private

Enlisted in Co. B on 7/8/1862 in Caswell Co. at age 22; called "Woodly"; married Virginia Foster on January 24, 1860 in Caswell Co.

Irvine, William: Private

Enlisted in Co. B; married Virginia A. Jeffreys on October 31, 1857 in Caswell Co.; paroled on 5/10/1865 at HQ, 3rd Div., 6th US Army Corps.

Jackson, John R.: Sergeant

Enlisted in Co. B on 7/8/1862 in Caswell Co. at age 28; mustered in as a corporal; appointed sergeant in May/June 1863; discharged Sept/Oct 1863.

Jeffreys, Arch W.: Private

Enlisted in Co. B on 7/8/1862 in Caswell Co. at age 30; called "Arch"; married Mary W. Taylor on May 12, 1858 in Caswell Co.; mustered into service on 8/12/1862; "no further [military] records."

Johnson, George W.: Private

Enlisted in Co. B on 7/8/1862 in Caswell Co. at age 18; captured 7/4/1863 on retreat from Gettysburg, held at Ft. McHenry; transferred 7/9/1863 to Ft. Delaware; released 6/19/1865 after taking Oath of Allegiance.

Jones, Robert T.: 3rd Lieutenant

Enlisted in Co. B on 7/8/1862 in Caswell Co. at age 26; appointed 3rd lieutenant to rank from date of enlistment; present or accounted for on muster rolls through August 1864.

Kimbrough, Alexander: Private

Enlisted in Co. B on 3/6/1863 in Caswell Co.; present or accounted for on muster rolls through October 1864.

Knighten, James W.: Private

Enlisted in Co. B on 3/6/1863 in Caswell Co.; captured 7/4/1863 on retreat from Gettysburg, held at Ft. McHenry; transferred 7/9/1863 to Ft. Delaware; died there 11/4/1863 of "inflamed tonsil."

Long, Thomas Ruffin: Ordnance Sergeant

Enlisted in Co. B on 7/8/1862 in Caswell Co. at age 26; son of William Long and Sarah Donoho Johnston; mustered in as a sergeant; transferred Sept/Oct 1863 to Field and Staff of regiment to serve as ordnance sergeant; present or accounted for on muster rolls through August 1864; died during the war according to family history.

Love, Apollos: Private

Enlisted in Co. B; paroled 4/9/1865 at Appomattox Court House.

Love, Cicero: Sergeant

Enlisted in Co. B on 7/8/1862 in Caswell Co. at age 21; previously served in 47th Reg. (Caswell Co.), 12th Brig. NC Conf. Militia, commissioned 2nd lieutenant on 9/5/1861; mustered into 4th NC Cavalry as a sergeant; discharged 5/16/1863 after providing Philip W. Duffy as a substitute.

Love, James C.: Sergeant

Enlisted in Co. B on 7/8/1862 in Caswell Co. at age 22; mustered in as a sergeant.

Maddin, Samuel Q.: Private

Enlisted in Co. B on 7/8/1862 in Caswell Co. at age 24; last name also appears in records as "Madden"; married Artelia S. Pleasants on October 8, 1861 in Caswell Co.; died 2/17/1863 in Weldon, NC hospital of "pneumonia."

Malone, James Thomas: Private

Enlisted in Co. B on 4/1/1864 in Caswell Co.; born May 20, 1827 in Caswell Co., NC; son of James Blackwell Malone and Sallie Baker Murray; married three times, first to Mildred A. Yancey on Jan. 2, 1849, second to Margaret Fannie Compton on May 12, 1856 and third to Margaret Parlee Murray on Dec. 12, 1872; farmer, tobacconist, and founder of the Mebane Bedding Company.

Malone, R. D.: Private
Enlisted in Co. B; paroled 5/10/1865 in Greensboro, NC.

Massey, Joseph Franklin: Private
Enlisted in Co. B on 7/8/1862 in Caswell Co. at age 31; married Mary Susan "Susie" Stadler (her second husband).

Massey, Levi P.: Private
Enlisted in Co. B on 7/8/1862 in Caswell Co. at age 25; married Sarah Boswell on December 12, 1861 in Caswell Co.; captured 7/4/1863 on retreat from Gettysburg, held at Ft. McHenry; transferred 7/9/1863 to Ft. Delaware; transferred 10/22/1863 to Pt. Lookout; exchanged 2/24/1865.

Massey, Nathan T.: Private
Enlisted in Co. B on 7/8/1862 in Caswell Co. at age 29; married twice in Caswell Co., first to Artelia Gooch on November 9, 1858 and second to Elizabeth Burke on September 25, 1866.

Matkins, John W.: Private
Enlisted in Co. B on 7/8/1862 in Caswell Co. at age 21; died 4/2/1865 in Rockingham Co., NC.

McCain, Henry David: Private
Enlisted in Co. B on 11/1/1863 in Caswell Co.; born 7/7/1845; son of Tillotson McCain and Elizabeth Elmore; died 7/3/1934, buried Green Hills Cemetery, Asheville, NC.

McCain, Samuel P.: Private
Enlisted in Co. B on 9/1/1863 in Caswell Co.; wounded in action (foot) on 10/15/1863, admitted to Richmond hospital; furloughed 11/3/1863 for 60 days; admitted 12/12/1864 to Danville, VA hospital with "rheumatismos acutis"; deserted from hospital 12/14/1864.

McKinney, David W.: Private
Enlisted in Co. B on 7/8/1862 in Caswell Co. at age 27; born circa 1835 in Caswell Co.; son of Drury and Susan McKinney of Caswell Co.; married Elizabeth F. Rudd on October 31, 1860 in Caswell Co.; died 12/15/1862 in Petersburg hospital of "typhoid fever."

McKinney, James Aaron: Private
Enlisted in Co. B on 7/8/1862 in Caswell Co. at age 34; born circa 1827; son of William W. and Jane McKinney; married Martha Frances Stadler on January 12, 1854 in Caswell Co.; died 11/11/1862 in Petersburg hospital of "measles"; his fourth child, James A. McKinney, Jr. was born two months after his death.

Miles, Hammond: Private
Enlisted in Co. B on 7/8/1862 in Caswell Co.; deserted 4/28/1863 in Washington, NC.

Miles, Henry: Private

Enlisted in Co. B; paroled 4/9/1865 at Appomattox Court House.

Miles, John: Private

Enlisted in Co. B; "deserted at Richmond May 14, 1863."

Miles, Warren W.: Private

Enlisted in Co. B on 7/8/1862 in Caswell Co. at age 26; paroled 4/9/1865 at Appomattox Court House.

Mitchell, James T.: Captain

Enlisted in Co. B on 7/8/1862 in Caswell Co. at age 31; resided in Caswell Co. as a mechanic prior to the war; previously served as captain of Company C, 13th NC Infantry (3rd NC Vol.), elected April 24, 1861; defeated for reelection as captain of the 13th NC in their reorganization on April 26, 1862; present or accounted for on muster rolls through August 1864.

Montgomery, Elvis L.: Private

Enlisted in Co. B on 7/8/1862 in Caswell Co.; resident of Caswell Co. at the time of enlistment; captured 7/4/1863 on retreat from Gettysburg, held at Ft. McHenry; transferred 7/9/1863 to Ft. Delaware; released 5/4/1865 after taking Oath of Allegiance.

Montgomery, Thomas L.: Corporal

Enlisted in Co. B on 7/8/1862 in Caswell Co. at age 27; mustered in as a private; appointed Corporal 8/31/1863.

Moore, Alexander: Private

Enlisted in Co. B on 7/8/1862 in Caswell Co. at age 23; deserted 1/3/1863; captured and returned to regiment 9/30/1863; transferred 4/15/1864 to Co. A, 13th NC Infantry.

Moore, Evans: Private

Enlisted in Co. B on 7/8/1862 in Caswell Co. at age 22; resident of Alamance Co. at the time of enlistment; captured 7/4/1863 on retreat from Gettysburg, held at Ft. McHenry; transferred 7/9/1863 to Ft. Delaware; released 6/19/1865 after taking Oath of Allegiance.

Moore, James P.: Private

Enlisted in Co. B on 9/1/1863 in Caswell Co.; present or accounted for on muster rolls through October 1864.

Morgan, Daniel: Private

Enlisted in Co. B on 4/1/1864 in Caswell Co.; present or accounted for on muster rolls through October 1864.

Morgan, Lorenzo D.: Private

Enlisted in Co. B on 7/8/1862 in Caswell Co. at age 32; married Sarah A. Evans on December 22, 1857 in Caswell Co.; listed as AWOL Jan. through Aug. 1864.

Morgan, Samuel W.: Corporal

Enlisted in Co. B on 7/8/1862 in Caswell Co. at age 21; mustered in as a private; appointed corporal March/April 1863; wounded in action on 6/17/1863 in Middleburg, VA; died there 6/19/1863 of wounds.

Murphy, William H.: Private

Enlisted in Co. B on 7/8/1862 in Caswell Co. at age 31; married Susan A. L. Smith on October 12, 1858 in Caswell Co.

Myers, John: Private

Enlisted in Co. B on 7/8/1862 in Caswell Co.; deserted 5/14/1863 in Richmond.

Neal, James William: Private

Enlisted in Co. B on 8/4/1863 in Caswell Co.; called "Bill"; born June 6, 1844 in Pittsylvania Co., VA; son of William David Neal and Sibyl Yeaman; moved to Caswell Co., NC in late 1850; brother of John T. Neal, also of Co. B; after the war he returned to Caswell Co. where he helped to raise his brother John's orphaned children; served as an overseer for T. D. Johnson and farmed; lived as a bachelor until he married Sarah Belle Riddle, a schoolteacher from Pittsylvania Co., VA on Nov. 26, 1895; died May 6, 1916 (in the Dan River Township) after being kicked by a horse in Danville, VA; both Bill and Belle were devout members of Moon's Creek Primitive Baptist Church and are buried in the cemetery there.

Neal, John T.: Private

Enlisted in Co. B on 7/8/1862 in Caswell Co. at age 23; born in 1838; son of William David Neal and Sibyl Yeaman; moved to Caswell Co., NC in late 1850; brother of James William "Bill" Neal, also of Co. B; on December 12, 1859 married Lucy A. Howard (died in childbirth on August 25, 1862); muster rolls list him serving as a courier to Gen. Wade Hampton Jan. 1864; died 5/25/1864 of typhoid fever, buried in Hollywood Cemetery, Richmond; his brother Bill raised his children after the war.

Nunn, James: Private

Enlisted in Co. B on 7/8/1862 in Caswell Co. at age 23; married Mary J. Waters on December 27, 1860 in Caswell Co.; captured 7/4/1863 on retreat from Gettysburg, held at Ft. McHenry; transferred 7/9/1863 to Ft. Delaware; died there 4/8/1864 of "diarrhea chronic"; buried in National Cemetery, Finn's Point (Salem), NJ.

Oakley, Thomas P.: Private

Enlisted in Co. B on 4/1/1864 in Caswell Co.; married Susan J. Cooper on December 21, 1856 in Caswell Co.; died 7/31/1864 in Petersburg hospital of "strictura ossophagus."

Oliver, Calvin C.: Private

Enlisted in Co. B on 3/6/1863 in Caswell Co.; previously served in 3rd Co. E, 59th Reg. VA Infantry; transferred back to 59th VA Infantry 4/15/1864.

Oliver, Iverson Lea: Private

Enlisted in Co. B; born 1828; son of Reuban Oliver and Nancy Lea; lived on

Country Line Creek about three miles southeast of Yanceyville, in an area later called Oliver's; married Mary Thomas Covington on Nov. 13, 1859; brother-in-law to Nathaniel R. Covington, also of Co. B; after the war he and his brother Monroe Oliver owned a grist mill on Country Line near Hightowers; died 1913.

Robert Calvin Payne, Company B, Caswell County (Norma B. Gordon).

Page, William C.: Private
Enlisted in Co. B on 7/8/1862 in Caswell Co. at age 33; paroled 4/9/1865 at Appomattox Court House.

Pass, John C.: Private
Enlisted in Co. B on 11/1/1863 in Caswell Co.; killed in action on 6/15/1864 near Petersburg.

Payne, Robert Calvin: Private
Enlisted in Co. B on 7/8/1862 in Caswell Co. at age 31; called "Calvin"; born on August 5, 1828; son of Robert Payne and Elizabeth McKinney; married Mary Stephens on May 1, 1856 in Rockingham Co.; present or accounted for on muster rolls through October 1864; after the war he farmed and did carpentry work; died on August 8, 1893, buried in the Pleasant Grove Primitive Baptist Church Cemetery in Caswell Co. with his wife.

Peterson, James O.: Private
Enlisted in Co. B on 3/6/1863 in Caswell Co.; married Mary F. Murray on May 30, 1858; resident of Caswell Co. at the time of enlistment; captured 7/4/1863 on retreat from Gettysburg, held at Ft. McHenry; transferred 7/9/1863 to Ft. Delaware; released 6/19/1865 after taking Oath of Allegiance.

Phillips, Paul George: Private
Enlisted in Co. B on 7/8/1862 in Caswell Co. at age 18; present or accounted for on muster rolls until his death (cause unknown) 7/7/1864 near Petersburg.

Pinnix, George W.: Private
Enlisted in Co. B on 7/8/1862 in Caswell Co. at age 33; married Mary Ursula Graves on September 19, 1854; discharged 5/16/1863 when he furnished Thomas Brown as substitute.

Pleasant, Stephen W.: Private
Enlisted in Co. B on 7/8/1862 in Caswell Co. at age 24; served as wagonmaster in 1862 and 1863.

Pleasant, W. Haywood: Private

Enlisted in Co. B on 6/1/1864 in Caswell Co.; present or accounted for on muster rolls through August 1864.

Pleasant, William Samuel: Private

Enlisted in Co. B on 7/8/1862 in Caswell Co. at age 26; born Nov. 9, 1834 near Baynes Store in Caswell Co.; son of Ruffin Pleasant and Sarah Enocks; married Martha Catholene Marshall of Person Co., NC on Sept. 13, 1855; farmer prior to the war; from 8/12/1863 to 9/5/1863 he returned to Caswell Co. on detached service to procure horses; captured 9/22/1863 at Jack's Shop, VA, held at Pt. Lookout, MD; recruited in prison to join the US Army; enlisted on 1/25/1864 and on 5/1/1864 mustered into Company G, 1st Reg. US Vol. Infantry in Norfolk, VA (such soldiers were dubbed "Galvanized Yankees"); died of consumption in a US Army hospital in Norfolk on July 25, 1864; buried in Section A, Grave 3561, Hampton National Cemetery, Hampton, VA.

Private William Samuel Pleasant, Company B, Caswell County (Henry N. Pleasant).

Cenephus Albert Reid, Company B, Caswell County (Emily Y. Ausband).

Pool, John T.: Private

Enlisted in Co. B on 7/8/1862 in Caswell Co. at age 29; 12/13/1863 "died at home."

Powell, Jarrell: Private

Enlisted in Co. B on 7/8/1862 in Caswell Co. at age 29; present or accounted for on muster rolls through October 1864.

Powell, Martin J.: Private

Enlisted in Co. B on 3/6/1863 in Caswell Co.; married Susan H. Gillispie on June 20, 1852 in Caswell Co.; present or accounted for on muster rolls through October 1864.

Reid, Cenephus Albert: Sergeant

Enlisted in Co. B on 7/8/1862 in Caswell Co. at age 19; born on March 25, 1843 in Caswell Co.; son of James William Reid and Susan Berry Thomas; mustered in as a corporal; 7/31/1863 roll reports him "absent wounded at home"; Nov/Dec 1863 promoted to sergeant; paroled

4/9/1865 at Appomattox Court House; married Sarah Jane Burton (daughter of Thomas Burton and Nancy Bradsher) on February 6, 1868; after the war he farmed in the Leasburg and Hightower Township areas of Caswell Co.; from April 23, 1897 to Nov. 19, 1900 he served as postmaster at Catawba Station in Catawba Co.; died on April 28,1928 in Buncombe Co., buried Catawba Methodist Church, Catawba, NC.

Richmond, Danie(l) W.: QM Sergeant
Enlisted in Co. B on 7/8/1862 in Caswell Co. at age 22; born in Caswell Co., where he resided at the time of enlistment; mustered in as a private; 12/23/1862 transferred to Field and Staff of regiment when appointed quartermaster sergeant; listed as sergeant major on Moore's roster; present or accounted for on muster rolls through October 1864.

Richmond, Henry C.: Sergeant
Enlisted in Co. B on 7/8/1862 in Caswell Co. at age 20; mustered in as a corporal; March/April 1863 appointed sergeant; captured 7/4/1863 on the retreat from Gettysburg, held at Ft. McHenry; 7/9/1863 transferred to Ft. Delaware; died there 9/28/1863 of "acute diarrhea"; buried in National Cemetery, Finn's Point (Salem), NJ.

Richmond, James Bethel: Private
Enlisted in Co. B on 3/6/1863 in Caswell Co.; may have previously served as a private in Company D, 13th NC Infantry (3rd NC Vol.); present or accounted for on muster rolls through October 1864.

Nathaniel Thomas Riggs, Company B, Caswell County (Neal F. Ganzert, Jr.).

Riggs, George Williamson: Private
Enlisted in Co. B on 4/1/1864 in Caswell Co.; married Fanny G. Burke on August 19, 1862 in Caswell Co.; present or accounted for on muster rolls through August 1864.

Riggs, Nathaniel Thomas: Private
Enlisted in Co. B on 7/8/1862 in Caswell Co. at age 18; born September 1844; son of Thomas Riggs, Sr. and Martha Bradsher; present or accounted for on muster rolls through October 1864; after the war he farmed and kept a store in Milton, NC; he was also very active in local affairs, serving as a charter member of the Farmer's Bank in Milton (1879) and as a charter member to restart the Milton and Yanceyville Railroad; also elected secretary of the County Line Agricultural Society, which was formed to solve issues of the changing labor market; he later moved to Winston-Salem, NC where he served as an Internal

Revenue agent; listed as a tobacco salesman in the 1900 Census; wife named Hyacinth (believed to be Hyacinth McCronie); no children.

Rudd, Lorenzo D.: Private

Enlisted in Co. B on 7/8/1862 in Caswell Co. at age 31; son of Joshua Rudd and Susannah "Susan" Culberson; married Arabella C. Chambers (daughter of Josias and Jane Chambers of Person Co.) on February 3, 1854 in Caswell Co.; was a farmer prior to enlistment, living in the Anderson Store area of southern Caswell Co.; captured 7/4/1863 on retreat from Gettysburg, held at Ft. McHenry; transferred 7/9/1863 to Ft. Delaware; died there 10/3/1863; buried at National Cemetery Finn's Pt. (Salem), NJ.

Slade, Elias M.: Private

Enlisted in Co. B on 7/8/1862 in Caswell Co. at age 29; captured on retreat from Gettysburg (July 1863), held at Ft. McHenry; transferred 7/9/1863 to Ft. Delaware; died there 8/26/1863 of "general debility"; buried in National Cemetery, Finn's Point (Salem), NJ.

Smith, Elijah R.: Private

Enlisted in Co. B on 4/1/1864 in Caswell Co.; married Nancy Miles on December 12, 1859 in Caswell Co.; present or accounted for on muster rolls through October 1864.

Smith, Thomas: Private

Enlisted in Co. B on 4/1/1864 in Caswell Co.; present or accounted for on muster rolls through August 1864.

Smith, William B.: Private

Enlisted in Co. B on 7/8/1862 in Caswell Co. at age 27; present or accounted for on muster rolls through October 1864.

Smith, William Rufus: Private

Enlisted in Co. B on 7/8/1862 in Caswell Co. at age 19; present or accounted for on muster rolls through October 1864; paroled 4/9/1865 at Appomattox Court House.

Snider, John: Private

Enlisted in Co. B on 7/8/1862 in Caswell Co.; deserted 5/14/1863 in Richmond.

Stadler, John Bentley: Private

Enlisted in Co. B in January 1864 in Caswell Co.; 10/2/1864 admitted to Danville, VA hospital with "febris remittens"; furloughed 10/20/1864 for 30 days; buried Bush Arbor Church Cemetery, Caswell Co., NC.

Stanfield, John O.: Private

Enlisted in Co. B on 5/1/1863 in Caswell Co.; captured 7/5/1863 on retreat from Gettysburg, held at Ft. McHenry; transferred 7/9/1863 to Ft. Delaware; died there 9/20/1863 of "typhoid fever"; buried in National Cemetery, Finn's Point (Salem), NJ.

Stephens, Benjamin: Private

Enlisted in Co. B; paroled 4/9/1865 at Appomattox Court House.

Tally, A. D.: Private

Enlisted in Co. B; detailed as a wagoner in 1864.

Tally, Daniel Y.: Private

Enlisted in Co. B on 2/1/1864 in Caswell Co.; present or accounted for on muster rolls through October 1864.

Tate, John C.: Private

Enlisted in Co. B on 7/8/1862 in Caswell Co. at age 22; present or accounted for on muster rolls through October 1864.

Teague, Aquilla: Private

Enlisted in Co. B; paroled 5/15/1865 in Greensboro, NC.

Terrell, David C.: Private

Enlisted in Co. B on 7/8/1862 in Caswell Co. at age 26; born in March 1835 in Caswell Co.; son of Paul Terrell and Sarah Rodgers; brother of Jesse Terrell and Joseph Terrell, also of Co. B; he married Tilley Hopkins; present or accounted for on muster rolls through October 1864; died in 1900.

Terrell, James R.: Private

Enlisted in Co. B on 2/1/1864 in Caswell Co.; deserted 5/1/1864 near Clarksville, VA; died 1/1/1891, buried Oakwood Cemetery, Raleigh, NC.

Terrell, Jesse R.: Private

Enlisted in Co. B on 7/8/1862 in Caswell Co. at age 23; born in October 1839 in Caswell Co.; son of Paul Terrell and Sarah Rodgers; brother of David Terrell and Joseph Terrell, also of Co. B; present or accounted for on muster rolls through October 1864; Jesse had several children with Flora Gennell Murphy, but they never married; oral family history states that Flora's father, Bazilla Murphy, killed Jesse after he did not show up for a wedding; he died in 1902 in Caswell Co.

Terrell, John: Private

Enlisted in Co. B on 8/1/1864 in Caswell Co.; born circa 1831; son of Solomon and Nancy Terrell; brother of Thomas Jefferson Terrell, also of Co. B; captured 8/20/1864 on Weldon Railroad; held at Pt. Lookout; paroled and exchanged 11/15/1864 at Venus Point, Savannah River, GA.

Terrell, Joseph W.: Private

Enlisted in Co. B on 7/8/1862 in Caswell Co. at age 20; son of Paul Terrell and Sarah Rodgers; brother of Jesse Terrell and David Terrell, also of Co. B; present or accounted for on muster rolls through October 1864; paroled 4/9/1865 at Appomattox Court House; never married; died in 1898.

Terrell, Thomas Jefferson: Private

Enlisted in Co. B on 7/8/1862 in Caswell Co. at age 23; he was born in April

1840; son of Solomon and Nancy Terrell; brother of John Terrell, also of Co. B; present or accounted for on muster rolls through October 1864; paroled 4/9/1865 at Appomattox Court House; married Sarah Cornelia Jackson on January 31, 1866 in Caswell Co.; listed living in Rockingham Co. in the 1870 Census and in Person Co. (Olive Hill Township) in the 1880 and 1900 Censuses.

Thaxton, Henry S.: 2nd Lieutenant

Enlisted in Co. B on 7/8/1862 in Caswell Co. at age 26; present or accounted for on muster rolls through August 1864; 12/1/1864 muster roll indicates "on detached service with dismounted men, Petersburg, VA"; on the 12/31/1864 roll reported as absent on detail; married Eugenia F. Currie on September 5, 1865 in Caswell Co.

Turner, James R.: Private

Enlisted in Co. B on 7/8/1862 in Caswell Co. at age 29; married Lucinda Roberts on October 21, 1854 in Caswell Co.; captured 7/4/1863 on retreat from Gettysburg, held at Ft. McHenry; transferred 7/9/1863 to Ft. Delaware; transferred 10/18/1863 to Pt. Lookout.

Turner, John: Private

Enlisted in Co. B on 7/8/1862 in Caswell Co. at age 22; present or accounted for on muster rolls through August 1864.

Vaughan, Warren T.: Private

Enlisted in Co. B on 7/8/1862 in Caswell Co. at age 25; married Dolly Miles on October 6, 1859 in Caswell Co.; born in Caswell Co., where he resided as a farmer at the time of enlistment; February 1863 detailed as a courier for Maj. Nethercutt; July/August 1863–October 1864 detailed as a teamster.

Vaughan, William: Private

Enlisted in Co. B on 7/8/1862 in Caswell Co. at age 32; born in Caswell Co., where he resided as a farmer at the time of enlistment; wounded in action on 7/12/1863 in Upperville, VA, admitted to Richmond hospital; transferred 7/20/1863 to Danville, VA; 8/4/1863 returned to duty.

Wade, John C.: Private

Enlisted in Co. B on 3/6/1863 in Caswell Co.; resident of Caswell Co.; captured 7/4/1863 on retreat from Gettysburg, held at Ft. McHenry; transferred 7/9/1863 to Ft. Delaware; died there 11/3/1863 of "smallpox"; buried in the National Cemetery, Finn's Point (Salem), NJ.

Ward, Alfred: Private

Enlisted in Co. B on 7/8/1862 in Caswell Co.; married Elizabeth Debrower on December 22, 1857 in Caswell Co.; January 1864–July 1864 muster rolls show him detailed as a teamster; admitted 12/12/1864 to Danville, VA hospital with "catarrhus."

Warren, Barteman H.: Private

Enlisted in Co. B on 7/8/1862 in Caswell Co. at age 27; born 4/15/1831; married E. C. Lea on February 16, 1860 in Caswell Co.; mustered into service on 8/12/1862; died 9/25/1899, buried Satterfield Family Cemetery, Prospect Hill, NC.

Warren, John: Private
Enlisted in Co. B on 4/1/1864 in Caswell Co.; present or accounted for on muster rolls through October 1864.

Warren, Shelby C.: Private
Enlisted in Co. B on 7/8/1862 in Caswell Co.; present or accounted for on muster rolls through October 1864.

Whitlow, William J.: Private
Enlisted in Co. B on 3/6/1863 in Caswell Co. at age 35; born in Caswell Co., where he resided as a farmer at the time of enlistment; wounded in action on 10/11/1863 at Brandy Station; "absent wounded" through October 1864; reported on the "retired list" by the Medical Examining Board in Raleigh, March 14, 1865; paroled on May 16, 1865 at Greensboro, NC.

Wickers, W.: Private
Enlisted in Co. B; on February 24, 1865 reported as a "deserter from the enemy" by the Federal provost marshal general, Army of the Potomac; received in Washington, DC on February 27, 1865; there he took the Oath of Allegiance and "was provided transportation to Farmington, MO."

Wiles, Thomas Alexander: Private
Enlisted in Co. B on 7/8/1862 in Caswell Co.; presented or accounted for on muster rolls through August 1864; January–August 1864 detailed as a clerk at brigade headquarters.

Wilkerson, Joseph: Private
Enlisted in Co. B on 4/1/1864 in Caswell Co.; present or accounted for on muster rolls through August 1864.

Willis, James H.: Private
Enlisted in Co. B on 7/8/1862 in Caswell Co. at age 19; born in Caswell Co., where he resided as a farmer at the time of enlistment; wounded in action near Petersburg August 15–18, 1864.

Wilson, Jordan: Private
Enlisted in Co. B on 7/8/1862 in Caswell Co. at age 25; present or accounted for on muster rolls through August 1864.

Wilson, L. J.: Private
Enlisted in Co. B on 7/8/1862 in Caswell Co.; admitted 2/10/1864 to Richmond hospital with "epilepsia"; returned to duty 3/15/1864; paroled 5/13/1865 in Raleigh.

Wilson, Thomas A.: Private
Enlisted in Co. B on 7/8/1862 in Caswell Co. at age 33; previously served in the 47th Reg. (Caswell Co.), 12th Brig. NC Confederate Militia, commissioned 1st lieutenant on 9/5/1861; mustered into 4th NC Cavalry as a 1st sergeant; November/December 1863 reduced to ranks; present or accounted for on muster rolls through October 1864.

Winstead, Charles S.: Private

Enlisted in Co. B on 7/8/1862 in Caswell Co.; present or accounted for on muster rolls through October 1864.

Wrenn, Hilman W.: Corporal

Enlisted in Co. B on 7/8/1862 in Caswell Co.; born 11/6/1843 near Yanceyville, Caswell Co. NC; first name also appears spelled as "Hillmon" in some records; mustered in as a private; appointed corporal 1/1/1864; reported as having pneumonia during Gettysburg Campaign, sent to Danville, VA hospital; stated that he had five different horses during war; on December 10, 1866 married Sinai Mitchell in Caswell Co.; member of the First Baptist Church; after her death (1889), married Emma DeLancey of Macon, GA in 1893; died on March 4, 1932 at his home on North Railroad Street in Leaksville, NC; buried in the family cemetery in Ruffin, NC.

Hilman Wrenn and wife, Company B, Caswell County (Ben Wrenn).

Wright, Sidney R.: Private

Enlisted in Co. B on 3/6/1863 in Caswell Co.; married Sarah T. Lockard on September 5, 1858 in Caswell Co.; captured 1/12/1864 in Fairfax Co., VA, held at Old Capitol Prison; transferred 2/3/1864 to Pt. Lookout; paroled and exchanged February 14–15, 1865 at Coxes Landing, James River, VA; listed on 2/1/1865 roll of exchanged prisoners at Camp Lee, near Richmond.

Yarbrough, George W.: Private

Transferred to Co. B on 5/25/1863; previously served in Co. B, 18th VA Infantry; present or accounted for on muster rolls through August 1864.

Yarbrough, Richard Loyston: Private

Enlisted in Co. B on 7/8/1862 in Caswell Co. at age 29; born 1833; married Rachel M. Pass on August 24, 1858 in Caswell Co.; present or accounted for on muster rolls through October 1864; died 1908, buried New Hope Methodist Church, Shattalon Dr., Forsyth Co., NC.

Company C

Anderson, James M.: Private

Enlisted in Co. C on 7/8/1862 in New Hanover Co. at age 33; married Catharine Ramsay on September 1, 1857 in New Hanover Co.; 8/17/1861 commissioned 1st lieutenant in the 22nd Regiment (New Hanover Co.) of the 6th Brigade, NC Confederate Militia; born in New Hanover Co., where he resided as a farmer at the time of enlistment; present or accounted for on muster rolls through October 1864.

Ashe, Alex S.: Private

Enlisted in Co. C on 7/7/1862 in New Hanover Co. at age 23; born and resided in Chatham Co.; physician; mustered in on 7/16/1862; served as an assistant surgeon in the Confederate Navy; died in 1866 in Texas.

Atkinson, Peter: Private

Enlisted in Co. C on 7/6/1862 in New Hanover Co. at age 18; born in New Hanover Co., where he resided as a farmer at the time of enlistment; present or accounted for on muster rolls through October 1864.

Bachman, August Charles: Private

Enlisted in Co. C on 7/7/1862 in New Hanover Co. at age 32; born in Bavaria; confectioner; previously served as corporal in Company A, 18th NC Infantry (8th NC Vol.); present or accounted for on muster rolls through October 1864; admitted 10/28/1864 to Petersburg hospital with a "gunshot, fracture of right ileum (partial)"; 11/16/1864 furloughed; paroled 5/1/1865 in Greensboro, NC.

Bannerman, Alexander W.: Private

Enlisted in Co. C on 7/15/1862 in New Hanover Co.; previously served in Co. K, 3rd NC Infantry; captured 7/4/1863 on retreat from Gettysburg, held at Ft. McHenry; transferred 7/9/1863 to Ft. Delaware; transferred to Pt. Lookout; paroled and exchanged February 20–21, 1865 at Boulwares and Coxes Wharf, James River, VA; present on 2/27/1865 roll of paroled and exchanged prisoners at Camp Lee, near Richmond; died near Richmond (date unknown) of "pneumonia."

Bass, Everett: Private

Enlisted in Co. C on 11/2/1864 (transferred); previously served as a private in Company H, 18th NC Infantry (8th NC Vol.).

Beam, G. W.: Private

Enlisted in Co. C on 4/8/1863 in Johnson Co., NC; wounded in action on 6/15/1864; present or accounted for on muster rolls through October 1864.

Beard, William: Private

Enlisted in Co. C; resident of Forsyth Co. at the time of enlistment; captured 4/3/1865 at Petersburg, held at Hart's Island, NY Harbor; released 6/19/1865 after taking Oath of Allegiance.

Beatty, Lucian Theophilus: Private

Enlisted in Co. C; he was born May 13, 1833 in Bladen Co., where he resided at the time of enlistment; captured 4/8/1865 at Sutherland Station, VA, held at Pt. Lookout; released 6/23/1865 after taking Oath of Allegiance; brother of William Henry Gore Beatty, also in Company C; died on March 3, 1899, buried in the Beatty Cemetery in Bladen Co.

Beatty, William Henry Gore: 1st Sergeant

Enlisted in Co. C on 5/26/1862 in New Hanover Co. at age 30; born on August 13, 1831 in Bladen Co., where he resided at the time of enlistment; mustered in as a sergeant; promoted 10/31/1862 to 1st sergeant; captured 4/8/1865 at Sutherland Station, VA, held at Pt Lookout; released 6/23/1865 after taking Oath of Allegiance; brother of Lucian Theophilus Beatty, also in Company C; died on November 27, 1906, buried in the Beatty Cemetery in Bladen Co.

Blake, Henry C.: Private

Enlisted in Co. C on 7/8/1862 in New Hanover Co. at age 19; born 10/7/1842, in Onslow Co., where he resided as a farmer at the time of enlistment; son of Henry T. Blake and Zelphia Harrell of Onslow Co.; brother of Wright Blake, also of Co. C; present or accounted for on muster rolls through October 1864; married Harriet Ann Eason; died on 10/24/1924, buried Mt. Williams Presbyterian Cemetery, Pender Co., NC.

Blake, Wright: Private

Enlisted in Co. C on 7/8/1862 in New Hanover Co. at age 29; born 9/10/1833 in Onslow Co., where he resided as a farmer at the time of enlistment; son of Henry T. Blake and Zelphia Harrell of Onslow Co.; brother of Henry C. Blake, also of Co. C; present or accounted for on muster rolls through October 1864; paroled 4/25/1865 in Raleigh; married Margaret Louise Ramsey on February 1, 1866 in New Hanover Co.; died 7/8/1906, buried in Blake Family Cemetery, Pender Co., NC.

Blanks, William: Private

Enlisted in Co. C on; listed on Aug. 7, 1862 *Wilmington Journal* muster roll; later served in 61st NC Infantry, Company G (New Hanover County).

Bloodworth, James Harriss: 1st Lieutenant

Enlisted in Co. C on 5/14/1862 in New Hanover Co. at age 27; born 2/14/1835; on 8/30/61 commissioned 1st lieutenant in the 22nd Regiment (New Hanover Co.) 6th Brigade, NC Confederate Militia; born in New Hanover Co., where he resided as a farmer at the time of enlistment; appointed 2nd lieutenant from rank 7/16/1862; promoted 9/22/1863 to 1st lieutenant; captured 10/11/1863 at Brandy Station, VA, held at Old Capitol Prison; transferred 11/11/1863 to Johnson's Island; transferred 2/9/1864 to Baltimore, MD, 2/14/1864 to Pt. Lookout, 7/16/1864 back to Old Capitol Prison, 7/22/1864 to Ft. Delaware; sent 8/20/1864 to Hilton Head, SC, 1/12/1865 sent back to Ft. Delaware; released 6/12/1865 after taking Oath of Allegiance; married Ann Jane Armstrong on February 1, 1866 in New Hanover Co.; died 4/23/1883, buried Pike Creek Presbyterian Church, Highway 117 S., Pender Co., NC.

Bloodworth, Robert N.: Private

Enlisted in Co. C on 5/15/1862 in New Hanover Co. at age 25; born May 14, 1837; he married Matilda L. Hand on December 22, 1859 in New Hanover Co.; on 11/4/1861 commissioned 2nd lieutenant in the 22nd Regiment (New Hanover Co.) of the 6th Brigade, NC Confederate Militia; militia roll states middle initial "M"; born and resided in New Hanover Co.; farmer; mustered in on 7/16/1862; "no further [military] records."

Bordeaux, John W.: Private
Enlisted in Co. C on 7/15/1862 in New Hanover Co. at age 33; born in New Hanover Co., where he resided as a farmer at the time of enlistment; discharged 7/16/1862.

Boswell, Uriah F.: Private
Enlisted in Co. C on 7/9/1862 in New Hanover Co. at age 34; born in Columbus Co., where he resided as a farmer at the time of enlistment; 7/16/1862 "furnished substitute."

Bowden, Bealy J.: Private
Enlisted in Co. C on 7/17/1862 in New Hanover Co.; born circa 1839 in New Hanover Co.; enlisted in regiment while on sick furlough from Co. G, 18th NC Infantry; arrested Nov/Dec 1863 as a deserter; Jan/Feb 1864 returned to Co. G, 18th NC Infantry.

Bowden, John D.: Corporal
Enlisted in Co. C on 6/13/1862 in New Hanover Co. at age 25; born in New Hanover Co., where he resided as a farmer at the time of enlistment; mustered in as a private; appointed corporal March/April 1863; wounded in action on 9/22/1863 at Jack's Shop; present or accounted for on muster rolls through October 1864.

Bowden, Joseph J.: Private
Enlisted in Co. C on 4/4/1863 in New Hanover Co.; born in 1847; on 1/19/1864 discharged due to "being a minor"; buried in the Oakdale Cemetery in Wilmington, NC; he may also have later served in Co. D of the 3rd NC Junior Reserves.

Bowden, Robert N.: Private
Enlisted in Co. C on 5/15/1862 in New Hanover Co. at age 17; born 7/30/1844; enlisted as a substitute; present or accounted for on muster rolls through October 1864; died 8/22/1925, buried Willowdale Cemetery, Goldsboro, NC.

Bowen, A.: Private
Enlisted in Co. C on 7/5/1862 in New Hanover Co. at age 19; born in Brunswick Co., where he resided as a farmer at the time of enlistment; discharged 7/16/1862.

Bowen, John W.: Private
Enlisted in Co. C on 7/9/1862 in New Hanover Co.; present or accounted for on muster rolls through October 1864.

Bradshaw, D. W.: Private
Enlisted in Co. C on 2/12/1863 in Duplin Co., NC; present or accounted for on muster rolls through October 1864.

Breece, George W.: Private
Enlisted in Co. C on 5/9/1862 in Onslow Co. at age 34; born in Onslow Co.,

where he resided as a farmer at the time of enlistment; absent sick Oct. 1862–August 1863; AWOL Sept. 1863–Feb. 1864.

Brown, E. A.: Private
Enlisted in Co. C on 2/6/1863 in New Hanover Co.; captured 4/9/1863 near Plymouth, NC; exchanged 5/28/1863 at City Point, VA; present or accounted for on muster rolls through October 1864.

Bruce, G. W.: Private
Enlisted in Co. C; listed on Aug. 7, 1862 *Wilmington Journal* muster roll; also served in Company I, 14th NC Infantry.

Burton, Blaney W.: Private
Enlisted in Co. C on 7/1/1862 in Duplin Co., NC at age 31; born April 18, 1831 in Duplin Co.; previously served in Company I, 1st NC Cavalry (9th NCST); present or accounted for on muster rolls through October 1864; he died on December 27, 1905, buried in the Sloan Family Cemetery in Duplin Co.

Burton, George W.: Private
Enlisted in Co. C on 7/8/1862 in New Hanover Co. at age 33; born October 15, 1828 in Cypress Creek, Duplin Co., where he resided as a farmer at the time of enlistment; son of John Burton of Duplin Co.; married Clementine Oglesby on February 1, 1850; discharged 7/10/1863 in Lynchburg, VA for "phthisis pulmonalis."

Cannady, William B.: Sergeant
Enlisted in Co. C on 5/5/1862 in New Hanover Co. at age 23; born 2/28/1839 in New Hanover Co., where he resided as a farmer at the time of enlistment; mustered in as a private; prior to 10/31/1862 appointed corporal; promoted 3/1/1864 to sergeant; present or accounted for on muster rolls through October 1864; paroled 4/9/1865 at Appomattox Court House; after the war he continued to farm; married Julia A. Harper on July 5, 1866 in New Hanover Co.; died on 5/3/1921, buried Wesley Chapel Methodist Church, Scott's Hill, NC.

Carter, Hill: Private
Enlisted in Co. C on 7/3/1862 in New Hanover Co. at age 34; born in Duplin Co., where he resided as a farmer at the time of enlistment; present or accounted for on muster rolls through October 1864.

Carter, Thomas J. Henry: Private
Enlisted in Co. C on 7/2/1862 in New Hanover Co. at age 18; born in Duplin Co., where he resided as a farmer at the time of enlistment; AWOL after August 1863.

Casteen, Ceyborn B.: Private
Enlisted in Co. C on 7/3/1862 in New Hanover Co. at age 26; his name also appears as "Cybun" and "Ceberon" in records; born in Duplin Co., where he resided as a farmer at the time of enlistment; son of Jacob C. Casteen and Kissey Lanier; AWOL after August 1863; married Bethany Lanier; died on April 3, 1919 in Duplin County, NC.

Chadwick, Josh J.: Private

Enlisted in Co. C on 7/6/1862 in New Hanover Co. at age 16; born in New Hanover Co., where he resided as a farmer at the time of enlistment; present or accounted for on muster rolls through October 1864.

Chancey, S. L.: Private

Enlisted in Co. C on 7/17/1862 in New Hanover Co.; last name also appears as "Chauncey" in records; present or accounted for on muster rolls through October 1864; buried Flynn Cemetery, Columbus Co., NC (no dates on stone).

Churchill, Thomas B.: Private

Enlisted in Co. C on 6/10/1862 in New Hanover Co. at age 39; born August 19, 1820 in Greene Co., where he resided as a farmer at the time of enlistment; son of William Churchill and Lany Freeman; according to an Oct. 4, 1846 letter, he was in the military (army) at Fort Moultrie, SC (Sullivan's Island), headed for Point Isabel, bound for Texas to fight in the Mexican War—he was a private and cook for 70 men; married Margaret Lynch (daughter of Cornelius Lynch) on March 4, 1851; a May 27, 1851 letter places him at Ft. Independence in Boston, Mass., in it he states that he would be returning home to NC by August 1851; on October 10, 1861 enlisted in New Hanover Co. in captain William C. Howard's Cavalry (raised "for local defense and special service in the District of the Cape Fear of NC—to be employed for the defense of the City of Wilmington and vicinity extending to the sea coast"); served as a corporal and was discharged on June 7, 1862 when Capt. Howard's Cavalry was disbanded (three days later he enlisted in the 4th NC Cavalry); died 1/3/1864 at Hanover Junction, VA of "pneumonia."

Congleton, Joseph: Private

Enlisted in Co. C on 7/7/1862 in New Hanover Co. at age 29; born in Lenoir Co., where he resided as a farmer at the time of enlistment; "discharged" on 7/16/1862 Wilmington muster roll.

Corbett, John: Private

Enlisted in Co. C on in New Hanover Co. at age 22; born in Onslow Co., where he resided at the time of enlistment; listed as "discharged" on 7/16/1862 Wilmington muster roll.

Corbett, Rubin A.: Sergeant

Enlisted in Co. C on 6/30/1862 in New Hanover Co. at age 26; born in Onslow Co., where he resided at the time of enlistment; mustered in as a private; 9/9/1862 appointed sergeant ; captured 7/4/1863 on retreat from Gettysburg, held at Ft. McHenry; 7/9/1863 transferred to Ft. Delaware; released 6/19/1865 after taking Oath of Allegiance.

Costin, William B. T.: Private

Enlisted in Co. C on 5/17/1862 in New Hanover Co. at age 34; born in New Hanover Co., where he resided as a farmer; mustered in as a corporal; reduced to ranks prior to 2/28/1863; present or accounted for on muster rolls through October 1864.

Cowan, John Wright: Private

Enlisted in Co. C on 7/11/1862 in New Hanover Co. at age 25; born in New Hanover Co. on March 23, 1834, where he resided as a farmer at the time of enlistment; married Mary Henderson on May 31, 1867 in New Hanover Co.; present or accounted for on muster rolls through October 1864; died on January 7, 1923, buried in the Burgaw Town Cemetery in Pender Co.

Damron, J. D.: Private

Enlisted in Co. C on 4/8/1863 in Johnston Co., NC; captured 7/4/1863 on retreat from Gettysburg, held at Ft. McHenry; transferred 7/9/1863 to Ft. Delaware.

Daniels, James H.: Private

Enlisted in Co. C on 7/7/1862 in New Hanover Co. at age 17; born in Craven Co., where he resided as a farmer at the time of enlistment; 10/6/1863 reported as sick with typhoid fever; 2/6/1864 furloughed 60 days for "inflammation of large joints following typhoid fever"; July/August 1864 "absent, permanently disabled but not retired."

Daniels, William T.: Private

Enlisted in Co. C on 5/15/1862 in New Hanover Co. at age 36; born in Craven Co., where he resided as a farmer at the time of enlistment; captured 7/4/1863 on retreat from Gettysburg, held at Ft. McHenry; transferred 7/9/1863 to Ft. Delaware; released May 1865 after taking Oath of Allegiance.

Davis, Alexander: Private

Enlisted in Co. C on 7/17/1862 in New Hanover Co.; resided in Robeson Co. at the time of enlistment; captured 7/4/1863 on retreat from Gettysburg, held at Ft. McHenry; transferred 7/9/1863 to Ft. Delaware; paroled and exchanged 8/1/1863 in City Point, VA; present or accounted for on muster rolls through October 1864; captured again 4/8/1865 at Sutherland Station, VA, held at Pt. Lookout; released 6/26/1865 after taking Oath of Allegiance; buried Toms Creek Baptist Church, Denton, NC.

Davis, William E.: Private

Enlisted in Co. C on 7/7/1862 in New Hanover Co. at age 27; born in Beaufort Co.; occupation listed as clerk; "discharged" on 7/16/1862 Wilmington muster roll; admitted 3/6/1865 to Richmond hospital with "pneumonia"; died 3/12/1865.

Deal, Isaac: Private

Enlisted in Co. C on 7/8/1862 in New Hanover Co. at age 21; born in New Hanover Co., where he resided as a farmer at the time of enlistment; married Hannah S. Henderson on September 16, 1860 in New Hanover Co.; present or accounted for on muster rolls through October 1864; paroled April 11–21, 1865 in Farmville, VA.

Dean, John J.: Private

Enlisted in Co. C on 3/21/1865 reported as a "deserter from the enemy" by provost marshal general, Army of the Potomac; 3/29/1865 took Oath of Allegiance in Washington, DC and furnished transportation to Boston, Mass.

Dempsey, George F.: Private

Enlisted in Co. C on 7/9/1862 in New Hanover Co. at age 30; born in Duplin Co., where he resided as a farmer at the time of enlistment; on 7/23/1863 he was transferred to Company B, 1st NC Heavy Artillery Battalion.

Earnhardt, A. S.: Private

Enlisted in Co. C; paroled 5/13/1865 in Salisbury, NC.

Edens, S. H.: Private

Enlisted in Co. C on 7/5/1862 in New Hanover Co. at age 19; born in Onslow Co., where he resided as a farmer at the time of enlistment; present or accounted for on muster rolls through October 1864.

Edens, T. H.: Private

Enlisted in Co. C on 7/5/1862 in New Hanover Co. at age 20; born in Onslow Co., where he resided as a farmer at the time of enlistment; present or accounted for on muster rolls through October 1864.

Ellen, S. F.: Private

Enlisted in Co. C on 2/25/1863 in Greene Co., NC; present or accounted for on muster rolls through October 1864.

English, Monroe: Corporal

Enlisted in Co. C on 7/2/1862 in New Hanover Co. at age 18; born in Duplin Co., where he resided as a farmer at the time of enlistment; mustered in as a private; in March 1864 he was appointed corporal; present or accounted for on muster rolls through October 1864.

Everett, Edward: Sergeant

Enlisted in Co. C on 5/17/1862 in New Hanover Co. at age 24; born in Brunswick Co. circa 1839; son of Dr. Sterling B. and Amelia Everett of Brunswick Co.; resided there as a farmer at the time of enlistment; only listed on one muster roll (June 17, 1862), afterwards "no further [military] record."

Fales, Stephen: Private

Enlisted in Co. C on 4/4/1863 in New Hanover Co.; present or accounted for on muster rolls through October 1864.

Flowers, W. H.: Corporal

Enlisted in Co. C on 10/8/1862 in Southampton Co., VA; mustered in as a private; appointed corporal prior to 2/28/1863; killed in action on 7/4/1863 at Monterey, PA; buried Oakwood Cemetery, Raleigh, NC.

Frink, John Solon: Private

Transferred to Co. C on 11/2/1864; previously served as a private in Company H, 18th NC Infantry (8th NC Vol.).

Fuller, Aug W.: Private

Enlisted in Co. C on 7/8/1862 in New Hanover Co. at age 30; born in Robeson Co., where he resided as a merchant at the time of enlistment; listed on only one muster roll (July 16, 1862), afterwards "no further [military] records."

Futch, Charles W.: Private

Enlisted in Co. C on 7/5/1862 in New Hanover Co. at age 27; married Hester Garrason on February 9, 1858 in New Hanover Co.; born in New Hanover Co., where he resided as a farmer at the time of enlistment; listed on only one muster roll (July 16, 1862), afterwards "no further [military] records."

Futch, J.: Private

Enlisted in Co. C on 7/5/1862 in New Hanover Co. at age 29; born in New Hanover Co.; farmer; "discharged" on 7/16/1862 Wilmington muster roll.

Garrison, Adolphus: Private

Enlisted in Co. C on 7/7/1862 in New Hanover Co. at age 32; born circa 1830 in New Hanover Co.; farmer; captured 7/4/1863 on retreat from Gettysburg, held at Ft. McHenry; transferred 7/9/1863 to Ft. Delaware; transferred 10/18/1863 to Pt. Lookout; paroled and exchanged 1/21/1865 at Boulware's Wharf, VA; present on 1/26/1865 roll of paroled prisoners at Camp Lee, Richmond.

Gillespie, James Flowers: Private

Transferred to Co. C on 7/31/1862; previously served in 2nd Company K, 3rd Regiment NC Artillery (40th NCST); captured 7/4/1863 on retreat from Gettysburg, held at Ft. McHenry; transferred 7/9/1863 to Ft. Delaware; paroled and exchanged 8/24/1863 in City Point, VA; absent wounded Nov./Dec. 1863; "on detached service" April–Oct. 1864; 3/6/1865 detailed "in the Quartermaster Department, (tax in kind) and will report to the quartermaster of Fourth Congressional District of North Carolina"; occupation: turpentine worker.

Hall, Nathan: Private

Enlisted in Co. C on 5/22/1862 in New Hanover Co. at age 22; born in Isle of Wight Co., VA; married Elizabeth Terry on February 2, 1860 in New Hanover Co.; captured 7/4/1863 on retreat from Gettysburg, held at Ft. McHenry; transferred 7/9/1863 to Ft. Delaware; died there 9/28/1863 of "acute diarrhea."

Hall, William J.: Private

Enlisted in Co. C on 5/22/1862 at age 18; born in Onslow Co.; farmer; present or accounted for on muster rolls through October 1864.

Hanchey, Owen R.: Private

Enlisted in Co. C on 7/3/1862 at age 34; born in Duplin Co.; farmer; married Eliza Robinson on May 12, 1853 in New Hanover Co.; present or accounted for on muster rolls through October 1864.

Hancock, John T.: Private

Transferred to Co. C on 8/19/1864; previously served in 2nd Company I, 1st NC

Artillery (10th NCST); present or accounted for on muster rolls through October 1864; on 12/3/1864 admitted to a Danville, VA hospital; on 1/2/1865 returned to duty; paroled 4/9/1865 at Appomattox Court House.

Hand, Patrick H.: Sergeant

Enlisted in Co. C on 5/14/1862 in New Hanover Co. at age 34; born in New Hanover Co., where he resided as a farmer at the time of enlistment; wounded in action on 7/4/1863 at Monterey, PA; present or accounted for on muster rolls through October 1864; paroled 4/9/1865 at Appomattox Court House; buried Burgaw Town Cemetery, Burgaw, NC.

Hand, William J.: Private

Enlisted in Co. C on 7/8/1862 in New Hanover Co. at age 36; born in New Hanover Co., where he resided as a farmer at the time of enlistment; 7/16/1862 Wilmington muster roll "substitute for July 22, 1862."

Hansley, M. L.: Private

Enlisted in Co. C on 5/16/1862 in New Hanover Co. at age 27; born in Onslow Co.; farmer; died 2/9/1864 in Weldon, NC hospital of "diarrhea chronic."

Hansley, R.: Private

Enlisted in Co. C on 7/5/1862 in New Hanover Co. at age 23; born in Onslow Co.; farmer; 7/16/1862 Wilmington muster roll states "discharged."

John Quency Henderson, Company C, New Hanover County (Melba Bonham Jones).

Hansley, Samuel G.: Private

Enlisted in Co. C on 7/4/1862 in New Hanover Co. at age 33; born Onslow Co.; farmer; 7/16/1862 Wilmington muster roll states "discharged"; married Mary E. Sanders on September 22, 1865 in New Hanover Co.

Hansley, William: Private

Enlisted in Co. C on 7/5/1862 in New Hanover Co. at age 34; born Onslow Co.; farmer; 7/16/1862 Wilmington muster roll states "discharged."

Harvey, William J.: Private

Enlisted in Co. C on 5/16/1862 in New Hanover Co. at age 18; born in Onslow Co.; farmer; present or accounted for on muster rolls through October 1864.

Henderson, John Quency: Private

Enlisted in Co. C on 7/8/1862 New Hanover Co. at age 29; born Nov. 16, 1833 in New Hanover Co.; married Minerva Jane Deal circa 1858; resided in New Hanover Co. as a farmer at the time of enlistment; muster rolls report him as "absent sick" after July 1863; May/June 1864 "absent. Permanently disabled and at home"; after the war he continued to farm, became a Methodist "circuit" minister and worked as a cobbler; about 1895 he moved to Georgia; returned to NC often via train to preach; died in March 1920 in Wayne County, GA.

Henderson, L. G.: Private
Enlisted in Co. C on 7/8/1862 in New Hanover Co. at age 24; born in New Hanover Co., where he resided as a farmer at the time of enlistment; present or accounted for on muster rolls through August 1863; AWOL Sept. 1863–Oct. 1864.

Hill, A. J., Jr.: Sergeant
Enlisted in Co. C on 7/17/1862 in New Hanover Co. at age 25; born in Chatham Co.; resided in New Hanover Co. at the time of enlistment; occupation, barber; mustered in as a private; appointed sergeant before 10/31/1862; present or accounted for on muster rolls through October 1864.

Hill, John F.: Private
Enlisted in Co. C on 5/5/1862 in New Hanover Co. at age 20; born in Onslow Co.; occupation, clerk; present or accounted for on muster rolls through October 1864.

Hollis, Joseph Ezekial: Private
Enlisted in Co. C on 7/5/1862 in New Hanover Co. at age 27; born 1835; born in Onslow Co.; occupation, farmer; present or accounted for on muster rolls through October 1864; died 1901, buried Johnston Family Cemetery, New Hanover Co., NC.

Horn, L. T.: Private
Enlisted in Co. C on 7/7/1862 in New Hanover Co. at age 22; born 7/3/1840 in Onslow Co.; occupation, farmer; present or accounted for on muster rolls through October 1864; captured 4/8/1865 at Sutherland Station, VA, held at Pt. Lookout; released 6/27/1865 after taking Oath of Allegiance; died 10/12/1924, buried Stump Sound Baptist Church, Stump Sound Church Rd., Onslow Co., NC.

Humphrey, Christopher McD.: Private
Enlisted in Co. C on 7/7/1862 in New Hanover Co. at age 37; born circa 1825 in Onslow Co.; occupation, farmer; present or accounted for on muster rolls through October 1864.

Ivey, Kader: Private
Enlisted in Co. C on 7/8/1862 in New Hanover Co.; present and accounted for on muster rolls until 2/28/1863 when he was reported as "absent sick."

Ivey, Napoleon B.: Private
Enlisted in Co. C on 7/7/1862 in New Hanover Co. at age 19; born circa 1843 in Brunswick Co.; on 8/30/1861 commissioned 1st lieutenant in the 22nd Regiment (New Hanover Co.) of the 6th Brigade, NC Confederate Militia; born in Brunswick Co.; machinist; mustered in as a corporal, reduced to ranks before 10/31/1862; transferred 1/3/1863 to 1st Company A, 2nd NC Artillery (36th NCST).

James, John: Private

Enlisted in Co. C on 7/8/1862 in New Hanover Co. at age 22; born in New Hanover Co., where he resided as a farmer at the time of enlistment; 7/16/1862 Wilmington muster role states "discharged."

James Theodore C.: Sergeant

Enlisted in Co. C on 7/8/1862 in New Hanover Co. at age 20; born in New Hanover Co., where he resided as a farmer; mustered in as a sergeant; listed as "QM & Comm. Sergeant" on Aug. 7, 1862 *Wilmington Journal* muster roll; transferred 1/26/1863 to Field and Staff, 3rd NC Infantry.

Jenkins, Jackson: Private

Enlisted in Co. C on 5/9/1862 in Onslow Co. at age 30; born in Onslow Co., where he resided as a farmer at the time of enlistment; 10/31/1862–2/28/1863 roll states "absent in Petersburg hospital"; March/April 1863 roll "absent in hospital. Reported dead but not officially."

Knight, James S.: Private

Transferred to Co. C on 7/7/1862; previously served in Company D, 23rd NC Infantry; transferred 8/12/1862 back to Co. D, 23rd NC Infantry upon appointment to 1st lieutenant.

Lamb, Elias: Private

Enlisted in Co. C; resident of Johnston Co.; paroled 5/2/1865 in Goldsboro, NC.

Lanier, Edward: Private

Enlisted in Co. C on 7/14/1862 in New Hanover Co. at age 27; born in New Hanover Co., where he resided at the time of enlistment; died 2/20/1863 in Raleigh hospital of "variola."

Lanier, J. N.: Corporal

Enlisted in Co. C on 5/16/1862 in New Hanover Co. at age 23; born in New Hanover Co., where he resided as a farmer at the time of enlistment; mustered in as a private; Sept./Oct. 1863 appointed corporal; present or accounted for on muster rolls through October 1864; 3/23/1865 reported as a "deserter from the enemy" by the provost marshall general, Army of the Potomac; 3/29/1865 took Oath of Allegiance and furnished transportation to Wilmington, NC.

Lee, John Hogan: Private

Enlisted in Co. C on 5/17/1862 in New Hanover Co. at age 32; born in New Hanover Co., where he resided as a farmer at the time of enlistment; present or accounted for on muster rolls through October 1864; married Martha Bannerman in May 1866 in New Hanover Co.

Leonard, Lewellyn: Private

Enlisted in Co. C on 7/7/1862 in New Hanover Co. at age 24; born in Brunswick Co. circa 1835; son of Nathaniel and Hulda Leonard of Brunswick Co.; occupation, farmer; previously served as 1st lieutenant of Company G, 20th NC Infantry (10 NC Vol.).

Love, Richard Sanders: Sergeant

Enlisted in Co. C on 7/7/1862 in New Hanover Co.; born January 21, 1836; occupation, clerk; previously served in Company I, 18th NC Infantry; mustered in as a private; appointed sergeant prior to 10/31/1862; captured 7/4/1863 on retreat from Gettysburg, held at Ft. McHenry; transferred 7/9/1863 to Ft. Delaware; transferred 10/15/1863 to Pt. Lookout; paroled and exchanged on 2/21/1865 at Boulwares and Coxes Wharf, James River, VA; present on 2/27/1865 roll of exchanged prisoners at Camp Lee, Richmond; died on June 6, 1907, buried in the Weyman Methodist Church Cemetery in Columbus Co.

Mashburn, J. B.: Private

Enlisted in Co. C on 6/10/1862 in New Hanover Co. at age 16; born in Duplin Co.; occupation, farmer; died 11/14/1862 in Garysburg, NC of "pneumonia."

Maultsby, W. Q.: Private

Enlisted in Co. C on 1/13/1864 in New Hanover Co.; detailed in Quartermaster Department; 4/11/1864 ordered to report to superintendent of Wilmington & Manchester RR for 60 days; detail extended 9/3/1864 for 60 days; present or accounted for on muster rolls through October 1864.

McIntire, Andrew: Captain

Enlisted in Co. C on 7/16/1862 in New Hanover Co. at age 50; uncle of Robert Motier McIntire, also of this company; born and resided in New Hanover Co. at the time of enlistment; physician; 9/5/1863 submitted resignation due to "physical disability resulting perhaps from advanced age"; 9/22/1863 resignation officially accepted.

McIntire, Gaston Calhoun: Musician

Enlisted in Co. C on 5/18/1862 in Duplin Co. at age 16; born June 7, 1845 in Duplin Co.; son of James McIntire and Julia Ann Williams of Muddy Creek (Duplin Co.); occupation, farmer; transferred 12/25/1862 to Field and Staff of regiment and to band as a musician; captured 7/4/1863 at South Mtn., held at Ft. McHenry; transferred 7/9/1863 to Ft. Delaware, 10/15/1863 to Pt. Lookout; paroled and exchanged 2/18/1865; present on 2/27/1865 roll of paroled and exchanged prisoners at Camp Lee, Richmond; married Lavinia Pierce Hendry on September 27, 1876 in Duplin Co.

McIntire, Robert Motier: Captain

Enlisted in Co. C on 5/17/1862 in New Hanover, Co. at age 26; nephew of Dr. Andrew McIntire, first captain of company; born and resided in Rocky Point, New Hanover Co. as a merchant at the time of enlistment; 7/16/1862 appointed 1st lieutenant; captured on the retreat from Gettysburg, PA, held at Ft. McHenry; transferred 7/9/1863 to Ft. Delaware; transferred 7/18/1863 to Johnson's Island; 9/22/1863 promoted to captain while a prisoner; 3/14/1865; paroled, 3/22/1865 exchanged at Coxes Landing, James River, VA.

McLendon, Evan C.: Private
Enlisted in Co. C on 5/17/1862 in New Hanover Co. at age 24; born in New Hanover Co., where he resided as a farmer at the time of enlistment; transferred 9/1/1864 to 2nd Company I, 1st NC Artillery (10th Regiment NCST).

Meeks, John W.: Private
Enlisted in Co. C on 7/8/1862 in New Hanover Co. at age 28; born in New Hanover Co., where he resided as a farmer at the time of enlistment; married Sarah A. Mott on June 26, 1855 in New Hanover Co.; present or accounted for on muster rolls through October 1864; on 3/21/1865 reported as a "deserter from the enemy" by the provost marshall general, Army of the Potomac; 3/29/1865 took Oath of Allegiance and furnished transportation to Wilmington, NC.

Mills, Jesse Jasper: Private
Enlisted in Co. C on 7/16/1862 in New Hanover Co. at age 16; born 12/7/1847 in New Hanover Co., where he resided as a farmer at the time of enlistment; present or accounted for on muster rolls through October 1864; died 5/26/1909, buried Antioch Church, Willard, NC.

Mitchell, W. T.: Private
Enlisted in Co. C on 7/17/1862 in New Hanover Co.; Oct. 1862–August reported as absent in Petersburg hospital; AWOL Sept. 1863–October 1864.

Moore, Patrick H.: Private
Enlisted in Co. C on 5/19/1862 in New Hanover Co. at age 25; born in Virginia; occupation, clerk; 7/16/1862 Wilmington muster roll states "discharged."

Moore, Wiley: Private
Transferred to Co. C on 1/3/1863; married Linda A. Wells on April 8, 1855; previously served in 1st Company A, 2nd NC Artillery (36th NCST); present or accounted for on muster rolls through October 1864.

Moore, Willohby: Private
Enlisted in Co. C on 7/9/1862 in New Hanover Co. at age 60; born in New Hanover Co., where he resided as a farmer at the time of enlistment; discharged 6/6/1863 in Richmond due to "the infirmities of age, etc."

Morgan, James M.: Private
Enlisted in Co. C on 7/5/1862 in New Hanover Co. at age 33; born in Sampson Co., NC; occupation, farmer; transferred 9/9/1864 to Company H, 18th NC Infantry.

Mott, Alonzo: Private
Enlisted in Co. C on 6/17/1862 in New Hanover Co. at age 17; born circa 1844 in New Hanover Co., where he resided as a machinist at the time of enlistment; 9/7/1863 detailed to work the Clarendon Iron Works, Wilmington, NC.

Ormsby, John C.: Corporal

Enlisted in Co. C on 6/30/1862 in New Hanover Co. at age 32; born 7/3/1829 in New Hanover Co., where he resided as a farmer at the time of enlistment; married Caroline A. Williams on March 17, 1853 in New Hanover Co.; mustered in as a private; appointed corporal Sept./Oct. 1864; present or accounted for on muster rolls through October 1864; died 8/20/1909, buried Wesley Chapel Methodist Church, Scott's Hill, NC.

Padgett, Benjamin: Private

Enlisted in Co. C on 7/5/1862 in Onslow Co. at age 24; born 1838 in Moors Ridge, Onslow Co., where he resided as a farmer at the time of enlistment; married Annie Sanders on January 8, 1861; present or accounted for on muster rolls through July 1863; reported as a "deserter" August 1863–October 1864; buried Maple Hill Baptist Church Cemetery, Maple Hill, NC.

Padgett, Isaac S.: Private

Enlisted in Co. C on 7/3/1862 in New Hanover Co. at age 17; born circa 1845 in New Hanover Co., where he resided at the time of enlistment; son of Spicer and Elisha Padgett; captured 7/4/1863 on retreat from Gettysburg, held at Ft. McHenry; transferred 7/9/1863 to Ft. Delaware; paroled 7/30/1863; exchanged 8/1/1863 at City Pont, VA; present or accounted for on muster rolls through October 1864.

Padgett, James H.: Private

Enlisted in Co. C on 7/5/1862 in New Hanover Co. at age 22; born in Onslow Co.; occupation, farmer; died 1/18/1863 in Petersburg hospital of "smallpox."

Padgett, Robert: Private

Enlisted in Co. C on 7/14/1862 in New Hanover Co. at age 20; born in Onslow Co.; farmer; March/April 1863 reported as "absent home with a broken leg"; reported as "deserted" after 7/31/1863; married Clara Pierce on September 3, 1867 in New Hanover, Co.

Person, E. O.: Private

Enlisted in Co. C on 11/2/1862 in Southampton Co., VA; present or accounted for on muster rolls through October 1864.

Pierce, David W.: Private

Enlisted in Co. C on 7/14/1862 at age 26; born in Duplin Co.; occupation, farmer; present or accounted for on muster rolls through October 1864.

Redd, Jacob H.: Private

Enlisted in Co. C on 5/16/1862 at age 21; born in Onslow Co.; 7/16/1862 Wilmington muster roll states "discharged."

Rhodes, Anthony H.: Private

Transferred to Co. C on 10/8/1863; previously served in Company G, 3rd NC Infantry; present or accounted for on muster rolls through October 1864.

Rhodes, Hardy B.: 3rd Lieutenant

Enlisted in Co. C on 5/5/1862 in Onslow Co. at age 24; born in Brunswick Co.; resided in New Hanover Co. as a farmer at the time of enlistment; mustered in as a corporal; promoted March/April 1863 to sergeant; on 3/1/1864 appointed to 3rd lieutenant; present or accounted for on muster rolls through February 1865; 2/20/1865 reported absent on leave.

Rhodes, Henry A.: Corporal

Enlisted in Co. C on 5/16/1862 in New Hanover Co. at age 32; born 1830 in Jones Co.; farmer; mustered in as a corporal; died 1/10/1863 in Greensboro, NC hospital of "pneumonia"; buried Green Hill Cemetery (CS Section), Greensboro, NC.

Richardson, R. S.: Private

Enlisted in Co. C on 7/14/1862 in New Hanover Co. at age 29; born circa 1831 in Columbus Co.; listed in the 1860 Columbus Co. Census as a carpenter living with his wife Caroline (of Edgecombe Co.); present or accounted for on muster rolls through October 1864.

Robeson, Neadham: Private

Enlisted in Co. C on 5/17/1862 in Onslow Co. at age 34; born in Onslow Co., where he resided at the time of enlistment; 7/16/1862 Wilmington muster roll states "discharged."

Rogers, George W.: Private

Enlisted in Co. C on 4/4/1863 in New Hanover Co.; present or accounted for on muster rolls through October 1864; married Nancy E. Kennedy on November 11, 1866 in New Hanover Co.

Rogers, John W.: Private

Enlisted in Co. C on 5/5/1862 in New Hanover Co. at age 25; 12/30/1861 commissioned 2nd lieutenant in the 22nd Regiment (New Hanover Co.) of the 6th Brigade, NC Confederate Militia; born in New Hanover Co., where he resided as a farmer at the time of enlistment; present or accounted for on muster rolls through October 1864; married Susan A. Williams on December 21, 1867 in New Hanover Co.

Rogers, William L.: Private

Enlisted in Co. C on 5/5/1862 in New Hanover Co. at age 21; born in New Hanover Co., where he resided as a farmer at the time of enlistment; present or accounted for on muster rolls through October 1864; married Cornelia Canady on December 7, 1865 in New Hanover Co.

Sanders, W. J.: Private

Enlisted in Co. C on 7/7/1862 in New Hanover Co. at age 18; born in Onslow Co.; farmer; wounded in action in Oct. 1863 at Jack's Shop, VA; admitted to Richmond hospital, died there 12/4/1863 of "gunshot wound of knee and typhoid fever."

Savage, Owen R.: Private

Enlisted in Co. C on 7/15/1862 in New Hanover Co. at age 30; born 11/18/1831 in Sampson Co.; resided in New Hanover Co. as a farmer at the time of enlistment; captured 7/4/1863 on retreat from Gettysburg, held at Ft. McHenry; transferred 7/9/1863 to Ft. Delaware; transferred 10/15/1863 to Pt. Lookout; released 7/13/1865 after taking Oath of Allegiance; died 7/25/1904, buried Black River Presbyterian Cemetery, Sampson Co., NC.

Savage, R.: Private

Enlisted in Co. C on 7/8/1862 in New Hanover Co. at age 28; born in New Hanover Co., where he resided as a farmer at the time of enlistment; 7/16/1862 Wilmington roll states "discharged."

Scott, P. B.: Private

Enlisted in Co. C on resident of Wilson Co. at the time of enlistment; paroled 5/2/1865 in Goldsboro, NC.

Simpson, Thomas: Private

Enlisted in Co. C on 5/9/1862 in New Hanover Co. at age 38; born in Carteret Co.; resided in New Hanover Co. as a farmer at the time of enlistment; present or accounted for on muster rolls through October 1864; captured 3/18/1865 in Goldsboro, NC, held at Hart's Island, NY; released 6/18/1865 after taking Oath of Allegiance.

Sloan, William H.: Private

Enlisted in Co. C on 7/7/1862 in New Hanover Co. at age 21; born in Duplin Co.; occupation, merchant; present or accounted for on muster rolls until transferred 9/9/1864 to Company H, 18th NC Infantry.

Smith, Thomas: Private

Enlisted in Co. C on 7/7/1862 in New Hanover Co. at age 30; born in New Hanover Co., where he resided as a fisherman at the time of enlistment; a July 16, 1862 muster roll lists him as present, afterwards "no further [military] records."

Smith, W. D.: Musician

Enlisted in Co. C; captured and paroled 4/20/1865 in Raleigh.

Sneeden, Silas: Private

Enlisted in Co. C on 7/7/1862 in New Hanover Co. at age 18; born circa 1844 in New Hanover Co., where he resided as a farmer at the time of enlistment; deserted to enemy in New Bern, NC, received at Camp Distribution, VA 1/29/1864; on 2/5/1864 sent to Norfolk, VA then to Ft. Monroe; 2/10/1864 took Oath of Allegiance.

Stokes, A. J.: Private

Enlisted in Co. C on 7/5/1862 in New Hanover Co.; present or accounted for on muster rolls through October 1864.

Stokes, Henry: Private

Enlisted in Co. C on 1/15/1863 in Lenoir Co.; captured 7/4/1863 on retreat from Gettysburg, held at Ft. McHenry; transferred 7/9/1863 to Ft. Delaware; later sent to Pt. Lookout; paroled and exchanged 3/14/1865 at Aiken's Landing, VA.

Stokes, Jacob: Private

    Enlisted in Co. C on 7/14/1862 in New Hanover Co. at age 27; married Elizabeth Anderson on February 2, 1857 in New Hanover Co.; present or accounted for on muster rolls through October 1864.

Swartz, Louis: Private

    Enlisted in Co. C on 7/29/1862 in New Hanover Co.; present or accounted for on muster rolls through October 1864.

Swinson, M.: Private

    Enlisted in Co. C on 2/12/1863 in Duplin Co.; present or accounted for on muster rolls through October 1864; on 4/21/1865 received as a "rebel deserter" by the provost marshal general, Washington, DC from City Point, VA; provided transportation to Wilmington, NC.

Sykes, M. M.: Private

    Enlisted in Co. C on 7/22/1862 in New Hanover Co. at age 36; his last name also appears as "Sikes" in records; born in Northampton Co.; farmer; "died while home on detail to mount in New Hanover County, NC, August 16, 1864"; believed to be Martin Sikes, born circa 1825 and living in Northampton Co. in the 1850 Census in house/dwelling 18.

Walker, George W.: Private

    Enlisted in Co. C on 6/12/1862 in New Hanover Co. at age 30; born in New Hanover Co., where he resided as a farmer at the time of enlistment; wounded in action on 10/15/1863 during Bristoe Campaign, admitted to Charlottesville hospital; 5/10/1864 furloughed for 60 days; 9/1/1864 retired to Invalid Corps.

Walker, Henry Dudley: Private

    Enlisted in Co. C on 7/8/1862 in New Hanover Co. at age 19; born 1/18/1843 in New Hanover Co., where he resided as a farmer at the time of enlistment; temporarily assigned to 2nd Company A, 2nd NC Artillery (36th NCST), appointed courier to Gen. W.H.C. Whiting; 8/10/1864 returned to Co. C of this regiment; present or accounted for on muster rolls through October 1864; may have previously served as private in Company I, 18th NC Infantry (8th NC Vol.); buried Oakdale Cemetery, Wilmington, NC.

Wall, William C.: Private

    Enlisted in Co. C on 7/7/1862 in New Hanover Co.; previously served in Company D, 23rd NC Infantry; transferred back to Company D, 23rd NC Infantry 5/22/1863 upon appointment to 2nd lieutenant.

Weiks, C. K.: Private

    Enlisted in Co. C on 7/7/1862 in New Hanover Co. at age 26; born in Carteret Co.; occupation, farmer; 7/16/1862 Wilmington roll states "discharged."

Wells, Joseph B.: Private

    Enlisted in Co. C on 7/15/1862 in New Hanover Co. at age 19; born in New

Hanover Co., where he resided as a farmer at the time of enlistment; wounded in action on 10/11/1863; present or accounted for on muster rolls through October 1864.

Westbrook, James Marion: Corporal
Enlisted in Co. C on 7/7/1862 in New Hanover Co. at age 18; born in New Hanover Co., where he resided as a farmer at the time of enlistment; mustered in as a private; appointed corporal March/April 1863; promoted to sergeant in July/August 1863; reduced to corporal Sept./Oct. 1863; present or accounted for on muster rolls through October 1864; captured 4/8/1865 near Petersburg, held at Pt. Lookout; released 6/21/1865 after taking Oath of Allegiance; married Mary E. Batson on January 17, 1867 in New Hanover Co.

Westbrook, James T.: Private
Enlisted in Co. C on 7/8/1862 in New Hanover Co. at age 22; born in New Hanover Co., where he resided as a farmer at the time of enlistment; present or accounted for on muster rolls through October 1864; married Caledonia E. Smith on December 6, 1866 in New Hanover Co.

Wilder, Jesse T.: 2nd Lieutenant
Enlisted in Co. C on 5/5/1862 in New Hanover Co. at age 23; born 1839 in Onslow Co., where he resided as a farmer at the time of enlistment; appointed 3rd lieutenant on 7/16/1862 from rank; promoted 9/22/1863 to 2nd lieutenant ; present or accounted for on muster rolls through October 1864; captured 4/8/1865 near Petersburg; held at Johnson's Island until taking Oath of Allegiance 6/20/1865; buried Bellevue Cemetery, Wilmington, NC.

Williams, Robert T.: Private
Enlisted in Co. C on 7/14/1862 in New Hanover Co. at age 27; born in New Hanover Co., where he resided as a farmer at the time of enlistment; discharged 12/1/1862 due to "family distress."

Wright, Joshua Granger, Jr.: 1st Sergeant
Enlisted in Co. C on 6/5/1862 in New Hanover Co. at age 21; born in New Hanover Co., where he resided as a farmer at the time of enlistment; mustered in as a 1st sergeant; transferred 8/1/1862 to Company E, 1st NC Infantry upon appointment to 2nd lieutenant.

Company D

Allen, Marcus A.: Private
Enlisted in Co. D on 1/1/1863 in Northampton Co.; present on 7/23/1863 roll of paroled and exchanged prisoners at Camp Lee, Richmond; present or accounted for on muster rolls through October 1864.

Askew, Abner H.: Private
Enlisted in Co. D on resident of Hertford Co. at the time of enlistment; previously

served as a private in Company C, 17th NC Infantry (2nd Organization); 4/11/1865 confined at Hart's Island, NY; released 6/19/1865.

Askew, Adolphus D.: Private

Enlisted in Co. D on 7/8/1862 in Hertford Co. at age 34; born circa 1828 in Hertford Co., where he resided as a farmer at the time of enlistment; present or accounted for on muster rolls through October 1864.

Askew, Edward S.: Private

Enlisted in Co. D on 7/8/1862 in Hertford Co. at age 18; born circa 1843; son of Zephaniah and Lucretia Askew; resided in Hertford Co. as a farmer at the time of enlistment; wounded in action on 9/21/1863 at Jack's Shop, VA; captured 3/31/1865 at Hatcher's Run, VA, held at Pt. Lookout; released 6/22/1865 after taking Oath of Allegiance.

Askew, William Jasper: Private

Enlisted in Co. D on 7/8/1862 in Hertford Co. age 34; born in Hertford Co., where he resided as a farmer at the time of enlistment; killed in action 6/21/1863 in Upperville, VA.

Barham, William: Private

Enlisted in Co. D on 2/5/1863 in Hertford Co.; died 1/3/1864; no further military records.

Beaman, Joseph T.: 3rd Lieutenant

Enlisted in Co. D on 7/12/1862 in Hertford Co.; born circa 1842 in Hertford Co., where he resided as a merchant at the time of enlistment; appointed 3rd lieutenant 8/9/1862 from rank; present or accounted for on muster rolls until transferred 9/8/1863 to Company A, 15th Battalion NC Cavalry upon appointment to 1st lieutenant.

Belch, Elisha: Private

Enlisted in Co. D on 7/5/1862 in Hertford Co. at age 23; born circa 1839 in Hertford Co., where he resided as a farmer at the time of enlistment; son of Jethro and Mary Belch; muster rolls list him as "deserted" prior to 2/28/1863; married Arramitta Holloman on December 27, 1868 in Hertford County.

Boone, John Wesley: Private

Enlisted in Co. D on 7/8/1862 in Northampton Co. at age 34; born 8/5/1828; present or accounted for on muster rolls through October 1864; died 8/6/1904 in Boone Family Cemetery, W.J. Duke Rd., Northampton Co., NC.

Boone, Lawrence: Private

Enlisted in Co. D on 7/8/1862 in Northampton Co. at age 24; born circa 1837 in Northampton Co., where he resided as a clerk at the time of enlistment; son of Thomas Boon(e) (farmer) and Rebecca Edwards; married Amanda J. Futrell on December 2, 1855 in Northampton Co.; present or accounted for on muster rolls through October 1864.

Boone, Simeon P.: Private

Enlisted in Co. D on 7/8/1862 in Northampton Co. at age 26; born in Northampton Co., where he resided as a farmer at the time of enlistment; present or accounted for on muster rolls through October 1864.

Bowen, William H: Sergeant

Enlisted in Co. D; born on June 3, 1837; "name appears on voucher for commutation of rations for the period August 8, 1863 to September 6, 1863"; "paid at Culpeper, VA, August 11, 1863"; died August 11, 1908.

Brett, Henry Thomas: Hospital Steward

Enlisted in Co. D on 7/6/1862 in Hertford Co. at age 20; born circa 1842 in Hertford Co., where he resided at the time of enlistment; doctor; son of Henry and Martha Brett; mustered in as a private; March/April 1863 detailed as "apothecary"; transferred 9/15/1863 to Field and Staff of regiment serving as a Hospital Steward; listed as "R. T. Brett" in Winborne's *The Colonial and State History of Hertford County*; present or accounted for on muster rolls through October 1864.

Bridgers, Andrew J.: Private

Enlisted in Co. D on 12/30/1862 in Northampton Co.; married Jane Coggins on December 22, 1859 in Northampton Co.; present or accounted for on muster rolls through October 1864.

Bridgers, Emory A.: Private

Enlisted in Co. D on 7/8/1862 in Northampton Co. at age 24; born circa 1838 in Northampton Co., where he resided as a farmer at the time of enlistment; married Martha Woodard on February 22, 1855 in Northampton Co.; captured 7/4/1863 on retreat from Gettysburg, held at Ft. McHenry; transferred 7/9/1863 to Ft. Delaware; died there 9/8/1863 of "typhoid fever."

Bridgers, George T.: Private

Enlisted in Co. D on 7/8/1862 in Northampton Co. at age 23; born circa 1839 in Northampton Co., where he resided as a farmer at the time of enlistment; present or accounted for on muster rolls through October 1864.

Britt, Albert G.: Private

Enlisted in Co. D on 7/8/1862 in Hertford Co.; born circa 1814; wife Susan; father of Richard Thomas Britt, also of Co. D; farrier; mustered in as a farrier; March/April 1864 reduced to ranks; present or accounted for on muster rolls through October 1864.

Britt, Richard Thomas: Private

Transferred to Co. D on 9/3/1862; born 12/3/1844 in Hertford Co. where he resided at time of enlistment; son of Albert G. and Susan Britt; his father Albert G. Britt also served in Co. D; previously served in Company C, 2nd NC Cavalry (enlisted 6/18/1861); Jan.–July 1863 detailed as a teamster; present or accounted for on muster rolls through October 1864; died 9/28/1925 in Raleigh, buried Oakwood Cemetery, Raleigh, NC.

Brown, James: Private

Enlisted in Co. D on 9/1/1862 in Northampton Co.; 8/30/1862 deserted at Garysburg, NC.

Brown, James Thomas: Private

Enlisted in Co. D on 7/8/1862 in Hertford Co. at age 18; born in Hertford Co., where he resided as a farmer at the time of enlistment; captured 7/4/1863 on retreat from Gettysburg, held at Ft. McHenry; transferred 7/9/1863 to Ft. Delaware; paroled and exchanged February 20–21, 1865 at Boulwares and Coxes Wharf, James River, VA; present on 2/27/1865 roll of paroled and exchanged prisoners at Camp Lee, Richmond.

Brown, William H.: Private

Enlisted in Co. D on 7/8/1862 in Hertford Co. at age 34; born in Hertford Co., where he resided as a farmer at the time of enlistment; wounded in action on 6/21/1863 in Upperville, VA; reported absent wounded through 10/1864.

Bryant, Charles J.: Private

Enlisted in Co. D on 7/8/1862 in Northampton Co. at age 34; born in Northampton Co., where he resided as a farmer at the time of enlistment; married Mary L. Hedgpeth in Northampton Co.; present or accounted for on muster rolls through October 1864; 11/1863–4/1864 detailed in Lynchburg, VA hospital.

Carter, Abner A.: Private

Enlisted in Co. D on 7/8/1862 in Hertford Co. at age 30; born circa 1834 in Hertford Co. where he resided as a farmer at the time of enlistment; son of Willie B. Carter and Winifred Cotton; in the 1850 Hertford Co. Census he is boarding with Daniel Valentine; present or accounted for on muster rolls through October 1864; married Sarah Ann Everett (the daughter of Thomas Everett).

Carter, Edward J.: Private

Enlisted in Co. D on 8/18/1862 in Northampton Co.; from 9/11/1863–11/1863 detailed in Richmond hospital; present or accounted for on muster rolls until he transferred in March 1864 to Company G, 68th NC Infantry.

Clark, William David: Private

Enlisted in Co. D on 7/5/1862 in Hertford Co. at age 25; born in Hertford Co., where he resided at the time of enlistment; present or accounted for on muster rolls through August 1864; buried in the Clark Family Cemetery (Wynn St.), Winton, NC (no dates on stone).

Cook, Joseph: Private

Enlisted in Co. D; paroled 4/9/1865 at Appomattox Court House.

Cook, Richard A.: Private

Enlisted in Co. D on 7/5/1862 in Hertford Co. at age 24; born in Hertford Co. where he resided as a farmer at the time of enlistment; mother's name, Martha Cook per 1850 Hertford Co. Census; captured 6/21/1863 near Upperville, VA, held at Old

Capitol Prison; paroled and exchanged 6/30/1863 at City Point, VA; present or accounted for on muster rolls through October 1864.

Cotton, Cullen: Private

Enlisted in Co. D on 7/5/1862 in Hertford Co. at age 32; born circa 1830 in Bertie Co.; present or accounted for on muster rolls through October 1864.

Cotton, Godwin: Private

Enlisted in Co. D on 5/10/1864 in Perquimans Co.; present or accounted for on muster rolls through October 1864.

Davis, James M.: Private

Enlisted in Co. D on 8/20/1864 in Northampton Co.; present or accounted for on muster rolls through August 1864.

Deans, James M.: Private

Enlisted in Co. D on 8/20/1864 in Northampton Co.; present or accounted for on muster rolls through October 1864.

Debeny, Henry T.: Private

Enlisted in Co. D on 8/18/1864 in Northampton Co.; present or accounted for on muster rolls through October 1864.

Dickens, Jesse: Private

Enlisted in Co. D on 8/20/1864 in Northampton Co.; present or accounted for on muster rolls through October 1864; paroled 9/20/1865 at Appomattox Court House.

Dilday, Henry E.: Private

Enlisted in Co. D on 7/5/1862 in Hertford Co. at age 19; born in Hertford Co., where he resided as a farmer at the time of enlistment; present or accounted for on muster rolls until deserted 9/15/1863.

Dilday, Jesse A.: Private

Enlisted in Co. D on 7/5/1862 in Hertford Co. at age 22; born circa 1840 in Hertford Co., where he resided as a farmer at the time of enlistment; son of Seth and Martha Dilday; muster rolls indicate that he "deserted at Franklin, VA, 25 September 1862."

Dilday, Thomas H.: Private

Enlisted in Co. D on 8/18/1862 in Northampton Co.; present or accounted for on muster rolls through October 1864.

Doughtie, Starkey J.: Private

Enlisted in Co. D on 7/3/1862 in Hertford Co. at age 21; born December 5, 1834 in Hertford Co., where he resided as a farmer at the time of enlistment; son of Joshua and Martha Doughtie; previously served as a private in Company D, 17th NC Infantry (1st Organization); present or accounted for on muster rolls through October 1864; on 12/6/1864 admitted to Richmond hospital and furloughed 60 days; died on March 20, 1920, buried in the Doughtie Family Cemetery in Hertford Co.

Doxey, Haywood D.: Private

Transferred to Co. D on 5/1/1864; previously served in Company G, 68th NC Infantry; present or accounted for on muster rolls through October 1864; 1/18/1865 received as a "deserter" in Norfolk, VA by Provost Marshall's Office.

Dukes, Thomas S.: Private

Enlisted in Co. D on 2/24/1863 in Northampton Co.; resident of Northampton Co. at the time of enlistment; wounded in action on 6/16/1863 in Middleburg, VA; absent wounded through August 1864.

Durman, J. W.: Private

Enlisted in Co. D; captured and paroled 4/3/1865 while in Richmond hospital

Private John Robert Early, Company D, Hertford County (Neil Hunter Raiford).

Early, John Robert: Private

Enlisted in Co. D on 7/8/1862 in Hertford Co. at age 30; born in Hertford Co. on October 16, 1833; mother's name Hester Holloman; married Sarah Matilda Dunning on March 29, 1859 in Bertie Co.; on 4/14/1862 commissioned captain in the 6th Regiment, 2nd Brigade, NC Confederate Militia; resided in Hertford Co. as a farmer at the time of enlistment; after the war he and his family settled in the Mitchell Township of Bertie Co., where he farmed; died on October 17, 1907, buried in the Wiley Dunning Cemetery in Aulander, NC (Bertie Co.).

Edwards, John T.: Private

Enlisted in Co. D on 7/8/1862 in Northampton Co. at age 26; born in Northampton Co., where he resided at the time of enlistment; missing in action June 1863 at Upperville, VA.

Edwards, John T., Jr.: Private

Enlisted in Co. D on 2/22/1863 in Greene Co.; died 5/23/1863 in Wilson, NC hospital of "phthisis pulmonalis"; Maplewood Cemetery, Wilson, NC.

Eure, Jethro H.: Private

Enlisted in Co. D on 7/25/1862 in Hertford Co.; resident of Gates Co.; present or accounted for on muster rolls until he transferred on 6/27/1864 to Company D, 2nd NC Cavalry (19th NCST).

Evans, David O.: Private

Enlisted in Co. D on 7/8/1862 in Hertford Co. at age 22; born circa 1840 in Hertford Co., where he resided as a farmer at time of enlistment; son of Freeman and Celia Evans; brother of Peyton H. Evans, also of Co. D; muster rolls indicate that he "deserted" 9/15/1863.

Evans, Meade: Private

Enlisted in Co. D on 7/8/1862 in Hertford Co. at age 18; born 5/18/1844 in Hertford Co.; called "Media" (listed as "Meady" in the 1850 Hertford Co. Census, age five); son of Noah Evans and Mary Cynthia Fairless; farmer; present or accounted for on all extant muster rolls; kept a diary during war and wrote a postwar recollection; married Margaret Evans on Nov. 29, 1872; died 3/11/1908, buried in Evan's Cemetery, Evanstown Rd. (five miles south of Harrellsville), Hertford Co., NC.

Evans, Peyton H.: Private

Enlisted in Co. D on 7/8/1862 in Hertford Co. at age 20; born circa 1842 in Hertford Co., where he resided as a farmer at time of enlistment; son of Freeman and Celia Evans; brother of David O. Evans, also of Co. D; present or accounted for on muster rolls through October 1864.

Meade "Media" Evans, Company D, Hertford County (Ernest L. Evans).

Fairless, Joseph J.: Private

Enlisted in Co. D on 7/8/1862 in Hertford Co. at age 18; born 1843 in Hertford Co., where he resided as a farmer at the time of enlistment; present or accounted for on muster rolls through October 1864; died in 1928, buried in Christian Harbor Church Cemetery, Christian Harbor Rd. (SR 1438), Hertford Co., NC.

Futrell, Benjamin J.: Private

Enlisted in Co. D on 2/27/1863 in Greene Co.; married Catherine Futrell on March 5, 1849 in Northampton Co.; present or accounted for on muster rolls through October 1864.

Futrell, Ira W.: Private

Enlisted in Co. D on 2/27/1863 in Greene Co.; present or accounted for on muster rolls until captured 10/1/1864 near Petersburg, held at Pt. Lookout; paroled and exchanged 3/17/1865 at Aiken's Landing, VA.

Futrell, James W.: Private

Enlisted in Co. D on 7/8/1862 in Hertford Co. at age 25; born in Bertie Co., where he resided as a farmer at the time of enlistment; married Catherine R. Mulden on April 2, 1957 in Northampton Co.; died prior to 2/28/1863.

Futrell, John: Private

Enlisted in Co. D on 7/5/1862 in Hertford Co.; present or accounted for on muster rolls through October 1864.

Garrett, James M.: Private

Enlisted in Co. D on 10/10/1864 "for the war."

Gatling, David C.: Private

Enlisted in Co. D on 7/6/1862 in Hertford Co.; born circa 1837 in Hertford Co., where he resided as a farmer at the time of enlistment; son of David and Milley Gatling; never mustered into service.

Henry Dolphus Godwin, Company D, Hertford County (Samuel L. Vaughan).

Godwin, Henry Dolphus: Corporal

Enlisted in Co. D on 7/8/1862 in Hertford Co. at age 27; born 4/13/1835 in Hertford Co., where he resided as a farmer at the time of enlistment; son of John Sparkman Godwin and Temperance Brown; married two times, first to Marinia Ann Susan Holloman on March 18, 1858 (daughter of Jalon and Judith Holloman), then to Lavenia Arthusa Jones on December 12, 1867 (daughter of Reddin Jones and Celia Belch); captured 5/3/1863 near Fredericksburg; exchanged 5/13/1863 at City Point, VA; recaptured 7/5/1863 in Waterloo, PA, held at Ft. McHenry; transferred 7/9/1863 to Ft. Delaware, 10/18/1863 to Pt. Lookout; paroled and exchanged 3/20/1864 at City Point; AWOL through October 1864; died 4/12/1906, buried Riverside Cemetery, Murfreesboro, NC.

Godwin, Isaac L.: Private

Enlisted in Co. D on 7/5/1862 in Hertford Co. at age 22; born in Hertford Co., where he resided as a farmer at the time of enlistment; "deserted December 15, 1862."

Grant, Jesse B.: Private

Enlisted in Co. D on 7/8/1862 in Northampton Co. at age 23; born in Northampton Co., where he resided as a farmer at the time of enlistment; present or accounted for on muster rolls through October 1864; married twice in Northampton Co., first to Emily B. Wells on January 2, 1866 and then Ella Jane Clary on February 6, 1867.

Grant, Jesse E.: Private

Enlisted in Co. D on 7/8/1862 in Northampton Co. at age 20; born in Northampton Co., where he resided as a farmer at the time of enlistment; present or accounted for on muster rolls through October 1864.

Griffin, Barnes: Private

Transferred to Co. D on 10/1/1862; previously served in Company B, 3rd Battalion NC Light Artillery; "deserted December 15, 1862."

Grizzard, William J.: Private

Enlisted in Co. D on 7/8/1862 in Northampton Co. at age 30; born in Northampton Co., where he resided as a farmer at the time of enlistment; married Martha D. Sumner on October 11, 1859 in Northampton Co.; present or accounted for on muster rolls through October 1864.

Hardy, James W.: Sergeant

Enlisted in Co. D on 9/1/1862 in Northampton Co.; mustered in as a private; appointed sergeant before 2/28/1863; present or accounted for on muster rolls through October 1864.

Hardy, John H.: QM Sergeant

Enlisted in Co. D on 7/8/1862 in Hertford Co. at age 23; born in Bertie Co.; farmer; previously served as a private in Company L, 1st NC Infantry (six months, 1861); mustered in as a private; Aug. 1862 assigned to Field and Staff of regiment detailed as quartermaster sergeant; returned to company Sept./Oct. 1863 and appointed corporal; 1864 "absent assigned to duty in Quartermaster Department, Raleigh, NC"; 2/1865 reported on detail at QM Dept. in Hillsboro, NC; captured 5/5/1865; paroled 5/6/1865 as a private in Raleigh.

Haste, Calvin A.: Private

Enlisted in Co. D on 7/8/1862 in Hertford Co. at age 30; born in Hertford Co., where he resided as a farmer at the time of enlistment; present or accounted for on muster rolls until transferred 10/1/1862 to Company B, 3rd Battalion NC Light Artillery.

Hayes, Elisha D.: Private

Enlisted in Co. D on 7/8/1862 in Hertford Co.; born circa 1834 in Hertford Co., where he resided at the time of enlistment; son of William and Penelope Hayes; 8/9/1862 Rich Square, NC muster roll states "absent sick"; "no further [military] records."

Hayes, Richard Adam: Corporal

Enlisted in Co. D on 7/3/1862 in Hertford Co. at age 22; born 1840 in Hertford Co., where he resided as a farmer at the time of enlistment; son of Methodist Rev. Thomas W. and Nancy Hayes; captured 6/21/1863 in Upperville, VA, held at Old Capitol Prison; paroled and exchanged 6/30/1863 at City Point, VA; Jan./Feb. 1864 appointed corporal; married twice, first to Mary Eleanor "Ella" Montgomery on January 28, 1869 in Hertford Co., then to her sister, Olive Montgomery; died in 1890, buried Montgomery Family Cemetery (at Frazier's Crossroads, junction of NC 561 and SR 1108), Hertford Co., NC.

Higgins, Thomas: Private
    Enlisted in Co. D on 9/8/1862 in Northampton Co.; the May/June 1863 muster roll states "died at Upperville, VA."

Hill, William E.: Private
    Enlisted in Co. D on 7/8/1862 in Hertford Co. at age 29; born in Hertford Co., where he resided as a farmer at the time of enlistment; present or accounted for on muster rolls through October 1864; 10/27/1864 admitted to Richmond hospital; 11/27/1864 furloughed for 60 days.

Hoggard, Joseph J.: Private
    Enlisted in Co. D on 7/8/1862 in Hertford Co. at age 34; born in Hertford Co., where he resided as a farmer at the time of enlistment; captured 6/21/1863 in Upperville, VA, held at Old Capitol Prison; paroled and exchanged 6/30/1863 at City Point, VA; 9/6/1863 deserted.

Holloman, James: Private
    Enlisted in Co. D on 7/5/1862 in Hertford Co. at age 22; born in Hertford Co., where he resided as a farmer at the time of enlistment; previously served as a private in Company D, 17th NC Infantry (1st Organization); deserted 10/3/1862 near Franklin, VA.

Holloman, William D.: Asst. QM
    Enlisted in Co. D on 7/8/1862 in Hertford Co. at age 34; born in Hertford Co., where he resided as a clerk at the time of enlistment; mustered in as a sergeant; transferred 8/16/1862 to Field and Staff of regiment upon appointment as captain, asst. quartermaster; present or accounted for on muster rolls through December 1864; after the war served as a justice of the peace in Hertford Co.

Jester, Charles W.: Private
    Enlisted in Co. D on 8/31/1862 in Southampton Co., VA; present or accounted for on muster rolls through October 1864; admitted 3/30/1865 to Petersburg hospital; captured there 4/3/1865; paroled 5/11/1865; may have previously served as a private in Company C, 17th NC Infantry (2nd Organization).

Jinkens, James P.: Private
    Enlisted in Co. D on 7/3/1862 in Hertford Co.; born in Hertford Co., where he resided as a farmer at the time of enlistment; present or accounted for on muster rolls through December 1863; Jan.–Oct. 1864 reported as a deserter.

Jones, Alexander: Private
    Enlisted in Co. D on 7/8/1862 in Hertford Co.; born in Hertford Co., where he resided as a farmer at the time of enlistment; previously served as a private in Company D, 17th NC Infantry (1st Organization); died 8/1/1864 in Petersburg hospital of "hepatitis acute, typhoid fever."

Jordan, Richard: Private
    Enlisted in Co. D on 9/4/1862 in Northampton Co.; born 11/16/1828; died 11/20/1862, buried in Jordan Family Cemetery, Winton, NC.

Joyner, William J.: Private

Enlisted in Co. D on 7/3/1862 in Hertford Co. at age 33; born in Northampton Co.; farmer; married Caroline Hart on January 1, 1861 in Northampton Co.; present or accounted for on muster rolls through October 1864.

Kidd, William H.: Private

Enlisted in Co. D on 4/28/1864 in Granville Co., NC; present or accounted for on muster rolls through October 1864.

Langston, Kindred D.: Private

Enlisted in Co. D on 7/3/1862 in Hertford Co. at age 24; born circa 1838 in Hertford Co., where he resided as a farmer at the time of enlistment; son of Abner and Jane Langston; wounded in action and captured 6/21/1863 in Upperville, VA, held at Old Capitol Prison; transferred 8/8/1863 to Pt. Lookout; died there 5/6/1864 of "chronic diarrhea"; buried in Confederate Cemetery, Pt. Lookout.

Lassiter, Junius: Private

Enlisted in Co. D on 7/3/1862 in Hertford Co. at age 24; born in Hertford Co., where he resided as a farmer at the time of enlistment; previously served as a Private in Company D, 17th NC Infantry (1st Organization); present or accounted for on muster rolls through October 1864.

Lewis, Daniel W.: 2nd Lieutenant

Enlisted in Co. D on 7/12/1862 in Hertford Co.; born 12/5/1839 in Hertford Co., where he resided at the time of enlistment; son of Watson (merchant) and Sally Lewis; appointed 2nd lieutenant on 8/9/1862 from rank; present or accounted for on muster rolls through January 1865; reported absent on leave after 2/8/1865; doctor; died 5/30/1909, buried Lewis Family Cemetery, NC Highway 903, Martin Co., NC.

Liverman, Albert Joseph: Private

Enlisted in Co. D on 7/5/1862 in Hertford Co. at age 24; born in Hertford Co., where he resided as a farmer at the time of enlistment; previously served as a private in Company D, 17th NC Infantry (1st Organization); captured 7/5/1863 in Waterloo, PA, held at Ft. McHenry; transferred 7/9/1863 to Ft. Delaware; died there 9/15/1863 of "acute dysentery"; buried in the National Cemetery, Finn's Point (Salem), NJ.

Liverman, John H.: Private

Enlisted in Co. D on 7/5/1862 in Hertford Co. at age 32; born in Hertford Co., where he resided as a farmer at the time of enlistment; present or accounted for on muster rolls through October 1864.

Liverman, William T.: Private

Enlisted in Co. D on 9/25/1862 in Southampton Co., VA; born 12/8/1830; first enlisted in 17th NC Infantry, Co. D on 5/22/1861; most of this unit surrendered at Ft. Hatteras on 8/28/1861, but Liverman escaped and joined the 31st NC Infantry, Co. G; then joined 12th Battalion NC Cavalry, Co. A; never reported to this regiment enlisting instead in the 4th NC Cavalry; captured 7/5/1863 in Waterloo, PA, held at Ft. McHenry; transferred 7/9/1863 to Ft. Delaware, 10/15/1863 to Pt. Lookout; February 14–15, 1865 paroled and exchanged at Coxes Landing, James River, VA; present on 2/17/1865 roll of exchanged prisoners at Camp Lee, Richmond; died 3/7/1907, buried Joe P. Austin Cemetery, Hertford Co., NC.

Livingston, John B.: Private

Transferred to Co. D on 7/27/1864; previously served in Company B, 2nd NC Cavalry (19th NCST); present or accounted for on muster rolls through October 1864.

Lowe, Jesse T.: Private

Enlisted in Co. D on 2/9/1863 in Lenoir Co., NC; substitute for Moses E. Newsom; present or accounted for on muster rolls through October 1864; paroled 4/9/1865 at Appomattox Court House.

Mann, Willis: Private

Enlisted in Co. D on 7/5/1862 in Northampton Co. at age 26; born in Northampton Co., where he resided as a farmer at the time of enlistment; married Martha Coggins on June 10, 1862 in Northampton Co.; died 2/27/1864 in Richmond hospital of "typhoid fever."

Marshall, John W.: Private

Enlisted in Co. D on 7/3/1862 in Hertford Co. at age 33; born 1831 in Hertford Co., where he resided as a farmer at the time of enlistment; captured 6/17/1863 in Middleburg, VA, held at Old Capitol Prison; paroled and exchanged 6/30/1863 at City Point, VA; died 1/21/1865 in Raleigh hospital of "pneumonia"; buried Oakwood Cemetery, Raleigh, NC.

Martin, James R.: Private

Enlisted in Co. D on 2/5/1863 in Lenoir Co., NC; captured 6/21/1863 in Upperville, VA, held at Old Capitol Prison; paroled and exchanged 6/30/1863 in City Point, VA; reported on Surgical Cases in CS Hospital, Petersburg for Oct. 1864 stating "Age 20. Gunshot wound left lung, ball remaining, mending October 28, 1864. Returned to duty November 29."

McGlohan, William D.: Private

Enlisted in Co. D on 7/8/1862 in Hertford Co. at age 19; born 11/10/1841 in Hertford Co., where he resided as a farmer at the time of enlistment; son of Luke and Mary McGlohan; present or accounted for on muster rolls through October 1864; died 5/30/1927, buried Holly Springs Baptist Church Cemetery (located off State Road 1400, three miles south of Winton), Hertford Co., NC; last name spelled "McGlaghon" in Winborne's *The Colonial and State History of Hertford County*.

McGuire, Frank: Private

Enlisted in Co. D on 9/6/1862 in Northampton Co.; present or accounted for on muster rolls through October 1864.

Mitchell, Joseph J.: Private

Enlisted in Co. D on 7/5/1862 in Hertford Co. at age 20; born circa 1842 in Hertford Co., where he resided as a farmer at the time of enlistment; son of Miles and Celia M. Mitchell; wounded in action in June 1863 in Upperville, VA; present or accounted for on muster rolls through October 1864.

Morris, Horatio E.: Private

Enlisted in Co. D on 7/8/1862 in Hertford Co. at age 26; born circa 1837 in Hertford Co., where he resided as a farmer at the time of enlistment; son of Noah and Martha Morris; brother of Noah W. Morris, also of Co. D; captured 7/5/1863 in Waterloo, PA, held at Ft. McHenry; transferred 7/9/1863 to Ft. Delaware, 10/15/1863 to Pt. Lookout; died there 2/19/1864 of "chronic diarrhea"; buried in the Confederate Cemetery, Pt. Lookout.

Morris, Noah W.: Private

Enlisted in Co. D on 7/8/1862 in Hertford Co. at age 21; born circa 1843 in Hertford Co., where he resided as a farmer at the time of enlistment; son of Noah and Martha Morris; brother of Horatio E. Morris, also of Co. D; previously served as a private in Company D, 17th NC Infantry (1st Organization); present or accounted for on muster rolls through October 1864.

Nelson, Woodard: Private

Enlisted in Co. D on 7/5/1862 in Northampton Co.; born in Northampton Co., where he resided as a farmer at the time of enlistment; 8/9/1862 Rich Square roll reports him "absent sick"; discharged prior to 2/28/1863.

Newsom(e), Eli: Private

Enlisted in Co. D on 7/8/1862 in Hertford Co. at age 30; born circa 1830 in Hertford Co., where he resided as a farmer at the time of enlistment; son of James and Mary Newsome; captured 7/3/1863 near Gettysburg, PA, held at Ft. Delaware; transferred 10/18/1863 to Pt. Lookout; died there 12/23/1863 of "pneumonia."

Newsom(e), Moses E.: Private

Enlisted in Co. D on 7/8/1862 in Hertford Co.; born circa 1832 in Hertford Co., where he resided as a farmer at the time of enlistment; son of Lemuel and Lavenia Newsom(e); discharged 2/9/1863 upon furnishing Jesse T. Lowe as a substitute.

Norfleet, Edward E.: Private

Enlisted in Co. D on 7/3/1862 in Hertford Co. at age 24; born in Hertford Co., where he resided as a saddler at the time of enlistment; mustered in as a saddler; reduced to ranks March/April 1863; captured 7/5/1863 in Waterloo, PA, held at Ft. McHenry; transferred 7/9/1863 to Ft. Delaware, 10/18/1863 to Pt. Lookout; paroled and exchanged February 14–15, 1865 at Coxes Landing, James River, VA; admitted 2/15/1865 to Richmond hospital.

Norvel, Blount: Private

Enlisted in Co. D on 7/8/1862 in Hertford Co. at age 26; born in Hertford Co., where he resided as a farmer at the time of enlistment; present or accounted for on muster rolls through October 1864.

Norvel, William L.: Private
Enlisted in Co. D on 7/8/1862 in Hertford Co. at age 23; born circa 1838 in Hertford Co., where he resided as a farmer at the time of enlistment; son of John and Liddia Norvel; present or accounted for on muster rolls through October 1864.

Odom, Jethro J.: Private
Enlisted in Co. D on 7/3/1862 in Hertford Co. at age 27; born circa 1836 in Hertford Co., where he resided as a farmer at the time of enlistment; son of Ira (blacksmith) and Nancy Odom; brother of William F. Odom, also of Co. D; present or accounted for on muster rolls through October 1864.

Odom, William F.: Private
Enlisted in Co. D on 7/8/1862 in Hertford Co. at age 24; born circa 1838 in Hertford Co., where he resided as a farmer at the time of enlistment; son of Ira (blacksmith) and Nancy Odom; brother of Jethro J. Odom, also of Co. D; muster rolls from March/April 1864 through August 1864 detailed as regimental blacksmith; present or accounted for on muster rolls through October 1864.

Outland, Richard Garner: Private
Enlisted in Co. D on 8/18/1862 in Northampton Co.; born 7/3/1844; son of Isaac Outland and Silvia Bridgers; wife Sarah; present or accounted for on muster rolls through October 1864; died of "tuberculosis of bowells [sic]" 10/9/1920; buried Liverman Graveyard, Murfreesboro, NC.

Overton, Andrew A. J.: Private
Enlisted in Co. D on 7/5/1862 in Hertford Co. at age 35; born in Hertford Co., where he resided as a farmer at the time of enlistment; muster rolls from March/April 1863–December 1863 list him as detailed in the Ambulance Corps; "deserted December 1863."

Overton, Freeman: Private
Enlisted in Co. D on 6/28/1862 in Hertford Co. at age 24; born circa 1837 in Hertford Co., where he resided as a merchant at the time of enlistment; son of William and Charlotte Overton; died 11/23/1862 in Petersburg hospital of "typhoid fever."

Overton, William A.: Private
Enlisted in Co. D on 7/18/1862 in Hertford Co.; 12/15/1862 deserted; may have previously served in as a private in Company D, 17th NC Infantry (1st Organization).

Parker, Benjamin T.: Private
Enlisted in Co. D on 7/8/1862 in Hertford Co.; born in Hertford Co., where he resided as a farmer at the time of enlistment; "Deserted December 1863"; may have previously served as a private in Company D, 17th NC Infantry (1st Organization).

Parker, James A.: Private

Enlisted in Co. D on 7/3/1862 in Hertford Co.; born in Hertford Co., where he resided at the time of enlistment; son of Abram and Harriet Parker; farmer; the 8/9/1862 Rich Square muster roll states "discharged on account of hernia"; married Susie A. Langston on January 25, 1872 in Hertford Co.

Parker, John A.: Corporal

Enlisted in Co. D on 7/5/1862 in Hertford Co. at age 27; born in Northampton Co.; farmer; July 8–Oct. 21, 1863 roll states "wounded on furlough at home"; present or accounted for on muster rolls through December 1863.

Parker, Orrin: Private

Enlisted in Co. D on 7/5/1862 in Hertford Co.; born in Hertford Co., where he resided as a farmer at the time of enlistment; 8/9/1862 Rich Square roll states "absent on leave"; "no further [military] records."

Perry, John D.: Sergeant

Enlisted in Co. D on 7/8/1862 in Hertford Co. at age 19; on 10/24/1861 commissioned captain in the 6th Regiment, 2nd Brigade, NC Confederate Militia; born in Hertford Co., where he resided as a farmer at the time of enlistment; present or accounted for on muster rolls through October 1864.

Pierce, Cincinnatus: Private

Enlisted in Co. D on 6/30/1862 in Hertford Co. at age 34; born circa 1828 in Hertford Co., where he resided as a farmer at the time of enlistment; wife, Milly; present or accounted for on muster rolls until he transferred on 9/3/1862 to Company C, 2nd NC Cavalry (19th NCST).

Pugh, George A.: Private

Enlisted in Co. D on 5/10/1864 in Perquimans Co., NC; present or accounted for on muster rolls through October 1864.

Rainey, James F.: Private

Enlisted in Co. D on 8/18/1862 in Northampton Co.; captured 7/12/1863 in Hagerstown, MD, held at Pt. Lookout; paroled and exchanged 3/6/1864 in City Point, VA; present or accounted for on muster rolls through October 1864.

Roundtree, Abner J.: Private

Enlisted in Co. D on 7/6/1862 in Bertie Co. at age 27; born circa 1834 in Bertie Co., where he resided as a farmer at the time of enlistment; married Mary Ann Lambertson on December 23, 1858 in Bertie Co.; present or accounted for on muster rolls through October 1864.

Ruffin, Thomas: 1st Lieutenant

Transferred to Co. D on 7/12/1862; previously served in Company A, 3rd Battalion NC Light Artillery; appointed 1st lieutenant on 8/9/1862 from rank; captured 7/4/1863 at South Mountain, PA, held at Ft. McHenry; transferred 7/10/1863 to Ft.

Delaware, 7/18/1863 to Johnson's Island; died 9/23/1864 at Johnson's Island and "buried on Island."

Russell, James T.: Private

Enlisted in Co. D on 9/4/1862 in Northampton Co.; present or accounted for on muster rolls through October 1864; 2/24/1865 received as a "deserter" by the provost marshal, Norfolk, VA; took Oath of Allegiance and retained.

Scott, Charles A.: Ordnance Sergeant

Enlisted in Co. D on 6/23/1862 in Hertford Co. at age 23; born in Norfolk, VA; gentleman; mustered in as an ordnance sergeant; wounded in action 6/21/1863 at Jack's Shop, VA; 11/23/1864 retired to Invalid Corps.

Sharp, William: Captain

Enlisted in Co. D on 7/12/1862 in Hertford Co.; born circa 1840 in Hertford Co., where he resided at the time of enlistment; son of Jacob (II) and Elizabeth Sharp; his brothers, Thomas H. Sharp and Henry Clay Sharp, also served in the CSA; appointed captain 8/9/1862 from rank; captured 7/5/1863 at Jack's Mtn., PA, held at Ft. Delaware; transferred 7/18/1863 to Johnson's Island; transferred 4/22/1864 to Pt. Lookout, 6/23/1864 back to Ft. Delaware; paroled 10/30/1864; exchanged 11/15/1864 at Venus Pt., Savannah River, GA; paroled in Greensboro, NC in 1865; he was a lawyer and after the war served as the county attorney for Hertford Co. 1865–1866; died in Charleston , SC.

Shaw, William P.: 3rd Lieutenant

Enlisted in Co. D on 7/8/1862 in Hertford Co. at age 18; born 10/13/1842 in Winton, NC (Hertford Co.) where he resided as a farmer at the time of enlistment; son of William and Matilda Shaw; mustered in as a corporal; appointed 3rd lieutenant on 11/1/1863; present or accounted for on muster rolls through October 1864; married Mollie R. Askew on September 29, 1869 in Hertford Co.; "prominent in church and state affairs of Hertford Co." after the war served as a member of the general assembly for the First Senatorial District from 1886–1889; died 11/27/1913, buried in the John O. Askew Family Cemetery, NC Highway 561, Hertford Co., NC.

Spiers, Duglass: Private

Enlisted in Co. D on 7/8/1862 in Hertford Co.; name also appears as "Spires"; born circa 1843 in Hertford Co., where he resided as a student at the time of enlistment; son of B. T. and Margaret Spiers; the 8/9/1862 Rich Square muster roll states "absent sick"; "no further [military] records."

Stevenson, John L.: Private

Enlisted in Co. D on 7/3/1862 in Hertford Co. at age 32; born in Northampton Co.; died 7/13/1864 in Petersburg hospital.

Stevenson, Thomas B.: Private

Enlisted in Co. D on 2/5/1863 in Lenoir Co., NC; present or accounted for on muster rolls through October 1864.

Taylor, Atlas S.: Sergeant

Enlisted in Co. D on 7/8/1862 in Northampton Co. at age 23; born in Northampton Co., where he resided as a farmer at the time of enlistment; present or accounted for on muster rolls until captured on 10/1/1864 near Petersburg, held at Pt. Lookout; released 6/21/1865 after taking Oath of Allegiance.

Taylor, Caleb: Private

Enlisted in Co. D on 2/20/1863 in Northampton Co.; deserted after April 1863.

Teaster, Jesse Joseph: Private

Enlisted in Co. D on 2/2063 in Hertford Co.; born on February 14, 1825 in North Carolina; son of William and Martha Teaster; wife, Celia; present or accounted for on muster rolls through October 1864; paroled 4/9/1865 at Appomattox Court House; after the war, returned to the St. John's area of Hertford Co. and farmed; he died on January 20, 1883 and is buried in the Teaster Family Cemetery, Hertford Co., NC.

Terry, Richard J.: Private

Enlisted in Co. D on 7/8/1862 in Hertford Co.; born in Northampton Co.; farmer; captured 7/4/1863 at South Mtn., held at Ft. McHenry; transferred 7/9/1863 to Ft. Delaware, 10/22/1863 to Pt. Lookout; paroled and exchanged 1/21/1865 at Boulware's Wharf, James River, VA; present on 1/26/1865 roll of exchanged prisoners at Camp Lee, Richmond.

Thompson, Mitchel: Private

Enlisted in Co. D; captured 7/3/1863 near Gettysburg, PA, held at Ft. Delaware; died there 11/14/1863 of "smallpox"; buried in the National Cemetery, Finn's Point (Salem), NJ.

Tyler, Luther R.: Private

Enlisted in Co. D on 7/8/1862 in Hertford Co. at age 19; born in Bertie Co.; farmer; captured 6/19/1863 in Middleburg, VA, held at Old Capitol Prison; paroled and exchanged 6/30/1863 at City Point, VA; admitted 11/29/1864 to Danville, VA hospital with "febris cont."; returned to duty 1/3/1865.

Vaughan, Jesse J.: Private

Enlisted in Co. D on 7/6/1862 in Hertford Co.; born circa 1828 in Northampton Co.; son of John D. L. Vaughan and Sarah "Sally" Edwards; married Martha Parker on September 28, 1854 in Northampton Co.; farmer at the time of enlistment; wounded in action on 6/10/1863 in Upperville, VA; family oral history states that he was wounded in both the ear and leg; present or accounted for on muster rolls through October 1864; died on February 17, 1897 in Hertford Co.

Wade, Henry R.: Private

Enlisted in Co. D on 7/8/1862 in Northampton Co. at age 32; born 1832 in Northampton Co., where he resided as a farmer at the time of enlistment; married Mary Grant on January 24, 1855 in Northampton Co.; present or accounted for on muster rolls through September 1863; AWOL after September 1863; died 9/22/1902 in Raleigh, buried Oakwood Cemetery, Raleigh, NC.

Whitehead, Micajah: Private
Enlisted in Co. D on 7/5/1862 in Perquimans Co., NC at age 37; born in Halifax Co.; merchant; mustered in as a corporal; promoted May/June 1863 to sergeant; reduced to corporal in July/Aug. 1863; reduced to ranks Sept./Oct. 1863; reappointed corporal in Jan./Feb. 1864; present or accounted for on muster rolls through October 1864; on 4/21/1865 received as a "rebel deserter" by provost marshal general, Washington, DC, giving rank as private; furnished transportation to Plymouth, NC.

Williams, James R.: Private
Enlisted in Co. D on 8/20/1862 in Northampton Co.; present or accounted for on muster rolls through October 1864.

Woodard, John: Private
Enlisted in Co. D on 7/8/1862 in Northampton Co. at age 27; born July 1837 in Northampton Co., where he resided as a farmer at the time of enlistment; son of James and Mary Woodard; present or accounted for on muster rolls through August 1864; married Sarah Parker Whitehorne; died 1904; buried at "Old Place" Woodard Farm, Pendleton, NC (Northampton Co.).

Company E

Alexander, Francis E.: Private
Enlisted in Co. E on 7/7/1862 in Mecklenburg Co. at age 24; resident of Mecklenburg Co. at the time of enlistment; previously served as a private in Company C, 1st NC Infantry (6 months, 1861); captured 7/4/1863 at South Mtn., held at Ft. McHenry; transferred 7/9/1863 to Ft. Delaware; released 6/19/1865 after taking Oath of Allegiance.

Allen, John: Private
Enlisted in Co. E on 7/7/1862 in Cabarrus Co. at age 29; resident of Cabarrus Co. at the time of enlistment; 6/2/1864 deserted at Bermuda Hundred, VA; 6/11/1864 took Oath of Amnesty.

Armstrong, G. Stanhope: Private
Enlisted in Co. E on 7/7/1862 in Mecklenburg Co.; "Captured Wilmington, NC"; present or accounted for on muster rolls through August 1864; received 4/21/1865 by provost marshal general, Defenses North of Potomac, "transportation ordered to Wilmington, NC."

Barbee, George: Private
Enlisted in Co. E on 7/7/1862 in Mecklenburg Co.; resident of Stanly Co., NC at the time of enlistment; "present or accounted for on company muster rolls from January through October 1864"; captured 4/3/1865 near Petersburg, held at Hart's Island, NY Harbor; released 6/1/1865 after taking Oath of Allegiance.

Barbee, Jonah (Jonas): Private

Enlisted in Co. E on 7/7/1862 in Mecklenburg Co.; born 1845; son of Benjamin and Matilda Barbee; cousin to Noah Barbee and George Barbee, also of Co. E; "present or accounted for on company muster rolls from January through October 1864"; paroled 5/20/1865 in Charlotte, NC; married Mary C. Tucker in Cabarrus Co., bond dated 1/24/1867; died before 1886.

Barbee, Noah: Private

Enlisted in Co. E on 7/7/1862 in Mecklenburg Co.; present or accounted for on muster rolls through August 1864.

Barnett, John T.: Private

Enlisted in Co. E on 7/7/1862 in Mecklenburg Co. at age 16; "Deserted 10 December 1862"; "Deserted to the enemy, and was shot by them as a deserter from their service."

Barnhardt, Charles: Private

Enlisted in Co. E on 5/16/1862 in Cabarrus Co. at age 30; married Milly L. C. McGraw on December 30, 1857 in Cabarrus Co.; May/June 1863 muster roll states "deceased last May"; July/August 1863 roll states "died on furlough."

Beattie, James O.: Private

Enlisted in Co. E on 7/7/1862 in Mecklenburg Co.; born April 30, 1823; last name also appears as "Beaty" in records; present or accounted for on muster rolls through October 1864; died July 30, 1890 and buried in the Pisgah Presbyterian Church Cemetery in Gastonia, NC.

Bender, J. H.: Private

Enlisted in Co. E; resident of Mecklenburg Co. at the time of enlistment; captured 4/3/1865 on Appomattox River, VA, held at Hart's Island, NY; released 6/19/1865 after taking Oath of Allegiance.

Benson, Henry A.: Private

Enlisted in Co. E on 7/7/1862 in Mecklenburg Co.; present or accounted for on muster rolls through October 1864.

Biggers, Alison H. C.: Private

Enlisted in Co. E on 8/13/1862 in Mecklenburg Co. at age 28; captured 7/4/1863 at South Mtn., held at Ft. McHenry; transferred 7/9/1863 to Ft. Delaware; died there 1/29/1865 of "apoplexy"; buried in the National Cemetery, Finn's Point (Salem) NJ.

Biggers, John: Private

Enlisted in Co. E on 8/13/1862 in Mecklenburg Co.; resident of Union Co. at the time of enlistment; present or accounted for on muster rolls through August 1864; admitted 12/26/1864 to Raleigh hospital with "debilitas"; returned to duty 12/6/1864.

Biggers, Robert W.: Private

Transferred to Co. E on 5/15/1863; previously served in Company F, 1st NC Cavalry (9th NCST); present or accounted for on muster rolls through October 1864; captured 4/3/1865 on Appomattox River, VA, held at Hart's Island, NY; released 6/19/1865 after taking Oath of Allegiance.

Biggers, William D.: Private

Enlisted in Co. E on 7/7/1862 in Mecklenburg Co.; born 11/20/1841; present or accounted for on muster rolls until captured 8/19/1864 on the Weldon RR, held at Pt. Lookout; paroled and exchanged 2/18/1865 at Aiken's Landing, VA; died 7/1/1899, buried Lexington City Cemetery, Lexington, NC.

Blackwelder, Daniel C.: Private

Enlisted in Co. E on 7/7/1862 in Mecklenburg Co. at age 27; wounded in action in October 1863 during Bristoe Campaign; present or accounted for on muster rolls through October 1864; paroled 4/9/1865 at Appomattox Court House.

Blythe, William: Private

Enlisted in Co. E on 8/13/1862 in Mecklenburg Co. at age 22; July 7–October 31, 1862 roll states "Not reported. Gone as conscript."

Boger, Martin Luther: Private

Enlisted in Co. E in September 1864 in Cabarrus Co.; born 1/11/1844; married A. E. Orchard on July 31, 1866 in Cabarrus Co.; died 4/1/1921, buried St. Martins Lutheran Church, NC Highway 200, Cabarrus Co., NC.

Bost, Henry Manilus: Private

Enlisted in Co. E on 3/1/1863 in Cabarrus Co. at age 18; born 11/10/1844; son of Frederick Bost and Caroline Faggart; resident of Cabarrus Co.; transferred 5/15/1863 to Company F, 1st NC Cavalry (9th NCST); wounded in action on 5/29/1864 in Ashland, VA; family history states lost leg; married Christina Dry Vickers, bond dated 11/9/1865; farmer and gold miner after war near Gold Hill, NC; died 8/30/1908, buried Cold Springs Methodist Church Cemetery, Township 11, Cabarrus County.

Bost, James K. Polk: Private

Enlisted in Co. E on 7/7/1862 in Mecklenburg Co.; son of Simon Bost and Jemina Holton; baptized 2/27/1845 at St. John's Lutheran Church; resident of Cabarrus Co. at the time of enlistment; present or accounted for on muster rolls through October 1864; captured 4/3/1865 near Petersburg, held at Hart's Island, NY; released 6/19/1865 after taking Oath of Allegiance.

Bost, Moses: Private

Enlisted in Co. E on 7/7/1862 in Mecklenburg Co.; born 5/28/1823, baptized same day at St. John's Lutheran Church; son of Paul Bost; married Melissa File on May 18, 1850 in Cabarrus Co.; present or accounted for on muster rolls through October 1864; died April 27, 1896, buried in the St. John's Lutheran Church Cemetery in Cabarrus Co.

Bost, Solomon Cicero: Private
Enlisted in Co. E on 7/7/1862 in Mecklenburg Co.; born 12/15/1844; son of Daniel Bost; married M. J. Furr on February 15, 1866 in Cabarrus Co.; present or accounted for on muster rolls through October 1864; died 7/6/1917, buried St. Martins Lutheran Church, NC Highway 200, Cabarrus Co., NC.

Boyd, T. B.: Private
Enlisted in Co. E; born circa 1837 in Mecklenburg Co.; listed on Aug. 6, 1862 Charlotte *Daily Observer* muster roll as "dec'd"; "Tribute of Respect" obituary from company appears in Aug. 7, 1862 Charlotte *Daily Observer*—listed as "Dr. T. B. Boyd"; also served in Company C, 1st NC Infantry (six months in 1861).

Broadstreet, Joseph Rawles: Private
Enlisted in Co. E on 8/14/1862 in Mecklenburg Co. at age 16; born in Jackson, VA; farmer; captured 11/9/1863 in Stephensburg, VA, held at Old Capitol Prison; transferred 2/3/1864 to Pt. Lookout; 2/13/1864 joined US service, mustered into Company E, 1st Regiment US Volunteer Infantry, Norfolk, VA; married Clara Amanda Josephine "Josie" Fleming in Bartow Co., GA on Sept. 20, 1874; settled in Texas; died in Wheeler Co., TX on Dec. 5, 1925.

Browning, James M.: Private
Enlisted in Co. E on 7/10/1862 in Mecklenburg Co. at age 17; deserted 12/15/1862.

Bryce, John Y.: Captain
Enlisted in Co. E on 7/7/1862 in Mecklenburg Co.; resident of Mecklenburg Co. at the time of enlistment; wounded in action on 11/27/1863; reported absent wounded until 3/27/1865 when he retired to the Invalid Corps; paroled 5/15/1865 in Charlotte.

Bryce, Robert S.: 1st Lieutenant
Enlisted in Co. E on 7/14/1862 in Mecklenburg Co. at age 22; previously served as 1st lieutenant in Company B, 1st NC Infantry (six months, 1861); killed on 9/22/1863.

Bryce, William H.: 3rd Lieutenant
Enlisted in Co. E on 5/14/1862 in Mecklenburg Co. at age 20; mustered in as a 1st sergeant; 3/1/1864 appointed 3rd lieutenant ; present or accounted for on muster rolls through August 1864; 10/5/1864 admitted to Danville, VA hospital with "abscesses left leg"; 10/6/1864 furloughed for 40 days; absent on leave through February 1865.

Burns, Richard: Private
Enlisted in Co. E on 6/25/1862 in Cabarrus Co. at age 24; the July 7–October 31, 1862 roll states "Not reported. Gone as conscript."

Burris, R.: Private
Listed on August 6, 1862 *Daily Bulletin* muster roll for Co. E.

Carriker, Solomon C.: Private
Enlisted in Co. E on 7/7/1862 in Cabarrus Co. at age 32; married Elizabeth Daniels on February 20, 1851; listed on Aug. 6, 1862 *Daily Bulletin* muster roll as "S. C. Canker"; present or accounted for on muster rolls through October 1864.

Carson, John L.: Private
Enlisted in Co. E on 7/5/1862 in Gaston Co. at age 17; born 1845; mustered in as a corporal; listed as 3rd corporal on Aug. 6, 1862 *Daily Bulletin* muster roll; reduced to ranks July/August 1863; present or accounted for on muster rolls through October 1864; buried Dallas Presbyterian Church, Dallas, NC.

Cauble, Henry: Private
Enlisted in Co. E on 5/17/1862 in Rowan Co. at age 27; residing in Rowan Co. as a carpenter at the time of enlistment; present or accounted for on muster rolls through August 1864; captured 10/27/1864 near Petersburg, held at Pt. Lookout; released 5/15/1865 after taking Oath of Allegiance.

Cauble, John: Private
Enlisted in Co. E on 5/9/1862 in Rowan Co. at age 41; born 10/4/1820; resident of Rowan Co. at the time of enlistment; mustered in as a corporal; wounded in action on 7/4/1863; reduced to ranks March/April 1864 while absent wounded; 6/9/1865 took Oath of Allegiance in Salisbury, NC; died 1902, buried Gold Hill Methodist Church, St. Stephens Church Rd., Rowan Co., NC.

Clay, James M.: Private
Enlisted in Co. E on 7/7/1862 in Mecklenburg Co.; born in Cabarrus Co.; farmer; captured 7/4/1863 at South Mtn., held at Ft. McHenry; transferred 7/9/1863 to Ft. Delaware, 10/22/1863 to Pt. Lookout; 2/22/1864 joined US service, 5/1/1864 mustered into Company A, 1st Regiment US Volunteer Infantry, Norfolk, VA.

Cline, Henry B.: Private
Enlisted in Co. E on 5/16/1862 in Cabarrus Co. at age 34; captured 6/13/1864 near City Point, VA, held at Pt. Lookout; transferred 7/9/1864 to Elmira, NY; died there 5/28/1865 of "pneumonia"; buried in Woodlawn National Cemetery (Elmira Prison Graveyard), Elmira, NY.

Cline, Wilson Davis: Private
Enlisted in Co. E on 7/7/1862 in Cabarrus Co.; born 5/10/1834; resident of Cabarrus Co. at the time of enlistment; married Elisabeth Joiner, bond dated 7/19/1852 in Cabarrus Co.; present or accounted for on muster rolls through October 1864; died 8/10/1897, buried St. Paul's Methodist Church Cemetery, NC Highway 200, Township 9, Cabarrus Co., NC.

Coster, C.: Private
Listed on an Aug. 6, 1862 *Daily Bulletin* muster roll for Co. E.

Cox, Jesse D.: Private
Enlisted in Co. E on 3/15/1863 in Cabarrus Co.; born 3/3/1827; married Lucy

Ann Hartsell, bond dated 11/1/1848 in Cabarrus Co.; brother-in-law of Nimrod Hartsell, also of Company E; present or accounted for on muster rolls through October 1864; died 10/9/1911, buried in Center Grove Methodist Church Cemetery, Township 9, Cabarrus Co., NC.

Craig, Alexander: Private
Enlisted in Co. E on 7/10/1862 in Mecklenburg Co. at age 16; present or accounted for on muster rolls through June 1864.

Cross, Daniel B.: Private
Enlisted in Co. E on 11/1/1862 in Mecklenburg Co.; present or accounted for on muster rolls through February 1864.

Cruse, Peter: Private
Enlisted in Co. E on 4/15/1862 in Cabarrus Co.; born 2/2/1827; son of John Cruse and Sophia Heilig Duke; married Mary Ann Hartman, bond dated 11/8/1847 in Cabarrus Co.; resident of Cabarrus Co. at the time of enlistment; present or accounted for on muster rolls through October 1864; captured 4/3/1865 near Petersburg, held at Hart's Island, NY; released 6/19/1865 after taking Oath of Allegiance; died 7/13/1887, buried Organ Lutheran Church Cemetery, Rowan County.

Davidson, James F.: Sergeant
Enlisted in Co. E on 7/7/1862 in Mecklenburg Co. at age 26; mustered in as a 1st corporal; listed as "J. Y. Davidson" on Aug. 6, 1862 Charlotte *Daily Bulletin* muster roll; promoted to sergeant before 2/28/1863; captured 6/19/1863 in Middleburg, VA, held at Old Capitol Prison; present or accounted for on muster rolls through October 1864; paroled and exchanged 6/30/1863 in City Point, VA; paroled 4/15/1865 in Lynchburg, VA; also served in the 1st NC Infantry, Company B (six months, 1861).

Davis, George C.: Private
Enlisted in Co. E on 7/5/1862 in Mecklenburg Co. at age 28; 7/8/1864 detailed in the Quartermaster Department for 60 days; present or accounted for on muster rolls through August 1864; paroled 5/12/1865 in Charlotte, NC.

Davis, James F.: Private
Enlisted in Co. E on 3/15/1863 in Mecklenburg Co.; captured 7/4/1863 at South Mtn., held at Ft. McHenry; transferred 7/9/1863 to Ft. Delaware, October 1863 to Pt. Lookout; paroled and exchanged 3/20/1864 in City Point, VA; present or accounted for on muster rolls through August 1864; paroled 5/9/1865 in Greensboro, NC.

Davis, John B.: Sergeant
Enlisted in Co. E on 5/9/1862 in Rowan Co. at age 26; born 1836; mustered in as a sergeant; captured 6/21/1863 in Upperville, VA, held at Old Capitol Prison; paroled and exchanged 6/30/1863 in City Point, VA; present or accounted for on muster rolls through October 1864; paroled 5/2/1865 in Salisbury, NC; buried Abbots Creek Baptist Church, Abbots Creek Church Rd., Davidson Co., NC.

Davis, John D.: Private
        Enlisted in Co. E on 7/5/1862 in Mecklenburg Co. at age 32; March/April 1864–September 1864 detailed at Fayetteville Arsenal and Armory; assigned to Company G, 2nd Battalion NC Local Defense Troops, while at armory.

Davis, Wallace E.: Private
        Transferred to Co. E on 7/21/1864; previously served as a private in Company F, 1st NC Cavalry (9th NCST); present or accounted for on company muster rolls through October 1864; paroled 4/16/1865 in Lynchburg, VA.

Dempster, John: Private
        Enlisted in Co. E on 7/7/1862 in Mecklenburg Co. at age 42; born 1820; killed in action on 7/4/1863 in Monterey, PA; buried Oakwood Cemetery, Raleigh, NC.

Dulin, Cyrus Q.: Private
        Enlisted in Co. E on 5/14/1862 in Mecklenburg Co. at age 31; died 2/8/1863 of "typhoid fever."

Dulin, Elias: Private
        Enlisted in Co. E on 8/1/1862 in Mecklenburg Co. at age 19; killed in action on 12/16/1862 in Whitehall, NC.

Endy, Paul: Private
        Enlisted in Co. E on 7/7/1862 in Cabarrus Co. at age 34; born August 2, 1829; present or accounted for on muster rolls through October 1864; died on July 8, 1902 and buried in the Rocky River Presbyterian Church Cemetery in Cabarrus Co.

Evans, George H. W.: Private
        Enlisted in Co. E; born 12/1/1835; died 2/5/1917, buried Oakwood Cemetery, Raleigh, NC (not found in roster of 4th NC Cavalry; information from military headstone).

Faggert, Daniel Cicero: Private
        Enlisted in Co. E on 4/15/1863 in Cabarrus Co.; born 2/23/1826; baptized St. John's Lutheran Church; son of John Faggart and Elizabeth Hartsell; married Rebecca House, bond dated 3/24/1851; present or accounted for on muster rolls through October 1864; 11/23/1864 furloughed from Richmond hospital for 60 days; admitted 1/17/1865 to Charlotte hospital with gunshot wound to "lower extremities left"; returned to duty 2/4/1865; died 5/22/1904, buried St. John's Lutheran Church Cemetery, Township 4, Cabarrus County.

Falls, William A.: Private
        Enlisted in Co. E on 4/1/1863 in Gaston Co., NC; present or accounted for on muster rolls through October 1864; buried Pisgah Presbyterian Church, Gastonia, NC.

File, John F.: Private
        Enlisted in Co. E on 4/15/1863 in Cabarrus Co.; resident of Cabarrus Co. at the time of enlistment; wounded (in leg) and captured 7/4/1863 at South Mtn., held

at Ft. McHenry; transferred 7/9/1863 to Ft. Delaware; released 6/19/1865 after taking Oath of Allegiance.

Finks, Simon Peter: Private

Enlisted in Co. E on 7/7/1862 in Cabarrus Co. at age 27; wounded in action on 6/21/1863 in Upperville, VA (wounded through the body, died in hospital).

Fisher, Caleb A.: Private

Enlisted in Co. E on 4/15/1863 in Cabarrus Co.; born 12/23/1827; baptized St. John's Lutheran Church; son of Daniel Fisher and Leah Faggart; married Martha A. Meanes, bond dated 12/17/1850 in Cabarrus Co.; captured 6/13/1864 near City Point, VA, held at Pt. Lookout; transferred 7/9/1864 to Elmira, NY; released 6/11/1865 after taking Oath of Allegiance; died 1/23/1900, buried Trinity Lutheran Church Cemetery, Township 4, Cabarrus County.

Flowers, Green F.: Private

Enlisted in Co. E on 5/10/1862 in Mecklenburg Co. at age 39; born 3/26/1821; captured 7/5/1863 in Monterey Springs, PA, held at Ft. Delaware; paroled and exchanged 4/30/1864 in City Point, VA; admitted 5/1/1864 to Richmond hospital with "rheumatismos chronic"; 5/6/1864 furloughed for 60 days; died 10/24/1895, buried Flowers Family Cemetery, Spencer Mountain Rd., Gaston Co., NC.

Floyd, William: Private

Enlisted in Co. E on 7/7/1862 in Mecklenburg Co.; present or accounted for on muster rolls March through August 1864; admitted 10/28/1864 to Richmond hospital; furloughed 11/18/1864 for 60 days.

Foard, E. M.: Private

Enlisted in Co. E on 7/7/1862 in Cabarrus Co.; present or accounted for on muster rolls through October 1864; captured 4/3/1865 near Petersburg, held at Hart's Island, NY; released 6/19/1865 after taking Oath of Allegiance.

Furr, Adam Monroe: Private

Enlisted in Co. E on 7/7/1862 in Cabarrus Co. at age 20; born 10/29/1841; son of Daniel Furr and Sophia Widenhouse; brother to Daniel Caleb Furr and first cousin of Allen Furr, both also in Co. E; captured 7/4/1863 at South Mtn., held at Ft. McHenry; transferred 7/9/1863 to Ft. Delaware, 10/22/1863 to Pt. Lookout; died there 1/28/1864 of an "incise wound," "killed in an affray"; buried in Confederate Cemetery, Pt. Lookout; memorial stone in Center Grove Methodist Church, Cabarrus Co., NC.

Furr, Allen: Private

Enlisted in Co. E on 6/14/1862 in Cabarrus Co. at age 42; born 7/24/1820; son of Paul Furr II and Rosinah Peck; married Eva "Eavy" A. Fink; CSA muster rolls show him present and accounted for through October 1864; family legend states that he "possessed great physical strength, reportedly he could lift a 50 gallon keg of liquor with his bare hands and drink from the spout"; first cousin of Adam M. Furr and

Daniel Caleb Furr, and uncle of Martin Luther Furr, Mathias Wilson Furr, and William Martin Furr, all of Co. E; died on 12/12/1879, buried Center Grove Methodist Church Cemetery, Township 9, Cabarrus County.

Furr, Daniel Caleb: Private

Enlisted in Co. E on 7/7/1862 in Cabarrus Co. at age 28; son of Daniel Furr and Sophia Widenhouse; brother of Adam M. Furr and first cousin of Allen Furr, both also in Co. E; married twice, first to Sarah Ann Clay, bond dated 11/29/1848 in Cabarrus Co.; then to Mary Ann Furr 2/12/1857 also in Cabarrus Co.; CSA muster rolls show him present and accounted for through October 1864.

Furr, Darling: Private

Enlisted in Co. E on 5/16/1862 in Cabarrus Co. at age 31; married twice, first to Elizabeth McDaniel, bond dated 6/7/1855 in Cabarrus Co.; then to Margaret McDaniel, bond dated 9/21/1865 also in Cabarrus Co.; paroled 5/18/1865 in Charlotte, NC; present or accounted for on muster rolls through October 1864.

Furr, John: Private

Listed on an Aug. 6, 1862 Charlotte *Daily Bulletin* muster roll for Co. E.

Furr, Martin L.: Private

Enlisted in Co. E on 7/7/1862 in Cabarrus Co. at age 18; mustered in as a private; appointed corporal March/April 1864; captured 4/3/1865 near Petersburg, held at Hart's Island, NY; released 6/19/1865 after taking Oath of Allegiance.

Furr, Martin Luther: Corporal

Enlisted in Co. E on 7/7/1862 in Cabarrus Co. at age 20; born 12/4/1842; son of Paul P. Furr and Eve Efird; married Catherine Dry; "discharged" before 10/31/1862; after the war became a very successful farmer near Mount Holly; his "plantation had its own granary, orchards and bee hives"; family lore recalls that he "was a dapper dresser, preferring black silk suits to coveralls." Died in June 1923, buried Greenwood Cemetery, Belmont, NC.

Furr, Mathias Wilson: Private

Enlisted in Co. E on 7/7/1862 in Cabarrus Co.; born 3/24/1832; son of W. Mathias (Tise) Furr and Mary (Polly) Page; his uncle Allen Furr also served in Co. E; married four times, first to Lovina Smith on 11/18/1852; second to Louisa Stallins, bond dated 10/23/1858; third to Ann Motley, and fourth to Louisa Snuggs; resident of Cabarrus Co. at the time of enlistment; captured 4/3/1865 on Appomattox River, VA, held at Hart's Island, NY; released 6/19/1865 after taking Oath of Allegiance; died 5/18/1893, buried in Furr Family Graveyard (near the Teeter Farm), Township 9, Cabarrus Co., NC.

Furr, William: Private

Enlisted in Co. E on 7/7/1862 in Cabarrus Co. at age 28; AWOL May 1863–August 1864; admitted 7/6/1864 to Richmond hospital with "scorbutus"; 8/7/1864 sent to Castle Thunder Prison, Richmond; readmitted 9/15/1864 to hospital with "febris int. tert."; 9/24/1864 returned to Castle Thunder Prison; readmitted 1/18/1865 to hospital with "typhoid pneumonia" and "died January 23, 1865."

Furr, William W.: Private

Enlisted in Co. E on 7/7/1862 in Mecklenburg Co.; present or accounted for on muster rolls through October 1864; admitted 3/27/1865 to Petersburg hospital with "rubiola"; captured there 4/3/1865; transferred 4/5/1865 to General Hospital, Point of Rocks, VA; admitted there 4/9/1865.

Gadd, Drury W.: Private

Enlisted in Co. E; married Martha H. Martin on 9/3/1860 in Cabarrus Co.; listed as "D. W. Gadd" on Aug. 6, 1862 Charlotte *Daily Bulletin* muster roll; also listed on Milton's infantry regiment muster roll.

Gadd, Robert: 1st Lieutenant

Enlisted in Co. E on 6/12/1862 in Cabarrus Co.; born c. 1833 in Great Britain; resident of Cabarrus Co. at the time of enlistment; miner and agent; wife, Mary A. Gadd; on 9/22/1863 appointed 1st lieutenant; 9/8/1864 submitted resignation stating that he was "a subject of Great Britain" and that his "father has recently deceased in England and left him heir to considerable property"; 8/19/1864 resignation officially accepted; his father, William Gadd, Sr. was apparently not dead according to the 1870 US Census; Gadd ran the Reed Gold Mine after the war; died 7/16/1908, buried Elmwood Cemetery (CS Section), Charlotte, NC.

Gatlin, George W.: Private

Enlisted in Co. E on 8/28/1862 in Mecklenburg Co. at age 22; resident of Mecklenburg Co. at the time of enlistment; wounded in action (leg) on 6/17/1863; on 7/29/1863 furloughed for 40 days; present or accounted for on muster rolls through August 1864; paroled 4/9/1865 at Appomattox Court House.

Griffin, Wesley: Private

Enlisted in Co. E on 7/5/1862 in Mecklenburg Co. at age 37; present or accounted for on muster rolls through June 1864; on July/August 1864 muster roll reported "absent without leave"; issued clothing 10/20/1864; admitted 1/23/1865 to Charlotte, NC hospital with "pneumonia"; 2/10/1865 furloughed; hospital records state unit as Provost Guard Conscript, NC and Capt. Howard's Prison Guard.

Groner, Austin: Private

Enlisted in Co. E on 4/1/1863 in Gaston Co.; reported as "deserted" May–December 1863; reported as "present" January/February 1864; reported as "absent without leave" after Feb. 1864.

Hagler, Allen: Private

Enlisted in Co. E on 5/16/1862 in Cabarrus Co. at age 40; son of Charles Hagler and Sarah "Sally" Linker; brother of Nelson Hagler, also of Co. E; married Elizabeth "Betsy" Lefler, bond dated 1/1/1848 in Cabarrus Co.; resident of Cabarrus Co. at the time of enlistment; present or accounted for on muster rolls through October 1864;

captured 4/3/1865 on Appomattox River, VA, held at Hart's Island, NY; released 6/19/1865 after taking Oath of Allegiance.

Hagler, J. A.: Private

Enlisted in Co. E on 7/7/1862 in Mecklenburg Co.; only present on muster rolls from January through August 1864; the July/August 1864 roll states "transferred by order of Secretary of War", reason not given; it is possible that this is John R. Hagler, brother to Allen and Nelson Hagler, also of Co. E, but no definitive proof discovered.

Hagler, Jacob: Private

Enlisted in Co. E on 6/14/1862 in Cabarrus Co. at age 47; born circa 1815; son of Leonard Hagler and Elizabeth Hartsell; married Nelly Dove, bond dated 1/30/1838 in Cabarrus Co.; captured 7/4/1863 at South Mtn., held at Ft. McHenry; transferred 7/9/1863 to Ft. Delaware; paroled and exchanged Feb. 14–15, 1865 at Coxes Landing, James River, VA; family history states that Jacob died in prisoner of war camp.

Hagler, Nelson: Private

Enlisted in Co. E on 3/1/1863 in Cabarrus Co.; last name also appears as "Hegler"; born 10/3/1825; son of Charles Hagler and Sarah "Sally" Linker; brother of Allen Hagler, also of Co. E; married Martha Ann Klutts (also spelled Kluttz), bond dated 7/9/1859 in Cabarrus Co.; occupation, farmer; present or accounted for on muster rolls through October 1864; after the war lived about seven miles south of Concord in Cabarrus Co.; on March 15, 1876 involved in a serious accident at home when a kerosene lamp exploded, severely burning him and nearly killing him; died on July 31, 1880, buried as Nelson Hegler, Rocky Ridge Methodist Church Cemetery, Township 11, Concord, NC.

Hartman, Henry L.: Private

Enlisted in Co. E on 7/7/1862 in Gaston Co. at age 30; resident of Rowan Co. at the time of enlistment; captured 7/4/1863 at South Mtn., held at Ft. McHenry; transferred 7/9/1863 to Ft. Delaware; paroled 7/30/1863; exchanged 8/1/1863 in City Point, VA; present or accounted for on muster rolls through October 1864; paroled 5/16/1865 in Salisbury, NC.

Hartness, John: Private

Enlisted in Co. E on 8/13/1862 in Mecklenburg Co.; July 7–October 31, 1862 roll states "Not reported."

Hartsell, Nimrod: Private

Enlisted in Co. E on 4/1/1863 in Cabarrus Co.; born 1824; son of Andrew Hartsell and Kitty Reed; married three times (all in Cabarrus Co.), first to Eliza J. Boger, bond dated 9/10/1845; second to Addelina Misenheimer, bond dated 4/21/1849; third to Sivly Matilda Kiser, 7/5/1856; brother-in-law to Jesse D. Cox also of Company E; captured 7/5/1863 in Monterey Springs, PA, held at Ft. McHenry; transferred 7/9/1863 to Ft. Delaware; died there 10/3/1863.

Hawkins, J. P.: Private
Listed on an Aug. 6, 1862 Charlotte *Daily Bulletin* muster roll in Co. E.

Helms, William: Private
Enlisted in Co. E on 7/4/1862 in Cabarrus Co. at age 26; "deserted" before 10/31/1862; married Evy C. Furr on 7/25/1865 in Cabarrus Co.

Hoffman, John Meloen: Private
Enlisted in Co. E on 7/16/1862 in Mecklenburg Co. at age 36; born 5/19/1825; reported as "deserted" May–December 1863; reported as "present" January/February 1864; reported as "absent without leave" after Feb. 1864; paroled 4/9/1865 at Appomattox Court House; died 11/23/1923, buried Long Creek Baptist Church, Lower Dallas Rd., Gaston Co., NC.

Hoffman, Jonas L.: Private
Enlisted in Co. E on 7/10/1862 in Mecklenburg Co. at age 25; captured 7/4/1863 at South Mtn., held at Ft. McHenry; transferred 7/9/1863 to Ft. Delaware; paroled and exchanged 9/22/1864 at Varina, VA; admitted 9/21/1864 to Richmond hospital, issue clothing there on 9/27/1864.

Hood, Thomas H.: Private
Enlisted in Co. E on 5/20/1862 in Mecklenburg Co. at age 30; died 2/14/1863 in Raleigh hospital of "febris typhoides."

Hope, James: Private
Enlisted in Co. E on 8/23/1862 in Mecklenburg Co. at age 45; May 1863–December 1864 reported as "deserted"; admitted 5/16/1864 to Richmond hospital.

Howell, William H.: Private
Enlisted in Co. E on 4/1/1863 in Cabarrus Co.; present or accounted for on muster rolls through October 1864; paroled 5/11/1865 in Charlotte, NC.

Hunsucker, Andrew Jackson: Private
Enlisted in Co. E on 7/7/1862 in Mecklenburg Co.; captured 6/21/1863 in Upperville, VA, held at Old Capitol Prison, Washington, DC; paroled 6/25/1863 and exchanged 6/30/1863 in City Point, VA; admitted to Winder Hospital #3 in Richmond, VA on 7/24/1863; listed in Ward #4 on 10/29/1863 muster roll; name also spelled Honsucker; present or accounted for on muster rolls through August 1864.

Irwin, Edward G.: Private
Enlisted in Co. E on 7/4/1862; July 7–October 31, 1862 roll states "Not reported"; last name spelled "Erwin" on Aug. 6, 1862 Charlotte *Daily Bulletin* muster roll.

Johnson, Jacob: Private
Enlisted in Co. E on 4/1/1863 in Gaston Co.; present or accounted for on muster rolls through October 1864; paroled 4/9/1865 at Appomattox Court House; buried Pisgah Presbyterian Church, Gastonia, NC.

Johnson, James Monroe: Private

Enlisted in Co. E on 8/20/1862 in Mecklenburg Co. at age 21; captured 12/27/1862 on Chowan River, NC; paroled 1/3/1863; captured again 7/4/1863 at South Mtn., held at Ft. McHenry; transferred 7/9/1863 to Ft. Delaware, 10/15/1863 to Pt. Lookout; date of parole and exchange not given; appears on an undated roll of paroled sick prisoners in 3rd Div. Gen. Hospital, Camp Winder, Richmond with remark paid on 3/3/1865.

Johnston, George W.: Private

Enlisted in Co. E on 2/1/1863 in Mecklenburg Co.; present or accounted for on muster rolls through August 1864.

Keiser, George A.: Private

Transferred to Co. E on 5/1/1863; previously served in Company F, 1st NC Cavalry (9th NCST); present or accounted for on muster rolls through October 1864.

Kimmons, R. M.: Private

Enlisted in Co. E on 7/7/1862 in Mecklenburg Co.; present or accounted for on muster rolls through October 1864.

King, John O.: Private

Enlisted in Co. E; paroled 5/17/1865 in Charlotte, NC.

Kiser, William D.: Private

Enlisted in Co. E on 7/7/1862 in Mecklenburg Co.; the July/August 1864 muster roll states "Died of disease."

Klutts, Julius Caesar: Private

Transferred to Co. E on 7/21/1864; previously served in Company F, 1st NC Cavalry (9th NCST); present or accounted for on muster rolls through October 1864.

Klutts, William H. A.: Sergeant

Enlisted in Co. E on 5/16/1862 in Cabarrus Co. at age 34; mustered in as a private; captured 6/21/1863 in Upperville, VA, held at Old Capitol Prison; paroled and exchanged 6/30/1863 in City Point, VA; appointed sergeant March/April 1864; present or accounted for on muster rolls through October 1864; paroled 5/12/1865 in Charlotte, NC.

Lay, Alford L.: Private

Enlisted in Co. E on 11/1/1862 in Mecklenburg Co.; present or accounted for on muster rolls through June 1864.

Lay, Cottsworth H.: Private

Enlisted in Co. E on 7/11/1862 in Gaston Co. at age 27; born 10/4/1834; present or accounted for on muster rolls through October 1864; died 7/15/1911, buried Edgewood Cemetery, Lowell, NC.

Lay, Isaac T.: Private

Enlisted in Co. E on 7/11/1862 in Gaston Co. at age 25; died 2/15/1864 in Richmond hospital of "typhoid pneumonia."

Lay, John W.: Private

Enlisted in Co. E on 7/7/1862 in Mecklenburg Co. at age 18; present or accounted for on muster rolls through August 1864; wounded in action (foot and shoulder) 9/1/1864 near Davis House on the Weldon RR, VA; 10/6/1864 furloughed for 60 days.

Lay, William J.: Private

Enlisted in Co. E on 8/26/1862 in Mecklenburg Co. at age 26; present or accounted for on muster rolls through June 1864.

Lee, Junius: Sergeant

Enlisted in Co. E on 7/5/1862 in Mecklenburg Co.; mustered in as a sergeant; July 7–October 31, 1862 roll states "Not reported."

Lefler, Michael Hoke: Private

Enlisted in Co. E on 7/7/1862 in Mecklenburg Co.; born 4/8/1845; resident of Cabarrus Co. at the time of enlistment; present or accounted for on muster rolls through October 1864; captured 4/3/1865 near Petersburg, held at Hart's Island, NY; released 6/19/1865 after taking Oath of Allegiance; died 11/3/1896, buried Cold Springs Methodist Church Cemetery, Township 11, Cabarrus Co., NC.

Linker, Aaron: Private

Enlisted in Co. E on 7/7/1862 in Mecklenburg Co.; born 8/15/1845; son of Jacob Linker and Sally Tucker; twin brother of Moses Linker and brother of James and William all of Company E; present or accounted for on muster rolls through October 1864; paroled 5/12/1865 in Charlotte, NC; married Leah C. Canup, bond dated 4/21/1866 in Cabarrus Co.; died 4/26/1909, buried Center Grove Methodist Church Cemetery, Township 9, Cabarrus Co., NC.

Linker, James A.: Private

Enlisted in Co. E on 5/16/1862 in Cabarrus Co.; at age 32; born 12/8/1829; son of Jacob Linker and Sally Tucker; brother of Aaron, Moses, and William also of Company E; married Abagail Northum, bond dated 9/15/1856 in Cabarrus Co.; present or accounted for on muster rolls through October 1864; captured 4/3/1865 near Petersburg, VA, held at Hart's Island, NY; released 6/19/1865 after taking Oath of Allegiance; died 5/24/1905, buried Willow Valley Cemetery, Mooresville, Iredell County.

Linker, Moses: Private

Enlisted in Co. E on 7/7/1862 in Mecklenburg Co.; born 8/15/1845; son of Jacob Linker and Sally Turner; twin brother to Aaron Linker and brother to James and William all of Company E; present or accounted for on muster rolls only from November 1863 through October 1864; died 1/2/1915, buried Poplar Trent Presbyterian Church Cemetery, Township 2 (now Concord), Cabarrus Co., NC.

Linker, William: Private

Enlisted in Co. E on 5/16/1862 in Cabarrus Co. at age 20; born 10/2/1842; son of Jacob Linker and Sally Tucker; wife, Catherine; captured 12/27/1862; paroled

1/3/1863 (no details given); 10/31/1862–2/28/1863 roll states "Ordered back to camp. Supposed to be exchanged."; Sept./Oct. 1863 roll states "Wounded and in the hands of the enemy."; reported on rolls as captured through April 1864; May–August 1864 reported as "absent sick"; died 1/20/1898, buried Center Grove Methodist Church Cemetery, Township 9, Cabarrus County.

Linker, William R.: Private
Enlisted in Co. E on 6/21/1865 in Cabarrus Co. at age 21; present or accounted for on muster rolls through October 1864; admitted 3/31/1865 to Petersburg hospital.

McCall, James A.: Private
Enlisted in Co. E on 7/7/1862 in Cabarrus Co.; present or accounted for on muster rolls through October 1862.

McCombs, William T.: Private
Enlisted in Co. E on 5/14/1862 in Mecklenburg Co. at age 19; died 12/8/1863 in Richmond hospital of "pneumonia."

McCoy, James R.: Private
Enlisted in Co. E on 8/23/1862 in Mecklenburg Co.; present or accounted for on muster rolls through June 1864; the July/August 1864 roll states "absent without leave."

McDonald, E. Alexander: Private
Enlisted in Co. E on 7/14/1862 in Gaston Co. at age 28; present or accounted for on muster rolls until transferred 4/15/1864 to Company C, 17th SC Infantry; name given as McDonald and McDaniel on records.

McDonald, Elisha B.: Private
Enlisted in Co. E on 7/14/1862 in Gaston Co. at age 30; present or accounted for on muster rolls until transferred 4/15/1864 to Company C, 17th SC Infantry; name given as McDonald and McDaniel on records.

McIntire, Marcus L.: Sergeant
Enlisted in Co. E on 5/17/1862 in Rowan Co. at age 27; mustered in as a sergeant; captured 7/4/1863 in Monterey, PA, held at Ft. McHenry; transferred 7/9/1863 to Ft. Delaware; released 1/26/1864 after taking Oath of Allegiance.

Michael, George W.: Corporal
Enlisted in Co. E on 6/10/1862 in Cabarrus Co. at age 36; born July 30, 1827; son of Jacob Michael and Annie Lontz; occupation prior to war: house carpenter; married Beizora on October 20, 1857; previously served as a sergeant in Company A, 52nd NC Infantry; mustered in as a private; appointed corporal March/April 1864; present or accounted for on muster rolls through August 1864; after the war he moved to Hillsboro, Illinois, where he continued to do carpentry work; he was also a hotel proprietor and farmer; member of the Lutheran Church and the Masonic fraternity.

Misenheimer, Jacob John: 1st Sergeant

Enlisted in Co. E on 4/15/1862 in Cabarrus Co.; born 11/8/1823; resident of Cabarrus Co. at the time of enlistment; mustered in as a private; captured 7/4/1863 at South Mtn., held at Ft. McHenry; transferred 7/9/1863 to Ft. Delaware; paroled and exchanged 7/31/1863; appointed 1st sergeant in March/April 1864; present or accounted for on muster rolls through October 1864; captured 4/3/1865 near Petersburg, held at Hart's Island, NY; released 6/19/1865 after taking Oath of Allegiance; died 11/4/1888, buried Mt. Pleasant Methodist Church, Mt. Pleasant, NC.

Misenheimer, John Henry: Private

Enlisted in Co. E on 4/15/1862 in Cabarrus Co.; born 8/23/1826; married Sophia E. Barringer, bond dated 10/2/1855 in Cabarrus Co. where he resided at the time of enlistment; present or accounted for on muster rolls through October 1864; captured 4/3/1865 near Petersburg, held at Hart's Island, NY; released 6/19/1865 after taking Oath of Allegiance; died 11/3/1899, buried St. John's Lutheran Church, St. John's Church Rd., Cabarrus Co., NC.

Moreton, William R.: Private

Enlisted in Co. E on 8/11/1862 in Mecklenburg Co. at age 35; present or accounted for on muster rolls through August 1864; paroled April 11–21, 1865 in Farmville, VA.

Osborn, Hyram: Musician

Enlisted in Co. E on 8/30/1862 in Mecklenburg Co. at age 26; mustered in as a private; transferred 12/25/1862 to Field and Staff of regiment and assigned to band as a musician; present or accounted for on muster rolls through March 1, 1863; the July/August 1864 roll states "Died of disease. This man was a member of the band and his name has not been on the roll (was taken off by order)."

Osborne, John F.: Private

Enlisted in Co. E on 3/21/1863 in Mecklenburg Co.; present or accounted for on muster rolls through August 1864; paroled 5/5/1865 in Greensboro, NC.

Osborne, Robert: Private

Enlisted in Co. E on 7/7/1862 in Mecklenburg Co.; resident of Mecklenburg Co. at the time of enlistment; present or accounted for on muster rolls through October 1864; captured 4/5/1865 at Amelia Court House, held at Pt. Lookout; released 6/29/1865 after taking Oath of Allegiance.

Pace, Young: Private

Enlisted in Co. E on 4/1/1862 in Mecklenburg Co.; son of Alsey Pace and Zilpha Hall; born c. 1837; apprenticed as an orphan in Guilford Co., NC to Jonathan Armfield in 1847, then to Isaac Armfield in 1850 as a cabinet maker; married Nancy Walls Jan. 22, 1858 in Mecklenburg Co., NC; residing in Mecklenburg Co. as a carpenter at the time of enlistment; captured 6/21/1863 in Upperville, VA, held at Old Capitol Prison; paroled and exchanged 6/30/1863 in City Point, VA; present or accounted for on muster rolls through October 1864; recaptured 4/3/1865 on the Richmond &

Danville RR, VA, held at Pt. Lookout; released 6/17/1865 after taking Oath of Allegiance; died c. 1890 in Mecklenburg Co.

Pendleton, William M.: Private

Enlisted in Co. E; captured 6/21/1863 in Upperville, VA, held at Old Capitol Prison; paroled and exchanged 6/30/1863 in City Point, VA.

Pendre, John H.: Private

Enlisted in Co. E on 8/23/1862 in Mecklenburg Co. at age 16; resident of Mecklenburg Co.; captured (place and date not given) and held at Hart's Island, NY; present or accounted for on muster rolls through October 1864; released 6/19/1865 after taking Oath of Allegiance.

Perkins, Asbury H.: Private

Enlisted in Co. E on 2/1/1863 in Mecklenburg Co.; present or accounted for on muster rolls through August 1864.

Plyler, F. S.: Private

Enlisted in Co. E on 7/7/1862 in Mecklenburg Co.; married Mary E. Ury, bond dated 10/27/1866 in Cabarrus Co.; last name also appears as "Pliler"; present or accounted for only on muster rolls from January 1864 through October 1864.

Popplein, Nicholas: Private

Enlisted in Co. E on 8/29/1862 in Mecklenburg Co. at age 19; captured 12/27/1862 (place not given); paroled 1/3/1863 (but not exchanged); reported as a deserter through Jan./Feb. 1864 when roll states "Marylander taken prisoner November 18, 1862. Went home and did not return."

Ray, Angus P.: Private

Enlisted in Co. E on 5/14/1862 in Mecklenburg Co. at age 31; present or accounted for on muster rolls through October 1864; paroled 4/9/1865 at Appomattox Court House.

Reaves, Franklin A.: Private

Enlisted in Co. E on 7/7/1862 in Mecklenburg Co. at age 21; present or accounted for on muster rolls through October 1864; paroled 5/13/1865 in Charlotte, NC.

Rhyne, Caleb M.: Private

Enlisted in Co. E on 7/7/1862 in Mecklenburg Co.; born on April 15, 1845; believed to be the son of Solomon H. Rhyne and Catherine Froneberger; present or accounted for only on muster rolls from March 1864 through August 1864; died in December 1928, buried Lutheran Chapel Cemetery, New Hope Rd., Gaston Co., NC.

Rhyne, Pinkney J.: Private

Enlisted in Co. E; born 7/9/1844; son of Joseph K. Rhyne and Susan C. Plonck; resident of Gaston Co. at the time of enlistment; captured 4/3/1865 near Petersburg, held at Hart's Island, NY; released 6/14/1865 after taking Oath of Allegiance; married Elizabeth Catherine Setzer circa 1867 in Gaston Co.; died on March 25, 1900, buried in the Philadelphia Lutheran Church Cemetery, Dallas, NC.

Rice, Moses: Private

Enlisted in Co. E on 7/7/1862 in Cabarrus Co. at age 46; married Margaret Fink on December 27, 1838 in Cabarrus Co.; present or accounted for on muster rolls through October 1864; paroled 5/15/1865 in Charlotte, NC.

Richards, William: Private

Enlisted in Co. E on 6/21/1862 in Cabarrus Co. at age 34; born 3/20/1827; present or accounted for on muster rolls through April 1864; received 6/2/1864 by federal provost marshal, Ft. Monroe as a "rebel deserter. Came into Federal lines at Bermuda Hundred, VA."; took Oath of Amnesty 6/11/1864; died 5/11/1911, buried Christ Lutheran Church Cemetery, Stanley, NC (Gaston Co.).

Rinehardt, Thomas Steadman: Private

Enlisted in Co. E on 7/7/1862 in Mecklenburg Co.; born 9/10/1845 in Cabarrus Co., NC; son of Mathias Rinehardt and Patsy Motley (first cousin of William David Rinehardt, also of Co. E); muster rolls for March through October 1864 list him as present (only ones located); issued clothing on 10/21/1864; married Ida Catherine Moser in Cabarrus Co. on Dec. 9, 1877; occupation: farmer and landowner; family resided on Cold Springs Road in Cabarrus Co.; died 4/15/1930, buried Cold Springs Methodist Church Cemetery, Township 11, Cabarrus County.

Rinehardt, William David: Private

Enlisted in Co. E on 7/7/1862 in Mecklenburg Co.; born 6/15/1845 in Cabarrus Co., NC; son of Paul R. Rinehardt and Catherine Dry (first cousin of Thomas Steadman Rinehardt, also of Co. E); resided near Mt. Pleasant, NC; captured 6/23/1864 near Petersburg, held at Pt. Lookout; "transferred to Elmira, NY, August 16, 1864"; after the war moved to Arkansas, where he met and married Lucinda J. Dingler (Feb. 14, 1868 in Monroe Co., AR); around 1870 moved back to Cabarrus Co. living and farming in Mt. Pleasant and later near Gold Hill; finally moving to Stanley Co., NC; died 3/7/1927, buried with his wife in Holy Trinity Lutheran Cemetery, Mount Pleasant, NC.

William David Rinehardt, Company E, Cabarrus County (Ben F. Callahan).

Samonds, Thomas K.: 2nd Lieutenant

Enlisted in Co. E on 4/1/1863 in Mecklenburg Co.; resident of Mecklenburg Co. at the time of enlistment; mustered in as a private; appointed corporal Nov./Dec. 1863; present or accounted for on muster rolls through August 1864; captured 4/3/1865 on Appomattox River, VA, held at Old Capitol Prison; transferred 4/21/1865 to Johnson's Island; rank on all POW records is 2nd lieutenant; released 6/20/1865 after taking Oath of Allegiance.

Saunders, Brantley H.: 1st Lieutenant

Enlisted in Co. E on 7/7/1862 in Cabarrus Co. at age 24; born 2/13/1838; married Sarah Bost 6/24/1858 in Cabarrus Co. where he resided at the time of enlistment; appointed 3rd lieutenant to rank from enlistment; 9/22/1863 promoted to 2nd lieutenant; 1/8/1865 promoted to 1st lieutenant; captured 4/3/1865 on Appomattox River, VA, held at Old Capitol Prison; transferred 4/21/1865 to Johnson's Island; released 6/20/1865 after taking Oath of Allegiance; died 12/15/1893; buried in St. Paul's Methodist Church Cemetery, Township 9, Cabarrus Co.

Seaford, Caleb M.: Private

Enlisted in Co. E on 7/7/1862 in Mecklenburg Co.; born 1845; present or accounted for only on muster rolls from March 1864 through October 1864; died 7/26/1921, buried Bethpage Presbyterian Church Cemetery, NC Highway 136, Cabarrus Co., NC.

Shinn, John Calvin: Sergeant

Enlisted in Co. E on 6/21/1862 in Cabarrus Co.; born 6/14/1837; son of Thomas Jefferson Shinn, Sr. and Mary Reed; married Susan C. Bost 9/16/1856 in Cabarrus Co.; mustered in as a 2nd sergeant; sent on detached service with 16 men for 30 days (8/8/1862 to 9/6/1862) to procure horses; killed in action on 10/9/1863 at Culpeper Court House, VA; three of his brothers who served in Co. B, 7th NC Infantry also died during the war.

Shoe, Noah: Corporal

Enlisted in Co. E on 7/7/1862 in Cabarrus Co. at age 18; mustered in as a private; appointed corporal March/April 1864; present or accounted for on muster rolls through October 1864; paroled 5/15/1865 in Charlotte, NC.

Simms, William B.: Private

Enlisted in Co. E on 7/8/1862 in Mecklenburg Co. at age 23; "Deserted December 10th January 1863, from Garysburg, NC."

Smith, Benjamin F.: Private

Enlisted in Co. E on 7/14/1862 in Mecklenburg Co.; born 1843; killed in action on 12/16/1862 in Whitehall, NC; buried Goshen Presbyterian Church Cemetery, Belmont, NC.

Smith, George F.: Private

Enlisted in Co. E on 7/7/1862 in Mecklenburg Co.; born 10/13/1843; 7/21/1864 ordered to report to Company F, 1st NC Cavalry (9th NCST) but remained with 4th NC Cavalry; died 7/27/1889, buried St. Paul's Methodist Church Cemetery, Township 9, Cabarrus County.

Smith, George Locke: Private

Enlisted in Co. E on 3/1/1863 in Mecklenburg Co.; captured 8/4/1863 at Kelly's Ford, VA, held at Pt. Lookout; paroled and exchanged 3/20/1864 in City Point, VA; present or accounted for on muster rolls through until transferred July/August 1864 to Company F, 1st NC Cavalry (9th NCST).

Smith, John B.: Private

Enlisted in Co. E on 7/14/1862 in Mecklenburg Co. at age 34; born 10/18/1829; present or accounted for on muster rolls through August 1864; paroled 4/19/1865 in Newton, NC; died 5/26/1903, buried Goshen Presbyterian Church, Belmont, NC.

Smith, Levi A.: Private

Enlisted in Co. E on 4/15/1863 in Gaston Co.; present or accounted for on muster rolls through October 1864; admitted 11/15/1864 to Danville, VA hospital with "rheumatisms chronic"; transferred 11/26/1864 to Raleigh hospital; returned to duty 12/6/1864; paroled April 11–21, 1865 in Farmville, VA.

Smith, Samuel B.: Private

Enlisted in Co. E on 7/7/1862 in Mecklenburg Co.; present or accounted for on muster rolls through October 1864.

Sossamon, David: Private

Enlisted in Co. E on 3/15/1863 in Cabarrus Co.; most likely the son of Christian Sossamon and Susan Kiser; present or accounted for on muster rolls through October 1864; believed to have migrated to Oklahoma after the war.

Sossamon, William Harvey: Private

Enlisted in Co. E on 6/21/1862 in Cabarrus Co.; born 1827; married Keziah Mottley on August 8, 1850 in Cabarrus Co.; present or accounted for on muster rolls through October 1864.

Sparks, Merit R.: Private

Enlisted in Co. E on 10/24/1862 in Mecklenburg Co.; "Deserted to the enemy April 10, 1863."

Starnes, Ephiran Wilson: Private

Enlisted in Co. E on 5/16/1862 in Cabarrus Co. at age 25; married Maceny Canup on November 5, 1860 in Cabarrus Co.; residing as a cooper in Cabarrus Co. at the time of enlistment; admitted 6/4/1864 to Danville, VA hospital with "bronchitis acute"; furloughed 6/14/1864; present or accounted for on muster rolls through August 1864; readmitted to Danville hospital 12/3/1864 with "endocarditis"; returned to duty 1/9/1865.

Starnes, John: Private

Enlisted in Co. E on 7/7/1862 in Cabarrus Co. at age 47; born in Cabarrus Co.; died 6/7/1864 in Petersburg hospital of "febris typhoides."

Stowe, Leroy P.: Private

Enlisted in Co. E on 4/15/1863 in Gaston Co.; born 10/7/1835; present or accounted for on muster rolls through October 1864; died 10/4/1906, buried Long Creek Baptist Church Cemetery, Lower Dallas Rd., Gaston Co., NC.

Stroub, John: Private

Enlisted in Co. E on 5/12/1862 in Mecklenburg Co. at age 29; last name spelled

"Strubb" on Aug. 6, 1862 Charlotte *Daily Bulletin* muster roll, also appears as "Strube" in some records; present or accounted for on muster rolls through October 1864; paroled 5/12/1865 in Charlotte, NC.

Stroub, Thomas Harris: Private
Enlisted in Co. E on 5/12/1862 in Mecklenburg Co. at age 34; married Martha J. Wall on April 4, 1853 in Cabarrus Co.; last name spelled "Strubb" on Aug. 6, 1862 Charlotte *Daily Bulletin* muster roll, also appears as "Strube" on some records; present or accounted for on muster rolls through October 1864.

Stroub, William: Private
Enlisted in Co. E on 5/12/1862 in Mecklenburg Co. at age 32; last name spelled "Strubb" on an Aug. 6, 1862 Charlotte *Daily Bulletin* muster roll, it also appears as "Strube" on some records; present or accounted for on muster rolls through October 1864.

Tanton, T.: Private
Enlisted in Co. E; admitted 7/13/1864 to Richmond hospital, transferred the next day.

Tate, Absolom M.: Private
Enlisted in Co. E on 7/5/1862 in Mecklenburg Co.; the July 7–October 31, 1862 muster roll states "Not reported."

Taylor, D. B.: Private
Enlisted in Co. E on 5/14/1862 in Mecklenburg Co.; the July 7–October 31, 1862 muster roll states "Not reported."

Thomas, Charles W.: Private
Enlisted in Co. E on 5/17/1862 in Rowan Co.; mustered in as a corporal; captured 7/4/1863 at South Mtn., held at Ft. McHenry; transferred 7/9/1863 to Ft. Delaware; paroled and exchanged 10/5/1864 at Aiken's Landing, VA; reduced to ranks March/April 1864 while a POW; admitted 10/8/1864 to Richmond hospital with diarrhea; furloughed 10/11/1864; paroled 5/22/1865 in Salisbury, NC.

Troutman, George: Private
Enlisted in Co. E on 4/15/1863 in Cabarrus Co.; born June 9, 1824; present or accounted for on muster rolls through October 1864; paroled 5/15/1865 in Salisbury, NC; died on October 6, 1903, buried in the Organ Lutheran Church Cemetery in Rowan Co.

Tucker, Joseph K.: Private
Enlisted in Co. E on 5/16/1862 in Cabarrus Co. at age 24; born in Cabarrus Co., where he resided as a minister at the time of enlistment; discharged 11/6/1863 due to "disability"; captured and paroled 5/20/1865 in Augusta, GA giving rank and unit on parole as "Chaplain, Company E, 4th Regiment NC Cavalry."

Turner, John S.: Private

Enlisted in Co. E on 3/15/1863 in Cabarrus Co.; captured 7/4/1863 at South Mtn., held at Ft. McHenry; transferred 7/9/1863 to Ft. Delaware; died there 10/21/1863 of "diarrhea chronic."

Turner, William D.: Private

Enlisted in Co. E on 8/16/1862 in Mecklenburg Co. at age 16; present or accounted for on muster rolls through October 1864; paroled 5/18/1865 in Charlotte, NC.

Vickers, George F.: Sergeant

Enlisted in Co. E on 6/21/1862 in Cabarrus Co. at age 24; present or accounted for on muster rolls until killed in action on 10/27/1864 near Burgess's Mill, Dinwiddie Co., VA.

Vickers, Martin L.: Private

Enlisted in Co. E on 6/21/1862 in Cabarrus Co. at age 26; married Elizabeth Plott on April 5, 1859 in Cabarrus Co.; muster rolls from June/July 1863 indicate that he was "wounded in shoulder"; Sept./Oct. 1863 roll states "Killed in action."

Wallace, John M.: Private

Enlisted in Co. E on 7/7/1862 in Cabarrus Co. at age 25; born 1837; resided in Cabarrus Co. at the time of enlistment; captured 6/21/1863 in Upperville, VA, held at Old Capital Prison; paroled and exchanged 6/30/1863 in City Point, VA; captured 4/4/1865 on the Richmond and Danville RR, VA, held at Pt. Lookout; released 6/22/1865 after taking Oath of Allegiance; died 8/31/1909 in Raleigh, buried Oakwood Cemetery, Raleigh, NC.

Wallace, Joseph R.: Private

Enlisted in Co. E on 11/1/1862 in Mecklenburg Co.; Jan./Feb. 1864 roll states "Discharged by habeas corpus. Was a minor"; present on May–August 1864 rolls; admitted 3/27/1865 to Petersburg hospital with "rubiola"; captured there 4/3/1865; admitted 4/11/1865 to Point of Rocks, VA hospital.

Watson, W. F.: Private

Enlisted in Co. E on 7/7/1862 in Mecklenburg Co.; "Deserted at Stephensburg, VA, July 1, 1863."

Williamson, James B.: Private

Enlisted in Co. E on 7/14/1862 in Mecklenburg Co. at age 30; born 6/7/1832; youngest son of John and Margaret Williamson; captured 7/4/1863 in Monterey, PA, held at Ft. McHenry; transferred 7/9/1863 to Ft. Delaware; paroled 9/28/1864; exchanged 10/5/1864 at Aiken's Landing, VA; present on 10/11/1864 roll of paroled and exchanged prisoners at Camp Lee, Richmond; after the war returned to Matthews and began farming; married twice, to sisters Mary and Malissa Knowles; was a member of Mecklenburg Camp, No. 382 U. C. V.; died 4/24/1924 at home in Matthews, NC, buried in family cemetery there; obituary in Confederate Veteran, Vol. XXXII, No. 6 (1924).

Williamson, John M.: Private
Enlisted in Co. E on 7/14/1862 in Mecklenburg Co. at age 45; present or accounted for on muster rolls through October 1864.

Wilson, John N.: Private
Enlisted in Co. E on 5/15/1862 in Mecklenburg Co. at age 26; resident of Mecklenburg Co. at the time of enlistment; present or accounted for on muster rolls through October 1864; captured 4/3/1865 near Petersburg, held at Hart's Island, NY; released 6/19/1865 after taking Oath of Allegiance.

Wilson, William M.: Private
Enlisted in Co. E on 1/12/1863 in Mecklenburg Co.; present or accounted for on muster rolls through October 1864; died 1/19/1895, buried Oakwood Cemetery, Gastonia, NC.

Company F

Acree, William A.: Private
Enlisted in Co. F on 8/9/1862 in Bertie Co. at age 22; born Oct. 12, 1839 in Bertie Co.; son of John Harrell Acree and Emeline "Emily" Harrell; resident of Bertie Co.; wounded in the foot at Brandy Station on 6/9/1863, admitted to General Hospital #22 and granted a 30 day furlough; surrendered at Appomattox; occupation: farmer; Mason; married three times, first to Elizabeth Mann on Jan. 28, 1866, next to Mary Lewis Cox on April 21, 1869, and then to Martha Cox Peele on June 28, 1874; member of Sandy Run Baptist Church; died Sept. 30, 1912; buried at the family homeplace.

Adkins, William D.: Corporal
Enlisted in Co. F on 8/9/1862 in Bertie Co.; mustered in as a private, appointed corporal May/June 1863; present or accounted for on muster rolls through October 1864.

Askew, David Cherry: Private
Enlisted in Co. F on 8/9/1862 in Bertie Co. at age 26; born circa 1836; son of Lawrence and Jane Askew; in the 1860 Bertie Co. Census he is living in the household of his future mother-in-law, Celia Jones; married Celia's daughter, Levina Arthusa Jones on December 20, 1860 in Bertie Co.; captured 6/21/1863 near Upperville, VA; paroled and exchanged 6/30/1863 in City Pt., VA; recaptured 1/26/1864 near Plymouth, NC, held at Pt. Lookout; paroled and exchanged 2/10/1865 at Aiken's Landing, VA; admitted 2/15/1865 to Richmond hospital with "scurvy"; died 3/11/1865.

Askew, William L.: Sergeant
Enlisted in Co. F on 8/9/1862 in Bertie Co. at age 26; born circa 1837; son of Willie and Eliza A. Askew; previously served as a private in Company L, 1st NC Infantry (six months, 1861); mustered in as a sergeant.

Barnes, Richard Higgs: Private

Enlisted in Co. F on 8/9/1862 in Bertie Co. at age 33 (records list date of birth as Feb. 1833); son of Richard Barnes and Judith Acree; 3rd cousin and later brother-in-law to William Acree, also of Co. F; listed as a laborer in the William and Jane Cox household in the 1850 Bertie Co. Census; married Georgeanna Cox on September 5, 1853 in Bertie Co.; listed as an overseer in the 1860 Bertie Co. Census; captured and paroled 4/13/1865 in Dinwiddie Co., VA; died in 1907 in Roxobel, NC.

Bazemore, H.: Private

Enlisted in Co. F on 8/9/1862 in Bertie Co.; no further military records.

Bazemore, Joseph Perry: Private

Enlisted in Co. F on 8/9/1862 in Bertie Co. at age 22; married Drucilla Bazemore on December 20, 1860; 3/12/1865 report of the provost marshall, Army of the Potomac, lists him as a "deserter from the enemy with horse and horse equipment"; received 3/18/1865 by provost marshal general, Washington, DC; took Oath of Allegiance and provided transportation to Norfolk, VA.

Bazemore, Kenneth: Private

Enlisted in Co. F on 8/9/1862 in Bertie Co. at age 28; born circa 1832; son of Elisha and Amilia Bazemore of Bertie Co.; listed as a student in his parent's household in the 1850 Bertie Co. Census; married Mary Butler on December 21, 1852 in Bertie Co.; listed as a farmer in the 1860 Bertie Co. Census; Oct. 1864 reported as "absent sick at home."

Bell, H. F.: Private

Enlisted in Co. F on 8/9/1862 in Bertie Co.; buried 10/14/1864 in Hollywood Cemetery.

Bowen, Frederick C.: Private

Enlisted in Co. F on 8/9/1862 in Bertie Co. at age 22; born circa 1840; son of Jesse Bowen and Margaret Gregory; brother to Thomas Bowen and William Bowen, also of Co. F; "wounded and paroled at Upperville, VA, June 21, 1863"; reported "absent on parole" through Feb. 1864.

Bowen, Hollaway E.: Private

Enlisted in Co. F on 8/9/1862 in Bertie Co.; born circa 1829; son of Cornelius Bowen and Charlotte Todd of Bertie Co.; name appears as "Holivid" in the 1850 Bertie Co. Census, in which he is listed as a laborer living in his parent's household; brother of James L. Bowen and Marcus H. Bowen, also of Co. F; married Francis A. White on October 18, 1853 in Bertie Co.; died 12/4/1863 of "pneumonia" in a Richmond hospital.

Bowen, James L.: Private

Enlisted in Co. F on 8/9/1862 in Bertie Co.; born circa 1838; son of Cornelius Bowen and Charlotte Todd of Bertie Co.; brother of Hollaway Bowen and Marcus H. Bowen, also of Co. F; living in the household of local merchant William H. Capehart in the 1860 Bertie Co. Census; present or accounted for on muster rolls through October 1864.

Bowen, Marcus H.: Private

Transferred to Co. F in or after June 1864; born circa 1843; son of Cornelius Bowen and Charlotte Todd; brother of James L. Bowen and Hollaway Bowen, also of Co. F; previously served in Company B, 12th Battalion NC Cavalry; present or accounted for on muster rolls through October 1864.

Bowen, Thomas E.: Private

Enlisted in Co. F on 8/9/1862 in Bertie Co. at age 27; born circa 1836; son of Jesse Bowen and Margaret Gregory; brother to Frederick Bowen and William Bowen, also of Co. F; killed in action on 6/18/1863 at Middleburg, VA.

Bowen, William H.: Private

Enlisted in Co. F on 8/9/1862 in Bertie Co.; born June 3, 1837; son of Jesse Bowen and Margaret Gregory; brother to Thomas Bowen and Frederick Bowen, also of Co. F; married Mary W. Butterton on July 12, 1860 in Bertie Co.; reported 3/17/1864 as a "rebel deserter" who "came into Federal lines, Plymouth [NC]" by Federal provost marshal, Ft. Monroe; released after taking Oath of Amnesty, provided transportation to Plymouth, NC; 12/31/1863–4/30/1864 roll states " absent prisoner of war"; reported 3/12/1865 as a "rebel deserter" by provost marshal general, Army of the Potomac; sent to provost marshal, Washington, DC 3/18/1865 where he took Oath of Allegiance and provided transportation to Norfolk, VA; died on August 11, 1908, buried in the Colerain Baptist Church Cemetery, Bertie Co.

Bridger, Robert M.: Private

Enlisted in Co. F on 8/9/1862 in Bertie Co. at age 32; born 10/3/1830; listed as a carpenter, living in the William Drake household in the 1850 Bertie Co. Census; married Hannah Bazemore on July 12, 1853 in Bertie Co.; died 5/27/1908, buried Reddin Bazemore Cemetery, Charles Taylor Rd., Bertie Co., NC.

Brogden, William T.: Private

Enlisted in Co. F on 10/1/1862 in Bertie Co.; born circa 1846; son of Henry and Millison Brogdin; last name also appears as "Brogdin" in records; reported as a "deserter" on rolls 11/1/1862–10/1/1864; paroled 5/13/1865 in Goldsboro, NC; married Mary Ann Rawls on November 22, 1866 in Bertie Co.

Bunch, William D.: Private

Enlisted in Co. F on 8/9/1862 in Bertie Co. at age 23; listed as a farmer in the 1860 Bertie Co. Census; present or accounted for on muster rolls through October 1864.

Burdin, Zachob Jackson: Private

Enlisted in Co. F on 8/9/1862 in Bertie Co. at age 34; name also appears as "Zadock"; married Emilla Jane Peele on December 29, 1853 in Bertie Co.; listed as a farmer in the 1860 Bertie Co. Census; captured 7/4/1863 in Waterloo, PA, held at

Ft. McHenry; transferred 7/9/1863 to Ft. Delaware, 10/8/1863 Pt. Lookout; died there December 1863; buried in Confederate Cemetery, Pt. Lookout.

Butler, James M.: Private

Enlisted in Co. F on 8/9/1862 in Bertie Co.; born circa 1830; son of Levin Butler (mechanic); listed as a laborer in his father's household in the 1850 Bertie Co. Census; muster rolls report him "absent with leave" through 9/1/1862; reported as a deserter September 1862–October 1864.

Butler, John Thomas: Corporal

Enlisted in Co. F on 8/9/1862 in Bertie Co. at age 31; born circa 1831; son of John and Louisa Butler of Bertie Co.; listed as a laborer living in his parent's household in the 1850 Bertie Co. Census; married Caroline Price on April 11, 1857 in Bertie Co.; listed as a farmer and living with his wife Caroline in the 1860 Bertie Co. Census; mustered in as a private, appointed corporal before 3/1/1863; present or accounted for on muster rolls through October 1864.

Butler, Joseph J.: Private

Enlisted in Co. F on 8/9/1862 in Bertie Co. at age 19; born circa 1842; son of Allen and Celia Butler of Bertie Co.; brother of Kenneth D. Butler and Worley Butler, also of Co. F.; reported as "absent without leave" and as a "deserter" after August 1863.

Butler, Kenneth D.: Private

Enlisted in Co. F on 8/9/1862 in Bertie Co. at age 30; born circa 1831; son of Allen and Celia Butler of Bertie Co.; brother of Joseph J. Butler and Worley Butler, also of Co. F.; married Harriette Pritchard on March 20, 1853 in Bertie Co.; resided in Bertie Co. as a farmer at the time of enlistment; reported "absent without leave" after August 1863; captured 3/15/1865 near Petersburg; 3/18/1865 took Oath of Allegiance, provided transportation to Baltimore, MD.

Butler, Worley: Private

Enlisted in Co. F on 8/9/1862 in Bertie Co. at age 24; born circa 1836; son of Allen and Celia Butler of Bertie Co.; brother of Kenneth D. Butler and Joseph J. Butler, also of Co. F.; captured 6/21/1863 in Upperville, VA; paroled and exchanged 6/30/1863 in City Point, VA; reported as a "deserter" after August 1863.

Casper, Cullen: Private

Enlisted in Co. F on 8/9/1862 in Bertie Co. at age 28; born circa 1835; son of Kenneth and Emilia "Milly" Casper; reported as "absent without leave" after August 1863.

Cherry, George O.: 1st Lieutenant

Enlisted in Co. F on 8/9/1862 in Bertie Co. at age 20; born circa 1841; son of Capt. Joseph B. (also in Co. F) and Sarah F. Cherry; brother of Joseph O. Cherry, also of Co. F; resident of Bertie Co. at the time of enlistment; previously served as a captain in 8th Regiment (Bertie Co.), 2nd Brigade NC Conf. Militia, commissioned

3/29/1862; appointed 1st lieutenant of 4th NC Cavalry to rank from date of enlistment; captured 7/4/1863 at South Mtn., PA, held at Ft. McHenry; transferred 7/9/1863 to Ft. Delaware, 7/18/1863 to Johnson's Island; transferred 2/24/1865 to City Pt., VA for exchange.

Cherry, Joseph B.: Captain

Transferred to Co. F and appointed captain on 8/9/1862; born circa 1824; wife Sarah; his sons George Cherry and Joseph O. Cherry also served in Co. F; listed as a farmer in the 1850 and 1860 Bertie Co. Census, owning $48,500 in real estate in 1860; previously served as adjutant on Field and Staff of 8th NC Infantry; resigned upon appointment to captain of Company F, 4th NC Cavalry; present or accounted for on muster rolls through October 1864; wounded in action on 4/1/1865 in Petersburg, died same day in Petersburg hospital.

Cherry, Joseph O.: Private

Enlisted in Co. F on 8/9/1862 in Bertie Co. at age 21; born circa 1841; son of Capt. Joseph B. (also in Co. F) and Sarah F. Cherry; resident of Bertie Co. at the time of enlistment; brother of George Cherry, also of Co. F; transferred 11/15/1862 to Company B, 12th Battalion NC Cavalry upon appointment to captain; transferred back to 4th NC Cavalry as captain of Company I 7/11/1864; 9/6/1864 submitted resignation for business reasons as administrator of a family estate; 9/19/1864 resignation accepted.

Clarke, Joseph B.: Private

Enlisted in Co. F on 8/9/1862 in Bertie Co. at age 21; present or accounted for on muster rolls through October 1864.

Cobb, George Washington: Private

Enlisted in Co. F on 8/9/1862 in Bertie Co.; born circa 1835 according to census records, but grave marker states year of birth as 1847; living with his mother Jennet Cobb during the 1860 Bertie Co. Census; previously served in 8th Regiment (Bertie Co.), 2nd Brigade NC Confederate Militia, commissioned 1st lieutenant on 11/2/1862 while enlisted in 4th NC Cavalry; married twice (both times in Bertie County), first to Celia A. Henry on April 30, 1867 then to Martha M. Shaw on March 5, 1868; died in 1923, buried in the Cobb-Britt Cemetery (NC Highway 45) in Bertie Co.

Cobb, Jesse B.: Private

Enlisted in Co. F on 8/9/1862 in Bertie Co.; born circa 1841; son of Thomas and Sarah "Sally" Cobb; received 3/12/1865 by provost marshal general, Army of the Potomac (from the provost marshal, 5th Army Corps); 3/18/1865 forwarded to Washington, DC as a "deserter from the enemy", took Oath of Allegiance and provided transportation to Norfolk, VA.

Cobern, Elezer: Private

Enlisted in Co. F on 8/9/1862 in Bertie Co.; born circa 1832; name also appears as "Eliazer" and "Leasor" in records; married Mary Temperance Butler on October 15,

1857 in Bertie Co.; listed as a farmer in the 1860 Bertie Co. Census; present or accounted for on muster rolls through October 1864.

Cofield, Alfred B.: Private
Enlisted in Co. F on 8/9/1862 in Bertie Co.; born circa 1845; son of Alfred and Delila Cobb of Bertie Co.; living with his mother during the 1860 Bertie Co. Census; present or accounted for on muster rolls until February 1864 when reported as "absent sick in hospital."

Daughtry, Edward A.: Private
Enlisted in Co. F on 8/9/1862 in Bertie Co.; captured 6/21/1863 in Upperville, VA; paroled and exchanged 6/30/1863 in City Point, VA; paroled 4/27/1865 at Provost Marshal's Office, District of Eastern VA.

Dilday, Joseph J.: Private
Enlisted in Co. F on 8/9/1862 in Bertie Co. at age 33; captured 6/21/1863 in Upperville, VA; paroled and exchanged 6/30/1863 in City Point, VA; after August 1863 reported as "absent without leave."

Francis, James H.: Private
Enlisted in Co. F on 8/9/1862 in Bertie Co. at age 23; born circa 1839; son of Charles and Emily Frances; married Delila Coffield on January 24, 1861 in Bertie Co.; on April 1863 muster roll reported as "absent sick."

Freeman, James C.: 1st Sergeant
Enlisted in Co. F on 8/9/1862 in Bertie Co. at age 30; born in Bertie Co., where he resided as a farmer at the time of enlistment; married Margaret E. Redditt on January 15, 1857 in Bertie Co.; mustered in as a 1st sergeant; captured 7/5/1863 near Gettysburg, PA, held at Ft. McHenry; transferred 7/9/1863 to Ft. Delaware, 10/22/1863 to Pt. lookout; paroled and exchanged 1/21/1865 at Boulware's Wharf, James River, VA; admitted 1/22/1865 to Richmond hospital; transferred 1/26/1865 to Camp Lee, Richmond.

Freeman, Reddick Norfleet: Private
Enlisted in Co. F on 8/9/1862 in Bertie Co.; born in 1836; name also appears as "Riddick"; resided at Wynn's Grove in Bertie Co., where he was farming at the time of enlistment; married Amanda Caroline White of Colerain, NC on March 15, 1859; after 4/30/1864 reported as a "deserter" on muster rolls; died 1887; a 1937 local history of Rosemead, NC by A. J. M. Perry states that "The late Reddick N. Freeman, a man of great energy and perseverance [...] moved into the wild woods, and cleared one of the largest farms in this vicinity. He went from a log hut to a spacious frame building; and was a good man and raised a large family of refined children."

Gill, Henry H.: Private
Enlisted in Co. F on 10/1/1862 in Bertie Co.; born circa 1843; son of John and Harriet Gill; wounded in action on 8/18/1864 (right hand), admitted to Petersburg hospital; 9/2/1864 furloughed; admitted 2/11/1865 to Raleigh hospital with "ascites";

2/21/1865 returned to duty; died 3/24/1865 in Raleigh hospital of "spinal meningitis."

Gilliam, John B.: Sergeant

Enlisted in Co. F on 8/9/1862 in Bertie Co. at age 30; born circa 1835 (age 25 in 1860 Bertie Co. Census); son of Wilie J. and Elizabeth Gilliam; previously served in 8th Regiment (Bertie Co.), 2nd Brigade NC Confederate Militia, commissioned 2nd lieutenant on 11/2/1862 while enlisted in 4th NC Cavalry; mustered in as a sergeant ; present or accounted for on muster rolls through October 1864.

Grimes, William T.: Private

Enlisted in Co. F on 8/9/1862 in Bertie Co. at age 29; wounded in action on 6/21/1863 in Upperville, VA ("arm shattered"); reported "absent wounded" through Oct. 1864.

Grover, A.: Private

Enlisted in Co. F; paroled April 11–21, 1865 in Farmville, VA.

Hale, James R.: Private

Enlisted in Co. F on 8/9/1862 in Bertie Co.; present or accounted for on muster rolls through October 1864.

Harmon, Eli: Private

Enlisted in Co. F on 8/9/1862 in Bertie Co. at age 30; born circa 1833; listed as a farmer and living with his wife Winny in the 1860 Bertie Co. Census; killed in action on 6/21/1863 in Upperville, VA.

Harrell, Joseph John: Private

Enlisted in Co. F on 8/9/1862 in Bertie Co. at age 22 (records list date of birth as October 1841); son of Marmaduke W. and Permelia Harrell; 1st cousin of William Acree, also of Co. F; captured 6/21/1863 in Upperville, VA; paroled and exchanged 6/30/1863 in City Point, VA; married twice, first to Anna Elizabeth Liverman on February 11, 1869 then to Gertrude Savage on April 7, 1898; after the war he farmed, became a large landowner and operated a lumber business.

Harrell, Wright: Private

Enlisted in Co. F on 8/9/1862 in Bertie Co. at age 23; born circa 1839; son of Jesse Harrell and Elizabeth Conner; listed as living in the Richard E. S. Cox household in the 1860 Bertie Co. Census; captured 6/21/1863 in Upperville, VA; paroled and exchanged 6/30/1863 in City Point, VA; after August 1863 reported as "absent without leave" and "deserted."

Hewson, John J.: Private

Enlisted in Co. F on 8/9/1862 in Bertie Co. at age 24; born circa 1837; last name also appears as "Housen" in records; listed as living in the Josiah Mitchell household in the 1860 Bertie Co. Census; after February 1864 reported as a "deserter."

Hoard, Willie: Private

Enlisted in Co. F on 8/9/1862 in Bertie Co.; name also appears as "Wiley"; married Mary E. Stallings on September 23, 1861 in Bertie Co.; wounded in action on 6/21/1863 in Upperville, VA; present or accounted for on muster rolls through October 1864.

Hobbs, Charles C.: Private

Enlisted in Co. F on 8/9/1862 in Bertie Co. at age 26; born circa 1836; son of Silas and Cynthia Hobbs; resident of Bertie Co. at the time of enlistment; present or accounted for on muster rolls through February 1864; deserted and entered Federal lines in Plymouth, NC, transported to Ft. Monroe, arrived there 4/23/1864; took Oath of Amnesty 5/10/1864 and furnished transportation to Baltimore, MD.

Hodder, James O.: Private

Enlisted in Co. F on 8/9/1862 in Bertie Co. at age 26; born circa 1836; listed as living in the Asa Phelps household in the 1860 Bertie Co. Census; previously served as a private in Company M, 1st NC Infantry (6 months, 1861); deserted and entered Federal lines in Plymouth, NC, transported to Ft. Monroe, arrived there 3/27/1864; released 4/1/1864 and sent to Plymouth, NC; took Oath of Amnesty there 4/4/1864; married Elenor Bayly on October 20, 1867 in Bertie Co.

Holder, Docton P.: Private

Enlisted in Co. F on 8/9/1862 in Bertie Co. at age 22; born circa 1841; son of Jethro M. and Oney Holder of Bertie Co.; married Sarah E. Thompson June 19, 1860 in Bertie Co.; listed as living with his wife Sarah in the Malicha Weston household in the 1860 Bertie Co. Census; present or accounted for on muster rolls through October 1864.

Holder, William A.: Sergeant

Enlisted in Co. F on 8/9/1862 in Bertie Co. at age 32; born circa 1832; married Francis "Fannie" Rhodes on November 23, 1858 in Bertie Co.; listed as an overseer, living with his wife Fannie in the 1860 Bertie Co. Census; mustered in as a corporal; promoted to sergeant in May/June 1863; "captured June 10, 1864."

Holloman, William E.: Private

Enlisted in Co. F on 8/9/1862 in Bertie Co.; born circa 1840; son of David and Jane Holloman; the 9/1/1862 Garysburg, NC roll states "absent without leave"; after September 1862 reported as a "deserter."

Holloman, William J.: Private

Enlisted in Co. F on 8/9/1862 in Bertie Co. at age 22; after August 1863 reported as "absent without leave."

Hughes, W.: Private

Enlisted in Co. F; the 12/31/1863–4/30/1864 muster roll states "exchanged 68th Regiment NC Troops"; 4/30/1864–8/31/1864 roll states: "Absent. Has not reported."

Jenkins, Kader: Private

    Enlisted in Co. F on 8/9/1862 in Bertie Co.; born circa 1836; son of Abner and Winnington Jenkins; first cousin of William A. Acree, also of Co. F; present or accounted for on muster rolls through October 1864.

Jernigan, James R.: Private

    Enlisted in Co. F on 8/9/1862 in Bertie Co. at age 19; born circa 1842; son of Nathan and Caroline Jernigan of Bertie Co.; muster roll of Jan./Feb. 1864 states "absent wounded at home"; present or accounted for on muster rolls through October 1864.

Lawrence, Jeremiah Baker: Private

    Enlisted in Co. F on 8/9/1862 in Bertie Co.; born circa 1843; listed at age seven and living in the Thomas O. Nichols (farmer) household in the 1850 Bertie Co. Census; called "Jerry"; present or accounted for on muster rolls through October 1864.

Lay, J. T.: Private

    Enlisted in Co. F; resident of Gaston Co.; captured 4/6/1865 at Harper's Farm, VA, held at Pt. Lookout; released 6/28/1865 after taking Oath of Allegiance.

Leary, James Edward: Private

    Transferred to Co. F on 1/9/1863; born circa 1839; son of Joseph and Harriet B. Leary; brother of John W. Leary, also of Co. F; previously served in Company G, 32nd NC Infantry; Jan./Feb. 1863 served as sergeant major; 2/28/1863–8/31/1863 served as ordnance sergeant , on detail to the Field and Staff of regiment; "no further [military] records."

Leary, John W.: Sergeant

    Enlisted in Co. F on 8/9/1862 in Bertie Co. at age 22; born circa 1841; son of Joseph and Harriet B. Leary; brother of James Edward Leary, also of Co. F; previously served in 8th Regiment (Bertie Co.), 2nd Brigade NC Confederate Militia, commissioned 2nd lieutenant on 9/21/1861; mustered in as a corporal; promoted to sergeant before 3/1/1863; present or accounted for on muster rolls through October 1864; admitted 10/27/1864 to Richmond hospital; furloughed 11/18/1864 for 60 days.

Mathews, James A.: Private

    Enlisted in Co. F on 8/9/1862 in Bertie Co. at age 25; born circa 1838; son of Jacob O. and Sarah Matthews; married Mary E. Mitchell on July 5, 1860 in Bertie Co.; present or accounted for on muster rolls through October 1864.

Mathews, Jordan T.: Private

    Enlisted in Co. F on 8/9/1862 in Bertie Co. at age 21; died 9/24/1863.

Mitchell, Joseph J.: Private

    Enlisted in Co. F on 8/9/1862 in Bertie Co. at age 20; born circa 1842; son of John H. Mitchell of Bertie Co.; brother of Rufus Mitchell, also of Co. F; captured 6/21/1863 in Upperville, VA, held at Old Capitol Prison; paroled and exchanged

6/30/1863 in City Point, VA; after August 1863 reported as "absent without leave" and as "deserted"; married Jarsey Ann Williams on September 23, 1866 in Bertie Co.

Mitchell, Rufus: Private

Enlisted in Co. F on 8/9/1862 in Bertie Co. at age 25; born circa 1836; son of John H. Mitchell of Bertie Co.; brother of Joseph J. Mitchell, also of Co. F; listed as a farmer in the 1860 Bertie Co. Census (Household 1049); received 3/12/1865 by provost marshal general, Army of the Potomac as a "deserter from the enemy"; 3/18/1865 sent to Washington, DC, where he took Oath of Allegiance and was furnished transportation to Norfolk, VA.

Mitchell, William L.: Private

Enlisted in Co. F on 8/9/1862 in Bertie Co. at age 30; born circa 1831; listed as a farmer and living with his wife, Mary M. Mitchell in the 1860 Bertie Co. Census; after August 1863 reported as "absent without leave" and "deserted."

Mizell, George W.: Private

Enlisted in Co. F on 8/9/1862 in Bertie Co. at age 27; born circa 1836; son of Josiah and Nancy Mizells; last name also appears as "Mizells" and "Mizelle" in records; Aug. 1863–Oct. 1864 reported as "absent sick."

Morris, Alpheus: Corporal

Enlisted in Co. F on 8/9/1862 in Bertie Co. at age 25; born on September 9, 1836 in Bertie Co.; son of James Layton Morris and Karen White; brother of Calvin J. Morris and William Morris, also of Co. F; married Christian Elizabeth Thompson on January 1, 1857 in Bertie Co.; listed as a farmer living with his two-year-old son William in the 1860 Bertie Co. Census; mustered in as a private; appointed corporal before 3/1/1863; received 3/12/1865 by provost marshal general, Army of the Potomac as a "deserter from the enemy"; 3/18/1865 sent to Washington, DC, where he took Oath of Allegiance and was furnished transportation to Norfolk, VA; after the war Alpheus remained in Norfolk, VA where he farmed; died on May 27, 1924 in Norfolk, buried in the Riverside Cemetery there.

Alpheus Morris, Company F, Bertie County (Bettie Morris Young).

Morris, Andrew: Private

Enlisted in Co. F on 8/9/1862 in Bertie Co. at age 25; born circa 1836; son of Allen and Sarah Morris; brother of George Morris, Edward Morris and James W. Morris, also of Co. F; after 11/1/1862 reported as a "deserter."

Morris, Calvin J.: Sergeant

Enlisted in Co. F on 8/9/1862 in Bertie Co. at age 22; born circa 1839 in Bertie Co.; son of James Layton Morris and Karen White; brother of Alpheus Morris and William Morris, also of Co. F; previously served as a private in Company L, 1st NC Infantry (six months, 1861); mustered in as a sergeant; present or accounted on muster rolls through October 1864.

Morris, Edward: Private

Enlisted in Co. F on 8/9/1862 in Bertie Co. at age 32; born circa 1831; son of Allen and Sarah Morris; brother of George Morris, Andrew Morris and James W. Morris, also of Co. F; listed as a farmer and living with his wife Mariah in the 1860 Bertie Co. Census; Sept./Oct. 1862 "absent without leave"; after November 1862 reported as "deserted."

Morris, George: Private

Enlisted in Co. F on 8/9/1862 in Bertie Co. at age 23; born circa 1837; son of Allen and Sarah Morris; brother of Andrew Morris, Edward Morris and James W. Morris, also of Co. F; present or accounted for on muster rolls through October 1864.

Morris, James W.: Private

Enlisted in Co. F on 8/9/1862 in Bertie Co. at age 19; born circa 1843; son of Allen and Sarah Morris; brother of George Morris, Edward Morris and Andrew Morris, also of Co. F; Sept./Oct. 1862 "absent without leave"; after November 1862 reported as "deserted."

Morris, William: Private

Enlisted in Co. F on 8/9/1862 in Bertie Co. at age 27; born March 9, 1827 in Bertie Co.; son of James Layton Morris and Karen White; brother of Calvin J. Morris and Alpheus Morris, also of Co. F; listed as a clerk in the 1850 Bertie Co. Census; present or accounted for on muster rolls through October 1864; died on April 11, 1882, buried in the Lane Cemetery in Pasquotank Co.

Morris, William S.: Private

Enlisted in Co. F on 8/9/1862 in Bertie Co. at age 22; born circa 1839; son of Joseph and Elizabeth Morris of Bertie Co.; died on 9/10/1863.

Myers, Ralph D.: Private

Enlisted in Co. F on 8/9/1862 in Bertie Co. at age 32; August 1863 "absent without leave"; after Feb. 1864 reported as a "deserter"; enlisted 6/1/1863 in Company B, 12th Battalion NC Cavalry while absent from 4th NC Cavalry.

Myers, Samuel L.: Private

Enlisted in Co. F on 8/9/1862 in Bertie Co. at age 22; previously served as a private in Company L, 1st NC Infantry (six months, 1861); present or accounted for on muster rolls through October 1864.

Newbury, George C.: Private

Enlisted in Co. F on 7/7/1862 in Bertie Co. at age 16; 9/1/1862 Garysburg, NC roll states "rejected and under age."

Northcutt, William T.: Private

Enlisted in Co. F; born circa 1842; son of Andrew and Sally Northcut(t) of Bertie Co.; 12/31/1863–4/30/1864 rolls state "Absent. Exchanged for F. C. Bowen"; Oct. 1864 "Absent. Has not reported." Married Octavia Rayner on November 19, 1865 in Bertie Co.

Outlaw, David C.: Sergeant

Enlisted in Co. F on 8/9/1862 in Bertie Co.; born circa 1846; son of attorney David Outlaw of Bertie Co.; previously served in Company L, 1st NC Infantry (six months, 1861); mustered in as a sergeant; transferred 11/15/1862 to Company B, 12th Battalion NC Cavalry upon appointment to 2nd lieutenant; 3/9/1864 resigned his commission and returned to Company F, 4th NC Cavalry; June 1864 transferred back to 12th Battalion NC Cavalry in exchange for Marcus H. Bowen; 7/11/1864 transferred as a sergeant from Company B, 12th Battalion NC Cavalry to Company I, 4th NC Cavalry.

Outlaw, George W.: Private

Enlisted in Co. F on 8/9/1862 in Bertie Co. at age 20; born circa 1842; son of Wilson and Penelope Outlaw of Bertie Co.; mustered in as a private; transferred 2/1/1863 to Field and Staff of regiment and assigned to band as a musician; present or accounted for on muster rolls through April 1863; May/June 1863 "at home on detail"; after August 1863 reported as "deserted"; married Sally Ann Cherry on January 30, 1867 in Bertie Co.

Page, William B.: Corporal

Enlisted in Co. F on 8/9/1862 in Bertie Co. at age 29; born circa 1832; son of Solomon and Sarah Page; listed as a student, living with his parents in the 1850 Bertie Co. Census; mustered in as a corporal; present or accounted for on muster rolls through October 1862.

Parker, Isaac: Private

Enlisted in Co. F on 8/9/1862 in Bertie Co. at age 27; born circa 1837; listed as living (age 13) in the Jordan Parker household in the 1850 Bertie Co. Census; after 11/1/1862 reported as "deserted"; married Ellen Hall on March 2, 1867 in Bertie Co.

Parker, James R.: Private

Enlisted in Co. F on 8/9/1862 in Bertie Co. at age 26; captured 6/21/1863 in Upperville, VA; 6/25/1863 confined to Old Capitol Prison; paroled and exchanged 6/30/1863 in City Point, VA; admitted 8/12/1863 to Richmond hospital with "febris typhoides"; 8/22/1863 sent to Castle Thunder Prison, Richmond; reported as a "deserter" after March 1864.

Parker, Joseph B.: Private

Enlisted in Co. F on 8/9/1862 in Bertie Co. at age 28; after August 1863 reported as "absent without leave" and as a "deserter."

Parker, Nazareth W.: Private

Enlisted in Co. F on 8/9/1862 in Bertie Co. at age 21; born circa 1841; son of Lemuel and Elizabeth Parker; resident of Bertie Co. at the time of enlistment; after 11/1/1862 reported as a "deserter"; 2/25/1864 received by provost marshal, Ft. Monroe as a "Rebel deserter. Came into Federal lines Plymouth, NC"; 3/3/1864 sent to Washington, DC; 3/14/1864 took Oath of Allegiance; he married Sarah Hall on August 22, 1866 in Bertie Co.

Peele, Joseph S.: Private

Enlisted in Co. F on 8/9/1862 in Bertie Co. at age 30; born circa 1834; son of Amos and Nancy Peell; brother of William E. Peele, also of Co. F; last name often appears as "Peell" in records; admitted on 12/9/1864 to a Richmond hospital with "gangrene knee"; 1/28/1865 furloughed for 60 days.

Peele, William E.: Private

Enlisted in Co. F on 8/9/1862 in Bertie Co. at age 21; born circa 1840; son of Amos and Nancy Peell; brother of Joseph S. Peele, also of Co. F; last name often appears as "Peell" in records; captured 1/26/1864 near Plymouth, NC, held at Pt. Lookout; died there 8/7/1864; buried in Confederate Cemetery, Pt. Lookout.

Perry, Freeman: Private

Enlisted in Co. F on 8/9/1862 in Bertie Co. at age 21; born circa 1841; son of John and Judia "Indy" Perry of Bertie Co., listed as living with them in the 1860 Bertie Co. Census; after August 1863 reported as "absent without leave" on muster rolls; married Harriet Ann Perry on February 6, 1868 in Bertie Co., NC.

Perry, Jacob B.: Private

Enlisted in Co. F on 8/9/1862 in Bertie Co. at age 22; born circa 1839; son of Wright and Kiddy Perry of Bertie Co.; captured 6/21/1863 in Upperville, VA, held at Old Capitol Prison; paroled and exchanged 6/30/1863 in City Point, VA; after August 1863 "absent without leave."

Perry, S.: Private

Enlisted in Co. F; the 12/31/1863–4/30/1864 muster roll states "Exchanged. 68th Regiment NC Troops. In place of James Francis"; 4/30/1864–8/31/1864 roll states "Has not reported."

Phelps, Henry P.: Private

Enlisted in Co. F on 8/9/1862 in Bertie Co. at age 26; born circa 1844 (age six in 1850 Bertie Co. Census); son of Micajah and Ann R. Phelps of Bertie Co.; 3/27/1864 received by provost marshal, Ft. Monroe as a "Rebel deserter. Came into Federal lines Plymouth, NC; 4/4/1864 took Oath of Amnesty and sent to Plymouth, NC"; married Margaret P. Shaw on June 7, 1866 in Bertie Co.

Pierce, James Richard: Private

Enlisted in Co. F on 8/9/1862 in Bertie Co. at age 17; born circa 1846; son of David Pierce of Bertie Co.; last name also appears as "Pearce"; after August 1863 "absent without leave"; married Sally Cherry Perry on October 18, 1866 in Bertie Co.

Pierce, John W.: Private

Enlisted in Co. F on 8/9/1862 in Bertie Co. at age 16; born circa 1845; son of Hardy and Hester Pierce of Bertie Co.; last name also appears as "Pearce"; captured 6/21/1863 in Upperville, VA, held at Old Capitol Prison; paroled and exchanged 6/30/1863 in City Point, VA; after August 1863 reported as "absent without leave"; married Harriet Ann Perry on February 7, 1867 in Bertie Co.

Pitman, John D.: Private

Enlisted in Co. F on 8/9/1862 in Bertie Co.; the 8/9/1863–9/31/1863 muster roll states "wounded and in hospital"; present or accounted for on muster rolls through October 1864; admitted 3/29/1865 to Petersburg hospital with gunshot wound (right knee); transferred 3/31/1865 to Richmond hospital; captured there 4/3/1865; "deserted" 5/9/1865 from hospital.

Rayner, John A.: Private

Enlisted in Co. F on 8/9/1862 in Bertie Co. at age 24; born circa 1838; son of William and Eliza Rayner of Bertie Co.; listed as living in the household of mechanic Thomas Hoggard in the 1860 Bertie Co. Census; present or accounted for on muster rolls through October 1864; received 3/15/1865 by provost marshal general, Army of the Potomac as a "rebel deserter"; forwarded to Washington, DC where he was received 3/18/1865; took Oath of Allegiance and furnished transportation to Norfolk, VA.

Rhea, John: Corporal

Enlisted in Co. F on 8/9/1862 in Bertie Co. at age 34; born circa 1829; listed as a farmer in the 1850 Bertie Co. Census (household 916), living with his mother Elizabeth; last name also appears as "Ray" in records; mustered in as a private; Sept./Oct. 1863 appointed farrier; May/June 1864 promoted to corporal; admitted 11/2/1864 to Richmond hospital with "feb. remitt."; 12/16/1864 returned to duty.

Rice, Dorsey: Private

Enlisted in Co. F on 8/9/1862 in Bertie Co. at age 34; born circa 1828; name also appears as "Dawry" and "Doweny" in records; son of John and Sarah Rice of Bertie Co.; listed as living with his wife Mary in the 1860 Bertie Co. Census; captured 6/21/1863 in Upperville, VA, held at Old Capitol Prison; paroled and exchanged 6/30/1863 in City Point, VA; admitted 8/18/1864 to Petersburg hospital with gunshot wound (right elbow); 9/1/1864 furloughed for 40 days.

Rice, Lemuel S.: Private

Enlisted in Co. F on 8/9/1862 in Bertie Co. at age 56; present or accounted for on muster rolls through October 1864.

Rice, William D.: Private

Enlisted in Co. F on 8/9/1862 in Bertie Co. at age 23; born circa 1840; son of William and Priscilla Rice of Bertie Co.; listed as living in the William D. Wynns household in the 1860 Bertie Co. Census; present or accounted for on muster rolls through October 1864.

Robinson, E. J.: Private

    Enlisted in Co. F on 8/9/1864 in Bertie Co.; born 10/13/1820; present or accounted for on muster rolls through October 1864; died 6/23/1899, buried Oakwood Cemetery, Gastonia, NC.

Shadgate, Charles: Private

    Enlisted in Co. F on 10/1/1862 in Bertie Co.; last name also appears as "Shadgett" and "Shadgell" in records; born circa 1845; son of William Shadgell (sailor, born in England) and Eliza Shadgell; listed as living with his mother Sally Eliza "Shadgett" in the 1860 Bertie Co. Census; transferred 1/9/1863 to Company G, 32nd NC Infantry.

Simmons, William J.: Private

    Enlisted in Co. F on 8/9/1862 in Bertie Co. at age 26; born circa 1835; son of Samuel and Pernecia Simmons of Bertie Co.; present or accounted for on muster rolls through October 1864; married Mary D. Burden on December 25, 1866 in Bertie Co.

Smithwick, John Thomas: Private

    Enlisted in Co. F on 8/9/1862 in Bertie Co. at age 18; born circa 1844; son of William Smithwick of Bertie Co.; May/June 1863 reported as "absent wounded and paroled"; present or accounted for on muster rolls through October 1864; married Elizabeth A. Pearce on December 21, 1865 in Bertie Co.

Speller, Charles B.: 3rd Lieutenant

    Enlisted in Co. F on 8/9/1862 in Bertie Co. at age 23; born circa 1840; son of Thomas H. and Mary F. Speller of Bertie Co.; resident of Bertie Co. at the time of enlistment; mustered in as a corporal; appointed sergeant before 3/1/1863; appointed 3rd lieutenant on 6/4/1863; wounded in action on 6/21/1863 in Upperville, VA; reported as absent wounded at home through 4/30/1864; present or accounted for on muster rolls through October 1864.

Sutton, Lewis Bond: 2nd Lieutenant

    Enlisted in Co. F on 8/9/1862 in Bertie Co. at age 22; name also appears as "Louis" in records; son of John A. Sutton and Esther Taylor Bond; born June 30, 1840 in Bertie Co., where he resided as a farm assistant at the time of enlistment; listed as living in his grandfather Lewis Bond's household in the 1850 Bertie Co. Census; listed as living in the William Moring household in 1860 Bertie Co. Census; previously served as a private in Company L, 1st NC Infantry (six months, 1861); appointed 2nd lieutenant to rank from date of enlistment; captured 6/21/1863 in Upperville, VA, held at Old Capitol Prison; transferred 8/8/1863 to Johnson's Island; transferred 2/24/1865 to City Pt., VA for exchange; married Sally A. Cooper on June 22, 1865 in Bertie Co.; died on September 29, 1907 in Bertie Co.

Swain, Thomas E.: Private

    Enlisted in Co. F; born circa 1836; listed as living in the William J. Cherry household in the 1850 Bertie Co. Census; 12/31/1863–4/30/1864 roll states "Exchanged

68th Regiment NC Troops in place of G. W. Cobb"; present or accounted for on muster rolls through October 1864.

Tayloe, George: Private
Enlisted in Co. F on 8/9/1862 in Bertie Co. at age 26; born circa 1834; last name also appears as "Taylor" in records; son of John and Mary Taylor of Bertie Co.; listed as a farmer and living with his wife Martha A. Tayloe in the 1860 Bertie Co. Census; the 9/1/1862 muster-in roll states "absent without leave"; Sept./Oct. 1862 roll states "never reported"; after November 1862 reported as a "deserter."

Tayloe, Henry: Private
Enlisted in Co. F on 8/9/1862 in Bertie Co. at age 19; resident of Bertie Co. at the time of enlistment; captured 4/6/1865 at High Bridge, VA, held at Pt. Lookout; released 6/30/1865 after taking Oath of Allegiance.

Tayloe, James: Private
Enlisted in Co. F on 8/9/1862 in Bertie Co. at age 21; born 12/25/1840; resident of Bertie Co. at the time of enlistment; captured 4/6/1865 at Amelia Court House, VA, held at Pt. Lookout; released 6/30/1865 after taking Oath of Allegiance; died 5/7/1930, buried James Tayloe Cemetery, Highway 305, Bertie Co., NC.

Thomas, Lewis: Private
Enlisted in Co. F on 8/9/1862 in Bertie Co. at age 37; married Esther Pierce on January 30, 1853 in Bertie Co.; listed as a farmer and living with his wife Esther in the 1860 Bertie Co. Census; muster rolls through 3/1/1863 report him as "absent sick"; after March 1863 reported as "deserted."

Watford, Joseph J.: 3rd Lieutenant
Enlisted in Co. F on 8/9/1862 in Bertie Co. at age 23; born circa 1838; listed as living in the James White household in the 1850 Bertie Co. Census; listed as a farmer in the 1860 Bertie Co. Census, with real estate valued at $10,600; appointed 3rd lieutenant to rank from date of enlistment; resigned 2/27/1863 due to health, also stated that his estate was near the enemy lines; resignation officially accepted 3/17/1863; may have previously served as private in Company L, 1st NC infantry (six months, 1861), may have later served as sergeant in Company B, 15th Battalion NC Cavalry.

White, James W.: Corporal
Enlisted in Co. F on 8/9/1862 in Bertie Co.; mustered in as a private; appointed corporal before 3/1/1863; present or accounted for on muster rolls through October 1864.

White, Joseph W.: Private
Enlisted in Co. F on 8/9/1862 in Bertie Co. at age 28; born circa 1834; son of Harvey J. and Martha White of Bertie Co.; living with his parents and listed as a student in the 1850 Bertie Co. Census; Sept./Oct. 1862–February 1864 reported as "deserted"; 12/31/1863–4/30/1864 roll states "Absent. Confined in prison." Released 7/29/1864 and returned to duty; present or accounted for on muster rolls through October 1864.

White, Zachariah: Private

Enlisted in Co. F on 8/9/1862 in Bertie Co.; born circa 1833; listed as living in the Martin White household in the 1850 Bertie Co. Census and with his brother Lodowick White in the 1860 Bertie Co. Census; present or accounted for on muster rolls through October 1864.

Williford, Alanson: Private

Enlisted in Co. F on 8/9/1862 in Bertie Co. at age 32; born circa 1831; married Martha Butler on April 5, 1855 in Bertie Co.; listed as a farmer and living with her in the 1860 Bertie Co. Census; last name also appears as "Willeford" and "Wilford"; captured 6/21/1863 in Upperville, VA, held at Old Capitol Prison; paroled and exchanged 6/30/1863 in City Point, VA; after August 1863 reported as "absent leg broken at hospital" and "absent wounded at home"; married Martha Butler on April 5, 1855 in Bertie Co.

Willoughby, John R.: Private

Enlisted in Co. F on 8/9/1862 in Bertie Co.; AWOL Sept. 1, 1862–April 1863 and August 1863–Oct. 1, 1864; 10/20/1864 issued clothing.

Willoughby, John W.: Private

Enlisted in Co. F on 8/9/1862 in Bertie Co. at age 30; resident of Hertford Co.; May/June 1863–August 1864 reported as "deserted"; returned to company Sept./Oct. 1864; admitted 2/3/1865 to Raleigh hospital with "febris typhoides"; 3/11/1865 returned to duty.

Willoughby, Winborn: Private

Enlisted in Co. F on 8/9/1862 in Bertie Co. at age 26; present or accounted for on muster rolls through October 1864.

Company G

Ballance, Caleb: Private

Enlisted in Co. G on 3/31/1862 in Currituck Co. at age 20; born on September 4, 1840 in Currituck Co. on the Mathias–John Harrell farm; son of Spence Ballance and Sivility Miller; listed as living in Peter Parker household in the 1850 Currituck Co. Census with his sister Mahala and brother Levin; resident of Currituck Co. at the time of enlistment; wounded in action (right arm) and captured on 6/19/1863 in Middleburg, VA, held at Old Capitol Prison; paroled and exchanged 6/30/1863 in City Point, VA; admitted 6/30/1863 to hospital; 8/8/1863 returned to duty; present or accounted for on muster rolls through October 1864; received by provost marshal general, Washington, DC 4/17/1865, on list of refugees and deserters with comment "Transportation ordered to Currituck County, NC"; occupation, farmer; died 4/12/1926 at Bell's Island, NC and buried in the Ballance-Snowden Cemetery, Maple Rd., Currituck Co., NC; a wonderful account of his life by Angeline M. Hayman is published in *The Heritage of Currituck County, North Carolina 1985* (Jo Anna Heath Bates, editor).

Ballance, Levi: Sergeant

Enlisted in Co. G on 3/31/1862 in Currituck Co. at age 29; resident of Currituck Co.; son of Wilson and Cynthia Ballance; mustered in as a corporal; wounded in action and captured on 6/19/1863 in Middleburg, VA, held at Old Capitol Prison; paroled and exchanged 6/30/1863 in City Point, VA; present or accounted for on muster rolls through October 1864; paroled 4/14/1865.

Ballance, Samuel: Private

Enlisted in Co. G on 3/31/1862 in Currituck Co. at age 19; son of Charlotte Ballance; present or accounted for on muster rolls through October 1864.

Barnett, John J.: Private

Enlisted in Co. G on 3/31/1862 in Currituck Co. at age 24; born in Camden Co.; died 5/18/1862 in a Petersburg hospital.

Baxter, Wallace B.: Private

Enlisted in Co. G on 12/6/1863 in Caroline Co., VA; born 1845; son of Thomas E. and Love Baxter; died 5/9/1864 in Raleigh hospital of "febris typhoides"; buried Oakwood Cemetery, Raleigh, NC.

Beasley, Malachi W.: Private

Enlisted in Co. G on 3/31/1862 in Currituck Co. at age 19; wounded in action (arm) on 6/19/1863 in Middleburg, VA; present or accounted for on muster rolls until transferred on 3/1/1864 to Company G, 68th NC Infantry.

Bell, Demosthenes: Captain

Enlisted in Co. G on 3/31/1862 in Currituck Co.; born circa 1838; son of Sarah Bell; listed as living with mother in household of Virginius and Mary Pitts in the 1850 Currituck Co. Census; previously served in Company I, 5th VA Cavalry (12 months, 1861–1862); appointed captain to rank 3/18/1862 of Company G, 4th NC Cavalry; captured 6/19/1863 in Middleburg, VA, held at Old Capitol Prison; transferred 8/8/1863 to Johnson's Island, 2/9/1864 to Baltimore, 2/14/1864 to Pt. Lookout; paroled and exchanged 3/3/1864 at Aiken's Landing, VA; present or accounted for on muster rolls through August 1864.

Bell, George F.: Ordnance Sergeant

Enlisted in Co. G on 3/31/1862 in Currituck Co. at age 30; born circa 1833; listed as living in Richard Flora's household in the 1850 Currituck Co. Census; resident of Camden Co. at the time of enlistment; mustered in as a corporal; promoted to sergeant in May/June 1862; present or accounted for on muster rolls through October 1864; paroled 4/25/1865 at Provost Marshal's Office, District of Eastern VA as an ordnance sergeant.

Bell, James H.: Private

Enlisted in Co. G on 5/1/1862 in Currituck Co.; resident of Currituck Co.; captured 10/14/1863 near Parksville (Perquimans Co.), NC while on detail to obtain a horse; held at Pt. Lookout, released May 12–14, 1865 after taking Oath of Allegiance.

Bell, John B.: Private

Enlisted in Co. G on 4/24/1862 in Currituck Co.; born circa 1838; son of James and Martha Bell; discharged 7/8/1862 upon providing John McGinniess as a substitute.

Brabbitt, J. B.: Private

Enlisted in Co. G; captured 6/19/1863 in Middleburg, VA, held at Old Capitol Prison; paroled and exchanged 6/30/1863 in City Point, VA.

Brabble, James J.: Private

Enlisted in Co. G on 3/31/1862 in Currituck Co. at age 27; son of James and Dorcas (or Doris) Brabble; brother of John W. Brabble, also of Co. G; resident of Currituck Co.; captured 3/3/1864 in Currituck Co., held at Pt. Lookout; released May 12–14, 1865 after taking Oath of Allegiance.

Brabble, John W.: Private

Enlisted in Co. G on 3/31/1862 in Currituck Co. at age 20; son of James and Dorcas (or Doris) Brabble; brother of James J. Brabble, also of Co. G; resident of Currituck Co. at the time of enlistment; present or accounted for on muster rolls through October 1864.

Bray, Wallace M.: Private

Enlisted in Co. G on 1/1/1864 in Caroline Co., VA; born circa 1848; son of Wallace Bray of Currituck Co., NC; present or accounted for on muster rolls through October 1864; paroled 4/14/1865 at HQ, 3rd Brigade, 1st Division, 9th Army Corps.

Bright, Isaac: Private

Enlisted in Co. G on 4/18/1862 in Currituck Co.; born circa 1841; son of Washington and Lovey Bright; present or accounted for on muster rolls through February 1864; after February 1864 reported as "absent without leave."

Brock, William: Private

Enlisted in Co. G; captured 9/14/1864 in Currituck Co.; held as a prisoner of war; released after war.

Brothers, William H., Jr.: Private

Enlisted in Co. G on 4/9/1862 in Currituck Co. at age 19; born August 3, 1840 in Pasquotank Co., where he resided as a farmer at the time of enlistment; previously served as a private in Company E, 17th NC Infantry (1st Organization); discharged 6/8/1862 in Petersburg due to "disease of the heart"; father also in this company; died April 1, 1895, buried in the Moriah Methodist Church Cemetery in Guilford Co.

Brothers, William H., Sr.: Private

Enlisted in Co. G on 5/1/1862 in Currituck Co.; "Deserted at Shingle Landing [Creek][Currituck Co.], NC, May 10, 1862"; son also in this company.

Brothers, Wilson: Private

Enlisted in Co. G on 11/1/1862 in Prince George Co., VA; born circa 1815; listed as living with his wife, Susan and five children in the 1850 Currituck Co. Census; farmer; previously served as a private in Company E, 17th NC Infantry; substitute for William R. Sears; captured 10/14/1863 near Newler's Bridge, NC, held at Pt. Lookout; died there 9/12/1864; buried in the Confederate Cemetery, Pt. Lookout.

Brumsey, John W.: Private

Enlisted in Co. G on 4/5/1862 in Currituck Co. at age 21; son of Augustus (carpenter) and Amelia Brumsey; brother of Malachi Brumsey, also of Co. G; resident of Currituck Co.; captured 6/19/1863 in Middleburg, VA, held at Old Capitol Prison; paroled and exchanged 6/30/1863 in City Point, VA; present or accounted for on muster rolls through October 1864; paroled 4/14/1865 at HQ, 3rd Brigade, 1st Division, 9th Army Corps.

Brumsey, Malachi J.: Private

Enlisted in Co. G on 3/31/1862 in Currituck Co. at age 19; son of Augustus (carpenter) and Amelia Brumsey; brother of John Brumsey, also of Co. G; resident of Currituck Co.; present or accounted for on muster rolls through October 1864; paroled 4/14/1865 at HQ, 3rd Brigade, 1st Division, 9th Army Corps.

Bunnill, Stephen D.: Private

Enlisted in Co. G on 5/1/1862 in Currituck Co.; born circa 1830; listed as living in the Jordan Bunnell household in the 1850 Currituck Co. Census; previously served as 2nd lieutenant in 1st Regiment (Currituck Co.), 1st Brigade NC Confederate Militia, commissioned 11/6/1861; discharged from 4th NC Cavalry 9/1/1862 at Sycamore Church, Prince George Co., VA upon furnishing a substitute.

Carsen, J. P.: Private

Enlisted in Co. G; captured 7/14/1863 at Falling Waters, MD, held at Pt. Lookout; "exchanged March 17, 1865."

Cayton, James S.: Private

Enlisted in Co. G on 3/31/1862 in Currituck Co. at age 23; son of John and Chloe Cayton; resident of Currituck Co.; captured 6/19/1863 in Middleburg, VA, held at Old Capitol Prison; paroled and exchanged 6/30/1863 in City Point, VA; recaptured 2/5/1864 in Currituck Co., held at Pt. Lookout; paroled and exchanged 2/24/1865 at Aiken's Landing, James River, VA; paroled 4/30/1865 at Provost Marshal's Office, Dist. of Eastern VA.

Cotter, Quinton T.: Private

Enlisted in Co. G on 4/8/1862 in Currituck Co. at age 25; son of William T. and Polly Cotter; resident of Currituck Co.; farmer; captured 3/24/1864 in Currituck Co., held at Pt. Lookout; released May 12–14, 1865 after taking Oath of Allegiance.

Cox, Davis M.: Private

Enlisted in Co. G on 4/7/1862 in Currituck Co. at age 29; captured 7/4/1863 South Mtn., held at Ft. Delaware; transferred 8/10/1863 to US Army General Hospital, Chester, PA; died there 9/10/1863 of "gangrene."

Jabez "Jabie" Cox, Company G, Currituck County (Bettie Morris Young).

Cox, Jabez: Private

Enlisted in Co. G on 3/31/1862 in Currituck Co. at age 35; called "Jabie"; born on March 24, 1827 at Old Trap in Camden Co.; son of Jabez Cox and Miriam Harrison; married Margaret Anderson; present or accounted for on muster rolls until transferred on 4/1/1864 to Company B, 68th NC Infantry; after the war he continued to farm in Currituck and Camden Counties; died circa 1899, buried "in the church yard of Shady Grove Church," Currituck Co.

Creekmore, Peter C.: Private

Enlisted in Co. G on 11/24/1862 in Prince George Co. VA; born circa 1843 in Camden Co., NC; son of Elliot and Harriet Creekmore; resident of Camden Co.; captured 6/19/1863 in Middleburg, VA, held at Old Capitol Prison; paroled and exchanged 6/30/1863 in City Point, VA; present or accounted for on muster rolls through October 1864; paroled 4/30/1865 at Provost Marshal's Office, Dist. of Eastern VA.

Creekmore, Samuel E.: Private

Enlisted in Co. G on 1/1/1864 in Caroline Co., VA; name also appears as Creekmur; born December 5, 1842; son of Horatio S. Creekmore and Susan Morse; brother of Wilson Preston Creekmore, also of Co. G.; present or accounted for on muster rolls through October 1864; admitted 3/30/1865 to Petersburg hospital with gunshot wound to face; admitted 4/5/1865 to Danville, VA hospital; furloughed 4/9/1865 for 30 days; family history states that he lost an arm during the war.

Creekmore, Wilson Preston: Private

Enlisted in Co. G on 1/1/1864 in Currituck Co.; name also appears as Creekmur; born April 15, 1847; son of Horatio S. Creekmore and Susan Morse; brother of Samuel E. Creekmore, also of Co. G.; resident of Currituck Co.; joined Company G at Milford Station, Caroline Co., VA; present or accounted for on muster rolls through October 1864; paroled 4/15/1865 at HQ, 3rd Brigade, 1st Division, 9th Army Corps; after the war he settled in Moycock, NC, where he opened a general store and became a landowner; married Adelaide Williams, died in 1904 of stomach cancer.

Wilson Preston Creekmore, Company G, Currituck County (Debbie Loefgren).

Culpeper, Hardy: Private

Enlisted in Co. G on 4/5/1862 in Currituck Co. at age 31; listed as living with his mother Rebecca Culpeper in the 1850 Currituck Co. Census; present or accounted for on muster rolls until transferred on 4/1/1864 to Company G, 68th NC Infantry.

Davis, Jeremiah: Private

Enlisted in Co. G on 5/1/1862 in Currituck Co.; residing as a farmer in Currituck Co. at the time of enlistment; captured 6/19/1863 in Middleburg, VA; paroled and exchanged 6/30/1863 in City Point, VA; recaptured 3/24/1864 at Shingle Landing (Creek), Currituck Co., NC, held at Pt. Lookout; released May 12–14, 1865 after taking Oath of Allegiance; may have previously served as private in Company E, 17th NC Infantry (1st Organization).

Davis, S.: Private

Enlisted in Co. G; captured 7/6/1863 near Gettysburg, PA, held at Ft. Delaware; paroled and exchanged 8/1/1863 in City Point, VA.

Divers, Henry H.: 1st Sergeant

Enlisted in Co. G on 3/31/1862 in Currituck Co. at age 39; listed as a tailor living with his wife, Mary and their daughter Jess Ann in the 1850 Currituck Co. Census; resident of Currituck Co.; mustered in as a sergeant; promoted to 1st sergeant July/August 1863; present or accounted for on muster rolls through October 1864; paroled 4/30/1865 at Provost Marshal's Office, Dist. of Eastern VA.

Dowdy, Benjamin: Private

Enlisted in Co. G on 3/31/1862 in Currituck Co. at age 22; son of William Dowdy of Currituck Co.; died 6/18/1862 in Petersburg hospital of "febris congestira."

Dozier, Noah J.: Private

Enlisted in Co. G on 4/9/1862 in Currituck Co. at age 25; born and resided in Camden Co.; listed as living in the Almond Jones household in the 1850 Currituck Co. Census; previously served as a private in Company H (1st), 32nd NC Infantry; transferred 5/6/1862 to Company A, 56th NC Infantry.

Dudley, Malachi: Private

Enlisted in Co. G on 3/31/1862 in Currituck Co. at age 37; born 1824 in Currituck Co., where he resided at the time of enlistment; captured 6/19/1863 in Middleburg, VA, held at Old Capitol Prison; paroled and exchanged 6/30/1863 in City Point, VA; present or accounted for on muster rolls through October 1864; paroled 4/27/1865 at Provost Marshal's Office, Dist. of Eastern VA.

Etheridge, Elias: Private

Enlisted in Co. G on 8/8/1862 in Petersburg, VA; born circa 1825; farmer residing in Currituck Co., NC; substitute for Thomas D. Sears; captured 6/19/1863 in Middleburg, VA, held at Old Capitol Prison; paroled and exchanged 6/30/1863 in City Point, VA; present or accounted for on muster rolls through August 1864.

Etheridge, Peter: Private

Enlisted in Co. G on 5/1/1862 in Currituck Co.; born circa 1834; son of Caleb and Elizabeth Etheridge; previously served in 1st Regiment (Currituck Co.), 1st Brigade NC Confederate Militia, commissioned 2nd lieutenant on 11/6/1861; killed in action on 6/19/1863 in Middleburg, VA.

Etheridge, Samuel A.: Corporal

Enlisted in Co. G on 4/18/1862 in Currituck Co.; born circa 1826; listed as living with wife Sarah in the 1850 Currituck Co. Census; mustered in as a Private; 5/1/1862 appointed corporal; captured 8/6/1863 at Mountain Run, VA, held at Pt. Lookout; died there October 1863; buried in Confederate Cemetery, Pt. Lookout.

Etheridge, Spence W.: Private

Enlisted in Co. G on 4/9/1862 in Currituck Co. at age 19; listed as living in household of Nathan Etheridge in 1850 Currituck Co. Census; captured 6/19/1863 in Middleburg, VA, held at Old Capitol Prison; paroled and exchanged 6/30/1865 in City Point, VA; present or accounted for on muster rolls until transferred on 3/1/1864 to Company G, 68th NC Infantry.

Etheridge, William A.: Private

Enlisted in Co. G on 4/28/1862 in Currituck Co.; present or accounted for on muster rolls through August 1864; reported as "absent sick" on muster rolls March/ April 1863–August 1864; 12/11/1864 appears on hospital record of 4th Div., General Hospital, Camp Winder, Richmond stating transferred to 6th Div. of same hospital.

Ferebee, Enoch D.: Private

Enlisted in Co. G on 3/31/1862 in Currituck Co. age 40; born 10/31/1821; son of Rev. Samuel Ferebee and Nancy Simmons; brother of Mitchel S. Ferebee and nephew of Col. Dennis D. Ferebee of this regiment; wife, Elizabeth; muster rolls for Jan./Feb. 1864 show him "On detail to remount"; present or accounted for on muster rolls until he transferred on 3/1/1864 to Company G, 68th NC Infantry; died 2/7/1889, buried in Walker Cemetery, Robert Walker Farm, Tulls Creek Rd, Currituck Co., NC.

Ferebee, Joseph B.: Private

Enlisted in Co. G on 11/24/1862 in Prince George Co., VA; born circa 1827; living in the Edwin Ferebee household in the 1850 Camden Co. Census; previously served in 2nd Regiment (Camden Co.), 1st Brigade NC Conf. Militia, commissioned 2nd lieutenant on 10/25/1861; discharged 4/25/1863 due to disability.

Ferebee, Mitchel Simmons: Private

Enlisted in Co. G on 3/31/1862 in Currituck Co. at age 42; born 4/7/1819, Currituck Co.; son of Rev. Samuel Ferebee and Nancy Simmons; brother of Enoch D. Ferebee and nephew of Col. Dennis D. Ferebee of this regiment; farmer; wife, Lotty; previously served in 1st Regiment (Currituck Co.), 1st Brigade NC Conf. Militia, commissioned 2nd lieutenant on 11/6/1861; mustered in as 2nd sergeant; 5/24/1862 appointed 1st sergeant; July/August 1863 reduced to ranks, also "on detail to purchase horse"; present or accounted for on muster rolls until transferred on 3/1/1864 to Company G, 68th NC Infantry; died 11/19/1889 in Currituck Co.; buried in private cemetery near corner of East Ridge Rd. and South Marshall Rd., Currituck Co. (a six-foot stone with Masonic seal marks his grave).

Field, Jerry H.: Private
Enlisted in Co. G; captured 2/24/1864 in Currituck Co.; confined 3/12/1864 to Pt. Lookout.

Forbes, Andrew Jackson: Private
Enlisted in Co. G on 3/31/1862 in Currituck Co. at age 24; son of Thomas Forbes; resident of Currituck Co.; called "Jackson"; wounded in action and captured on 6/19/1863 in Middleburg, VA, held at Old Capitol Prison; paroled and exchanged 6/30/1863 in City Point, VA; admitted 6/30/1863 to Petersburg hospital; furloughed 8/13/1863 for 40 days; present or accounted for on muster rolls through October 1864; served as a courier to Brig. Gen. William P. Roberts until the surrender at Appomattox; paroled 4/15/1865 at HQ, 3rd Brigade, 1st Division, 9th Army Corps.

Forbes, Isaac W.: Private
Enlisted in Co. G on 5/1/1862 in Currituck Co.; captured 6/19/1863 in Middleburg, VA, held at Old Capitol Prison; paroled and exchanged 6/30/1863 in City Point, VA; present or accounted for on muster rolls until transferred on 4/1/1864 to Company G, 68th NC Infantry.

Forbes, Jeremiah: Private
Enlisted in Co. G on 3/31/1862 in Currituck Co. at age 24; listed as living in the William D. Knight household in the 1850 Camden Co., NC Census; admitted 7/13/1863 to Petersburg hospital as a "paroled prisoner" for "diarrhea chronic"; returned to duty 8/14/1863; after July 1863 reported as absent without leave.

Frost, Alfred P.: 3rd Lieutenant
Enlisted in Co. G on 3/31/1862 in Currituck Co. at age 22; resident of Currituck Co.; appointed 3rd lieutenant to rank from date of enlistment; submitted resignation 8/10/1863 due to health; resignation officially accepted 9/11/1863.

Fulford, George: Private
Enlisted in Co. G on 4/24/1862 in Currituck Co.; resident of Currituck Co.; previously served as a private in Company E, 17th NC Infantry (1st Organization); present or accounted for on muster rolls through October 1864; paroled 4/15/1865 at HQ, 3rd Brigade, 1st Division, 9th Army Corps.

Fulford, James: Private
Enlisted in Co. G on 4/5/1862 in Currituck Co. at age 37; captured 10/14/1863 at Catlett Station, VA, held at Old Capitol Prison; transferred 10/27/1863 to Pt. Lookout; died there 12/8/1863 of "chronic diarrhea"; buried in Confederate Cemetery, Pt. Lookout.

Gammon, James: Private

Enlisted in Co. G on 3/31/1862 in Currituck Co. at age 25; born circa 1837; son of Josiah (carpenter) and Mary A. Gammon; present or accounted for on muster rolls until transferred on 4/1/1864 to Company B, 68th NC Infantry.

Gilbert, Walter Raleigh: Private

Enlisted in Co. G on 11/2/1862 in Prince George Co., VA; born circa 1834; listed as living in the Franklin (farmer) and Elizabeth Gilbert household in the 1850 Currituck Co. Census; captured 6/17/1863 in Middleburg, VA, held at Old Capitol Prison; paroled and exchanged 6/30/1863 in City Point, VA; present or accounted for on muster rolls through October 1864; recaptured and paroled 4/13/1865 in Dinwiddie Co., VA; may have previously served as a private in Company I (1st), 32nd NC Infantry.

Grandy, Abner: Private

Transferred to Co. G on 5/1/1864; previously served in Company G, 68th NC Infantry; present or accounted for on muster rolls through August 1864.

Grandy, Thomas J., Jr.: Private

Enlisted in Co. G on 10/1/1862 in Prince George Co., VA; captured 7/4/1863 at South Mtn., held at Ft. McHenry; transferred 7/9/1863 to Ft. Delaware; paroled and exchanged February 20–21, 1865 at Boulware's and Coxes Wharf, James River, VA; 2/27/1865 present on roll of paroled and exchanged prisoners Camp Lee, Richmond; father also in this company; may have previously served as a private in Company I (1st), 32nd NC Infantry.

Grandy, Thomas J., Sr.: Private

Enlisted in Co. G on 11/1/1862 in Prince George Co., VA; muster rolls indicate he was present through April 1863; absent sick until "deserted to the enemy on or about the first day of August 1863."

Gray, Thomas C.: Private

Enlisted in Co. G on 5/1/1862 in Currituck Co.; previously served as a private in Company E, 17th NC Infantry (1st Organization); present or accounted for on muster rolls through October 1864.

Griggs, Jerome: Private

Enlisted in Co. G on 3/31/1862 in Currituck Co. at age 35; born circa 1828; boarding in the Inn of Abraham Baum (innkeeper) in the 1850 Currituck Co. Census; captured 2/24/1864 in Currituck Co.; paroled and exchanged 5/3/1864; recaptured 9/14/1864 in Currituck Co., held at Pt. Lookout; paroled and exchanged 2/18/1865 at Aiken's Landing, James River, VA; 2/27/1865 present on roll of exchanged and paroled prisoners at Camp Lee, Richmond; admitted 2/26/1865 to Richmond hospital; transferred 4/1/1865 to Farmville, VA; paroled April 1865 in Lynchburg, VA.

Halstead, James R.: Private

Enlisted in Co. G on 4/24/1862 in Currituck Co.; born circa 1836; son of Tully (farmer) and Sarah Halstead of Currituck Co.; resident of Norfolk Co., VA at the time of enlistment; previously served as a corporal in Company E, 17th NC Infantry (1st Organization); present or accounted for on muster rolls through August 1864; paroled 4/27/1865 at Provost Marshal's Office, Dist. of Eastern VA.

Hill, Walter: Private
Enlisted in Co. G; captured 9/14/1864 in Currituck Co.; released after war.

Hines, Leonard P.: Private
Enlisted in Co. G on 3/31/1862 in Currituck Co. at age 18; previously served as a private in Company A, 17th NC Infantry (1st Organization); present or accounted for on muster rolls until transferred on 8/1/1862 to Company D, 17th NC Infantry (2nd Organization).

Hughes, Marshall: Private
Transferred to Co. G on 5/1/1864; previously served in Company B, 68th NC Infantry; present or accounted for on muster rolls through October 1864.

Humphries, Gideon M.: Corporal
Enlisted in Co. G on 3/31/1862 in Currituck Co. at age 19; last name also appears as "Humphreys"; born circa 1842; mother: Adelia Humphreys (appears to be widowed in the 1850 Currituck Co. Census); mustered in as a private; appointed corporal 12/31/1863; present or accounted for on muster rolls through October 1864.

Jennings, Gardner: Private
Enlisted in Co. G on 3/31/1862 in Currituck Co. at age 22; died 2/11/1864 in Richmond hospital of gunshot wound.

Jones, Dempsey: Private
Enlisted in Co. G on 4/14/1862 in Currituck Co.; previously served as a private in Company H (1st), 32nd NC Infantry; wounded in action in June 1863 at Middleburg, VA; died 6/28/1863 of wounds.

Kemp, William: Private
Enlisted in Co. G on 3/31/1862 in Currituck Co. at age 34; captured 12/17/1863 in Currituck Co., held at Pt. Lookout; paroled and exchanged 2/24/1865; admitted 3/8/1865 to Richmond hospital with "debilitas"; furloughed 3/9/1865 for 30 days.

Lane, Holloman: Private
Enlisted in Co. G on 3/31/1862 in Currituck Co. at age 21; resident of Princess Anne County, VA; "deserted on or about the 10th of April 1864"; received 4/27/1864 by provost marshal, Ft. Monroe as a "Rebel Deserter, came into Federal lines, Chowan River, VA [NC]"; released 5/2/1864 after taking Oath of Amnesty, taken to Norfolk, VA.

Lay, J. T.: Private
Enlisted in Co. G; admitted 7/2/1865 to Pt. Lookout hospital with "scorbutus"; died there 7/4/1865.

Lee, Daniel W., Jr.: Sergeant

Enlisted in Co. G on 3/31/1862 in Currituck Co. at age 28; mustered in as a private; appointed sergeant on 10/31/1863; 3/16/1865 reported as "absent without leave" by Conscript Bureau.

Lee, Daniel W., Sr.: Private

Enlisted in Co. G on 10/1/1862 in Prince George Co., VA; substitute for David J. Lee; present or accounted for on muster rolls through October 1864; captured 4/13/1865 in Raleigh hospital; paroled 4/23/1865.

Lee, David J.: Private

Enlisted in Co. G on 5/1/1862 in Currituck Co.; born circa 1831; son of Moses (farmer) Lee; discharged 10/1/1862 at Sycamore Church, Prince George Co., VA upon furnishing Daniel W. Lee, Sr. as substitute.

Lee, Jerome Bunnill: 2nd Lieutenant

Enlisted in Co. G on 3/31/1862 in Currituck Co. at age 26; born March 27, 1835 in Currituck Co. (Tulls Creek); son of Jesse and Mary Bunnill Lee (died in 1836); listed as living with his sister Mary in their uncle John Bunnell's household in the 1850 Currituck Co. Census; married Lydia Grace Baxter (daughter of Thomas Baxter) on July 21, 1858; member of the Shady Grove Baptist Church; occupation, planter; previously served as a sergeant in Company E, 17th NC Infantry (1st Organization); mustered in as a private; 5/24/1862 appointed corporal; captured 6/19/1863 in Upperville, VA, held at Old Capitol Prison; paroled and exchanged 6/30/1863 in City Point, VA; 12/28/1863 elected 2nd lieutenant ; present or accounted for on muster rolls through October 1864; paroled 4/30/1865 at Provost Marshal's Office, Dist. of Eastern VA; Lydia died on June 29, 1875; on October 29, 1876 he married Mary A. Hutchins; married a third time in December 1886 to Sarah Rebecca Messick of Norfolk, VA; active in the Henry M. Shaw Camp of NC Confederate Veterans (No. 1304), serving as adjutant general; died on March 16, 1919 and per his request was buried in his Confederate uniform.

Jerome Bunnill Lee, Company G, Currituck County (Margaret Pritchard).

Lee, Jesse W.: Private
Transferred to Co. G on 7/23/1864; previously served in Company I, 15th VA Cavalry; present or accounted for on muster rolls through October 1864; paroled 4/15/1865 at HQ, 3rd Brigade, 1st Division, 9th Army Corps.

Lindsey, Joseph J.: Private
Enlisted in Co. G on 4/18/1862 in Currituck Co.; previously served as a private in Company E, 17th NC Infantry (1st Organization); mustered in as a private; May/ June 1862 appointed sergeant; July/ August 1863 reduced to ranks; present or accounted for on muster rolls through August 1864.

Lindsey, William: Private
Enlisted in Co. G on 4/5/1862 in Currituck Co. at age 23; born 1839; resident of Currituck Co.; present or accounted for on muster rolls through October 1864; paroled 4/14/1865 at HQ, 3rd Brigade, 1st Division, 9th Army Corps; died 1898, buried Oakwood Cemetery, Raleigh, NC.

Litchfield, Jeremiah B.: Private
Enlisted in Co. G on 3/31/1862 in Currituck Co. at age 46; resided in Currituck Co. as a farmer at the time of enlistment; wife: Patsy; captured 2/24/1864 in Currituck Co., held at Pt. Lookout; released May 12–14, 1865 after taking Oath of Allegiance.

Martin, John: Private
Enlisted in Co. G on 6/4/1862 in Petersburg, VA; substitute for Henry J. Wilson; "Deserted 2 September 1862 at Sycamore Church, Prince George County, VA."

Mathias, Benjamin F.: Private
Enlisted in Co. G on 4/8/1862 in Currituck Co. at age 21; born circa 1840; son of John (farmer) and Olive Mathias of Currituck Co.; present or accounted for on muster rolls through August 1864.

Mathias, John E.: Private
Enlisted in Co. G on 3/31/1862 in Currituck Co. at age 21; born in Isle of Wight Co., VA; died 10/7/1862 in Petersburg hospital of "typhoid fever."

Mathias, Wiley: Private
Enlisted in Co. G on 4/8/1862 in Currituck Co. at age 21; born circa 1840; mother: Sarah Mathias; captured 2/3/1864 in Currituck Co., held at Pt. Lookout; paroled and exchanged 2/24/1865.

McGinniess, John: Private
Enlisted in Co. G on 7/8/1862 in Petersburg, VA; substitute for John B. Bell; "Deserted 2 September 1862 at Sycamore Church, Prince George County, VA."

Morrisette, Peter: Private
Enlisted in Co. G on 3/31/1862 in Currituck Co. at age 36; born 1824 in Currituck Co. where he resided as a farmer at the time of enlistment; son of Cason B.

and Elizabeth West Morrisette; listed as living with four of his siblings in the Jesse Mercer household in the 1850 Currituck Co., NC Census; discharged 6/8/1862 in Petersburg due to "disease of the heart"; died 1888, buried in Morrisette Family Cemetery, US Highway 158, Currituck Co., NC.

Morse, James W.: Corporal

Enlisted in Co. G on 3/31/1862 in Currituck Co. at age 44; born circa 1817; wife, Susan; residing in Currituck Co. as a farmer at the time of enlistment; mustered in as a corporal; admitted 4/2/1865 to Farmville, VA hospital with gunshot wound (right hand and right thigh); present or accounted for on muster rolls through October 1864; paroled between April 11–22, 1865 in Farmville, VA; admitted 6/18/1865 to Norfolk, VA hospital; died there 6/25/1865.

Morse, John J.: Private

Enlisted in Co. G on 2/1/1864 in Caroline Co., VA; born circa 1844; son of James (farmer) and Chloe Morse; resident of Currituck Co. at the time of enlistment; present or accounted for on muster rolls through October 1864; paroled 4/15/1865 at HQ, 3rd Brigade, 1st Division, 9th Army Corps.

Moss, William T.: Private

Transferred to Co. G on 5/1/1864; previously served in Company G, 68th NC Infantry; present or accounted for on muster rolls through October 1864.

O'Neal, Simmons: Private

Enlisted in Co. G on 3/31/1862 in Currituck Co. at age 38; born 2/10/1823; listed as "Simon" Oneal in the 1850 Currituck Co. Census, living with his wife Sarah and their three-month-old son, Wilson; present or accounted for on muster rolls through August 1864, after which reported as "absent without leave"; died 8/23/1891, buried Dunton Family Cemetery, Narrow Shore Rd., Currituck Co., NC.

Owens, James F.: Private

Enlisted in Co. G on 5/1/1862 in Currituck Co.; "Deserted at Shingle Landing [Creek], Currituck County, NC, May 10, 1862."

Owens, Thomas Steward: Private

Enlisted in Co. G on 4/5/1862 in Currituck Co. at age 21; born Sept. 11, 1839 in Tyrrell Co., NC; resident of Currituck Co.; previously served as a private in Company E, 17th NC Infantry (1st Organization); captured 6/19/1863 in Middleburg, VA, held at Old Capitol Prison, Washington, DC; paroled and exchanged 6/30/1863 in City Point, VA; present or accounted for on muster rolls through August 1864; paroled 4/27/1865 at Provost Marshal's Office, Dist. of Eastern VA; married Martha Arcena Creef of Tyrrell Co. on July 27, 1871; died April 15, 1916 in Elizabeth City; buried Hollywood Cemetery, Elizabeth City, NC.

Owens, Warren: Private

Enlisted in Co. G on 3/31/1862 in Currituck Co. at age 31; "Captured and paroled at Middleburg, VA, June 19, 1863"; after September 1862 reported as absent without leave; captured 5/5/1864 in Currituck Co., held at Pt. Lookout; paroled and exchanged 11/15/1864 Venus Pt., Savannah River, GA; recaptured 12/19/1864 in Currituck Co., held at Pt. Lookout; died there 4/18/1865; buried in Confederate Cemetery, Pt. Lookout.

Parsons, George W.: Private

Enlisted in Co. G on 3/31/1862 in Currituck Co. at age 44; born circa 1818 in Virginia; occupation, carpenter; wife, Mary; July/August 1863 rolls report him as "Commissary Sergeant"; Sept./Oct. 1863 "Discharged and appointed Sutler for Regiment."

Payne, Samuel: Private

Enlisted in Co. G on 3/31/1862 in Currituck Co. at age 32; born circa 1832 in Currituck Co.; son of Thomas (farmer) and Margaret Payne; "Died at Camp Blandford near Petersburg, VA, July 2, 1862."

Perkins, Jeremiah: Private

Enlisted in Co. G on 3/31/1862 in Currituck Co. at age 42; born circa 1825 (age 25 in 1850 Census); married Edney Flora and listed as living in the household of his brother-in-law, Isaac Flora, in the 1850 Currituck Co. Census; muster rolls through December 1863 report him as "absent sick"; after January 1864 "absent without leave."

Perkins, John: Private

Enlisted in Co. G on 4/8/1862 in Currituck Co.; previously served as a private in Company H (1st), 32nd NC Infantry; present or accounted for on muster rolls through October 1863; November 1863–August 1864 "absent without leave."

Pugh, William H., Jr.: Private

Enlisted in Co. G on 3/31/1862 in Currituck Co. at age 24; present or accounted for on muster rolls through August 1864.

Pugh, William H., Sr.: Private

Enlisted in Co. G on 4/29/1862 in Currituck Co.; "Deserted to the enemy on or about the 15th of September 1863."

Richardson, Joseph S.: Private

Enlisted in Co. G on 3/31/1862 in Currituck Co. at age 26; July 1864–August 26, 1864 detailed as acting steward, Gen. Hospital, No. 7, Raleigh; 8/26/1864 appointed hospital steward, transferred to Medical Dept.

Sanderlin, Dorsey S.: Corporal

Enlisted in Co. G on 4/18/1862 in Currituck Co.; born in 1839; resident of Camden Co. at the time of enlistment; mustered in as a private; appointed corporal 12/31/1863; present or accounted for on muster rolls through October 1864; paroled 4/30/1865 at Provost Marshal's Office, Dist. of Eastern VA; may have previously served as a private in Company I (1st), 32nd NC Infantry; died in 1904, buried in the East Lake Methodist Church Cemetery in Dare Co.

Sanderlin, John W.: Private

Transferred to Co. G on 11/1/1862; joined the company at Sycamore Church, Prince George Co., VA; previously served in Company F, 15th VA Cavalry; present or accounted for on muster rolls through August 1864.

Sanderson, Thomas: Private

Enlisted in Co. G on 3/31/1862 in Currituck Co. at age 26; born circa 1835; son of Thomas (farmer) and Ruth Sanderson; captured 6/19/1863 in Middleburg, VA, held at Old Capitol Prison; paroled and exchanged 6/30/1863 in City Point, VA; present or accounted for on muster rolls until recaptured on 9/14/1864 in Currituck Co., held at Pt. Lookout; paroled and exchanged 3/17/1865.

Sawyer, George W.: Corporal

Enlisted in Co. G in March 1862 in Currituck Co.; 4/8/1862 Currituck, NC muster-in roll states "Not transferred."

Sawyer, John L. F.: Private

Enlisted in Co. G on 4/1/1864 in Halifax Co.; present or accounted for on muster rolls through October 1864.

Sawyer, Maxey: Private

Enlisted in Co. G on 4/8/1862 in Currituck Co. at age 28; born circa 1833 in Currituck Co.; June 1863 muster roll states "absent without leave"; after July 1863 reported as "deserted."

Sears, Thomas D.: Private

Enlisted in Co. G on 3/31/1862 in Currituck Co. at age 33; born circa 1828; son of John (farmer) and Polly Sears; discharged 8/8/1862 upon furnishing Elias Etheridge as a substitute.

Sears, William Riley: Private

Enlisted in Co. G on 5/1/1862 in Currituck Co.; born on March 8, 1832; son of Thomas Cooper Sears and Ruth Bright; listed as boarding in the James Parsons household in the 1850 Currituck Co. Census; married Mary Ethridge (daughter of William and Elisa Mercer Ethridge) on November 13, 1851; discharged 11/1/1862 upon furnishing Wilson Brothers as a substitute; died on August 7, 1907.

Seymour, Silas C.: Sergeant

Enlisted in Co. G on 3/31/1862 in Currituck Co. at age 21; born circa 1840 in Currituck Co., where he resided at the time of enlistment; mustered in as a sergeant; captured 7/4/1863 in Monterey, PA, held at Ft. Delaware; transferred 10/15/1863 to Pt. Lookout; paroled and exchanged 4/27/1864; admitted 5/1/1864 to Richmond hospital with "diarrhea chronic"; furloughed 5/12/1864 for 60 days; paroled 4/30/1865 at Provost Marshal's Office, Dist. of Eastern VA; married Angelicia Wilson on July 27, 1865 in Currituck, Co.

Stanley, William: Private

Enlisted in Co. G on 5/1/1862 in Currituck Co.; born circa 1837; son of Benjamin (farmer) and Mary Stanley; died 7/7/1862 in Petersburg hospital of "pleuritis."

Sykes, Caleb F.: Private

Enlisted in Co. G on 1/1/1864 in Currituck Co.; born circa 1844; last name also appears as "Sikes"; son of William (farmer) and Mary Sikes; resident of Currituck Co. at the time of enlistment; present or accounted for on muster rolls through October 1864; paroled 4/27/1865 at Provost Marshal's Office, Dist. of Eastern VA.

Tatem, David T.: Private

Enlisted in Co. G on 1/1/1864 in Currituck Co.; born August 31, 1844 in Currituck Co.; son of Peter (farmer) and Lovey Tatem; four of his brothers (Hollowell, John, Thaddeus, and William) also served in Co. G; present or accounted for on muster rolls through October 1864; married Sarah ("Sallie") Mercer on March 27, 1866 in Currituck Co.; died September 29, 1908 in Norfolk, VA.

Tatem, Holowell: Private

Enlisted in Co. G on 5/1/1862 in Currituck Co.; born circa 1840 in Currituck Co.; his first name also appears as "Holoway" in records; son of Peter (farmer) and Lovey Tatem; four of his brothers (David, John, Thaddeus and William) also served in Co. G; married Caroline Whitehall on August 23, 1861 in Currituck Co.; "Deserted at Currituck Court House, NC, May 10, 1862."

Tatem, John J.: Private

Enlisted in Co. G on 5/1/1862 in Currituck Co.; born circa 1838 in Currituck Co.; son of Peter (farmer) and Lovey Tatem; four of his brothers (Hollowell, David, Thaddeus and William) also served in Co. G; captured 6/19/1863 in Middleburg, VA, held at Old Capitol Prison; paroled and exchanged 6/30/1863 in City Point, VA; present or accounted for on muster rolls through October 1864.

Tatem, Thaddeus C.: Private

Enlisted in Co. G on 3/31/1862 in Currituck Co. at age 21; born circa 1840 in Currituck Co.; son of Peter (farmer) and Lovey Tatem; four of his brothers (Hollowell, John, David and William) also served in Co. G; captured 12/17/1863 in Currituck Co., held at Pt. Lookout; paroled and exchanged 3/25/1865 at Aiken's Landing, James River, VA; died 12/10/1915 in Raleigh, buried Oakwood Cemetery, Raleigh, NC.

Tatem, William B.: Private

Enlisted in Co. G on 5/1/1862 in Currituck Co.; born circa 1836 in Currituck Co.; son of Peter (farmer) and Lovey Tatem; four of his brothers (Hollowell, John, Thaddeus and David) also served in Co. G; captured 12/17/1863 in Currituck Co., held at Pt. Lookout; paroled and exchanged 2/25/1865 at Aiken's Landing, James River, VA.

Taylor, J. M.: Private

Enlisted in Co. G; retired 9/20/1864 to the Invalid Corps.

Taylor, Malachi C.: Private

Enlisted in Co. G on 3/31/1862 in Currituck Co. at age 27; born circa 1833; mother, Dinah Taylor; resident of Currituck Co. at the time of enlistment; wounded in action (right thigh) and captured in Middleburg, VA on 6/19/1863; right leg amputated on 6/20/1863; date of release not available; admitted 10/24/1863 to Richmond hospital; furloughed 11/3/1863 for 60 days; readmitted 3/23/1864 to Richmond hospital; transferred 3/30/1864 to Charlottesville, VA; furloughed 4/6/1864 for 60 days; retired 9/20/1864 to the Invalid Corps.

Temple, William S.: Private

Transferred to Co. G in or after August 1864; previously served in Company I, 15th VA Cavalry; paroled 4/14/1865 at HQ, 3rd Brigade, 1st Division, 9th Army Corps.

Thouroughgood, Paul: Private

Enlisted in Co. G on 4/24/1862 in Currituck Co.; captured 10/14/1863 at Newberry Bridge, NC, held at Pt. Lookout; died there on 4/27/1864 of "pneumonia"; buried in Confederate Cemetery, Pt. Lookout.

Tillet, Isaac N.: 2nd Lieutenant

Enlisted in Co. G on 3/31/1862 in Currituck Co. at age 27; born 1835; resident of Currituck Co. at the time of enlistment; appointed 2nd lieutenant to rank 3/18/1862; captured 6/19/1863 in Middleburg, VA, held at Old Capitol Prison; transferred 8/8/1863 to Johnson's Island, 3/14/1865 to Pt. Lookout; released; after the war became a teacher in Elizabeth City and "lived in the community (as) a cultured gentleman, a kind friend and teacher, a good citizen"; died 11/8/1907 (obituary in *Confederate Veteran*, Volume XVI, 1908), buried Old Episcopal Cemetery, Elizabeth City, NC.

Upton, Joseph E.: Private

Enlisted in Co. G on 9/1/1863 in Currituck Co.; resident of Camden Co. at the time of enlistment; May–August 1864 "Absent on furlough. Wounded"; paroled 4/30/1865 at Provost Marshal's Office, Dist. of Eastern VA.

Walch, John: Private

Enlisted in Co. G on 3/31/1862 in Currituck Co.; "Deserted 2 September 1862 at Sycamore Church, Prince George County, VA."

Walker, Charles R.: Private

Enlisted in Co. G on 3/31/1862 in Currituck Co. at age 35; born circa 1827; son of Levi (farmer) and Eliza Walker; muster rolls March–August 1864 indicate he was "absent without leave"; Oct.–Dec. 1864 performing extra duty as a teamster.

Walker, Griffin B.: Private

Enlisted in Co. G on 3/31/1862 in Currituck Co. at age 18; born circa 1844 in Currituck Co.; son of Benjamin (farmer) Walker; captured 6/17/1863 in Middleburg, VA, held at Old Capitol Prison; paroled and exchanged 6/30/1863 in City Point, VA; present or accounted for on muster rolls through October 1864; paroled 4/14/1865 at HQ, 3rd Brigade, 1st Division, 9th Army Corps.

Walker, Thomas D.: Private
Enlisted in Co. G on 3/31/1862 in Currituck Co. at age 21; captured 6/19/1863 in Middleburg, VA, held at Old Capitol Prison; paroled and exchanged 6/30/1863 in City Point, VA; present or accounted for on muster rolls through October 1864.

Walker, Wiley O.: Private
Transferred to Co. G on 2/2/1864; born circa 1836; son of Thomas (farmer) and Elizabeth Walker; previously served in Company I, 15th VA Cavalry; present or accounted for on muster rolls through October 1864.

Waller, Turners: Private
Enlisted in Co. G on 3/31/1862 in Currituck Co. at age 27; discharged 6/10/1862 in Petersburg due to "inability to do military duty."

West, Charles E.: Private
Enlisted in Co. G on 4/8/1862 in Currituck Co. at age 18; captured 7/4/1863 at South Mtn., held at Ft. McHenry; transferred 7/9/1863 to Ft. Delaware; died there 10/11/1863; buried in National Cemetery, Finn's Point (Salem), NJ.

West, Dennis: Private
Enlisted in Co. G on 3/31/1862 in Currituck Co. at age 39; born circa 1823; wife, Marina; resident of Currituck Co. at the time of enlistment; admitted 10/3/1864 to Raleigh hospital with "debilitas"; 11/30/1864 returned to duty; 3/13/1865 reported as "absent without leave" by Conscript Bureau.

West, Willoughby: Private
Enlisted in Co. G on 5/1/1862 in Currituck Co.; born 1828; son of farmer Willoughby West of Currituck Co.; present or accounted for on muster rolls through October 1864; died in 1880, buried in the West Family Cemetery in Currituck Co.

Whitehurst, Peter H.: Private
Enlisted in Co. G on 3/31/1862 in Currituck Co. at age 21; born circa 1841; son of Luke (farmer) and Courtney Whitehurst; resident of Currituck Co. at the time of enlistment; present or accounted for on muster rolls through October 1864; paroled 4/23/1865 at Provost Marshal's Office, Dist. of Eastern VA.

Whitehurst, Peter R.: Private
Enlisted in Co. G on 5/1/1862 in Currituck Co.; born circa 1829; son of Olly Whitehurst; residing in Currituck Co. as a farmer at the time of enlistment; previously served in 1st Regiment (Currituck Co.), 1st Brigade NC Confederate Militia, commissioned 1st lieutenant on 11/6/1861; reported "absent sick" through May/June 1863 when discharged "from disability."

Whitehurst, Travis: Private
Enlisted in Co. G on 3/31/1862 in Currituck Co. at age 40; born circa 1827 (age 23 in the 1850 Currituck Co. Census, living in the household of Thomas Mercer); called "Travey"; present or accounted for on muster rolls through October 1864.

Williams, Charles C.: Sergeant
Enlisted in Co. G on 3/31/1862 in Currituck Co. at age 38; mustered in as a 1st sergeant; "Discharged May 24, 1862, being exempt from military duty on account of age."

Williamson, Samuel: Private
Enlisted in Co. G on 3/31/1862 in Currituck Co. at age 32; resident of Currituck Co. at the time of enlistment; present or accounted for on muster rolls through October 1864; paroled 4/14/1865 at HQ, 3rd Brigade, 1st Division, 9th Army Corps.

Wilson, Henry J.: Private
Enlisted in Co. G on 5/1/1862 in Currituck Co.; born circa 1842; son of Samuel (born in VA, farmer) and Margaret Wilson; discharged 6/4/1862 in Petersburg upon furnishing John Martin as a substitute.

Wilson, Stephen Pendleton: 1st. Lieutenant
Enlisted in Co. G on 3/31/1862 in Currituck Co. at age 27; born 1835; resident of Currituck Co. at the time of enlistment; appointed 1st lieutenant from rank 3/18/1862; wounded in action on 6/18/1863 in Middleburg, VA; furloughed 8/17/1863 from Richmond hospital for 60 days; 1/28/1865 absent on furlough; present or accounted for on muster rolls through February 1865; paroled 4/14/1865 at HQ, 3rd Brigade, 1st Division, 9th Army Corps; buried Wilson Family Cemetery, Currituck Co., NC.

Woodhouse, Samuel F.: Corporal
Enlisted in Co. G on 3/31/1863 in Southampton Co., VA; born circa 1840; son of Elihu (farmer) and Penelope Woodhouse; resident of Currituck Co., NC at the time of enlistment; mustered in as a private; captured 6/19/1863 in Middleburg, VA, held at Old Capitol Prison; paroled and exchanged 6/30/1863 in City Point, VA; 12/31/1863 promoted to corporal; present or accounted for on muster rolls through October 1864; paroled 4/27/1865 at Provost Marshal's Office, Dist. of Eastern VA.

Wright, Major: Private
Enlisted in Co. G on 3/31/1862 in Currituck Co. at age 39; resident of Currituck Co. at the time of enlistment; present or accounted for on muster rolls through October 1864; paroled 4/30/1865 at Provost Marshal's Office, Dist. of Eastern VA; may have previously served as private in Company E, 17th NC Infantry (1st Organization).

Wright, Willoughby: Private

Enlisted in Co. G on 3/31/1862 in Currituck Co. at age 26; present or accounted for on muster rolls through October 1864; paroled 4/9/1865 at Appomattox Court House.

Wright, Wilson Campbell: Private

Enlisted in Co. G on 4/15/1862 in Currituck Co.; born on January 7, 1843 at Campbell's Landing, Pungo, VA (Princess Anne Co.); son of Davis Wright and Francis Campbell; previously served as private in Company E, 17th NC Infantry (1st Organization); captured 6/19/1863 in Middleburg, VA, held at Old Capitol Prison; paroled and exchanged 6/30/1863 at City Point, VA; present or accounted for on muster rolls through October 1864; paroled 4/9/1865 at Appomattox Court House; married Amelia "Emily" Etheridge on January 12, 1888; "he lived out his life as a local politician and farmer"; died on November 11, 1926 in Shawboro, NC (Currituck Co.) and buried there.

Wilson Campbell Wright, Company G, Currituck County (Bettie Morris Young).

Company H

Abernathy, Joshua C.: Private

Enlisted in Co. H on 1/2/1863 in Wilson Co.; present or accounted for on muster rolls through August 1864.

Adams, Elbert A.: Private

Enlisted in Co. H on 1/2/1863 in Wilson Co.; born in Wilson Co., where he resided at the time of enlistment; present or accounted for on muster rolls until discharged 1/15/1864 at Guinea Station, VA.

Adams, James H.: Private

Enlisted in Co. H on 1/2/1863 in Wilson Co.; present or accounted for on muster rolls through August 1864.

Adams, John D.: Private

Enlisted in Co. H on 12/19/1862 in Wilson Co.; discharged 3/12/1863 upon furnishing a substitute.

Amerson, Elisha: Private

Enlisted in Co. H on 1/2/1863 in Wilson Co.; present or accounted for on muster rolls through September 1864; paroled 1865 in Goldsboro, NC.

Applewhite, Jonathan H.: Corporal

Enlisted in Co. H on 1/2/1863 in Wilson Co.; born 10/9/1833; only appears on muster rolls from December 31, 1863 to September 1864; died 7/22/1910, buried Maplewood Cemetery, Wilson, NC.

Arthur, E. R.: Private

Enlisted in Co. H; 5/16/1864 admitted to Richmond hospital, transferred the next day.

Atkinson, Ashley: Private

Enlisted in Co. H on 12/17/1862 in Wilson Co.; born 2/8/1822; captured 6/19/1863 in Middleburg, VA, held Old Capitol Prison; paroled and exchanged 6/30/1863 in City Point, VA; admitted 4/3/1865 to Danville, VA hospital with "rubiola"; died 8/1/1908, buried Atkinson Family Cemetery, Holland Rd., Wilson Co., NC.

Atkinson, Calvin: Private

Enlisted in Co. H on 12/17/1862 in Wilson Co.; born on September 22, 1825; married Eliza Bass (daughter of Wright Bass and Annis Umflet) circa 1848; listed in the 1850 Wayne Co. Census (entry 685—north of Neuse); resident of Wilson Co. at the time of enlistment; present or accounted for on muster rolls through September 1864; paroled 1865 in Goldsboro; qualified to vote in 1902 in the Springhill township of Wilson Co.; died August 24, 1908 in Wilson Co.

Bailey, John L.: Private

Enlisted in Co. H on 12/17/1862 in Nash Co.; resident of Wilson Co. at the time of enlistment; present or accounted for on muster rolls through September 1864; paroled 5/4/1865 in Goldsboro, NC.

Bailey, Reddin: Private

Enlisted in Co. H on 12/17/1862 in Wilson Co.; present or accounted for on muster rolls until transferred on 11/11/1863 to Company K, 66th NC Infantry.

Baker, James: Private

Enlisted in Co. H on 12/17/1862 in Wilson Co.; resident of Wilson Co. at the time of enlistment; present or accounted for on muster rolls through September 1864; paroled 5/15/1865 in Goldsboro, NC.

Barfield, Sol. J.: Private

Enlisted in Co. H; resident of Wayne Co. at the time of enlistment; paroled 1865 in Goldsboro.

Barnes, (unknown): Private

Enlisted in Co. H on 12/17/1862 in Wilson Co.; discharged 1/2/1863.

Barnes, A. J.: Private

Enlisted in Co. H; resident of Wayne Co. at the time of enlistment; paroled 1865 in Goldsboro, NC.

Barnes, Arthur: Captain

Enlisted in Co. H on 11/25/1862 in Wilson Co.; born 4/24/1837; resident of Wilson Co. at the time of enlistment; appointed captain to rank from date of enlistment; resigned 5/26/1864 being "permanently disabled from service by disease" and because he was "at the time of enlistment into the service the solicitor for the county of Wilson, NC and was re-elected to the same office"; resignation officially accepted 6/8/1864; died 11/10/1926, buried Maplewood Cemetery, Wilson, NC.

Barnes, Columbus C.: Private

Enlisted in Co. H on 12/17/1862 in Nash Co.; discharged 1/2/1863.

Barnes, Frank Washington: 2nd Lieutenant

Enlisted in Co. H on 12/19/1862 in Wilson Co. at age 18; born 9/10/1844 in Edgecombe Co. (now Wilson Co.); resident of Wilson Co. at the time of enlistment; mustered in as a private; appointed 1st sergeant in March/April 1863, 2nd lieutenant on 12/17/1864; present or accounted for on muster rolls through December 1864; admitted April 1865 to Wilson, NC hospital, captured there, but escaped to Goldsboro; after war "engaged in the management of his agricultural interests in Wilson County and of the First National bank of Wilson"; became vice-president of bank in 1874; served as president 1875–1897; married Mattie Bynum in 1869; died 5/30/1910, buried Maplewood Cemetery, Wilson, NC.

Barnes, John T.: Private

Enlisted in Co. H on 12/18/1862 in Nash Co.; present or accounted for on muster rolls through August 1864; reported "absent sick" May/June 1863–August 1864.

Barnes, Peter L.: Private

Enlisted in Co. H on 12/17/1862 in Nash Co.; resident of Wilson Co. at the time of enlistment; present or accounted for on muster rolls through September 1864; paroled 5/9/1865 in Goldsboro, NC.

Bass, Isaac: Private

Enlisted in Co. H on 12/17/1862 in Wilson Co.; present or accounted for on muster rolls through September 1864; buried in the Knight Family Cemetery in Edgecombe Co.

Bass, James Ball: Private

Enlisted in Co. H on 1/2/1863 in Wilson Co.; resident of Wilson Co. at the time of enlistment; present or accounted for on muster rolls through September 1864; paroled 5/4/1865 in Goldsboro, NC.

Bass, Jeremiah: Private

Enlisted in Co. H on 12/17/1862 in Wilson Co.; present or accounted for on muster rolls through September 1864; paroled 1865 in Goldsboro, NC.

Belch, Benjamin: Private

Enlisted in Co. H on 12/17/1862 in Wilson Co.; discharged 1/2/1863 upon furnishing William Stocks as a substitute.

Bell, Henry E.: Private

Enlisted in Co. H on 12/18/1862 in Wilson Co.; resident of Wilson Co. at the time of enlistment; present or accounted for on muster rolls through September 1864; paroled 1865 in Goldsboro, NC.

Bell, Joseph J.: Private

Enlisted in Co. H on 12/17/1862 in Wilson Co.; resident of Halifax Co. at the time of enlistment; present or accounted for on muster rolls through September 1864; captured 4/3/1865 on Appomattox River, VA, held at Hart's Island, NY; released 6/19/1865 after taking Oath of Allegiance.

Bunn, William H.: Private

Enlisted in Co. H on 1/2/1863 in Wilson Co.; listed on the September 1864 muster roll as "Commanding Company"; killed in action on 10/27/1864 near Burgess Mill, Dinwiddie Co., VA.

Clark, Sidney Phineas: Captain

Enlisted in Co. H on 9/24/1862 in Wilson Co.; born 5/25/1842; resident of Wilson Co. at the time of enlistment; appointed 1st lieutenant to rank 9/24/1862; captured on 6/19/1863 in Middleburg, held at Old Capitol Prison; transferred 8/8/1863 to Johnson's Island; promoted captain 6/8/1864 while POW; transferred 2/20/1865 to Pt. Lookout; paroled 5/1/1865 in Goldsboro; died 5/10/1896, buried Maplewood Cemetery, Wilson, NC.

Davis, John A.: Private

Enlisted in Co. H on 12/18/1862 in Wilson Co.; born 1842; present or accounted for on muster rolls through September 1864; paroled 5/4/1865 in Goldsboro, NC; died 3/20/1915, buried Davis-Hooks-Yelverton Cemetery, Franklin Price Church Rd., Wilson Co., NC.

Deans, Robert Benton: Private

Enlisted in Co. H on 12/18/1862 in Wilson Co.; present or accounted for on muster rolls through September 1864; paroled 4/9/1865 at Appomattox Court House.

Eastman, W.: Private

Enlisted in Co. H; resident of Wilson Co. at the time of enlistment; paroled 5/16/1865.

Edwards, William H.: Sergeant

Enlisted in Co. H on 12/18/1862 in Wilson Co.; previously served in Company E, 2nd NC Cavalry (19th NCST); mustered in as a private; appointed sergeant in March/April 1863; "killed in battle June 15, 1864 near Petersburg, VA."

Ellis, James L.: Private

Enlisted in Co. H on 12/18/1862 in Wilson Co.; present or accounted for on muster rolls until 8/18/1864 when admitted to Petersburg hospital with gunshot wound; transferred 9/30/1864 to Danville, VA hospital; furloughed 10/7/1864 for 60 days.

Everitt, William L.: Private

Enlisted in Co. H on 12/18/1862 in Wilson Co.; resident of Wilson Co. at the time of enlistment; present or accounted for on muster rolls through September 1864; paroled 5/9/1865 in Goldsboro, NC.

Farmer, Ceburn: Private

Enlisted in Co. H on 12/18/1862 in Wilson Co.; captured 7/4/1863 at South Mtn., held at Ft. McHenry; transferred 7/9/1863 to Ft. Delaware; paroled and exchanged 11/15/1864 at Venus Point, Savannah River, GA.

Farmer, Isaac T.: Private

Enlisted in Co. H on 12/18/1862 in Wilson Co.; present or accounted for on muster rolls through September 1864.

Farmer, Jacob D.: Private

Enlisted in Co. H on 12/18/1862 in Wilson Co.; present or accounted for on muster rolls through September 1864.

Farmer, John W.: Private

Enlisted in Co. H on 12/18/1862 in Wilson Co.; present or accounted for on muster rolls through September 1864; admitted 12/10/1864 to Richmond hospital.

Farmer, Joseph: Private

Enlisted in Co. H on 12/18/1862 in Wilson Co.; born 5/17/1827; present or accounted for on muster rolls through August 1864; admitted 8/12/1864 to Petersburg hospital with shell wound (left knee); furloughed 9/16/1864; died 1/22/1892, buried Farmer-Daniel Family Cemetery, Wilson Christian Rd., Wilson Co., NC.

Farmer, T. R.: Private

Enlisted in Co. H on 12/17/1862 in Wilson Co.; discharged 1/8/1863.

Farmer, Walter: Sergeant

Enlisted in Co. H on 12/18/1862 in Wilson Co.; mustered in as a private; appointed sergeant in March/April 1863; captured 6/19/1863 in Middleburg, VA, held at Old Capitol Prison; paroled and exchanged 6/30/1863 in City Point, VA; killed in action on 10/11/1863 at Brandy Station, VA.

Ferrell, P. L.: Private

Enlisted in Co. H on 1/2/1863 in Wilson Co.; name only appears on muster rolls from December 31, 1863 to September 1864.

Ferrell, William Burton: Private

Enlisted in Co. H on 1/2/1863 in Wilson Co.; son of William Ferrell and Isley Crowell; brother of William Crockett "Crock" Ferrell, also of Co. H; name only appears on muster rolls from December 31, 1863 to September 1864.

Ferrell, William Crockett: 2nd Lieutenant

Transferred to Co. H on 10/18/1862; called "Crock"; born April 17, 1840 in Nash Co., NC; son of William Ferrell and Isley Crowell; brother of William Burton Ferrell, also of Co. H; resident in Wilson Co.; previously served as a private in Company B, 2nd NC Infantry; shot in the foot at Battle of Malvern Hill and came back home to NC to recuperate; joined the 4th NC Cavalry and appointed 2nd lieutenant to rank 10/18/1862; captured 6/19/1863 in Middleburg, held at Old Capitol Prison; transferred 8/8/1863 to Johnson's Island; paroled 2/24/1865 for exchange in City Point, VA; after the war moved back to Nash Co. where he married Sarah Elizabeth Deans; he farmed, was a Justice of the Peace and a member of the Nash Co. chapter of the UCV; died April 26, 1909, buried near Nashville.

Finch, Joachim Lane: Sergeant

Enlisted in Co. H on 12/18/1862 in Nash Co.; resident of Nash Co. at the time of enlistment; mustered in as a private; appointed corporal March/April 1863; present or accounted for on muster rolls through September 1864; captured 3/31/1865 at Hatcher's Run, VA, held at Pt. Lookout; released 6/26/1865 after taking Oath of Allegiance.

Finch, John Christopher: Private

Enlisted in Co. H on 12/18/1862 in Wilson Co.; born in 1840; resident of Wilson Co. at the time of enlistment; present or accounted for on muster rolls through September 1864; paroled 5/9/1865 in Goldsboro, NC; died in 1908, buried in the David Daniel Bottoms Cemetery in Wilson Co.

Flora, John: Private

Enlisted in Co. H on 12/18/1862 in Nash Co.; wounded and captured 6/19/1863 in Middleburg, VA; exchanged 6/30/1863 in City Point, VA; August 1864 reported as "absent in Wilson hospital sick"; 12/31/1864 in General Hospital No. 2, Wilson, NC.

Ford, William G.: Private

Enlisted in Co. H; born on June 1, 1830; admitted to hospital 12/15/1862 with gunshot wound (head), deserted from hospital 2/2/1863; received 3/12/1865 by provost marshal general, Army of the Potomac with remark "Deserted from the enemy with horse and horse equipment"; forwarded 3/18/1865 to Washington, DC where took Oath of Allegiance and provided transportation to Norfolk, VA; he died May 7, 1922, buried in the Good Hope Baptist Church Cemetery in Wake Co.

Founes, B.: Private

Enlisted in Co. H; resident of Wilson Co. at the time of enlistment; paroled 5/15/1865 in Goldsboro, NC.

Glover, H. H.: Private

Enlisted in Co. H on 12/18/1862 in Wilson Co.; present or accounted for on muster rolls through September 1864.

Glover, W. G.: Private

Enlisted in Co. H on 12/17/1862 in Wilson Co.; discharged 1/28/1863.

Godwin, Erwin L.: Private
Enlisted in Co. H on 12/18/1862 in Wilson Co.; admitted 6/14/1863 to Richmond hospital; transferred 6/19/1863 to Castle Thunder Prison (Richmond); deserted 9/15/1863.

Godwin, Jesse H.: Private
Enlisted in Co. H on 12/18/1862 in Wilson Co.; resident of Johnston Co. at the time of enlistment; present or accounted for on muster rolls until retired 9/1/1864 to Invalid Corps; paroled 5/8/1865 in Goldsboro, NC.

Godwin, Ransom: Private
Enlisted in Co. H on 12/18/1862 in Wilson Co.; present or accounted for on muster rolls through December 1863 when reported "absent without leave"; January 1864–August 1864 reported as "deserted."

Godwin, Tobias T.: Private
Enlisted in Co. H on 12/18/1862 in Wilson Co.; present or accounted for on muster rolls through February 1864; from March 1864–August 1864 reported as "deserted."

Griffin, James J.: Private
Enlisted in Co. H on 12/18/1862 in Wilson Co.; present or accounted for on muster rolls through September 1864; paroled 5/9/1865 in Goldsboro, NC.

Hayes, Levi M.: Private
Enlisted in Co. H on 12/18/1862 in Wilson Co.; born 3/7/1823; admitted 3/27/1865 to Petersburg hospital with gunshot wound (leg); captured there 4/3/1865, transferred April 8–9, 1865 to Federal hospital at Point of Rocks, VA; died 5/20/1882, buried Elm City Cemetery, Elm City, NC.

Haynes, G. H.: Private
Enlisted in Co. H on 12/17/1862 in Wilson Co.; discharged 1/28/1863; paroled 1865 in Goldsboro, NC.

Haynes, Jesse K.: Private
Enlisted in Co. H on 12/18/1862 in Wilson Co.; born circa 1823 in Edgecombe Co.; son of William Haynes and Nancy Knight; brother of Willis Haynes and William Haynes, also of Co. H; married Polly Barnes on February 17, 1848 in Edgecombe Co.; wounded (right thigh) and captured 6/19/1863 in Middleburg, VA; paroled 8/23/1863 in Baltimore, MD; exchanged 8/24/1863 in City Point, VA; Sept./Oct. 1863–Sept. 1864 reported as "absent sick"; married a second time to Martha Woodard on February 28, 1888; died in 1898 in Wilson Co.

Haynes, William: Private
Enlisted in Co. H on 1/2/1863 in Wilson Co.; born on December 26, 1837 in Nash Co.; son of William Haynes and Nancy Knight; brother of Willis Haynes and Jesse K. Haynes, also of Co. H; he married Tempie Ann Mercer; captured 6/19/1863 in Middleburg, VA, held at Old Capitol Prison; paroled and exchanged 6/30/1863

in City Point, VA; died on November 8, 1893 in Wilson Co., buried in the Barnes/Haynes Cemetery in Wilson, NC.

Haynes, Willis: Private

Enlisted in Co. H on 12/18/1862 in Wilson Co.; son of William Haynes and Nancy Knight; brother of Jesse K. Haynes and William Haynes, also of Co. H; captured 7/12/1863 in Hagerstown, MD, held at Pt. Lookout; paroled and exchanged 3/20/1864 in City Point, VA; present or accounted for on muster rolls through September 1864; paroled 1865 in Goldsboro.

Hinnant, James H.: Private

Enlisted in Co. H on 12/18/1862 in Wilson Co.; born 7/18/1828; son of Jesse and Nancy Hinnant; married twice, first to Rebecca Raper and then to Sallie Barnes; resident of Wilson Co. at the time of enlistment; present or accounted for on muster rolls through September 1864; paroled 5/2/1865 in Goldsboro, NC; died 4/6/1895, buried John Raper Cemetery, NC Highway 581, Wilson, NC.

Jenkins, Henry: Private

Enlisted in Co. H on 12/18/1862 in Wilson Co.; captured 7/4/1863 at South Mtn., held at Ft. McHenry; transferred 7/9/1863 to Ft. Delaware; died there 8/11/1863 of "chronic diarrhea"; buried in National Cemetery, Finn's Point (Salem), NJ.

Johnson, John W.: Private

Enlisted in Co. H on 1/2/1863 in Wilson Co.; present or accounted for on muster rolls from July 1864 through September 1864.

Johnson, Woodard: Private

Enlisted in Co. H on 12/18/1862 in Wilson Co.; captured 6/19/1863 in Middleburg, VA, held at Old Capitol Prison; paroled and exchanged 6/30/1863 in City Point, VA; present or accounted for on muster rolls through September 1864; paroled 4/9/1865 at Appomattox Court House.

Jordan, Cornelius: Private

Enlisted in Co. H on 12/18/1862 in Wilson Co.; born 12/4/1824; present or accounted for on muster rolls through September 1864; died 2/13/1881, buried Jordan Family Cemetery, NC Highway 42, Wilson Co., NC.

Keene, C.: Private

Enlisted in Co. H; resident of Wilson Co. at the time of enlistment; paroled 5/12/1865 in Goldsboro, NC.

Lamb, Larry: Private

Enlisted in Co. H on 12/18/1862 in Wilson Co.; discharged 3/15/1863.

Lewis, Barna B.: Private

Enlisted in Co. H on 12/18/1862 in Wilson Co.; wounded (left shoulder) and captured 6/19/1863 in Middleburg, VA, held at Old Capitol Prison; paroled and exchanged 6/30/1863 in City Point, VA; admitted 6/30/1863 to Petersburg hospital;

furloughed 7/16/1863 for 60 days; present or accounted for on muster rolls through September 1864; paroled 5/25/1865 in Goldsboro, NC.

Lucus, William D.: Private
Enlisted in Co. H on 12/18/1862 in Wilson Co.; captured 6/19/1863 in Middleburg, VA, held at Old Capitol Prison; paroled and exchanged 6/30/1863 in City Point, VA; present or accounted for on muster rolls through September 1864.

Mason, Robertson: Private
Enlisted in Co. H on 12/18/1862 in Wilson Co.; present or accounted for on muster rolls through September 1864; paroled 4/9/1865 at Appomattox Court House.

Mattox, William Riley: Corporal
Enlisted in Co. H on 12/18/1862 in Wilson Co.; born 11/9/1825; mustered in as a private; appointed corporal before 6/30/1864; present or accounted for on muster rolls through September 1864; died 4/8/1883, buried Mattox-Jones Family Cemetery, Gardner's School Rd., Wilson Co., NC.

Mercer, William Henry: Private
Enlisted in Co. H on 12/18/1862 in Wilson Co.; born 11/17/1844; resident of Wilson Co. at the time of enlistment; present or accounted for on muster rolls through September 1864; captured 4/2/1865 near Petersburg, VA, held at Pt. Lookout; released 6/29/1865 after taking Oath of Allegiance; died 12/3/1924, buried Maplewood Cemetery, Wilson, NC.

Moore, E. L.: Private
Enlisted in Co. H; paroled 5/25/1865 in Raleigh, NC.

Moore, M.: Private
Enlisted in Co. H; resident of Wilson Co. at the time of enlistment; paroled 1865 in Goldsboro.

Newson, Redding B.: Private
Enlisted in Co. H on 12/17/1862 in Wilson Co.; died 1/18/1863.

Oliver, Daniel: Private
Enlisted in Co. H on 12/18/1862 in Wilson Co.; born 6/1813; resident of Wilson Co. at the time of enlistment; wounded (right arm) 6/19/1863 in Middleburg, VA; absent at home through August 1863; paroled 5/13/1865 in Goldsboro, NC; died 2/24/1914, buried Oakwood Cemetery, Raleigh, NC.

Owens, Kinchen: Private
Enlisted in Co. H on 12/18/1862 in Wilson Co.; captured 6/19/1863 in Middleburg, VA, held at Old Capitol Prison; paroled and exchanged 6/30/1863 in City Point, VA; present or accounted for on muster rolls through September 1864.

Peel, Stephen J.: Private
Enlisted in Co. H on 12/18/1862 in Wilson Co.; present or accounted for on muster rolls through August 1864; 8/18/1864 admitted to Petersburg hospital with gunshot wound (left hip); furloughed 8/25/1864 for 30 days.

Perry, William E.: Private

Enlisted in Co. H on 12/18/1862 in Nash Co.; resident of Wayne Co. at the time of enlistment; present or accounted for on muster rolls through September 1864; paroled 5/8/1865 in Goldsboro, NC.

Perry, Willie K.: Private

Enlisted in Co. H on 12/18/1862 in Nash Co.; resident of Nash Co. at the time of enlistment; captured 7/4/1863 at South Mtn., held at Ft. McHenry; transferred 7/9/1863 to Ft. Delaware; no record of parole, exchange or release found; admitted 11/26/1864 to Pettigrew General Hospital No. 12, Raleigh with "debilitas"; returned to duty 12/18/1864.

Pittman, Joseph: Private

Enlisted in Co. H on 12/18/1862 in Wilson Co.; present or accounted for on muster rolls through September 1864.

Pittman, Warren: Private

Enlisted in Co. H on 12/18/1862 in Wilson Co.; present or accounted for on muster rolls through September 1864.

Powell, Richard H.: Private

Enlisted in Co. H on 12/18/1862 in Wilson Co.; mustered in as a private; appointed sergeant in March/April 1863; captured 7/4/1863 at South Mtn., held at Ft. McHenry; transferred 7/9/1863 to Ft. Delaware; transferred 7/19/1863 to Chester Hospital, Chester, PA; died there 7/29/1863 of "pneumonia"; reduced to ranks after capture and death.

Raper, Robert: Private

Enlisted in Co. H on 12/18/1862 in Wilson Co.; born 5/26/1827; resident of Wilson Co. at the time of enlistment; present or accounted for on muster rolls through September 1864; paroled 5/2/1865 in Goldsboro, NC; died 11/11/1910, buried John Raper Cemetery, NC Highway 581, Wilson, NC.

Raper, William: Private

Enlisted in Co. H on 1/2/1863 in Wilson Co.; resident of Wilson Co. at the time of enlistment; captured 3/31/1865 at Dinwiddie Court House, VA, held at Pt. Lookout; released 6/17/1865 after taking Oath of Allegiance; buried Mt. Olivet Methodist Church, Mt. Olivet Church Rd., Davidson Co., NC.

Rentfrow, William V.: Sergeant

Enlisted in Co. H on 12/18/1862 in Nash Co.; resident of Nash Co. at the time of enlistment; mustered in as a private; appointed corporal in March/April 1863; promoted sergeant before 6/30/1864; present or accounted for on muster rolls through September 1864; paroled 1865 in Goldsboro.

Resly, T.: Private

Enlisted in Co. H; resident of Wilson Co. at the time of enlistment; paroled 1865 in Goldsboro, NC.

Ricks, Garland Duke: Private

Enlisted in Co. H on 1/2/1863 in Wilson Co.; born 12/16/1844; "name appears only on muster rolls for the period December 31, 1863 through September 1864" on which he is listed as present; died 8/6/1913, buried Oakdale Cemetery, Spring Hope, NC.

Robbins, Elias S.: Private

Enlisted in Co. H on 12/18/1862 in Wilson Co.; wounded in action on 10/11/1863; absent wounded in Wilson, NC hospital through September 1864.

Robbins, James R.: Private

Enlisted in Co. H on 12/18/1862 in Wilson Co.; present or accounted for on muster rolls until transferred 5/1/1864 to Company I, 17th NC Infantry (2nd Organization).

Robinson, S.: Lieutenant

Enlisted in Co. H; resident of Johnston Co. at the time of enlistment; paroled 5/15/1865 in Goldsboro, NC.

Sharp, G. B.: Private

Enlisted in Co. H; resident of Wilson Co. at the time of enlistment; paroled 5/9/1865 in Goldsboro, NC.

Sneed, William B.: Private

Enlisted in Co. H on 12/18/1862 in Wilson Co.; "Never reported for duty."

Sneed, William L.: Private

Enlisted in Co. H on 1/2/1863 in Wilson Co. "for the war."

Stinson, W. C.: Private

Enlisted in Co. H; captured 7/3/1863 near Gettysburg, PA; present 8/10/1863 in Letterman General Hospital, Gettysburg, PA.

Stocks, William: Private

Enlisted in Co. H on 12/18/1862 in Wilson Co.; substitute for Benjamin Belcher; present or accounted for on muster rolls through September 1864.

Strickland, William D.: Private

Enlisted in Co. H on 12/18/1862 in Nash Co.; resident of Nash Co. at the time of enlistment; present or accounted for on muster rolls through September 1864; paroled 5/15/1865 in Goldsboro, NC.

Thigpen, John Q. A.: Private

Enlisted in Co. H on 12/18/1862 in Wilson Co.; captured 6/19/1863 in Middleburg, VA, held at Old Capitol Prison; paroled and exchanged 6/30/1863 in City Point, VA; present or accounted for on muster rolls through September 1864.

Thigpen, LaFayette: Private

Enlisted in Co. H on 12/18/1862 in Wilson Co.; present or accounted for on muster rolls through September 1864; paroled 4/9/1865 at Appomattox Court House.

Thomas, Hilliard: Private

Enlisted in Co. H on 12/18/1862 in Wilson Co.; born 1824; present or accounted for on muster rolls through September 1864; died 1884, buried in the Sharp-Thomas Cemetery, Varnell Rd., Wilson Co., NC.

Thorne, Raymond C.: Private

Enlisted in Co. H on 12/18/1862 in Wilson Co.; present or accounted for on muster rolls through September 1864.

Tomlinson, Larry D.: Private

Enlisted in Co. H on 12/18/1862 in Wilson Co.; present or accounted for on muster rolls through September 1864.

Tomlinson, William: Private

Enlisted in Co. H; resident of Wilson Co. at the time of enlistment; paroled 1865 in Goldsboro.

Tyson, William A.: Corporal

Enlisted in Co. H on 1/2/1863 in Wilson Co.; "name reported only on muster rolls for the period December 31, 1863 through September 1864" on which he is listed as present with the rank of corporal; paroled 4/9/1865 at Appomattox Court House.

W____, B.: Private

Enlisted in Co. H on 12/17/1862 in Wilson Co.; discharged 1/28/1863.

Waran, P. W.: Private

Enlisted in Co. H; resided in Wilson Co. at the time of enlistment; paroled 5/16/1865 in Goldsboro, NC.

Ward, George W.: Private

Enlisted in Co. H on 12/18/1862 in Wilson Co.; wounded in action on 6/22/1863; sent to hospital in Jordan Springs, VA; captured there 7/26/1863; paroled 8/2/1863; admitted 12/18/1863 to Richmond hospital and furloughed; August 1864 "in Wilson hospital wounded."

Watson, Ephraim: Private

Enlisted in Co. H on 12/18/1862 in Wilson Co.; killed in action on 6/22/1863 near Upperville, VA.

Weaver, Benjamin W.: Private

Enlisted in Co. H on 12/18/1862 in Wilson Co.; resident of Wilson Co. at the time of enlistment; admitted 8/22/1864 to Raleigh hospital with "rheumatismos"; furloughed 9/8/1864 for 60 days; paroled 1865 in Goldsboro, NC.

Whitehead, James G.: Private

Enlisted in Co. H on 12/18/1862 in Wilson Co.; captured 7/4/1863 at South Mtn., held at Ft. McHenry; transferred 7/9/1863 to Ft. Delaware, 10/22/1863 to Pt. Lookout; died there 11/22/1863; buried in the Confederate Cemetery, Pt. Lookout.

Wilford, W. T.: Private
Enlisted in Co. H; resident of Wilson Co. at the time of enlistment; paroled 5/1/1865 in Goldsboro, NC.

William, R.: Private
Enlisted in Co. H; resident of Wilson Co. at the time of enlistment; paroled 1865 in Goldsboro, NC.

Williams, James Haywood: Private
Transferred to Co. H on 5/1/1864; previously served in Company I, 17th NC Infantry (2nd Organization); present or accounted for on muster rolls through August 1864; paroled 1865 in Goldsboro, NC.

Williams, Malachia M.: 1st Lieutenant
Enlisted in Co. H on 10/13/1862 in Wilson Co.; resident of Wilson Co. at the time of enlistment; appointed 2nd lieutenant to rank from date of enlistment; promoted 6/8/1864 to 1st lieutenant; after 9/11/1864 absent by authority of Gen. Lee; present or accounted for on muster rolls through February 1865; paroled 5/10/1865 in Goldsboro, NC.

Williamson, Thomas: Private
Enlisted in Co. H on 12/18/1862 in Wilson Co.; born 11/2/1824; resident of Wilson Co. at the time of enlistment; present or accounted for on muster rolls through September 1864; paroled 1865 in Goldsboro, NC; died 9/29/1890, buried Williamson Family Cemetery, Old Raleigh Rd., Wilson Co., NC.

Company I

Balfour, Charles H.: Private
Transferred to Co. I on 7/11/1864; resided in Tyrrell Co. at the time of enlistment in 12th Battalion; previously served in Company B, 12th Battalion NC Cavalry (enlisted in Bertie Co.); captured 4/2/1865 near Petersburg, held at Pt. Lookout; released 6/24/1865 after taking Oath of Allegiance.

Barbour, Ezekial E.: Private
Transferred to Co. I on 7/11/1864; previously served in Company B, 12th Battalion NC Cavalry (enlisted in Johnston Co.); last name also appears as "Barber"; born circa 1845; son of Larkin and Welthey Barber of Johnston Co.; present or accounted for on muster rolls through October 1864; married Mary Francis Johnson on February 14, 1867 in Johnston Co.

Barnes, William P.: Private
Transferred to Co. I on 7/11/1864; previously served in Company B, 12th Battalion NC Cavalry, the 8th (Dearing's) Confederate Cavalry and the 3rd Battalion NC Light Artillery; captured 4/3/1865 in Petersburg hospital where he was recovering from a gunshot wound to left arm; died in hospital 5/21/1865.

Boswell, Edwin G.: Private

Transferred to Co. I on 7/11/1864; previously served in Company B, 12th Battalion NC Cavalry (enlisted in Bertie Co.); 1/3/1865 reported by medical director, Richmond "appointed and forwarded to Assistant Adjutant General."

Bowen, Jesse T.: Private

Transferred to Co. I on 7/11/1864; born circa 1828; listed as a farmer in the 1850 and 1860 Bertie Co. Census, living with his mother Tobithy (also spelled Talitha) Bowen; previously served in Company B, 12th Battalion NC Cavalry (enlisted in Bertie Co.); present or accounted for on muster rolls through October 1864.

Brewer, Andrew J.: Private

Transferred to Co. I on 7/11/1864; previously served in Company B, 12th Battalion NC Cavalry; transferred to 12th Battalion NC Cavalry 4/20/1864 from Company B, 3rd Battalion NC Light Artillery; present or accounted for on muster rolls through October 1864.

Brickle, J. D.: Private

Transferred to Co. I on 7/11/1864; previously served in Company B, 12th Battalion NC Cavalry; AWOL at time of transfer to 4th NC Cavalry, reported as a deserter.

Brown, Daniel E.: Corporal

Transferred to Co. I on 7/27/1864; previously served in Company G, 16th Battalion NC Cavalry; present or accounted for on muster rolls through October 1864.

Bulloch, Bythiel: Private

Transferred to Co. I on 7/11/1864; previously served in Company B, 12th Battalion NC Cavalry (enlisted in Bertie Co.); present or accounted for on muster rolls through October 1864.

Clifton, Rufus R.: Private

Transferred to Co. I on 7/11/1864; born circa 1830; listed as living in the Bud and Elizabeth Youngblood household as a laborer in the 1850 Johnston Co. Census; believed to be the son of Rivers and Thitus Clifton; married Marzilla Byrd on February 17, 1864 in Johnston Co.; previously served in Company B, 12th Battalion NC Cavalry (enlisted in Johnston Co.); AWOL when transferred to 4th NC Cavalry; returned to regiment before 10/20/1864; captured and paroled April 19–20, 1865 in Raleigh.

Cook, Henry H.: 1st Sergeant

Transferred to Co. I on 7/11/1864; previously served in Company B, 12th Battalion NC Cavalry; captured 4/2/1865 near Petersburg, held at Pt. Lookout; released 6/26/1865 after taking Oath of Allegiance.

Cook, S. D.: Private

Transferred to Co. I on 7/11/1864; previously served in Company B, 12th Battalion NC Cavalry (enlisted in Northampton Co.); "deserted" August 1864.

Early, B. A.: Private
Transferred to Co. I on 7/11/1864; previously served in Company B, 12th Battalion NC Cavalry (enlisted in Hertford Co.); present or accounted for on muster rolls through October 1864.

Easom, Jacob: Private
Transferred to Co. I on 7/11/1864; previously served in Company B, 12th Battalion NC Cavalry (enlisted in Lenoir Co.); present or accounted for on muster rolls through October 1864.

Farmer, Thomas: Private
Transferred to Co. I on 7/11/1864; previously served in Company B, 12th Battalion NC Cavalry (enlisted in Hertford Co.); 9/14/1864 discharged by order of Gen. R. E. Lee.

Grimes, Benjamin F.: Private
Transferred to Co. I on 7/11/1864; born circa 1829; son of William and Pherebah Grimes; previously served in Company B, 12th Battalion NC Cavalry (enlisted in Johnston Co.); present or accounted for on muster rolls through October 1864; married Milly Ennis on March 7, 1867 in Johnston Co.

Guyun, J. B.: Private
Transferred to Co. I on 7/11/1864; previously served in Company B, 12th Battalion NC Cavalry; transferred to 4th NC Cavalry while absent in Charlotte, NC hospital with "rheumatism chro."; 7/31/1864 returned to duty.

Hagatha, Thomas: Private
Transferred to Co. I on 7/11/1864; previously served in Company B, 12th Battalion NC Cavalry (enlisted in Hertford Co.); present or accounted for on muster rolls through October 1864.

Hall, Alvin: Private
Transferred to Co. I on 7/11/1864; previously served in Company B, 12th Battalion NC Cavalry (enlisted in Greene Co.); August 1864 "detailed as courier for General Hoke"; present or accounted for on muster rolls through August 1864.

Harrington, James O.: Private
Transferred to Co. I on 7/11/1864; previously served in Company B, 12th Battalion NC Cavalry (enlisted in Bertie Co.); in prison for desertion at time of transfer to 4th NC Cavalry; 8/3/1864 released under presidential pardon for service in the Winder Legion in defense of Richmond during the Sheridan raid.

Hill, Moses P.: Private
Transferred to Co. I on 7/11/1864; previously served in Company B, 12th Battalion NC Cavalry (enlisted in Hertford Co.); present or accounted for on muster rolls through October 1864.

Hill, William: Private

Transferred to Co. I on 7/11/1864; previously served in Company B, 12th Battalion NC Cavalry (enlisted in Johnston Co.); present or accounted for on muster rolls through October 1864.

Hinton, William Hillary: Private

Transferred to Co. I on 7/11/1864; previously served in Company B, 12th Battalion NC Cavalry (enlisted in Johnston Co.); present or accounted for on muster rolls through October 1864; captured 4/17/1865 on Raleigh; paroled 4/20/1865.

Holloman, Samuel J.: Sergeant

Transferred to Co. I on 7/11/1864; born 8/26/1826; previously served in Company B, 12th Battalion NC Cavalry (enlisted in Hertford Co.); present or accounted for on muster rolls through October 1864; 4/5/1865 admitted to Danville, VA hospital with "diarrhea chronic"; died 11/19/1905, Ahoskie Cemetery, Ahoskie, NC.

Horne, Hardee: Corporal

Transferred to Co. I on 7/11/1864; previously served in Company B, 12th Battalion NC Cavalry (enlisted in Johnston Co.); present or accounted for on muster rolls through October 1864; captured 4/3/1865 near Petersburg, held at Hart's Island, NY; released 6/19/1865 after taking Oath of Allegiance.

Johnson, A. E.: Private

Transferred to Co. I on 7/11/1864; previously served in Company B, 12th Battalion NC Cavalry (enlisted in Hertford Co.); present or accounted for on muster rolls through October 1864.

Johnson, Henry: Private

Transferred to Co. I on 7/11/1864; previously served in Company B, 12th Battalion NC Cavalry (enlisted in Hertford Co.); present or accounted for on muster rolls through October 1864.

Johnson, John W. H.: Private

Transferred to Co. I on 7/11/1864; previously served in Company B, 12th Battalion NC Cavalry (enlisted in Bertie Co.); present or accounted for on muster rolls through October 1864; 4/22/1865 took Oath of Allegiance in Raleigh.

Johnson, Sir William: Private

Transferred to Co. I on 7/11/1864; previously served in Company B, 12th Battalion NC Cavalry (enlisted in Johnston Co.); present or accounted for on muster rolls through October 1864; paroled 5/10/1865 in Raleigh.

Jones, Kile A.: Private

Transferred to Co. I on 7/11/1864; previously served in Company B, 12th Battalion NC Cavalry (enlisted in Johnston Co.); 8/18/1864 admitted to Petersburg hospital with a gunshot wound to back; 9/1/1864 furloughed for 60 days; paroled 4/20/1865 at Bunn's House, Nash Co., NC.

Jones, William A.: Private

Transferred to Co. I on 7/11/1864; previously served in Company B, 12th Battalion NC Cavalry (enlisted in Johnston Co.); present or accounted for on muster rolls through October 1864; captured and paroled 4/13/1865 in Dinwiddie Co., VA.

Lamb, William Mark: Private

Transferred to Co. I; resided in Wilson Co.; paroled 5/1/1865 in Goldsboro, NC.

Lassiter, Henry B.: Private

Transferred to Co. I; resided in Hertford Co.; captured 4/3/1865 on Appomattox River, VA, held at Hart's Island, NY; released 6/19/1865 after taking Oath of Allegiance.

Lassiter, Joel: Private

Transferred to Co. I on 7/11/1864; previously served in Company B, 12th Battalion NC Cavalry (enlisted in Hertford Co.); present or accounted for on muster rolls through October 1864.

Lassiter, Wiley J.: Private

Transferred to Co. I; son of Bryant and Penelope Lassiter; resided in Hertford Co. at the time of enlistment; captured 4/3/1865 on Appomattox River, VA, held at Hart's Island, NY; released 6/19/1865 after taking Oath of Allegiance; married Imogen Womble on October 1, 1872 in Hertford Co.

Lassiter, William H.: Private

Transferred to Co. I on 7/11/1864; married Rebecca Rich on October 6, 1859 in Northampton Co.; previously served in Company B, 12th Battalion NC Cavalry (enlisted in Hertford Co.); present or accounted for on muster rolls through October 1864.

Lee, Blythan D.: Private

Transferred to Co. I on 7/11/1864; born circa 1827; listed as an overseer and living with his wife Elizabeth in the 1850 Johnston Co. Census; previously served in Company B, 12th Battalion NC Cavalry (enlisted in Johnston Co.); present or accounted for on muster rolls through October 1864.

Lee, Troy: Private

Transferred to Co. I on 7/11/1864; previously served in Company B, 12th Battalion NC Cavalry (enlisted in Johnston Co.); present or accounted for on muster rolls through October 1864; 4/19/1865 took Oath of Allegiance in Raleigh, paroled 4/20/1865.

Lipscomb, Joshua: Private

Transferred to Co. I on 7/11/1864; last name also appears as "Liscombe" in records; born circa 1844; listed as living with Sydney Liscombe (female, age 54) in shoemaker Joseph Johnston's household in the 1850 Bertie Co. Census; previously served in Company B, 12th Battalion NC Cavalry (enlisted in Bertie Co.); present or accounted for on muster rolls through October 1864; wounded in action on 3/28/1865 on the Boydton Plank Road, Dinwiddie Co., VA; 3/29/1865 admitted to Petersburg hospital; captured there 4/3/1865; 5/17/1865 sent to Point of Rocks Hospital; 5/25/1865 sent to Military Prison, Camp Hamilton, VA; released 5/31/1865.

Lovejoy, Charles C.: 3rd Lieutenant

Transferred to Co. I on 7/11/1864; residing in Wake Co. as a student prior to the war; previously served in Company B, 12th Battalion NC Cavalry; wounded 6/23/1864 and on sick furlough at time of transfer; furloughed remainder of war; captured 5/11/1865 at Raleigh hospital; paroled 5/11/1865.

Lynch, Josephus: Private

Transferred to Co. I; muster rolls indicate that he was issued clothing in October 1864.

McCoy, Robert A.: Private

Transferred to Co. I on 12/5/1864; previously served as a private in Company H, 27th NC Infantry.

McLeod, Alexander: Private

Transferred to Co. I on 7/11/1864; previously served in Company B, 12th Battalion NC Cavalry (enlisted in Wayne Co.); present or accounted for on muster rolls through October 1864.

Menshaw, John V.: Private

Transferred to Co. I on 7/11/1864; previously served in Company B, 12th Battalion NC Cavalry (enlisted in Wayne Co.); transferred to 4th NC Cavalry while POW in Elmira, NY; paroled 10/11/1864; exchanged 11/15/1865 at Venus Pt., Savannah River, GA; paroled 5/2/1865 in Goldsboro, NC.

Minton, Thomas: Private

Transferred to Co. I on 7/11/1864; previously served in Company B, 12th Battalion NC Cavalry (enlisted in Hertford Co.); transferred to 4th NC Cavalry while on sick leave; AWOL August 1864.

Mitchell, Franklin V.: Sergeant

Transferred to Co. I on 7/11/1864; born circa 1843; son of Wright and Martha Mitchell; previously served in Company B, 12th Battalion NC Cavalry (enlisted in Bertie Co.); present or accounted for on muster rolls through October 1864.

Myers, Ralph: Private

Transferred to Co. I on 7/11/1864; previously served in Company B, 12th Battalion NC Cavalry (enlisted in Hertford Co.); present or accounted for on muster rolls through October 1864.

Parrish, Albert: Private

Transferred to Co. I on 7/11/1864; previously served in Company B, 12th Battalion NC Cavalry (enlisted in Johnston Co.); transferred to 4th NC Cavalry while AWOL; August 1864 reported as a "deserter."

Pate, Henry H.: Private

Transferred to Co. I on 7/11/1864; previously served in Company B, 12th Battalion NC Cavalry (enlisted in Johnston Co.); present or accounted for on muster rolls through October 1864.

Peoples, Henry: Private

Transferred to Co. I on 7/11/1864; previously served in Company B, 12th Battalion NC Cavalry (enlisted in Greene Co.); present or accounted for on muster rolls through 12/15/1864 when transferred to Company A, 33rd NC Infantry.

Perry, Martin: Private

Transferred to Co. I on 7/11/1864; previously served in Company B, 12th Battalion NC Cavalry (enlisted in Bertie Co.); transferred to 4th NC Cavalry while AWOL.

Powell, William B.: Sergeant

Transferred to Co. I on 7/11/1864; married Maria Cook on January 10, 1854 in Northampton Co.; previously served in Company B, 12th Battalion NC Cavalry (Northampton Co.); present or accounted for on muster rolls through October 1864.

Rand, Marcellus Ferdinand: 2nd Lieutenant

Transferred to Co. I on 7/11/1864; born 7/13/1834; previously served in Company B, 12th Battalion NC Cavalry (enlisted in Johnston Co.); transferred with rank of corporal; appointed 2nd lieutenant on 10/7/1864; captured 4/3/1865 on Appomattox River, VA, held at Old Capitol Prison; transferred 4/21/1865 to Johnson's Island; released 6/20/1865 after taking Oath of Allegiance; died 1/29/1916, buried Holland Methodist Church, Ten-Ten Rd., Wake Co., NC.

Rodgerson, Job C.: Private

Transferred to Co. I on 7/11/1864; previously served in Company B, 12th Battalion NC Cavalry; transferred to 4th NC Cavalry while AWOL; 8/3/1864 released from prison under presidential pardon for service in the Winder Legion in defense of Richmond during Sheridan's raid.

Scoggins, Henry M.: Private

Transferred to Co. I on 7/11/1864; previously served in Company B, 12th Battalion NC Cavalry; died 10/7/1864 in Lynchburg, VA hospital of gunshot wounds; buried in the Old City Cemetery, Confederate Section, Lynchburg, VA.

Scott, William B. F.: Private

Transferred to Co. I on 7/11/1864; previously served in Company B, 12th Battalion NC Cavalry (enlisted in Bertie Co.); transferred to 4th NC Cavalry while AWOL.

Sessoms, A. S.: Private

Transferred to Co. I on 7/11/1864; previously served in Company B, 12th Battalion NC Cavalry (enlisted in Hertford Co.); present or accounted for on muster rolls through October 1864.

Smith, James A.: Private

Transferred to Co. I on 7/11/1864; married Martha Byrd on July 13, 1852 in Johnston Co.; previously served in Company B, 12th Battalion NC Cavalry (enlisted in Johnston Co.); 12/12/1864 admitted to Danville, VA hospital with "nephritis"; returned to duty 1/28/1865; paroled 5/18/1865 in Raleigh.

Stancill, James H.: Private

Transferred to Co. I on 7/11/1864; previously served in Company A, 55th Regiment NC Troops and Company B, 12th Battalion NC Cavalry; present or accounted for on muster rolls through October 1864.

Strickland, Edward Day: Private

Transferred to Co. I on 12/15/1864; previously served as a private in Company A, 33rd NC Infantry.

Thomas, Admiral: Private

Transferred to Co. I on 7/11/1864; previously served in Company B, 12th Battalion NC Cavalry (enlisted in Lenoir Co.); present or accounted for on muster rolls through October 1864; captured 4/2/1865 on the Appomattox River, VA, held at Pt. Lookout; released 6/5/1865 after taking Oath of Allegiance.

Thomas, Isaiah: Corporal

Transferred to Co. I on 7/11/1864; previously served in Company B, 12th Battalion NC Cavalry (enlisted in Wayne Co.); present or accounted for on muster rolls through October 1864; transferred to 4th NC Cavalry as a private; Sept./Oct. 1864 appointed corporal.

Tyler, Joseph: Private

Transferred to Co. I on 7/11/1864; previously served in Company B, 12th Battalion NC Cavalry (enlisted in Hertford Co.); transferred to 4th NC Cavalry while AWOL.

Tynch, Josephus: Private

Transferred to Co. I on 7/11/1864; previously served in Company B, 12th Battalion NC Cavalry (enlisted in Bertie Co.); present or accounted for on muster rolls through October 1864.

Waldo, Samuel Pearce: Private

Transferred to Co. I; resident of Granville Co., NC; captured 3/29/1865 at Hatcher's Run, VA, held at Pt. Lookout; released 6/21/1865 after taking Oath of Allegiance; married Alice Margarette Owen on December 31, 1868 in Granville Co.

Ward, George D.: Captain

Transferred to Co. I on 7/11/1864; born circa 1841; listed as living with his mother Sarah Ward in the 1860 Bertie Co. Census; resident of Bertie Co. at the time of enlistment; previously served in Company B, 12th Battalion NC Cavalry; transferred with rank of 1st lieutenant; 12/20/1864 promoted to captain; present or accounted for on muster rolls through January 1865; 2/21/1865 absent on furlough.

White, David: Private

Transferred to Co. I on 7/11/1864; previously served in Company B, 12th Battalion NC Cavalry (enlisted in Bertie Co.); transferred to 4th NC Cavalry while in confinement for desertion; returned to company before 10/13/1864 when he was issued clothing.

White, George W.: Private

Transferred to Co. I on 7/11/1864; born circa 1834; son of Hamilton and Nancy White of Bertie Co.; previously served in Company B, 12th Battalion NC Cavalry (enlisted in Hertford Co.); transferred to 4th NC Cavalry while AWOL; August 1864 reported as "deserted."

White, Henderson W.: Private

Transferred to Co. I on 7/11/1864; born circa 1842; son of Cader and Harriet White; previously served in Company B, 12th Battalion NC Cavalry (enlisted in Bertie Co.); reported as "absent sick at hospital" and "absent without leave."

Company K

Askew, Lemuel: Private

Transferred to Co. K on 7/11/1864; previously served in Company A, 12th Battalion NC Cavalry (enlisted in Northampton Co.); present or accounted for on muster rolls through October 1864.

Baggett, Jesse: Private

Transferred to Co. K on 7/11/1864; previously served in Company A, 12th Battalion NC Cavalry (enlisted in Northampton Co.); present or accounted for on muster rolls through October 1864.

Baggett, John: Private

Enlisted in Co. K on 8/1/1864 in Northampton Co.; present or accounted for on muster rolls through October 1864; wounded in action on 12/10/1864 near Petersburg, VA.

Baggett, Shadrack: Private

Transferred to Co. K on 8/1/1864 in Northampton Co.; 1/6/1865 reported as a POW by 3rd NY Cavalry (Bernard's Mill, VA) with the remark "deserted."

Baker, Henry: Private

Transferred to Co. K on 7/11/1864; previously served in Company A, 12th Battalion NC Cavalry (enlisted in Northampton Co.); present or accounted for on muster rolls through October 1864.

Baker, John: Private

Transferred to Co. K on 7/11/1864; previously served in Company A, 12th Battalion NC Cavalry (enlisted in Hertford Co.); present or accounted for on muster rolls through October 1864.

Baker, Thomas: Private

Transferred to Co. K; "issued clothing during the third quarter of 1864."

Ballance, Daniel: Sergeant

Transferred to Co. K on 7/11/1864; married Sarah E. Smith on December 5, 1861 in Northampton Co.; previously served in Company A, 12th Battalion NC Cavalry (enlisted in Northampton Co.); present or accounted for on muster rolls through October 1864; Nov. 1864 admitted to Richmond hospital; 11/29/1864 furloughed for 60 days; 2/27/1865 reported as a "deserter."

Baugham, John: Private

Transferred to Co. K on 7/11/1864; previously served in Company A, 12th Battalion NC Cavalry (enlisted in Northampton Co.); present or accounted for on muster rolls through October 1864.

Baugham, Nathaniel: Corporal

Transferred to Co. K on 7/11/1864; previously served in Company A, 12th Battalion NC Cavalry (enlisted in Northampton Co.); present or accounted for on muster rolls through October 1864.

Beal, Drewry: Private

Transferred to Co. K on 7/11/1864; previously served in Company A, 12th Battalion NC Cavalry (enlisted in Hertford Co.); present or accounted for on muster rolls through October 1864; married Susan Blythe on December 8, 1866 in Northampton Co.

Beal, R. S.: Private

Transferred to Co. K; "signed undated receipt roll for clothing issued."

Beale, Dallas M.: 3rd Lieutenant

Transferred to Co. K on 7/11/1864; born 11/8/1844 in Northampton Co.; son of Jordan Beale and Eliza Martin of Northampton Co.; previously served in Company A, 12th Battalion NC Cavalry; transferred to 4th NC Cavalry as a 3rd lieutenant; present or accounted for on muster rolls through October 1864; paroled 4/28/1865 at Gen. Hospital No. 12, Greensboro, NC; after the war was a merchant in Potecasi, NC; married Cicely F. Powell on January 30, 1873 in Northampton Co.; from 1890–1891 served as editor and publisher of the local newspaper *Roanoke Patron*; died on June 4, 1911 in Northampton Co.; buried in the Beale-Cale Family Cemetery, Potecasi, NC.

Bennett, John S.: Private

Transferred to Co. K; paroled 4/9/1865 at Appomattox Court House.

Bolton, James: Private

Transferred to Co. K on 7/11/1864; married Lavenia McDaniel on July 1, 1856 in Northampton Co.; previously served in Company A, 12th Battalion NC Cavalry (resided and enlisted in Northampton Co.); present or accounted for on muster rolls through October 1864.

Bolton, Lemuel: Private

Transferred to Co. K on 7/11/1864; married Margaret J. Lassiter on February 24, 1859 in Northampton Co.; previously served in Company A, 12th Battalion NC Cavalry (enlisted in Northampton Co.); present or accounted for on muster rolls through October 1864.

Bowers, Thomas: Private

Transferred to Co. K on 7/11/1864; married Elizabeth Roan on January 1, 1855 in Northampton Co.; previously served in Company A, 12th Battalion NC Cavalry (enlisted in Northampton Co.); present or accounted for on muster rolls through October 1864.

Boyce, Daniel: Private

Transferred to Co. K on 7/11/1864; previously served in Company A, 12th Battalion NC Cavalry (enlisted in Northampton Co.); present or accounted for on muster rolls through October 1864.

Boyce, Thomas: Private

Transferred to Co. K on 7/11/1864; born circa 1840; last name also appears as "Boice" in records; son of William and Ann Boice of Northampton Co.; previously served in Company A, 12th Battalion NC Cavalry (enlisted in Northampton Co.); present or accounted for on muster rolls through October 1864; he married Nancy McDaniel on January 11, 1867 in Northampton Co.

Bradley, Joseph: Private

Transferred to Co. K on 7/11/1864; previously served in Company A, 12th Battalion NC Cavalry (enlisted in Northampton Co.); present or accounted for on muster rolls through October 1864; 2/27/1865 reported as a "deserter."

Britt, Elisha: Private

Transferred to Co. K on 7/11/1864; previously served in Company A, 12th Battalion NC Cavalry (enlisted in Northampton Co.); transferred to 4th NC Cavalry while AWOL; July/August 1864 muster roll states "absent in arrest"; a notice in the April 1919 *Confederate Veteran*, p. 122 (Vol. XXVII, No. 4) has him seeking help to endorse his pension application (listed as Elijah Britt); a similar notice appears on page 119 of the March 1920 *Confederate Veteran* (correctly listed as Elisha Britt).

Bryant, Peterson: Private

Transferred to Co. K on 7/11/1864; previously served in Company A, 12th Battalion NC Cavalry (enlisted in Northampton Co.); present or accounted for on muster rolls through October 1864.

Bryant, Wiley: Private

Transferred to Co. K on 7/11/1864; previously served in Company A, 12th Battalion NC Cavalry (enlisted in Northampton Co. on September 25, 1862); present or accounted for on muster rolls through October 1864.

Bryant, Wiley A.: Private

Transferred to Co. K on 7/11/1864; previously served in Company A, 12th Battalion NC Cavalry (enlisted in Northampton Co. on September 1, 1863); present or accounted for on muster rolls through October 1864.

Burkett, William Henry: Private

Transferred to Co. K on 7/11/1864; previously served in Company A, 12th Battalion NC Cavalry (enlisted in Northampton Co.); born August 1843 in Northampton Co., NC; son of William Burkett and Elizabeth Harris; present and accounted for on the last muster roll, October 1864; after the war returned to Bertie Co. where he began farming; on December 9, 1868 married Mary Newsome; they had two children; he died on January 22, 1923 in Bertie Co., buried at "The Raby Place."

Cole, Mark: Private

Transferred to Co. K; resident of Richmond Co., NC; captured 3/30/1865 near Hatcher's Run, VA, held at Pt. Lookout; released 6/26/1865 after taking Oath of Allegiance.

Conner, James W.: Private

Transferred to Co. K on 7/11/1864; previously served in Company B, 15th Battalion NC Cavalry and Company A, 12th Battalion NC Cavalry; present or accounted for on muster rolls through October 1864.

Conwell, Joshua: Private

Transferred to Co. K on 7/11/1864; previously served in Company A, 12th Battalion NC Cavalry (resided and enlisted in Northampton Co.); transferred to 4th NC Cavalry while absent sick.

Cook, George W.: Private

Transferred to Co. K on 7/11/1864; previously served in Company A, 12th Battalion NC Cavalry (enlisted in Northampton Co.); transferred to 4th NC Cavalry while AWOL; married Rizzie A. Monger on December 17, 1864 in Northampton Co.

Curl, Redmond: Private

Enlisted in Co. K on 8/1/1864 in Northampton Co.; born circa 1827 in Northampton Co.; last name also appears as "Cure" in records; married Mariah Nelson on November 23, 1849 in Northampton Co.; wounded in action on 8/20/1864 (in head); died 8/22/1864 in Petersburg hospital.

Dement, Fidel: Private

Transferred to Co. K on 7/11/1864; previously served in Company A, 12th Battalion NC Cavalry (enlisted in Granville Co.); present or accounted for on muster rolls through October 1864.

Dunning, James W.: Private

Transferred to Co. K on 7/11/1864; previously served in Company A, 12th Battalion NC Cavalry (enlisted in Hertford Co.); present or accounted for on muster rolls through October 1864; wounded in action on 3/29/1865 (in left hand), admitted to

Petersburg hospital; transferred 4/1/1865 to Richmond hospital; captured there 4/3/1865; released 6/22/1865 after taking Oath of Allegiance.

Elliot, John F.: Sergeant

Transferred to Co. K on 7/11/1864; previously served in Company A, 12th Battalion NC Cavalry (resided and enlisted in Northampton Co.); present or accounted for on muster rolls through October 1864.

Evans, Samuel F.: Private

Transferred to Co. K on 7/11/1864; previously served in Company A, 12th Battalion NC Cavalry (enlisted in Hertford Co.); present or accounted for on muster rolls through October 1864.

Fespeman, Cornelius Monroe: Private

Transferred to Co. K; paroled 5/12/1865 in Salisbury, NC.

Futrell, Exum: Sergeant

Transferred to Co. K on 7/11/1864; previously served in Company A, 12th Battalion NC Cavalry (resided and enlisted in Northampton Co.); present or accounted for on muster rolls through October 1864.

Futrell, Harrison: Private

Transferred to Co. K on 7/11/1864; previously served in Company A, 12th Battalion NC Cavalry (enlisted in Northampton Co.); present or accounted for on muster rolls through October 1864.

Greene, Silas M.: Private

Enlisted in Co. K in July 1864; born May 11, 1810 in Burke Co., NC; son of William and Elizabeth Green; died August 7, 1892.

Harmon, Henry: Private

Transferred to Co. K on 7/11/1864; previously served in Company A, 12th Battalion NC Cavalry (enlisted in Northampton Co.); present or accounted for on muster rolls through October 1864; captured 3/29/1865 near Hatcher's Run, VA, held at Pt. Lookout; released 6/27/1865 after taking Oath of Allegiance.

Hays, J. M.: Private

Transferred to Co. K on 7/11/1864; previously served in Company A, 12th Battalion NC Cavalry (enlisted in Northampton Co.); transferred to 4th NC Cavalry while AWOL.

Hoggard, Jesse H.: Private

Transferred to Co. K on 7/11/1864; previously served in Company B, 1st NC Cavalry (9th NCST) and Company A, 12th Battalion NC Cavalry; transferred to 4th NC Cavalry while AWOL.

Hoggard, John O.: Private

Transferred to Co. K on 7/11/1864; previously served in Company A, 12th Battalion NC Cavalry (resided and enlisted in Hertford Co.); transferred to 4th NC Cavalry while absent sick.

Hoggard, Nathan S.: 1st Sergeant
Transferred to Co. K on 7/11/1864; previously served in Company A, 12th Battalion NC Cavalry (enlisted in Northampton Co.); present or accounted for on muster rolls through October 1864; on 4/10/1865 admitted to a Danville, VA hospital.

Hudson, Charles W.: Private
Transferred to Co. K on 7/11/1864; previously served in Company A, 12th Battalion NC Cavalry; Aug. 1864 "absent without leave"; 9/10/1864 issued clothing at General Hospital, Kittrell, NC.

Hunter, Marcus G.: Private
Enlisted in Co. K on 8/1/1864 in Northampton Co.; present or accounted for on muster rolls through October 1864; 2/27/1865 received by federal provost marshal, Norfolk, VA "with instructions that the Oath of Allegiance be administered and he be allowed to go to his home to reside."

Hunter, Wiley J.: Private
Transferred to Co. K on 7/11/1864; previously served in Company A, 12th Battalion NC Cavalry (enlisted in Northampton Co.); present or accounted for on muster rolls through October 1864.

Joyner, Joseph B.: Private
Transferred to Co. K on 7/11/1864; married Harriot Benthal on September 30, 1850 in Northampton Co.; previously served in Company A, 12th Battalion NC Cavalry (resided and enlisted in Northampton Co.); transferred to 4th NC Cavalry while absent sick.

Joyner, William T.: Corporal
Transferred to Co. K on 7/11/1864; previously served in Company A, 12th Battalion NC Cavalry (enlisted in Northampton Co.); present or accounted for on muster rolls through October 1864.

Knight, Adam: Private
Transferred to Co. K on 7/11/1864; married Elizabeth M. Vaughan on January 11, 1855 in Northampton Co.; previously served in Company A, 12th Battalion NC Cavalry (enlisted in Northampton Co.); transferred to 4th NC Cavalry while AWOL.

Lassiter, John W.: Private
Transferred to Co. K on 7/11/1864; previously served in Company A, 12th Battalion NC Cavalry (enlisted in Hertford Co.); present or accounted for on muster rolls through October 1864.

Leak, James R.: Sergeant
Transferred to Co. K on 7/27/1864; previously served in Company B, 1st NC Cavalry (9th NCST); present or accounted for on muster rolls through October 1864.

Manning, Phil S. P.: Private
Transferred to Co. K on 7/11/1864; previously served in Company A, 12th Bat-

talion NC Cavalry (enlisted in Hertford Co.); transferred to 4th NC Cavalry while "missing in action."

Parker, Denison Wilson: Private
Transferred to Co. K on 7/11/1864; previously served in Company A, 12th Battalion NC Cavalry (enlisted in Northampton Co.); present or accounted for on muster rolls through October 1864; transferred to 4th NC Cavalry as a corporal; paroled April 11–21, 1865 in Farmville, VA as a private; married three times in Northampton Co., first to Elizabeth Wiggins on March 1, 1868; second to Burnettie Powell on October 12, 1871; third to Marcilla Eddie Bridgers on March 15, 1880.

Parker, Jesse: Private
Transferred to Co. K on 7/11/1864; previously served in Company A, 12th Battalion NC Cavalry (resided and enlisted in Northampton Co.); present or accounted for on muster rolls through October 1864.

Pledger, Benjamin W.: Private
Transferred to Co. K; wounded in action on 3/29/1865 (right shoulder) near Hatcher's Run, VA, admitted to Petersburg hospital that same day; captured in hospital 4/3/1865; transferred 4/8/1865 to US Army General Hospital, Ft. Monroe; transferred 5/30/1865 to Military Prison, Camp Hamilton, VA; released 5/31/1865.

Roan, James L.: Private
Transferred to Co. K on 7/11/1864; previously served in Company A, 12th Battalion NC Cavalry (enlisted in Northampton Co.); present or accounted for on muster rolls through October 1864; 3/4/1865 reported by federal provost marshal, Suffolk, VA as a "deserter", forwarded to asst. adjutant general, Capt. S. L. McHenry; married Emily Hall on January 12, 1867 in Northampton Co.

Robertson, B. A.: Private
Transferred to Co. K on 7/11/1864; previously served in Company A, 12th Battalion NC Cavalry (enlisted in Northampton Co.); present or accounted for on muster rolls through October 1864.

Sauls, James V.: 1st Lieutenant
Transferred to Co. K on 7/11/1864; born circa 1837 in Northampton Co.; previously served in Company A, 12th Battalion NC Cavalry; transferred to 4th NC Cavalry as a 1st lieutenant; 10/17/1864 admitted to Richmond hospital with a gunshot wound to right side of face; 10/26/1864 furloughed; 1/25/1865 tendered resignation that was officially accepted 2/10/1865.

Sauls, Warren: Private
Transferred to Co. K on 7/11/1864; previously served in Company A, 12th Battalion NC Cavalry (enlisted in Northampton Co.); transferred to 4th NC Cavalry while "absent in arrest."

Savage, John L.: Private
Transferred to Co. K on 7/11/1864; previously served in Company A, 12th Bat-

talion NC Cavalry (enlisted in Northampton Co.); present or accounted for on muster rolls through October 1864.

Skiles, William H.: Corporal

Transferred to Co. K on 7/11/1864; previously served in Company A, 12th Battalion NC Cavalry (resided and enlisted in Northampton Co.); present or accounted for on muster rolls through October 1864; Sept./Oct. 1864 absent sick in Petersburg and Raleigh hospitals.

Sumner, William W.: Private

Transferred to Co. K on 7/11/1864; previously served in Company A and C, 12th Battalion NC Cavalry (resided and enlisted in Northampton Co.); transferred 7/27/1864 to Company B, 1st NC Cavalry (9th NCST).

Vann, Joseph: Private

Transferred to Co. K on 7/11/1864; previously served in Company A, 12th Battalion NC Cavalry (enlisted in Northampton Co.); present or accounted for on muster rolls through October 1864.

Vann, William: 2nd Lieutenant

Transferred to Co. K on 7/11/1864; previously served in Company A, 12th Battalion NC Cavalry; transferred to 4th NC Cavalry as a 2nd lieutenant; 12/31/1864 absent on seven day furlough; 1/18/1865 dropped from rolls as an officer due to "absence beyond leave" and "inefficiency."

Vaughan, Turner: Private

Transferred to Co. K on 7/11/1864; previously served in Company A, 12th Battalion NC Cavalry (enlisted in Northampton Co.); transferred to 4th NC Cavalry while AWOL.

Ward, W. R.: Private

Transferred to Co. K on 8/1/1864; resident of Northampton Co.; captured 4/3/1865 in Petersburg, held at Hart's Island, NY; released 6/19/1865 after taking Oath of Allegiance.

Warren, James C.: Private

Transferred to Co. K on 7/11/1864; previously served in Company A, 12th Battalion NC Cavalry (enlisted in Northampton Co.); present or accounted for on muster rolls through October 1864.

Webb, James: Private

Transferred to Co. K on 10/25/1864; previously served in Company G, 27th NC Infantry; transferred from 27th NC Infantry in exchange for Lemuel K. Woodard; paroled 5/1/1865 in Greensboro, NC.

Woodward, Harrison E.: Private

Transferred to Co. K on 7/11/1864; born circa 1835 in Northampton Co.; married twice in Northampton Co., first to Tabais Darden on November 27, 1850 and then to Rebecca Lewter on January 16, 1859; previously served in Company A, 12th Battalion NC Cavalry (enlisted in Northampton Co.); present or accounted for on muster rolls through October 1864.

Woodward, Lemuel K.: Private

Transferred to Co. K on 7/11/1864; born circa 1821 in Northampton Co.; married Susan Bridgers on September 30, 1851 in Northampton Co.; previously served in Company A and C, 12th Battalion NC Cavalry (enlisted in Northampton Co.); transferred 10/25/1864 to Company G, 27th NC Infantry.

Unknown

Keever, Daniel: Private

Born 4/6/1833; died 12/14/1920, buried Oakwood Cemetery, Hickory, NC (not found on rolls of 4th NC Cavalry; info from grave marker).

Listing of
Missing Troops

Reason not present on muster roll	Brigade Command	F & S	Co. A	Co. B	Co. C	Co. D	Co. E	Co. F	Co. G	Co. H	Co. I	Co. K	Unknown	Total
Captured		3	21	33	23	24	54	23	47	23	9	3		263
Deserted/AWOL			2	14	11	15	18	33	18	3	12	14		140
Wounded	1		18	12	7	7	7	9	5	8	2	3		79
Discharged			4	4	19	3	2	1	13	10	1			57
Died (during war)			7	10	8	9	10	4	6	1	1			56
Transferred			2	1	10	5	3	4	8	2	1	2		38
Killed in action			3	1	1	1	8	3	3	3		1		24
Furnished substitute			1	2	2	1			5	2				13
Absent (not AWOL)			2		1			2				3		8
Resigned		2			1		1	2	1	1				8
Never mustered in			6			1								7
Never reported							3			1				4
Hospital										1	1			2
Missing in action						1				1				2
Invalid Corps									1			1		2
Disabled					1									1
Furloughed											1			1
Not transferred									1					1
POW at transfer											1			1
Relieved of duty		1												1
Total Not Present	1	6	66	77	84	67	106	81	108	56	29	27		708
Total Enlistment	5	13	163	184	149	132	178	119	139	116	69	70	1	1337

Notes

1. Independent Companies of Partisan Rangers

1. *War of the Rebellion: A Compilation of the Official Records of the Union and Confederate Armies*, Series IV, Volume 1, p. 1094–1095. Hereafter referred to as O.R. (all references are to Series 1 unless otherwise noted); Wadesboro *North Carolina Argus*, December 12, 1861, p. 3; Ferebee Family Genealogy, copy in possession of author; Robert K. Krick, *Lee's Colonels: A Biographical Register of the Field Officers of the Army of Northern Virginia*, Dayton, Ohio, 1979, p. 123, 396; Richard L. Zuber, *Jonathan Worth: A Biography of a Southern Unionist*, Chapel Hill, 1965, p. 218–219; Stephen E. Bradley, *North Carolina Confederate Militia Officers Roster As Contained in the Adjutant-General's Officers Roster*, Wilmington, 1992, p. 9; Frontis W. Johnston, editor, *Zebulon B. Vance Letters, Volume One: 1843–1862*, Raleigh, 1963, p. 341.

2. Wadesboro *North Carolina Argus*, December 12, 1861, p. 3.

3. Johnston, p. 119–120.

4. Johnston, p. 133.

5. Wadesboro *North Carolina Argus*, May 1, 1862, p. 2.

6. Johnston, p. xl.

7. Louis A. Manarin, *North Carolina Troops 1861–1865: A Roster, Volume II, Cavalry*, Raleigh, 1968, p. 268.

8. Bradley, p. 218–222.

9. Wadesboro *North Carolina Argus*, May 22, 1862, p. 3.

10. Wadesboro *North Carolina Argus*, July 3, 1862, p.1.

11. *Ibid.*

12. *Ibid.*

13. *Ibid.*

14. *Ibid.*

15. *Ibid.*

16. Wadesboro *North Carolina Argus*, July 3, 1862, p.1; Johnston, p. 141–142.

17. Manarin, p. 268.

18. D. D. McLaurin to Hugh McLaurin, letter of August 23, 1862, in the McLaurin Family Papers, Southern Historical Collection, University of North Carolina, Chapel Hill, North Carolina.

19. Wadesboro *North Carolina Argus*, September 25, 1862, p.2–3.

20. Manarin, p. 275.

21. Bradley, p. 126–127.

22. Manarin, p. 275.

23. Manarin, p. 284.

24. Bradley, p. 55–61; James Sprunt, *Chronicles of the Cape Fear River: 1660–1916*, Raleigh, 1916, p. 339.

25. Manarin, p. 284.

26. *Wilmington Journal*, September 4, 1862.

27. Manarin, p. 292.

28. Bradley, p. 17–18.

29. Media Evans Collection, Private Manuscript Collection (482), North Carolina Department of Archives and History, Raleigh, North Carolina, p. 1–2.

30. Charlotte *Daily Bulletin*, February 4, 1862.

31. Charlotte *Daily Bulletin*, February 19, 1862.

32. Manarin, p. 299.

33. Bradley, p. 207–209, 228–235.

34. Manarin, p. 299; Charlotte *Daily Bulletin*, July 31, 1862.

35. Manarin, p. 309.

36. Bradley, p. 21–24.

37. Manarin, p. 309.

38. Manarin, p. 315–316.

39. Bradley, p. 7–8.

40. Manarin, p. 315–316.

41. O.R., Volume 18, p. 750.

42. Manarin, p. 315–316.

43. Evans, p. 2; Walter Clark, *Histories of the Several Regiments and Battalions from North Carolina in the Great War, 1861–1865*, Volume III, Wendell, NC, 1982 (reprint), p. 458.

2. First Taste of Fire: Skirmishes Along the Blackwater

1. Evans, p. 2.

2. O.R., Volume 18, p. 18–19.

3. Wadesboro *North Carolina Argus*, August 4, 1862, p. 1.

4. O.R., Volume 18, p. 745, 748.

5. O.R., Volume 18, p. 18.

6. *Official Records of the Union and Confederate Navies in the War of the Rebellion*, Series 1, Volume 8, p. 105. Hereafter referred to as O.R.N.

7. O.R.N., Volume 8, p. 104–5, 108; John M. Coski, *Capital Navy: The Men, Ships and Operations of the James River Squadron*, Campbell, California, 1996, p. 197; Tony Gibbons, *Warships and Naval Battles of the Civil War*, New York, 1989, p. 110; Navy Department, *Dictionary of American Naval Fighting Ships Volume II*, Washington, 1963, p. 155; Navy Department, *Dictionary of American Naval Fighting Ships Volume III*, Washington, 1968, p. 395–396; James L. Mooney, editor, *Dictionary of American Naval Fighting Ships Volume VIII*, Washington, 1981, p. 271 .

8. Clark, Volume I, p. 587.

9. O.R., Volume 18, p. 17.

10. O.R., Volume 18, p. 16.

11. O.R., Volume 18, p. 15.

12. O.R., Volume 18, p. 17.

13. O.R., Volume 18, p. 15.

14. C. T. Chaplain and J. M. Keeling, "Operations on the Blackwater River," *Confederate Veteran*, Volume 27 (August 1919), p. 304–305; Wadesboro *North Carolina Argus*, October 23, 1862.

15. Wadesboro *North Carolina Argus*, October 23, 1862, p. 2.

16. O.R.N., Volume 8, p. 108.

17. Evans, p. 2; Wadesboro *North Carolina Argus*, October 23, 1862.

18. O.R., Volume 18, p. 18–19; Chaplain and Keeling, p. 305.

19. O.R., Volume 18, p. 18–19; Evans, p.2–3; Wadesboro *North Carolina Argus*, October 23, 1862; Clark, Volume III, p. 458–459.

20. O.R.N., Volume 8, p. 108; Evans, p. 2–3; Wadesboro *North Carolina Argus*, October 23, 1862; Clark, Volume III, p. 458–459.

21. O.R.N., Volume 8, p. 108; Evans, p. 3.

22. O.R.N., Volume 8, p. 108.

23. O.R.N., Volume 8, p. 108

24. O.R.N., Volume 8, p. 106.

25. O.R.N., Volume 8, p. 108

26. O.R.N., Volume 8, p. 108–111.

27. O.R., Volume 18, p.19.

28. O.R., Volume 18, p.17.

29. O.R., Volume 18, p.19.

30. O.R., Volume 18, p.17.

31. O.R., Volume 18, p.19; Wadesboro *North Carolina Argus*, October 23, 1862.

32. O.R., Volume 18, p.17.

33. O.R.N., Volume 8, p. 107.

34. Wadesboro *North Carolina Argus*, October 23, 1862.

35. O.R., Volume 18, p. 1; Evans, p. 3.

36. O.R., Volume 18, p. 755.

37. Ezra Warner, *Generals in Gray: Lives of the Confederate Commanders*, Baton Rouge, 1959, p. 259–260.

38. Clark, Volume III, p. 530.

39. Abe Jones to mother, Letter of October 9, 1862, in the Abraham G. Jones Papers, East Carolina University Manuscript Collection, J.Y. Joyner Library, East Carolina University, Greenville, North Carolina.

40. Wadesboro *North Carolina Argus*, November 27, 1862.

41. Wadesboro *North Carolina Argus*, November 24, 1862; Charles Dana Gibson, "Hay: The Linchpin of Mobility," *North & South*, Volume 2 Number 2 (January 1999), p. 51–53.

42. Wadesboro *North Carolina Argus*, December 1, 1862.

43. *Ibid.*

44. O.R., Volume 18, p. 33.

45. Wadesboro *North Carolina Argus*, December 1, 1862.

46. Wadesboro *North Carolina Argus*, November 27, 1862.

47. Evans, p. 3.

3. The Battle of Whitehall

1. Evans, p. 3; Clark, Volume III, p. 553.

2. O.R., Volume 18, p. 54.

3. W. W. Howe, *Kinston, Whitehall and Goldsboro North Carolina Expedition, December, 1862*, New York, 1890, p. 49.

4. O.R., Volume 18, p. 54.

5. Howe, p. 11.

6. O.R., Volume 18, p. 112–113.

7. Howe, p. 13–14.

8. Evans, p. 4; Clark, Volume III, p. 459.
9. O.R., Volume 18, p. 55.
10. O.R., Volume 18, p. 55–56; Howe, p. 15.
11. O.R., Volume 18, p. 56; Howe, p. 23–24.
12. O.R., Volume 18, p. 121; *Spirit of the Age*, January 5, 1863.
13. O.R., Volume 18, p. 121.
14. Clark, Volume V, p. 86–87.
15. Leslie S. Bright, William H. Rowland, and James C. Bardon, *C.S.S. Neuse: A Question of Iron and Time*, Raleigh, 1981, p. 6.
16. O.R., Volume 18, p. 56–57.
17. Clark, Volume V, p. 87.
18. Howe, p. 25–26; Clark, Volume I, p. 584–585; Clark, Volume V, p. 88.
19. Evans, p. 4.
20. J. C. Warlick, "Battle of White Hall, N.C.," *Confederate Veteran*, Volume 12, p. 178.
21. Clark, Volume V, p. 88.
22. O.R., Volume 18, p. 57, 64, 121–122.
23. O.R., Volume 18, p. 57, 76, 93.
24. O.R., Volume 18, p. 93.
25. O.R., Volume 18, p. 64.
26. O.R., Volume 18, p. 122.
27. O.R., Volume 18, p. 57, 64, 83.
28. Clark, Volume V, p. 89.
29. O.R., Volume 18, p. 83, 85; Howe, p. 31.
30. O.R., Volume 18, p. 804–805; O.R. Supplement, Part I, Volume 3, p. 397.
31. O.R., Volume 18, p. 57.
32. Evans, p. 5.

4. Movements in Eastern North Carolina

1. Evans, p. 5; Abe Jones to Ellick [brother], Letter of December 24, 1862, in the Abraham G. Jones Papers, East Carolina University Manuscript Collection, J. Y. Joyner Library, East Carolina University, Greenville, North Carolina.
2. *Spirit of the Age*, February 9, 1863.
3. Raleigh, *State Journal*, January 8, 1863.
4. O.R., Volume 18, p. 824.
5. Evans, p. 5.
6. O.R., Volume 18, p. 854.
7. *Spirit of the Age*, February 9, 1863.
8. O.R., Volume 18, p. 529.
9. Abe Jones to Parents, Letter of January 28, 1863, in the Abraham G. Jones Papers, East Carolina University Manuscript Collection, J. Y. Joyner Library, East Carolina University, Greenville, North Carolina; *Spirit of the Age*, February 9, 1863.
10. O.R., Volume 18, p. 896.
11. O.R., Volume 18, p. 894.
12. John G. Barret, *The Civil War in North Carolina*, Chapel Hill, 1963, p. 149.
13. O.R., Volume 18, p. 891.
14. O.R., Volume 18, p. 950–951.
15. Barrett, p. 151.
16. O.R., Volume 18, p. 197.
17. O.R., Volume 18, p. 197.

18. O.R., Volume 18, p.197–198.

19. O.R., Volume 18, p. 188–189.

20. O.R., Volume 18, p. 198.

21. Raleigh *Daily Progress*, April 30, 1863; Evans, p. 5; O.R., Volume 18, p. 602.

22. Evans, p. 5.

23. Evans, p. 5–6.

24. Raleigh *Daily Progress*, April 30, 1863.

25. Evans, p. 6.

26. O.R., Volume 18, p. 992–993.

27. O.R., Volume 18, p. 1020.

28. Evans, p. 6.

29. Steven A. Cormier, *The Siege of Suffolk: The Forgotten Campaign: April 11–May 4, 1863*, Lynchburg, 1989, p. 318.

30. O.R., Volume 18, p. 1044.

5. J.E.B. Stuart's Cavalry: Brandy Station

1. O.R., Volume 51, Part II, p. 704–706; O.R., Volume 18, p. 1051; Clark, Volume II, p. 87–88.

2. Evans, p. 7; Wadesboro *North Carolina Argus*, May 28, 1863; O.R., Volume 51, Part II, p. 928; O.R., Volume 18, p. 1059.

3. Evans, p. 7; Clark, Volume III, p. 531.

4. H. B. McClellan, *The Life and Campaigns of Stuart's Cavalry*, Secaucus, NJ, 1993, p. 261.

5. Evans, p. 7; W. W. Blackford, *War Years with J. E. B. Stuart*, New York, 1945, p. 210.

6. George M. Neese, *Three Years in the Confederate Horse Artillery*, Dayton, OH, 1983, p. 166.

7. Evans, p. 7.

8. Emory M. Thomas, *Bold Dragoon: The Life of J. E. B Stuart*, New York, 1986, p. 219; Stephen Z. Starr, *The Union Cavalry in the Civil War*, Volume I, Baton Rouge, 1979, p. 371.

9. Heros Von Borcke, *Memoirs of the War for Independence*, Volume II, New York, 1938, p. 264.

10. Neese, p. 167.

11. Gary W. Gallagher, "Battle of Brandy Station," *Blue & Gray Magazine*, Volume XIII, Number 1 (October 1990), p.13.

12. Blackford, p. 212.

13. Von Borcke, Volume II, p. 265; Neese, p. 167–168.

14. Blackford, p. 211; Edward G. Longacre, *The Cavalry at Gettysburg: A Tactical Study of Mounted Operations During the Civil War's Pivotal Campaign, 9 June–14 July, 1863*, Rutherford, NJ, 1986, p. 40.

15. Neese, p. 167.

16. Blackford, p. 211–212; McClellan, p. 261; Longacre, p. 40.

17. Neese, p. 169; Blackford, p. 212–213; Daniel Branson Coltrane, *The Memoirs of Daniel Branson Coltrane*, Raleigh, 1956, p. 11.

18. Blackford, p. 212; McClellan, p. 262; Neese, p. 169; Longacre, p. 41.

19. John W. Thomason, Jr., *Jeb Stuart*, New York, 1992, p. 400; Jack Coggins, *Arms and Equipment of the Civil War*, Wilmington, 1989, p. 52; Wilbur Sturtevant Nye, *Here Come the Rebels!*, Baton Rouge, 1965, p.50; Gallagher, p. 13; Longacre, p. 42; McClellan, p. 262.

20. Starr, Volume I, p. 366, 373; Patrick A. Bowmaster, *Confederate Brig. Gen. B. H. Robertson and the 1863 Gettysburg Campaign*, Master's Thesis, Virginia Polytechnic Institute and State University, Blacksburg, VA, 1995, p. 30–31; Longacre, p. 62–63; Gallagher, p. 11.

21. Gallagher, p. 12; Starr, Volume I, p. 377; Longacre, p. 62–63.
22. Gallagher, p. 14; O.R., Volume 27, Part II, p. 734–735.
23. Gallagher, p. 20; O.R., Volume 27, Part II, p. 734–735; Bowmaster, p. 31–32.
24. O.R., Volume 27, Part II, p. 734–735.
25. *Ibid.*
26. O.R., Volume 27, Part II, p. 734–736.
27. O.R., Volume 27, Part II, p. 735.
28. O.R., Volume 27, Part II, p. 734–736; Bowmaster, p. 43–44.
29. Bowmaster, p. 44; O.R., Volume 27, Part II, p. 735–736.
30. Bowmaster, p. 44; O.R., Volume 27, Part II, p. 736.
31. O.R., Volume 27, Part II, p. 733–736.
32. O.R., Volume 27, Part II, p. 736.
33. O.R., Volume 27, Part II, p. 720.

6. Fights in the Loudon Valley

1. Gallagher, p. 13; Starr, Volume I, p. 397; Evans, p. 78.
2. Gallagher, p. 1314; Starr, Volume I, p. 397.
3. Gallagher, p. 14; Evans, p. 8; O.R., Volume 27, Part II, p. 687–688; Nye, p. 169.
4. O.R., Volume 27, Part II, p. 688; Nye, p. 169–170.
5. George Bliss, *Personal Narratives...The Rhode Island Cavalry at Middleburg, VA*, Providence, RI, 1889, p. 6–10; Robert F. O'Neill, Jr., *The Cavalry Battles of Aldie, Middleburg and Upperville, ...June 10-27, 1863*, Lynchburg, VA, 1993, p. 69–70; Frederic Denison, *Sabres and Spurs: The First Regiment Rhode Island Cavalry in the Civil War, 1861-1865*, Baltimore, 1994, p. 223.
6. Bliss, p. 10–11; O'Neill, p. 72.
7. Clark, Volume III, p. 562; O'Neill, p. 72; Bowmaster, p. 49–50; Nye, p. 184.
8. O'Neill, p. 72–73; Bowmaster, p. 50; Denison, p. 234; Clark, Volume III, p. 563.
9. Evans, p. 8; Nye, p. 188.
10. Nye, p. 189–190; Clark, Volume II, p. 564.
11. Nye, p. 189–190; O'Neill, p. 102; O.R., Volume 27, Part II, p. 689.
12. Evans, p. 8; O'Neill, p. 104–105; O.R., Volume 27, Part II, p. 689–690; Roster analysis by the author.
13. O.R., Volume 27, Part II, p. 689–690.
14. Nye, p. 194–195; O.R., Volume 27, Part II, p. 689–690; Evans, p. 8.
15. O.R., Volume 27, Part II, p. 690–691.
16. O.R., Volume 27, Part II, p. 690–691; Nye, p. 198; O'Neill, p. 121–123; Evans, p. 8.
17. O.R., Volume 27, Part II, p. 690–691; Nye, p. 199–200; O'Neill, p. 122–124; Evans, p. 9.
18. O'Neill, p. 147–153; Nye, p. 200.
19. Clark, Volume III, p. 461.
20. Nye, p. 208–209.
21. O'Neill, p. 156–157; Clark, Volume III, p. 462; Roster analysis by the author.
22. Evans, p. 9.

7. Gettysburg

1. Nye, p. 210; J. E. B. Stuart, "The Gettysburg Campaign," *Southern Historical Society Papers* (S.H.S.P.), Volume 7, Number 9 (September 1879), p. 408; Evans, p. 9; *Richmond Whig*, July 30, 1863.

2. Robert E. Lee, "Report of the Gettysburg Campaign," *S.H.S.P.*, Volume 2 (1876), p. 38; Bowmaster, p. 64–65; Roster analysis by the author.

3. O.R., Volume 27, Part III, p. 927–928.

4. *Ibid.*

5. O.R., Volume 27, Part II, p. 629; Robert Underwood Johnson and C. C. Buel (editors), "The Opposing Forces at Gettysburg," *Battles and Leaders of the Civil War* (*Battles and Leaders*), Volume III, Secabeus, 1991 (reprint), p. 439; *The Memphis Weekly Appeal*, Wednesday, December 26, 1877.

6. O.R., Volume 27, Part II, p. 766; Bowmaster, p. 69–70.

7. *Battles and Leaders*, Volume III, p. 252; O.R., Volume 27, Part II, p. 321.

8. O.R., Volume 27, Part II, p. 751–752; Neese, p. 184–185; Coltrane, p. 15; Evans, p. 10; Clark, Volume III, p. 462; W.E. Jones, "Summer Campaign of 1863," *S.H.S.P.*, Volume 9 (1881), p. 115–119.

9. Evans, p. 10; Clark, Volume III, p. 462; Neese, p. 186–187; *The Memphis Weekly Appeal*, Wednesday, December 26, 1877.

10. O.R., Volume 27, Part II, p. 232; *The Memphis Weekly Appeal*, Wednesday, December 26, 1877; Neese, p. 187; Clark, Volume III, p. 463.

11. Bowmaster, p. 77; Evans, p. 10; Clark, Volume III, p. 463.

12. *Ibid.*

13. Clark, Volume III, p. 463; Neese, p. 190; Bowmaster, p. 85.

14. Clark, Volume III, p. 463.

15. W.E. Jones, "Summer Campaign of 1863," *S.H.S.P.*, Volume 9 (1881), p. 117.

16. Clark, Volume III, p. 463; O.R., Volume 27, Part II, p. 699, 753.

17. *Richmond Whig*, July 30, 1863; O.R., Volume 27, Part II, p.700–703; Neese, p. 192, 196, 197.

18. Clark, Volume III, p. 464; O.R., Volume 27, Part II, p.703; Neese, p. 197.

19. Neese, p. 197–198.

20. Coltrane, p. 18; Clark, Volume III, p. 464; Neese, p. 198–199.

21. Clark, Volume III, p. 464; *North Carolina Presbyterian*, August 8, 1863; Evans, p. 11; O.R., Volume 27, Part III, p. 761; Abe Jones to parents, Letter of August 21, 1863, in the Abraham G. Jones Papers, East Carolina University Manuscript Collection, J. Y. Joyner Library, East Carolina University, Greenville, North Carolina.

22. O.R., Volume 27, Part III, p. 791, 1006; *Richmond Whig*, July 30, 1863; Hugh Buckner Johnston, editor, *The Confederate Letters of William Henry Edwards*, Wilson, NC, 1952, copy from the North Carolina Department of Archives and History (hereafter referred to as Edwards Letter(s), Letters of August 5, 1863; August 9, 1863; August 16, 1863; August 21, 1863; September 6, 1863; Abe Jones to brother, Letter of September 4, 1863, in the Abraham G. Jones Papers, East Carolina University Manuscript Collection, J. Y. Joyner Library, East Carolina University, Greenville, North Carolina.

8. The North Carolina Cavalry Brigade

1. O. R., Volume 29, Part II, p. 707, 726.

2. Johnston, *Zebulon B. Vance Letters, Volume One: 1843-1862*, p. 248; D. H. Hill, Jr., *Confederate Military History* (*C.M.H.*), Volume V (North Carolina), Wilmington, NC 1987 (reprint), p. 291–294; Abe Jones Letter of September 20, 1863, in the Abraham G. Jones Papers, East Carolina University Manuscript Collection, J. Y. Joyner Library, East Carolina University, Greenville, North Carolina; Warner, *Generals in Gray*, p. 14–15; Chris J. Hartley, *Stuart's Tarheels: James B. Gordon and His North Carolina Cavalry*, Baltimore, 1996, p. 85.

3. Abe Jones Letters of September 11, 1863 and September 14, 1863, in the Abraham

G. Jones Papers, East Carolina University Manuscript Collection, J. Y. Joyner Library, East Carolina University, Greenville, North Carolina; William D. Henderson, *The Road to Bristoe Station: Campaigning with Lee and Meade, August 1–October 20, 1863*, Lynchburg, VA, 1987, p. 51–53; Clark, Volume III, p. 572.

4. Clark, Volume III, p. 449, 572; Henderson, p. 53.

5. Abe Jones to parents, Letter of September 24, 1863, in the Abraham G. Jones Papers, East Carolina University Manuscript Collection, J. Y. Joyner Library, East Carolina University, Greenville, North Carolina; Clark, Volume III, p. 450–453; Henderson, p. 53–60.

6. Henderson, p. 60–68.

7. Abe Jones Letters of September 24, 1863 and October 7, 1863, in the Abraham G. Jones Papers, East Carolina University Manuscript Collection, J. Y. Joyner Library, East Carolina University, Greenville, North Carolina.

8. Warner, *Generals in Gray*, p. 110–111; Hill, *C.M.H.*, Volume V, p. 312; Kerr Craige, "General James B. Gordon," *Confederate Veteran*, Volume 6, Number 5 (1898), p. 216; William H. Cowles, "Oration on James B. Gordon," *Carolina and the Southern Cross*, Volume 1, Number 6, p. 19–20.

9. Clark, Volume III, p. 465; Clark, Volume IV, p. 581; O.R., Volume 29, Part I, p. 460; Henderson, p. 78.

10. O.R., Volume 29, Part I, p. 460; Henderson, p. 81, 244.

11. Clark, Volume III, p. 465, 575–576; O.R., Volume 29, Part I, p. 460; Wadesboro *North Carolina Argus*, October 29, 1863.

12. Clark, Volume III, p. 576–577.

13. Clark, Volume III, p. 576; O.R., Volume 29, Part I, p. 386.

14. Wadesboro *North Carolina Argus*, October 29, 1863; O.R., Volume 29, Part I, p. 460; Hartley, p. 284; Henderson, p. 144–149, 239–240.

15. Clark, Volume III, p. 579; Henderson, p. 146–148.

16. O.R., Volume 29, Part I, p. 443, 449–451, 456, 460–461, 581; Clark, Volume III, p. 582.

17. O.R., Volume 29, Part I, p. 450.

18. O.R., Volume 29, Part I, p. 451–452; Henderson, p. 201–205; Abe Jones Letter of October 21, 1863, in the Abraham G. Jones Papers, East Carolina University Manuscript Collection, J. Y. Joyner Library, East Carolina University, Greenville, North Carolina.

19. Abe Jones Letters of October 21, October 23, and October 31, 1863, in the Abraham G. Jones Papers, East Carolina University Manuscript Collection, J. Y. Joyner Library, East Carolina University, Greenville, North Carolina; Edwards Letters of November 1, November 4, November 7, November 9, November 10, November 12, 1863; Raleigh *Spirit of the Age*, December 14, 1863; Hartley, p. 300; O.R., Volume 29, Part I, p. 898–901; Clark, Volume III, p. 585

20. Raleigh *Spirit of the Age*, December 14, 1863; O.R., Volume 29, Part I, p. 898–903.

21. Clark, Volume III, p. 586; O.R., Volume 29, Part I, p. 900; Raleigh *Spirit of the Age*, December 14, 1863.

9. Defending Petersburg

1. O.R., Volume 33, p. 1088–1089, 1143; John A. Smith to sister, Letter of January 24, 1864, in the John A. Smith Papers, Special Collections Department, William R. Perkins Library, Duke University, Durham, North Carolina.

2. Wadesboro *North Carolina Argus*, March 31, 1864; Edwards Letters of February 26, February 29, March 17, April 16, April 18, and April 20, 1864; Henry C. Wall Diary, in the Private Manuscript Collection (1276), North Carolina Department of Archives and History, Raleigh, NC, April 14, 1864 entry (hereafter referred to as Wall Diary).

3. Edwards Letter of April 23, 1864; O.R., 36, Part II, p. 958.

4. Richard N. Current, editor, *Encyclopedia of the Confederacy*, Volume 2, New York, 1993, p. 459; Warner, *Generals in Gray*, p. 69–70; William L. Parker, *General James Dearing, CSA*, Lynchburg, VA, 1990, p. 2; Chris M. Calkins, *The Appomattox Campaign*: March 29–April 9, 1865, Conshohocken, PA, 1997, p. 140–142.

5. William Glenn Robertson, *Back Door to Richmond: The Bermuda Hundred Campaign*, *April-June 1864*, Baton Rouge, LA, 1987, p. 13; General Johnson Hagood, "General P. G. T. Beauregard," *S.H.S.P.*, Volume 28 (1900), p. 318–319.

6. William Glenn Robertson, *The Petersburg Campaign: The Battle of Old Men and Young Boys, June 9, 1864*, Lynchburg, VA, 1989, p. 8–11; O.R., Volume 51, Part II, p. 919.

7. O.R., 36, Part II, p. 998, 1002–1003, 1008; O.R., Volume 51, Part II, p. 928.

8. O.R., 36, Part II, p. 251, 1008; Robertson, *Back Door*, p. 171.

9. Robertson, *Back Door*, p. 210.

10. Robertson, *Back Door*, p. 212.

11. O.R., 36, Part III, p. 821, 833, 859, 868.

12. Robertson, *Petersburg*, p. 17–24; Noah Andre Trudeau, *The Last Citadel: Petersburg, Virginia, June 1864–April 1865*, Baton Rouge, LA, 1991, p. 6.

13. Wadesboro *North Carolina Argus*, June 23, 1864; Edwards Letter of June 8, 1864.

14. O.R., 36, Part I, p. 303; Robertson, *Petersburg*, p. 32–34.

15. Robertson, *Petersburg*, p. 4–5.

16. Robertson, *Petersburg*, p. 59–60.

17. O.R., 36, Part III, p. 884; Robertson, *Petersburg*, p. 41.

18. Robertson, *Petersburg*, p. 48–56.

19. Robertson, *Petersburg*, p. 60; Fletcher H. Archer, "The Defense of Petersburg on the 9th of June, 1864," *War Talks of Confederate Veterans*, George S. Bernard, editor, Petersburg, VA, 1892, p. 139.

20. Robertson, *Petersburg*, p. 60–61.

21. Robertson, *Petersburg*, p. 73.

22. Robertson, *Petersburg*, p. 73–74.

23. Robertson, *Petersburg*, p. 75–78.

24. Dennis D. Ferebee Report of June 20, 1864 to Captain William E. Hinton, 44th VA Battalion, North Carolina Department of Archives and History.

25. Thomas J. Howe, *The Petersburg Campaign: Wasted Valor, June 15–18, 1864*, Lynchburg, VA, 1988, p. 11.

26. Ferebee Report, June 20, 1864.

27. *Ibid.*

28. O.R., Volume 40, Part II, p. 669.

29. Clark, Volume I, p. 432–435.

30. Clark, Volume III, p. 612; Clark, Volume I, p. 433–435.

10. Reams' Station, the Cattle Raid, and Hatcher's Run

1. O.R., Volume 40, Part III, p. 763; Clark, Volume III, p. 340; Clark, Volume IV, p. 339–340.

2. Wadesboro *North Carolina Argus*, July 28, 1864.

3. R. P. Allen to Companion, Letters of July 28, 1864 and August 1, 1864, in the Eleanor S. Brockenbrough Library, The Museum of the Confederacy, Richmond, VA.

4. John W. Gordon Diary (Private, Company C, 2nd NC Cavalry), in the Eleanor S. Brockenbrough Library, The Museum of the Confederacy, Richmond, VA, p. 9; O.R., Volume 42, Part II, p. 199, 1365.

5. Trudeau, p. 75–76.

6. O.R., Volume 42, Part I, p. 857; O.R., Volume 42, Part II, p. 1187, 1365; Trudeau, *The Last Citadel*, p. 160–161; Parker, *Dearing*, p. 75; Clark, Volume IV, p. 207; Gordon Diary, p. 9.

7. Clark, Volume V, p. 207; O.R., Volume 42, Part II, p. 407; O.R., Volume 51, Part II, p. 1037; Colonel U. R. Brooks, "Battle of Reams Station," *Confederate Veteran*, Volume 22 (1914), p. 554–555; Trudeau, *Citadel*, p. 171.

8. Wadesboro *North Carolina Argus*, September 15, 1864; O.R., Volume 42, Part II, p. 1205, 1224–1225, 1228, 1244, 1267; Clark, Volume III, p. 681.

9. Brantley H. Saunders to Abigail Smith, Letter of September 12, 1864, in the Local History Collection, Lore Room, Charles A. Cannon Memorial Library, Concord, NC; Parker, *Dearing*, p. 79.

10. Bennett H. Young, *Confederate Wizards of the Saddle: Being Reminiscences and Observations of One Who Rode With Morgan*, Boston, 1914, p. 42–59; O.R., Volume 42, Part I, p. 944–955; Trudeau, *The Last Citadel*, p. 192–201; Parker, *Dearing*, p. 79–82; Clark, Volume III, p. 622; Wadesboro *North Carolina Argus*, September 29, 1864.

11. Parker, *Dearing*, p. 83; O.R., Volume 42, Part I, p. 947.

12. O.R., Volume 42, Part III, p. 1133, 1146.

13. Trudeau, *The Last Citadel*, p. 222.

14. Trudeau, *The Last Citadel*, p. 230–231; O.R., Volume 42, Part I, p. 949–950.

15. O.R., Volume 42, Part I, p. 949–950.

16. *Ibid.*

17. O.R., Volume 42, Part I, p. 950.

18. O.R., Volume 42, Part III, p. 449, 485, 626, 1192, 1209; Risden B. Gaddy to Cousin, Letter of November 25, 1864, in the Fannie (Bennett) Gaddy Papers, Special Collections Library, Duke University, Durham, North Carolina.

19. Gordon Diary, p. 23; W. H. Roberts, *Drums and Guns Around Petersburg*, Bowie, MD, 1995, p. 29.

11. To Appomattox: The Final Months of the War

1. Clark, Volume III, p. 541; Wall, p. 59–61; Fred C. Foard Reminiscences, Fred C. Foard Papers, Department of Archives and History, Raleigh, North Carolina; O.R., Volume 46, Part I, p. 384–385; Neill McLaurin to Margaret McLaurin, Letter of January 23, 1865, in the McLaurin Family Papers, Southern Historical Collection, University of North Carolina, Chapel Hill, North Carolina.

2. O.R., Volume 46, Part I, p. 150, 385; O.R., Volume 46, Part II, p. 368, 369, 1175, 1183; Wadesboro *North Carolina Argus*, February 23, 1865.

3. Clark, Volume III, p. 466–467; Warner, *Generals in Gray*, p. 258–259; *S.H.S.P.* Volume 18 (1890), p. 386; *Current*, Vol. 3, p. 1340–1341; *Hill*, Volume V (NC), p. 348.

4. Clark, Volume III, p. 467; D. D. Ferebee to Col. G. W. Little, Letter of March 3, 1865, in the Zebulon Baird Vance Papers, Department of Archives and History, Raleigh, North Carolina.

5. O.R., Volume 46, Part II, p. 630–631, 633, 963–964, 966; Clark, Volume III, p. 467; Roberts, p. 59.

6. O.R., Volume 46, Part III, p. 7, 29, 1319; Roberts, p. 63.

7. O.R., Volume 46, Part III, p. 76, 1327, 1329.

8. Chris Calkins, "The Battle of Five Forks: Final Push for the South Side," *Blue & Gray Magazine*, Volume IX, Number 4 (April 1992), p. 9; Chris Calkins, *The Appomattox Campaign*, Conshohocken, PA, 1997, p. 10–14.

9. Clark, Volume III, p. 467–468.

10. Clark, Volume III, p. 468–469; O. R., Volume 46, Part III, p. 1371; Calkins, *"Battle of Five Forks,"* p. 18–22; Calkins, *The Appomattox Campaign,* p. 20; Roberts, p. 65.

11. Clark, Volume III, p. 469; Calkins, *"Battle of Five Forks,"* p. 18–22; Calkins, *The Appomattox Campaign,* p. 20, 30; David Cardwell, "The Battle of Five Forks," *Confederate Veteran,* Volume 22 (1914), p. 117–120; David Cardwell, "The Eleventh at Five Forks," *S.H.S.P.,* Volume 35 (1907), p. 357–362; Robert M. Stribling, "Story of Battle of Five Forks," *S.H.S.P.,* Volume 37 (1909), p. 172–178.

12. Starr, Volume 2, p. 454; Calkins, *The Appomattox Campaign,* p. 36; Clark, Volume III, p. 470.

13. Calkins, *The Appomattox Campaign,* p. 69–70; Clark, Volume III, p. 470.

14. Calkins, *The Appomattox Campaign,* p. 70–72; Clark, Volume III, p. 470; W. R. Webb, "The Capture of Gen. Rufus Barringer," *The Daily Observer,* April 9, 1911.

15. Clark, Volume III, p. 470–471; Chris Calkins, *The Battles of Appomattox Station and Appomattox Court House, April 8-9, 1865,* Lynchburg, VA, 1987, p. 53–54, 60–62; Roberts, p. 67.

16. Clark, Volume III, p. 471; Current, Volume 1, p. 186–187.

17. North Carolina Literary and Historical Association, *Five Points in the Record of North Carolina in the Great War of 1861-5,* Goldsboro, NC, 1904, p. 71–72; Calkins, *The Appomattox Campaign,* p. 161; O.R., Volume 46, Part I, p. 1303–1304.

18. North Carolina Literary and Historical Association, *Five Points,* p. 72; Calkins, *The Appomattox Campaign,* p. 161–174.

19. Clark, Volume III, p. 471.

Bibliography

Books

Alexander, J.B., MD. *The History of Mecklenburg County from 1740 to 1900*. Charlotte, NC: Observer Printing House, 1902.

Almasy, Sandra Lee. *Bertie County, North Carolina 1850 Census: Free Population and Slave Population*. Joliet, IL: Kensington Glen, 1991.

_____. *Bertie County, North Carolina Census 1860: Population Schedule of the Eighth Census of the United States*. Middleton, WI: Kensington Glen Publishing, 1996.

Archer, Fletcher H. "The Defense of Petersburg on the 9th of June, 1864." In *War Talks of Confederate Veterans*, George S. Bernard, editor: pp. 107–148, Petersburg, VA: Fenn & Owen, 1892.

Barrett, John G. *The Civil War in North Carolina*. Chapel Hill: University of North Carolina Press, 1963.

Bates, Jo Anna Heath, editor. *The Heritage of Currituck County, North Carolina 1985*. Winston-Salem, NC: Hunter, 1985.

Beale, G. W. *A Lieutenant of Cavalry in Lee's Army*. Baltimore, MD: Butternut and Blue, 1994 (reprint of 1918 edition).

Beale, R. L. T. *History of the Ninth Virginia Cavalry in the War Between the States*. Richmond, VA: B.F. Johnson, 1899.

Bearss, Edwin, and Christopher Calkins. *The Battle of Five Forks*. Lynchburg, VA: H.E. Howard, 1985.

Birdsong, James C. *Brief Sketches of the North Carolina State Troops in the War Between the States*. Raleigh, NC: Edwards & Broughton, 1894.

Blackford, W. W. *War Years with J. E. B. Stuart*. New York: Charles Scribner's Sons, 1945.

Bliss, George. *Personal Narratives of Events in the War of the Rebellion, Fourth Series, No. 4: The Rhode Island Cavalry at Middleburg, Va*. Providence, RI: Rhode Island Soldiers and Sailors Historical Society, 1889.

Boatner, Mark Mayo III. *The Civil War Dictionary*. New York: David McKay, 1959.

Bradley, Stephen E. *North Carolina Confederate Militia Officers Roster As Contained in the Adjutant-General's Officers Register*. Wilmington, NC: Broadfoot, 1992.

Bright, Leslie S., William H. Rowland and James C. Bardon. *C.S.S. Neuse: A Question of Iron and Time*. Raleigh, NC: North Carolina Division of Archives and History, 1981.

Cain, Barbara T., Ellen Z. McGrew and Charles E. Morris. *Guide to Private Manuscript Collec-*

tions in the North Carolina State Archives. Raleigh, NC: North Carolina Department of Cultural Resources, 1993.

Calkins, Christopher. *The Appomattox Campaign: March 29–April 9, 1865*. Conshohocken, PA: Combined Books, 1997.

_____. *The Battles of Appomattox Station and Appomattox Court House, April 8–9, 1865*. Lynchburg, VA: H. E. Howard, 1987.

_____. *From Petersburg to Appomattox, April 2–9, 1865*. Farmville, VA: Farmville Herald Publishing Company, 1983.

_____. *Thirty-Six Hours Before Appomattox: The Battles of Sayler's Creek, High Bridge, Farmville and Cumberland Church, April 6–7, 1865*. Farmville, VA: Farmville Herald, 1980.

Carpenter, Reva Nance. *Anson County, North Carolina: Abstract of Wills 1750–1880*. San Diego: Grasshopper Press, 1976.

Clark, Walter. *Histories of the Several Regiments and Battalions from North Carolina in the Great War 1861–1865*, 5 volumes. Wendell, NC: Broadfoot, 1982 (reprint).

Coggins, Jack. *Arms and Equipment of the Civil War*. Wilmington, NC: Broadfoot, 1989.

Coltrane, Daniel Branson. *The Memoirs of Daniel Branson Coltrane*. Raleigh, NC: Edwards & Broughton, 1956.

Cormier, Steven A. *The Siege of Suffolk: The Forgotten Campaign, April 11–May 4, 1863*. Lynchburg, VA: H. E. Howard, 1989.

Coski, John M. *Capital Navy: The Men, Ships and Operations of the James River Squadron*. Campbell, CA: Savas, 1996.

Cullum, George W. Bvt. Maj.-Gen. *Biographical Register of the Officers and Graduates of the U. S. Military Academy at West Point, N. Y. (Volume II: Nos. 1001 to 2000)*. Boston and New York: Houghton, Mifflin, 1891.

Current, Richard N., editor. *Encyclopedia of the Confederacy*, 4 volumes. New York: Simon and Schuster, 1993.

Davis, Burke. *To Appomattox: Nine April Days*. New York: Rinehart & Company, 1959.

Denison, Frederic. *Sabres and Spurs: The First Regiment Rhode Island Cavalry in the Civil War, 1861–1865*. Baltimore: Butternut and Blue, 1994 (reprint of 1876 edition).

Dornbusch, C. E. *Military Bibliography of the Civil War*, 3 volumes. New York: The New York Public Library, 1961.

Dowd, Jerome. *Sketches of Prominent Living North Carolinians*. Raleigh, NC: Edwards & Broughton, Printers and Binders, 1888.

Downey, Fairfax. *Clash of Cavalry: The Battle of Brandy Station*. New York: David McKay Company, Inc., 1959.

Eliot, Ellsworth Jr. *West Point in the Confederacy*. New York: G. A. Baker & Co., Inc., 1941.

Foote, Shelby. *The Civil War: A Narrative*, 3 volumes. New York: Vintage Books, 1974.

Forty-Fourth Massachusetts Volunteer Militia Historical Committee. *Record of the Service of the Forty-Fourth Massachusetts Volunteer Militia in North Carolina: August 1862 to May 1863*. Boston: University Press, 1887.

Fouts, Raymond Parker. *Marriages of Bertie County, North Carolina: 1762–1868*. Baltimore: Genealogical Publishing Co., 1982.

Freeman, Douglas Southall. *Lee Lieutenants*, 3 volumes. New York: Charles Scribner's Sons, 1942–44.

Gammon, David B., and Stephen E. Bradley, Jr. *Northampton County North Carolina, The 1850 Census: All Schedules*. Lawrenceville, VA: Stephen E. Bradley, Jr., 1996.

Garnett, Theodore Stanford. *Riding with Stuart: Reminiscences of an Aide-de-camp*. Robert J. Trout, editor. Shippensburg, PA: White Maine Publishing Company, 1994.

Gibbons, Tony. *Warships and Naval Battles of the Civil War*. New York: Gallery Books, 1989.

Graham, Martin F. and George F. Skoch. *Mine Run: A Campaign of Lost Opportunities*. Lynchburg, VA: H. E. Howard, 1987.

Hartley, Chris J. *Stuart's Tarheels: James B. Gordon and His North Carolina Cavalry*. Baltimore: Butternut and Blue, 1996.

Henderson, William D. *Petersburg in the Civil War: War at the Door*. Lynchburg, VA: H. E. Howard, 1998.

_____. *The Road to Bristoe Station: Campaigning with Lee and Meade, August 1–October 20, 1863*. Lynchburg, VA: H. E. Howard, 1987.

Hendrickson, Robert. *The Road to Appomattox*. New York: John Wiley & Sons, 1998.

Hill, D.H., Jr. *Confederate Military History Volume 5, North Carolina*. Wilmington, NC: Broadfoot, 1987.

Horn, John. *The Petersburg Campaign: June 1864–April 1865*. Conshohocken, PA: Combined Books, Inc., 1993.

_____. *The Petersburg Campaign, The Destruction of the Weldon Railroad: Deep Bottom, Globe Tavern, and Reams Station, August 14–25, 1864*. Lynchburg, VA: H. E. Howard, 1991.

Howe, Thomas J. *The Petersburg Campaign: Wasted Valor, June 15–18, 1864*. Lynchburg, VA: H. E. Howard, 1988.

Howe, W. W. *Kinston, Whitehall and Goldsboro (North Carolina) Expedition, December 1862*. New York: W. W. Howe, 1890.

Humphreys, Andrew A. *The Virginia Campaign of '64 and '65: The Army of the Potomac and the Army of the James*. New York: Charles Scribner's Sons, 1883.

Ingmire, Frances Terry. *Cabarrus County North Carolina Marriage Records: 1793–1868*. Athens, GA: Iberian, 1984 (1993 reprint).

_____. *Caswell County North Carolina Marriage Records: 1778–1876*. St. Louis: Ingmire Publications, 1984.

_____. *Johnston County North Carolina Marriage Records: 1767–1867*. Athens, GA: Iberian Publishing Company, 1993 (reprint).

_____. *New Hanover County North Carolina Marriage Records: 1779–1868*. Athens, GA: Iberian Publishing Company, 1993.

_____. *Northampton County North Carolina Marriage Records: 1812–1867*. St. Louis: Frances Terry Ingmire, 1984.

Johnson, Clint. *Touring the Carolina's Civil War Sites*. Winston-Salem, NC: John F. Blair, 1996.

Johnson, Robert Underwood, and C. C. Buel, editors. *Battles and Leaders of the Civil War*, 4 volumes. Secaucus, NJ: Castle, 1991 (reprint of original).

Johnston, Frontis W., editor. *Zebulon B. Vance Letters, Volume One: 1843–1862*. Raleigh, NC: State Department of Archives and History, 1963.

Johnston, Hugh Buckner, editor. *The Confederate Letters of William Henry Edwards*. Wilson, NC: privately published, 1952.

Jones, Richard L. *Dinwiddie County: Carrefour of the Commonwealth*. Richmond, VA: Whittet & Shepperson, 1976.

Jordan, Weymouth T., Jr. *North Carolina Troops 1861–1865, A Roster: Volume II Addenda*. Wilmington, NC: Broadfoot, 1988.

Kendall, Jerry T. *The Kendall Family: Descendants of William Kendall, Westmoreland County, Virginia*. Bennettsville, SC: Jerry T. Kendall, 1998.

Krick, Robert K. *Lee's Colonels: A Biographical Register of the Field Officers of the Army of Northern Virginia*. Dayton, OH: Morningside Bookshop, 1979.

Longacre, Edward G. *The Cavalry at Gettysburg: A Tactical Study of Mounted Operations During the Civil War's Pivotal Campaign, 9 June–14 July 1863*. Rutherford, NJ: University of Nebraska Press, 1986.

_____. *Mounted Raids of the Civil War*. South Brunswick and New York: A. S. Barnes, 1975.

Lowry, Don. *No Turning Back: The Beginning of the End of the Civil War: March–June, 1864*. New York: Hippocrene, 1992.

_____. *Towards an Infinite Shore: The Final Months of the Civil War: December 1864–May 1865.* New York: Hippocrene Books, Inc., 1995.

Luvaas, Jay, and Joseph P. Cullen. *Appomattox Court House.* Washington, DC: US Department of the Interior, 1980.

Manarin, Louis H. *A Guide to Military Organizations and Installations, North Carolina: 1861–1865.* Raleigh, NC: The North Carolina Confederate Centennial Commission, 1961.

_____. *North Carolina Troops 1861–1865: A Roster (Volume II, Cavalry).* Raleigh, NC: North Carolina Division of Archives and History, 1968.

_____. *North Carolina Troops 1861–1865: A Roster (Volume V, Infantry).* Raleigh, NC: North Carolina Division of Archives and History, 1968.

McClellan, H. B. *The Life and Campaigns of Stuart's Cavalry.* Secaucus, NJ: Blue & Grey Press, 1993.

Mooney, James L., editor. *Dictionary of American Naval Fighting Ships, Volume VIII.* Washington, DC: Naval Historical Center, 1981.

Moore, John W. *Roster of North Carolina Troops in the War Between the States, Volume III.* Raleigh, NC: Edwards, Broughton & Co., 1882.

Moore, Robert H., II. *Graham's Petersburg, Jackson's Kanawha and Lurty's Roanoke Horse Artillery.* Lynchburg, VA: H. E. Howard, 1996.

Mosby, John S. *Stuart's Cavalry in the Gettysburg Campaign.* New York: Moffat, Yard, 1908.

Neal, Carl B. *The Beaver Pond Neals of Virginia.* Olympia, WA: Sherwood Press and Patterson Book Binding, 1965.

Neese, George M. *Three Years in the Confederate Horse Artillery.* Dayton, OH: Morningside, 1911.

Nesbitt, Mark. *Saber and Scapegoat, J. E. B. Stuart and the Gettysburg Controversy.* Mechanicsburg, PA: Stackpole, 1994.

North Carolina Literary and Historical Association. *Five Points in the Record of North Carolina in the Great War of 1861–5.* Goldsboro, NC: Nash Brothers, 1904.

Nye, Wilbur Sturtevant. *Here Come the Rebels!* Baton Rouge, LA: Louisiana State University Press, 1965.

O'Neill, Robert F., Jr. *The Cavalry Battles of Aldie, Middleburg and Upperville: Small But Important Riots, June 10–27, 1863.* Lynchburg, VA: H. E. Howard, 1993.

Opie, John N. *A Rebel Cavalryman with Lee, Stuart and Jackson.* Chicago: W. B. Conkey, 1899.

Papers of the Military Historical Society of Massachusetts: The Shenandoah Campaigns of 1862 and 1864 and the Appomattox Campaign of 1865 (Volume 6). Wilmington, NC: Broadfoot, 1989 (reprint of 1907 original).

Parker, William L. *General James Dearing, CSA.* Lynchburg, VA: H. E. Howard, 1990.

Parramore, Thomas C., F. Roy Johnson and E. Frank Stephenson, Jr. *Before the Rebel Flag Fell.* Murfreesboro, NC: Johnson, 1965.

Perrin, William Henry, editor. *History of Bond and Montgomery Counties, Illinois.* Chicago: O. L. Baskin & Co., 1882.

Powell, William S. *The North Carolina Gazetteer: A Dictionary of Tar Heel Places.* Chapel Hill, NC: University of North Carolina Press, 1968.

_____, editor. *Dictionary of North Carolina Biography: Volume 1, A–C.* Chapel Hill, NC: University of North Carolina Press, 1979.

Pugh, Jesse Forbes. *Three Hundred Years Along the Pasquotank: A Biographical History of Camden County.* Durham, NC: Seeman Printery, 1957

Roberts, W. H. *Drums and Guns Around Petersburg.* Bowie, MD: Heritage Books, 1995.

Robertson, William Glenn. *Back Door to Richmond: The Bermuda Hundred Campaign, April–June 1864.* Baton Rouge, LA: Louisiana State University Press, 1987.

_____. *The Petersburg Campaign: The Battle of Old Men and Young Boys, June 9, 1864.* Lynchburg, VA: H. E. Howard, 1989.

Rumple, the Rev. Jethro. *A History of Rowan County North Carolina: Containing Sketches of Prominent Families and Distinguished Men with an Appendix.* Salisbury, NC: J. J. Bruner, 1881.

Sauers, Richard A., and Will D. Gorges. *The Battle of New Bern and Related Sites in Craven County, NC, 1861–1865.* New Bern, NC: Griffin & Tilghman, 1994.

Schildt, John W. *Roads from Gettysburg.* Shippensburg, PA: Burd Street Press, 1998.

Shannonhouse, Edna Morrisette. *Census of 1850: Camden and Currituck Counties.* Elizabeth City, NC: Pasquotank Historical Society, 1977.

Shiman, Philip. *Fort Branch and the Defense of the Roanoke Valley, 1862–1865.* Raleigh, NC: North Carolina Division of Archives and History, Fort Branch Battlefield Commission, 1990.

Shoemaker, John J. *Shoemaker's Battery: Stuart Horse Artillery, Pelham's Battalion, Army of Northern Virginia.* Memphis: S. C. Toof & Company, 1907.

Sommers, Richard J. *Richmond Redeemed: The Siege at Petersburg.* New York: Doubleday, 1981.

Sprunt, James. *Chronicles of the Cape Fear River: 1660–1916.* Raleigh, NC: Edwards & Broughton, Co., 1916.

Stackpole, Edward J. *They Met at Gettysburg.* Harrisburg, PA: Stackpole, 1996 (40th Anniversary Edition).

Starr, Stephen Z. *The Union Cavalry in the Civil War,* 3 volumes. Baton Rouge, LA: Louisiana State University Press, 1979.

Stroupe, Vernon S., Robert J. Stets, Ruth Y. Wetmore and Tony L. Crumbley, editors. *Post Offices and Postmasters of North Carolina: Colonial to USPS, Volume 1-Alamance through Durham.* Charlotte, NC: North Carolina Postal History Society, 1996.

Taylor, Anne Hatcher. *Marriage Register of Hertford County North Carolina: August 1868 through December 1872 (Volume 1).* Winton, NC: Hatcher-Taylor Press, 1986.

Thomas, Emory M. *Bold Dragoon: The Life of J. E. B. Stuart.* New York: Harper & Row, 1986.

Thomas, Gerald W. *Divided Allegiances: Bertie County during the Civil War.* Raleigh, NC: Division of Archives and History, North Carolina Department of Cultural Resources, 1996.

Thomason, John W. Jr. *JEB Stuart.* New York: Mallard Press, 1992 (reprint of Scribner's 1930 edition).

Thompson, Doris Lancaster. *1850 Federal Census of Brunswick County, North Carolina.* New Bern, NC: Owen G. Dunn Co., 1976.

Tilberg, Frederick. *Gettysburg, National Military Park Pennsylvania.* Washington, DC: National Park Service, 1962.

Trudeau, Noah Andre. *Civil War Series: The Campaign to Appomattox.* Conshohocken, PA: Eastern National Park & Monument Association, 1998.

_____. *Civil War Series: The Siege of Petersburg.* Conshohocken, PA: Eastern National Park & Monument Association, 1995.

_____. *The Last Citadel: Petersburg, Virginia, June 1864–April 1865.* Baton Rouge, LA: Louisiana State University Press, 1991.

_____. *Out of the Storm: The End of the Civil War, April–June 1865.* Baton Rouge, LA: Louisiana State University Press, 1994.

Trotter, William R. *Ironclads and Columbiads: The Civil War in North Carolina; The Coast.* Winston-Salem, NC: John F. Blair, 1989.

United States Department of the Navy. *Civil War Naval Chronology 1861–1865.* Washington, DC: Naval History Division, 1971.

_____. *Dictionary of American Naval Fighting Ships, Volume II.* Washington, DC: Naval History Division, 1963.

_____. *Dictionary of American Naval Fighting Ships, Volume III.* Washington, DC: Naval History Division, 1968.

Vann, J. A., and W. L. Daniel. *1850 Census of Hertford County, North Carolina.* Winton, NC: Albemarle Regional Library, no date.

Von Borcke, Heros. *Memoirs of the Confederate War,* 2 volumes. New York: Peter Smith, 1938 (reprint of the 1866 edition).

_____, and Justus Scheibert. *The Great Cavalry Battle of Brandy Station, 9 June 1863.* Gaithersburg, MD: Olde Soldier Books, Inc., 1976.

Wakelyn, Jon L. *Biographical Dictionary of the Confederacy.* Westport, CT: Greenwood Press, 1977.

Warner, Ezra J. *Generals in Blue: Lives of the Union Commanders.* Baton Rouge, LA: Louisiana State University Press, 1964 (1991 printing).

_____. *Generals in Gray: Lives of the Confederate Commanders.* Baton Rouge, LA: Louisiana State University Press, 1959 (1992 printing).

Wells, Edward L. *Hampton and His Cavalry in '64.* Richmond, VA: Owens, 1991.

Whitlow, Jeannine D, editor. *The Heritage of Caswell County North Carolina.* Winston-Salem, NC: Hunter, 1985.

Winborne, Benjamin B. *The Colonial and State History of Hertford County, North Carolina.* Baltimore, MD: Genealogical Publishing Co., 1976.

Wittenberg, Eric J. *Gettysburg's Forgotten Cavalry Actions.* Gettysburg, PA: Thomas, 1998.

Yearns, W. Buck, and John G. Barrett, editors. *North Carolina Civil War Documentary.* Chapel Hill, NC: University of North Carolina Press, 1980.

Young, Bennett H. *Confederate Wizards of the Saddle: Being Reminiscences and Observations of One Who Rode with Morgan.* Boston: Chapple, 1914.

Zuber, Richard L. *Jonathan Worth: A Biography of a Southern Unionist.* Chapel Hill, NC: University of North Carolina Press, 1965.

Newspapers

Asheville News 1862
Daily Bulletin (Charlotte) 1862
The Daily Observer (Charlotte) 1911
Daily Progress (Raleigh) 1863
The Memphis Weekly Appeal 1877
Milton Chronicle 1863
North Carolina Argus (Wadesboro) 1862–1865
North Carolina Presbyterian (Fayetteville) 1863
Richmond Whig 1863
Spirit of the Age (Raleigh) 1863
State Journal (Raleigh) 1863
Wilmington Journal 1862

Articles

Brooks, Col. U. R. "Battle of Reams Station." *Confederate Veteran,* Volume 22 (1914): pp. 554–555.

Calkins, Chris. "The Battle of Five Forks: Final Push for the South Side." *Blue & Gray Magazine,* Volume IX, Number 4 (April 1992): pp. 8–22, 41–52.

Cardwell, David. "The Battle of Five Forks." *Confederate Veteran,* Volume 22 (1914): pp. 117–120.

_____. "The Eleventh at Five Forks." *Southern Historical Society Papers,* Volume 35 (1907): pp. 357–362.

Chaplain, C. T., and J. M. Keeling. "Operations on the Blackwater River." *Confederate Veteran,* Volume 27 (1919): pp. 304–305.

Cowles, William H. "Oration on James B. Gordon." *Carolina and the Southern Cross,* Volume 1, Number 6: pp. 17–23.

Craige, Kerr. "General James B. Gordon." *Confederate Veteran,* Volume 6 (1898): p. 216.

Dunn, the Rev. Joseph B. " Eulogy of General Lawrence S. Baker. St. Paul's Parish, Suffolk, VA, April 12, 1907." North Carolina State Archives, Raleigh, NC—Military Collection—Civil War Collection Box 70, Folder #7: pp. 1–2.

Gallagher, Gary W. "Battle of Brandy Station." *Blue & Gray Magazine*, Volume XIII, Number 1 (October 1990): p. 13.

Gibson, Charles Dana. "Hay: The Linchpin of Mobility." *North & South*, Volume 2, Number 2 (January 1999): pp. 51–53.

Hagler, John Blair. "Two Adam Monroe Furrs." *Cabarrus Genealogical Society Journal*, Volume 4, Number 1 (March 1996): pp. 11–12.

Hagood, Gen. Johnson. "General P. G. T. Beauregard." *Southern Historical Society Papers*, Volume 28 (1900): pp. 318–319.

Jones, W. E. "Summer Campaign of 1863." *Southern Historical Society Papers*, Volume 9 (1881): pp. 115–119.

Krimminger, Betty L. "Frightful Accident: A Kerosene Lamp Explodes and Burns a Man Nearly to Death." *Cabarrus Genealogical Society Journal*, Volume 4, Number 2 (June 1996): p. 68—reprinted from *Concord Register*, April 11, 1876.

Lee, Robert E. "Report of the Gettysburg Campaign." *Southern Historical Society Papers*, Volume 2 (1876).

"The Opposing Forces at Gettysburg." *Battles and Leaders of the Civil War*, Volume 3: pp. 434–440.

Roberts, William P. "Statement of Brigadier General W.P. Roberts as to His Staff and Command." *Southern Historical Society Papers*. Volume 18 (1890): p. 386.

Stribling, Robert M. "Story of Battle of Five Forks." *Southern Historical Society Papers*, Volume 37 (1909): pp. 172–179.

Stuart, J. E. B. "The Gettysburg Campaign." *Southern Historical Society Papers*, Volume 7, Number 9 (September 1879): pp. 401–434.

Warlick, J. C. "Battle of White Hall, N.C." *Confederate Veteran*, Volume 12: p. 178.

Webb, W. R. "The Capture of Gen. Rufus Barringer." *The Daily Observer*, April 9, 1911.

Weeks, Stephen Beauregard. "The University of North Carolina in the Civil War." *Southern Historical Society Papers*, Volume 24 (1896): pp. 1–38.

Official Documents

Atlas to Accompany the Official Records of the Union and Confederate Armies. Washington, DC: Government Printing Office, 1891–1895.

Official Records of the Union and Confederate Navies in the War of the Rebellion. 31 volumes. Washington, DC: Government Printing Office, 1900–1901.

Supplement to the Official Records of the Union and Confederate Armies. 100 volumes. Wilmington, NC: Broadfoot Publishing Company, 1994–2001

The War of the Rebellion: A Compilation of the Official Records of the Union and Confederate Armies. 70 volumes in 128 parts. Washington, DC: Government Printing Office, 1881–1902. (Broadfoot reprint)

Manuscript Sources

Charles A. Cannon Memorial Library, Local History Collection, Lore Room, Concord, North Carolina—Brantley H. Saunders Letter

Duke University, Special Collections Library, Durham, North Carolina—Fannie (Bennett)

Gaddy Papers: R. B. Gaddy Letters; Lizzie Nelms(?) (Smith) Parker Papers: W. T. Smith Letters; John A. Smith Letter

East Carolina University, Manuscript Collection, J. Y. Joyner Library, Greenville, North Carolina—Abraham G. Jones Papers; Charles F. Glover Papers

Library of Congress, Manuscript Division, Washington, DC—Mercer Green Johnston Papers: James Steptoe Johnston Letters

Museum of the Confederacy, Eleanor S. Brockenbrough Library, Richmond, Virginia—R. P. Allen Letters; John W. Gordon Diary

North Carolina State Archives, North Carolina Division of Archives and History, Raleigh, North Carolina—Media Evans Collection; Dennis D. Ferebee Report, June 20, 1864; Fred C. Foard Papers; Hugh Buckner Johnston Collection: William Henry Edwards Letters; John W. Lay Reminiscences; Zebulon Baird Vance Papers; Henry C. Wall Diary

University of North Carolina at Chapel Hill, Southern Historical Collection, Chapel Hill, North Carolina—McLaurin Family Papers, 1861–1865, #4659z; H. G. Worsley Memoir, #1851

Wake Forest University, Z. Smith Reynolds Library, Winston-Salem, North Carolina—John Alexander Oates Papers: Charles C. Lovejoy letter

Thesis

Bowmaster, Patrick. *Confederate Brig. Gen. B. H. Robertson and the 1863 Gettysburg Campaign.* Master's Thesis, Virginia Polytechnic Institute and State University, Blacksburg, VA, 1995.

Index

Numbers in bold refer to pages with photographs